The Canadian General Election of 2004

The Canadian General Election of 2004

Edited by Jon H. Pammett and
Christopher Dornan

THE DUNDURN GROUP
TORONTO

Copyright © Jon H. Pammett and Christopher Dornan, 2004

All rights reserved. No part of this publication may be reproduced, stored in a retrieval system, or transmitted in any form or by any means, electronic, mechanical, photocopying, recording, or otherwise (except for brief passages for purposes of review) without the prior permission of Dundurn Press. Permission to photocopy should be requested from Access Copyright.

Copy-Editor: Jennifer Bergeron
Design: Jennifer Scott
Printer: AGMV Marquis

Library and Archives Canada Cataloguing in Publication

The Canadian general election of 2004 / edited by Jon H. Pammett and Christopher Dornan.

Includes bibliographical references.
ISBN 1-55002-516-3

1. Canada. Parliament--Elections, 2004. I. Pammett, Jon H., 1944- II. Dornan, Chris

FC635.C366 2004 324.971'071 C2004-906623-4

1 2 3 4 5 08 07 06 05 04

Conseil des Arts du Canada Canada Council for the Arts

We acknowledge the support of the Canada Council for the Arts and the Ontario Arts Council for our publishing program. We also acknowledge the financial support of the Government of Canada through the Book Publishing Industry Development Program and The Association for the Export of Canadian Books, and the Government of Ontario through the Ontario Book Publishers Tax Credit program, and the Ontario Media Development Corporation's Ontario Book Initiative.

Care has been taken to trace the ownership of copyright material used in this book. The author and the publisher welcome any information enabling them to rectify any references or credits in subsequent editions.

J. Kirk Howard, President

Printed and bound in Canada.
Printed on recycled paper.

www.dundurn.com

Dundurn Press
8 Market Street, Suite 200
Toronto, Ontario, Canada
M5E 1M6

Gazelle Book Services Limited
White Cross Mills
Hightown, Lancaster, England
LA1 4X5

Dundurn Press
2250 Military Road
Tonawanda, NY
U.S.A. 14150

TABLE OF CONTENTS

CHAPTER ONE

Election Night in Canada: *The Transition Continues*

by Jon H. Pammett and Christopher Dornan

THE CONTEXT OF THE 2004 VOTE

If elections are contests over how the country is to be governed and by whom, then the election of 2004 was an aftershock to a more seismic contest that had been going on for years. By 2002, there were open calls in the media for Prime Minister Jean Chrétien to step down. His opponents within the Liberal party, led by Prime-Minister-in-Waiting Paul Martin, were determined that he should go sooner rather than later. Chrétien and his supporters were equally resolved to remain in power until they decided the time was right to depart. Canadians were treated to a contest over who would govern them during the inter-election period between 2000 and 2004, but not one in which they had any meaningful say.

The fight between Chrétien and Martin was carried out through meetings in hotel rooms, whispers in corridors, harsh words in riding offices, icy stares in Cabinet, and a tremendous trumpet of leaks, counter-leaks, and heated opinions in the press. Not even Liberal Party members got to vote on the outcome. All they got to vote on in the end was a leadership contest between Paul Martin and Sheila Copps. Thus the context for the 2004 campaign was a bitter internecine power struggle within the Liberal Party.

The other crucial feature that set the stage for the 2004 election was the "sponsorship scandal," which is described later in this book. This was true not simply because it triggered sustained public outrage and galvanized widespread infuriation with the Liberals, but because it was the first true test of the new Martin regime. How this volatile political problem was handled would surely give the electorate a glimpse of how a Martin government might behave. The Martinite camp had been waiting in the wings for almost two years, unpestered by awkward questions from the media and content to let Chrétien take the barbs from the opposition in the House. They billed themselves as cool and ultra-competent technocrats who, the instant they took power, would install a government of rationalism, expertise, sound judgment, and good management, as opposed to the government of grease and favours and threats run by the wily old codger and his circle of backroom boys.

For political operatives preparing not only to run a government but also to win an election, they had plenty of time to prepare and still fumbled the file badly. It seemed as though they were taken by surprise at the depth and particularly the longevity of the animosity that attached to the sponsorship scandal. It did not blow over. It was as though the Martinites had assumed that the opprobrium would attach to Chrétien and that Canadians would join together in wishing him good riddance. When that did not happen, when it became apparent that the scandal was sticking to the party and — more ominously — to the new leader, they tripped all over themselves. What Canadians saw was not Paul Martin as unflappable chief executive officer, but the stammering Paul Martin, the one who could not get his tongue around the proper response because the response changed from day to day.

The timeline for the run-up to the 2004 general election went as follows:

- In early June 2002, with the drumbeats already out for his resignation, Jean Chrétien delivered a speech in Winnipeg. The Auditor General had by then given advance notice that she would be looking into the allocation of federal sponsorship monies in Quebec. In an unscripted departure from his text, Chrétien allowed that "perhaps a few million dollars were stolen," but that the program itself was necessary. "I had to make sure the presence of Canada was known in Quebec." He refused to apologize.

- Within a fortnight, Paul Martin was no longer in the Cabinet, despite the fact that by this point his supporters had sewn up by far the majority of the Liberals' 301 constituency associations. It became obvious that the sitting prime minister could not win this fight if it went to mandatory leadership review.

- At almost the same time, Alexa McDonough announced she was stepping down as NDP leader.

- In August, Joe Clark announced he would be retiring as leader of the Progressive Conservative Party.

- On August 21, Chrétien announced that he would be stepping down as leader of the Liberal Party, but not until February 2004.

- Martin then went on tour, outlining his vision on radio call-in shows and at speaking engagements. As a sitting MP, however, he could not be seen to be proposing a legislative agenda that differed from that of his own government. As a result, he spoke in generalities and bromides, while surrendering the legislative agenda to Chrétien, who crafted a series of "legacy" bills.

- In November 2002, in the wake of a series of ethics scandals, and immediately upon the forced resignation of Solicitor General Lawrence MacAuley, Chrétien unveiled an "ethics package" that would govern the conduct of elected members of Parliament and senators. Other initiatives included an Aboriginal governance package, the ratification of the Kyoto agreement, a promise to fix health care, and a measure to decriminalize possession of small amounts of marijuana.

- In January 2003 prominent Cabinet Minister Allan Rock dropped out of the lopsided contest to replace Jean Chrétien.

- In February, John Manley, the man who replaced Paul Martin as finance minister and at this point was still a leadership rival, delivered his first budget. It was widely seen as a Chrétienite budget, tying up government spending and taxation for the next five years and therefore hamstringing Martin.

- In March 2003 Chrétien declined the U.S. invitation for Canada to join the "coalition of the willing" in attacking Iraq.

- In June, Peter MacKay won the leadership of the Progressive Conservative Party in a bizarre deal with party gadfly David Orchard, in which MacKay promised in writing that he would not — among other things — countenance a merger with the Alliance.

- In August, John Manley bowed out of the race to replace Chrétien as leader of the Liberal Party. Like Rock before him, he confronted the reality that the contest was unwinnable. The eligible party voters had been ruthlessly conscripted by the Martin camp and no amount of stumping or backroom dealing was going to turn the tide.

- Meanwhile, Jack Layton had become leader of the NDP, and the negotiations between MacKay of the Progressive Conservatives and Stephen Harper of the Alliance about finally "uniting the right" had begun in earnest. All the opposition parties recognized that they had very little time to get organized. Martin might call a spring election, if only to catch his opponents exhausted and off guard.

- On October 3, 2003, Dalton McGuinty's Liberals won the Ontario provincial election, forming a government with 72 of 103 seats and reducing the Tories to 24. Almost immediately, though, McGuinty reneged on campaign promises having to do with spending and taxation. He insisted he was forced to do so once he discovered the financial mess the Ontario Conservatives had left him, but his reversal was popularly seen as more evidence of Liberal perfidy: they will say anything to get elected and then do what they want once they are in power. The resentment stuck to the federal Liberal Party like a Limpet mine.

- Paul Martin was elected leader of the Liberal Party and prime minister in November 2003. In February 2004 the House reconvened and heard the Speech from the Throne. The following week, Auditor General Sheila Fraser released her report into the federal sponsorship program in Quebec and all hell broke loose.

- By the time the snow melted in southern Canada in 2004, the Liberals had lost any hope of inroads in Quebec, where the sponsorship scandal was playing out especially badly — Quebecers were insulted by the revelations that the feds were trying to buy them off, and further incensed that they were seen as corrupt sponges for federal money. The Liberals' promises of a new accord with Western Canada were dashed by their own performance and the emergence of Stephen Harper as leader of the Conservative Party. They might have hoped to hold their own in Atlantic Canada, but the Maritimes are not sufficiently rich in seats to deliver a government. Meanwhile, vote-rich Ontario, which the Liberals were counting on, became troublesome terrain. If the Conservatives carried the West, the NDP took the Maritimes, the Bloc controlled Quebec, and the Conservatives captured enough seats in Ontario, the result might be the Balkanization of the country.

With that calculus in mind, the Martinites still called an election for early summer 2004. Did they win or did they lose? They certainly failed to form a majority government. On the other hand, they denied the Conservatives and the NDP what they had hoped for. Only the Bloc Québécois was returned in numbers that were decisive. Quite apart from the returns, however, are the patterns of voting and the political realities that gave us this result.

CAMPAIGN TRENDS AND DEVELOPMENTS

After putting aside their plans for an early 2004 election and rejecting the temptation to call a late 2004 or spring 2005 election (partly because they felt this was what the Conservatives wanted), the Liberals were left with a mid-2004 election. By all accounts, many within the party had misgivings about this strategy. The sponsorship scandal was still in the news, and the government's popularity had not fully recovered from its effects. Public reaction to putative planks in the election platform around health care renewal and democratic reform could best be characterized as indifferent. As the weeks went by, the Paul Martin team became less and less "fresh-faced" in the public mind, and more like "the same old gang." And more and more the question became, "What exactly is their New Agenda anyway?" The answer, "Wait till the election campaign," locked the party in to holding the election before the height of summer, lest the public and media cynicism level rise unacceptably.

Governments in Canada seeking re-election appear to stumble into "bad campaigns" about every ten years. The spectres of the Progressive Conservative campaign of 1993 under Kim Campbell and the Liberal campaigns of 1984 and 1972, under John Turner and Pierre Trudeau respectively, appeared to haunt the Martin Liberals in 2004. Looking further back, the Diefenbaker re-election campaign of 1962 and the final St. Laurent campaign of 1957 provided further examples of ineptitude. In all of these cases, the incumbents failed to generate the image of a government with a fresh approach to problems and a set of plans for the future. Rather, they gave the impression that they didn't quite know what they wanted to do in the next mandate they sought from the electorate. They appeared to assume that, the party having achieved office, they were entitled to stay there. They strove to give an example of competence, but the more self-consciously they did so, the more they created the opposite impression. The "arrogance of power" was always in the background, blinding leaders of government parties to reality. And contrary to what one might expect, new leaders taking over governments, like Kim Campbell, John Turner, and Paul Martin, seemed to suffer even more than experienced ones seeking re-election of administrations they had headed for a full term.

What did Campbell, Turner, and Martin have in common? Primarily, they all replaced prime ministers who, for one reason or another, were reluctant to leave. Brian Mulroney, Pierre Trudeau, and Jean Chrétien all felt they had been successful leaders and that they had more work to do. They thought back to their more popular days and felt that these could return under the right circumstances. They certainly felt that they were not only more experienced but also more creative in generating plans and ideas, and more resourceful in finding ways to bring them about, than their successors. Mulroney had changed the nature of the country's trade relationships for the foreseeable future; Trudeau had changed and rehabilitated the constitution; and Chrétien had steadied the economy, passed the Clarity Act, and committed the country to the Kyoto agreement. Despite the fact that their popularity had dropped (to some extent because of the aforementioned actions) they were hard acts to follow. Once they realized that their departure was inevitable, they hung on as long as possible. And their shadows hung ominously over the parties their successors inherited.

For Paul Martin, the Chrétien legacy was not necessarily the problem that Mulroney had posed for Campbell or that Trudeau had caused Turner. As finance minister, Martin had been a major part of the Chrétien government and the main architect of its fiscal policy. While some of the spending cuts were controversial, the results in terms of financial stability and deficit reduction were generally supported by public opinion; they helped to undercut the main policy agenda of the opposition Reform and Alliance parties. Recent policy actions spearheaded by Chrétien, like the commitment to the Kyoto Agreement on Climate Change and the decision not to send troops to support the American invasion of Iraq, were popular in the country at large. The sponsorship scandal did not need to be handled by blaming Chrétien, as Martin ended up doing by implication. Chrétien was in fact reasonably popular personally throughout the country, even in Quebec. Martin's decision to distance himself from Chrétien and pursue what looked like a vendetta against him and his supporters within the party, as Stephen Clarkson writes in Chapter Two, was the product of a personal decision, and it gave a negative cast to the public image of the Liberal Party.

If we look back to the chain of three Liberal victories during the Chrétien years, the party had the advantage of being "closest to the public" on all three of the major issue areas: economic issues, national unity issues, and social issues.[1] When the economic issues were defined as unemployment, the deficit, and the debt, or taxes (except in 1997), the Liberals had the edge as the party closest to where the electorate stood. And, ironically enough, this edge came from Paul Martin, the co-author of the Red Book from 1993 that created the short-term jobs program and the finance minister who led the government's economic policy into the elections of 1997 and 2000. To the extent that national unity or constitutional issues were important to the public, there again the Liberals had the edge, a traditional Liberal strength dating back to the time of Laurier. And finally, social policy, defined as issues of health, pensions, education, and welfare, was associated with the Liberal Party because it had carefully cultivated the image (deserved or not) of being responsible, not only for introducing these programs, but also for defending them in the face of conservative attacks.

In 2004, even at the outset of the campaign, the Liberals maintained the advantage in only one of these issue areas — social policy (see Chapter Eleven). The sponsorship scandal, where sums of money were paid illicitly, supposedly to promote national feeling in Quebec, undermined Liberal credibility, particularly in Quebec itself, where the prevailing attitude among citizens was resentment at being bought with one's own money (see Chapter Five). In some other areas of the country, resentment at supposed "special treatment" for Quebec soured public attitudes towards the Liberals. Jean Chrétien would have defended these expenditures as necessary to save Canada, as he did at earlier stages in the revelations of sponsorship money going astray. Paul Martin backed away from it in horror, but convinced few, in or out of Quebec, that he didn't know about the scandal, or that he could be the new champion of national unity.

Then came the leaders' debates, in which Martin was outclassed by Gilles Duceppe, the leader of the Bloc Québécois. The Liberal campaign at that point almost seemed to abandon Quebec, and the number of seats they lost in that province went a long way toward losing them their majority.

If the national unity area slipped away from the Liberals because of the sponsorship scandal, the economic issue domain slipped away through neglect. Aside from some potential aid for cities, the Liberals made little mention of the economy apart from the occasional reference to the desirability of "prosperity." This left the economic area to be defined by the other parties, which did so primarily in the realm of taxation. The Conservatives promised to cut taxes, and the Liberals were content to ridicule the notion that such a tax cut could go along with the increased spending on social programs that the Tories also promised. The Liberals foresaw no changes in taxation in the implementation of their program. This strategy forfeited the ground of economic voting to the Conservatives (see Chapter Eleven, Table 5). While indeed tax reduction turned out to be the most important issue to relatively few Canadian voters, those who did value it heavily favoured the Conservatives. More important for the Liberals, however, was their abdication of the whole issue area of economic stimulation, which might have gained some votes for them. They opted instead to put all their eggs in the social policy basket.

From the beginning, the Liberals decided that "fixing health care for a generation" was to be their main campaign plank, though as the campaign went on "reducing waiting times" became a more familiar refrain for Paul Martin, perhaps in an effort to be more specific about how it would be fixed. The health care issue did work in the Liberals' favour and appears to be a major factor in the limited victory they eventually achieved. However, promises to fix health care have been a staple of Liberal campaigns since the 1993 Red Book, and a decade of federal-provincial infighting (interspersed with a couple of Health Care Accords) has certainly succeeded in persuading Canadians that a quick fix is not possible. This was especially true in 2004, since the Liberal plan consisted essentially of allocating sums of money (the most frequently mentioned number at the beginning of the campaign was $9 billion) to existing programs rather than implementing any reforms to the system. And as many commentators remarked, the Canadian health care system is capable of soaking up as much money as is available to it.

The Conservatives were well aware that the Liberals had an advantage on the health care issue as the campaign began. The Alliance Party had suffered in the 2000 election because the Liberals successfully linked them, despite their protestations, with plans to change the system in favour of more private medical care. Their efforts to escape this image are best exemplified by the decision of leader Stockwell Day to hold up a homemade card during the leaders' debate which said "No 2-tier health care." This time, the Stephen Harper Conservatives were determined to fight the Liberals on their own ground by promising even more money for health care than the Liberals were and adding that they would implement a national plan to cover drug expenses. To a considerable extent, the health policy area was the centrepiece in Harper's attempt to improve the credibility of the new Conservative Party by moving it to the centre of the political spectrum and styling it to resemble the Liberals. If this was "uniting the right," the strategy appears to have been to get it together and move it to the centre. The strategy likely worked when health policy alone is considered — the problem was the combination of promises of increased health care spending with substantial proposed tax cuts. The combination of policies allowed critics and other parties to ridicule the "black hole" in the Conservatives' budget that would result from both raising spending and cutting revenues.

The shift in the overall issue agenda of Canadian federal elections (see Chapter Eleven, Table 4) has been dramatic. Over the last four elections, the emphasis of the electoral campaign discourse has changed from economics to the social policy agenda, and particularly health. This change has not been gradual, though 1997 appears in retrospect to have been a transitional election that, while still weighted toward issues of unemployment and job creation, gave substantial attention to both national unity and social issues. Since that time, the issue of unemployment has virtually disappeared from election discourse, as have questions of job creation and overall economic stimulation. The one exception to this was the issue of regional economic development, which continued to be a political theme in the Atlantic region.

It is hard to think of another substantial period of time since Confederation when the economic development, growth, or policy of the country has not been front and centre during a series of federal elections. The Conservatives' national policy, and ensuing debates over the height and nature of the tariff, dominated elections from 1878 until the First World War, and even beyond, as the economic reintegration of servicemen was the concern in 1921. Elections in the 1930s debated ways out of the economic depression, while post-war economic stimulation and reorientation dominated the agenda in the second half of the 1940s. Gallup Polls in the 1950s and 1960s show that the public issue agenda was dominated by economic concerns, and the National Election Studies since their inception in 1965 gave the same result. What has happened in the twenty-first century to make the public and the politicians forget about economics?

It is one answer, though not a terribly convincing one, to cite the good performance of the economy in the last half-decade. The 1993 election was held in the atmosphere of an 11 percent unemployment rate, and in 1997 more than 9 percent of the workforce was looking for jobs. By November of 2000, however, the unemployment rate had dropped to 6.9 percent, and for the 2004 election it had risen only slightly to 7.2 percent.[2] On the face of it, however, these unemployment numbers are not particularly low in absolute terms and might be thought to have merited at least a moderate amount of concern. After all, in the 1979 Canadian federal election, an unemployment rate of 7 percent caused 10 percent of the public to cite it as the most important election issue. This occurred despite the fact that two other issues were important in 1979: inflation, which had dominated the previous election discourse, was still high, and the upcoming referendum in Quebec meant that the Liberals were orienting their campaign around their self-proclaimed advantage in promoting the national unity of the country.[3]

Since that time, the persistence of unemployment rates above 5 percent has occurred for so many years that the public has come to accept this as normal. In addition, the public has become rather cynical about the efforts of modern politicians to mount offensives to reduce the jobless rate. Brian Mulroney's cry that the only issue in the 1984 election was "jobs, jobs, jobs" was not followed by any conspicuous action to provide them, and Jean Chrétien's 1993 Red Book promise of a short-term job creation program made only a very modest contribution to the employment situation. It appears that the unemployment problem can shoulder its way back onto the election agenda in a major way only when it exceeds 10 percent. When it does so, it tends to dominate the election rhetoric; the public identifies it as a problem, and the media promote it as an agenda item. When the unemployment rate drops back to a position around 7 percent, it now seems to fall off the election radar screen altogether.

In addition, the existence of the free trade agreements within North America has made it more difficult for national governments in this hemisphere to promise to take a hand in directly creating jobs. Under these agreements, jobs are supposed to move within the continent according to the ability of different economic sectors to enjoy a comparative advantage. The election rhetoric around the free trade agreement issue in the 1988 campaign debated whether these treaties would create jobs for Canada or lose jobs because they would move to the United States, where wage rates were lower and unionization less entrenched. In the period since 1988, the extension of the free trade agreement into NAFTA has brought job competition from Mexico into the picture. It has also, however, allowed governments in all three countries to avoid responsibility for any negative aspects of the state of the economy by saying that the operation of NAFTA takes time to evaluate and that any job losses in one area are compensated for by gains in another. And, more generally, the argument that globalization has made it difficult for any party or government to pull the levers of the national economy and achieve results is widely accepted and generally bemoaned. This public perception of the power of global economic forces has persuaded many that participation at the national level has less relevance than in the past.

In addition, the non-Quebec parties in the Canadian federal opposition in recent years, Reform, the Alliance, the Progressive Conservatives, and the Conservatives, have championed ideologies that do not favour interventionist economic policies to promote jobs or stimulate the economy. Rather their agenda has advocated restraint in government commitments and reductions in taxation. With the exception of the Progressive Conservatives, now no longer in existence, these parties have opposed the implementation of the Kyoto agreement, which commits the country to strict future controls on greenhouse gas emissions. Their position is that such commitments might inhibit economic growth and cost jobs. Therefore, in a sense, they are able to escape any campaign dialogue on the issue of job creation by deflecting the discussion to the environment area and arguing that others are at fault for accepting restrictions on the activities of business.

Perhaps more important, however, than a lack of public attention to the economy has been the increased public concern in the last decade about the state of the Canadian health care system. Relentless publicity about hospital or bed closings, hospital debt, long waiting lists, and lack of proper equipment has raised the alarm. Many people have experienced the impact of these problems on their own treatment or those of family and friends. Provincial governments have stated over and over again that the federal government has produced this situation by cutting back on the share of medical care funding originally envisioned when the programs were implemented, and the federal government has in turn criticized the provinces for not implementing services properly or diverting money to other purposes. The federal government thinks it is "paying the piper without calling the tune," and the provincial governments think the federal government has been "calling the tune without paying the piper." Either way, sweet music has not been the result.

Pleased as the general public might be to cease paying attention to this inter-governmental dispute, personal interest has made this impossible. The demographic trends of a lower birth rate and higher life expectancy have meant the aging of the population overall. People are living longer and there are more and more older people in the citizenry. These people are not just concerned with health issues when they get sick; they are vitally interested in modern health procedures, such as hip and joint replacements, which can contribute to their quality of life. Publicity about diagnostic tests or machines and expensive new drugs leads to a demand for access to them where appropriate. Demands on the health service have seemingly exceeded the ability of all governments to provide the supply.

Finally, we note the fact that the older segments of the population are the ones who vote at very high levels in elections. In the 2000 federal election, more than 80 percent of those aged sixty-five or over cast a ballot.[4] Older people have health care on their minds and are inclined to evaluate the political parties on this issue. It is no wonder that the political parties in 2004 headed into the election campaign with promises to rectify the health care system. Even the Green Party and the Bloc Québécois, whose main issue domains lay in other areas, produced health care improvement plans (see chapters Five and Six). Young people turn out to vote at lower levels, and the dominance of electoral discussion by health care is one reason for this; after all, many young people feel primarily healthy and are concerned with other things. But the presence of so many seniors and middle-aged people (often also dealing with parents who need medical care) in the active electorate means that, short of an economic crisis, health policy issues will be at the forefront of electoral discourse for many elections to come.

If the Liberals entered the 2004 election campaign with an advantage in only one of the three main issue clusters, they counted on being able to convince the voters that, on three other attitudinal measures, they merited a fourth term in office. But here again there were problems. A major one had to do with ratings of the leaders themselves. Paul Martin counted, in his appeal to the Liberal Party, on a degree of popularity Jean Chrétien had never achieved. Not only was Martin considered to be more popular in their home province of Quebec, but he intended to make inroads into opposition support in the West on the basis of his personal appeal. The Martin vision was to be a truly national one, which would free the Liberal Party from its dependence on central Canadian votes and seats. While this vision might have propelled Martin to finally challenge Chrétien and win the leadership of the Liberal Party (see Chapter Two), it ultimately did not play out the same way during the election campaign. Martin's popularity exceeded Chrétien's in only two regions of the country, Quebec and the Atlantic, and ultimately did not benefit the party in these areas (see Chapter Eleven, Table 9). In particular, Chrétien was more popular than Martin in the West and in Ontario.

The same factors that eroded the possibility of Martin making a personal appeal affected another aspect of public opinion where the Liberals felt they had an initial advantage — the image of competence and the repositories of public trust. Establishing their credentials in this area was particularly important to the Liberal campaign, since it had been vital in the three previous election victories where the other parties had been successfully portrayed as erratic and inexperienced. The Liberals, the traditional party of government for much of the twentieth century, could be counted on to manage the affairs of state, to steer a centrist course, to operate in a brokerage manner giving something to everyone, and to touch enough nationalistic chords to engender a bit of patriotism on occasion. When the country tired of the Mulroney interregnum in 1993, it was clearly the Liberals to whom they could safely turn.

The sponsorship scandal undermined the image of trust and competence that normally attended the Liberal Party. It was not so much the sums of money involved, but rather the revelation that a privileged position had been used to benefit the friends of the party. The fact that those responsible for the sponsorship program had been friends and appointees of the Chrétien Liberal Party rather than the allies of incoming Paul Martin gave the Martinites a false sense of security about being able to deal with the revelations. Although they didn't do it, they felt they could say, they would clean it up. The problems with that strategy inside and outside of the Liberal Party were quite different. Inside the party, where relations were already strained between the Martin and Chrétien camps, blaming the other faction was seen as disloyalty. Outside the party, the electorate was not paying the same kind of attention to the fine details of who was getting along with whom — weren't these new Liberals the same as the old Liberals? How could Paul Martin, who had been minister of finance when money was being spent in places it should not have been, not have known about it? In the crudest terms, if he did know he was now lying about it, and if he didn't know he was incompetent. In such a no win situation, the Martin Liberals suffered from a diminution of the public trust.

Neither was Paul Martin the fresh face and personable leader he might have been had he won the Liberal leadership in 1990. In 2004, he was by a considerable margin the oldest of the leaders. Though energetic, the bursts of energy looked at times forced and unconvincing, perhaps not in keeping with a politician of his years, who should project an image of calmness and wisdom. That had worked for Macdonald, Laurier, King, St. Laurent, and Trudeau in their later years. In contrast, Martin looked rather frantic, with his hurried speaking style and his waving arm movements. If Jack Layton acted much the same way, at least he wasn't so old and he smiled a lot. If Stephen Harper appeared wooden in comparison, at least he wasn't trying to act like this on purpose. The personae of the other leaders made Gilles Duceppe look positively presidential.

So the Liberals, having failed to appeal on leadership and trust, fell back on the only other factor on which they had an advantage — values. "Choose your Canada," said a Liberal fundraising appeal inserted into several of the country's newspapers during the campaign. It continued, "Help us Build the Canada you Want. For the Liberal Party of Canada, this election is about the values we share as Canadians. Together, we can build a Canada that reflects your values as we strengthen the social foundations of Canadian life." The patina of social and moral conservatism that had attended the Reform Party from its inception and persisted in the Alliance Party led by the fundamentalist Christian Stockwell Day continued to attach itself to the Conservative Party in 2004. This latent public view of the Conservatives existed despite strenuous efforts of Stephen Harper and many of his associates to clamp down on statements by members of the party in favour of such things as dismantling official bilingualism and outlawing abortion. It was accentuated by statements made by several former members of the Progressive Conservative Party who were opposed to the merger that formed the Conservatives, including former leader Joe Clark, that they could not support the values of the Alliance, which they feared would dominate the new party. Some Progressive Conservative MPs crossed the floor of the House of Commons to join the Liberals. Liberal advertising took advantage of these public doubts about the Conservatives — choose *your* Canada, voters were exhorted, not theirs.

In summation, of six possible areas in which public opinion might have been on their side, the Liberals called the election with the advantage in only two, social policy and values. Two others, leadership and national unity, might charitably be considered a saw-off. And on economic issues and the trust/competence factor, the Liberals suffered in comparison with the other parties, primarily the Conservatives. Why they went ahead with the election under these circumstances is unclear. Despite the fact that there was a new prime minister at the helm, the 2000 election had occurred less than four years before, so there was certainly no stigma of potential defeat that could have been attached to waiting till fall 2004 or even spring 2005. And they had already waited too long to use the "we need a new mandate for a new leader" argument. In any event, the Liberal advantage in the social policy and value domains was enough to win them only a plurality of seats, and even then, as many of the chapters in this book point out, they might consider themselves lucky to have achieved even that dubious victory.

If the Liberal campaign strategy remains a point of contention, the main puzzle about the Conservatives relates to the meaning for them of the election results. The party's campaign made the most of their opportunities to capitalize on the manifest public discontent with the Liberals. Their message was the classic exhortation to vote for the opposition if one wants a change from the government. "Demand Better," they said, an effective slogan that combined the point that the Liberals had disappointed people over the recent scandals with a reminder that the Conservatives were the alternative, a party that had overtly positioned itself to become a viable alternative government. They made, no doubt, a few missteps, as is pointed out in Chapter Three. They reacted to favourable public opinion polls partway through the campaign by setting up a "transition team" to smooth the transfer of power after they formed a government. This struck many people as arrogant (neutralizing somewhat their advantage over the Liberals in that department), but also brought home to people the real possibility that they could wake up the morning after the voting to find the Conservatives in power. Similarly, the inability of the Conservatives to silence some of the "loose cannons" in their ranks who promoted their opposition to same-sex marriage, a woman's right to abortion, and francophone rights to bilingual services and opportunities hurt the party by reminding some voters of why they had not felt comfortable supporting the Reform or Alliance parties. Nevertheless, the Conservatives ran an effective campaign, and it is difficult to conceive how they could have done much better under the circumstances.

So how do we interpret the Conservative results? Did they make a further significant advance on Alliance and Reform, taking the popular vote to a new high of almost 30 percent, a gain of 5 percent from the 2000 election? Or did they make a spectacular failure in uniting the right, falling back almost 8 percentage points from the combined Alliance and

Progressive Conservative vote total in the previous election? All in all, the former interpretation seems more persuasive. For one thing, academics and journalists united in pointing out, nobody believed that the new Conservative Party would be able to count on the combined vote of the two parties that merged to produce it. In particular, Progressive Conservative supporters in previous elections looked much more like Liberal voters than Alliance or Reform voters. The most that realistically could be expected from the merger was to position the Conservatives as a stronger official opposition, without the Progressive Conservatives nipping at their heels by telling all and sundry that *they* were the real "national opposition" by virtue of having some seats outside the West and having a bit more vote share in Quebec. The most credible claim for Conservative gains in 2004 was their vastly improved seat total of ninety-nine, enough to position the party to make a strong impact in the next Parliament. The 5 percent improvement in the vote from the Alliance total in 2000, given the dominance of the new party by Alliance stalwarts, is a significant achievement. (A more pessimistic view of the election outcome for the Conservatives is offered in Chapter Eleven.)

The question for the Conservatives is whether they have achieved their natural limit in growth. Certainly, it is reasonable for the party to aspire to further gains in Ontario, but they will not likely be able to form a government without improvement in Quebec. Even if they managed to do so, it would probably be counterproductive for the Conservatives in much the same way that it was for the Diefenbaker Progressive Conservatives in 1957. That party was able to get a one-time cadre of Quebec MPs elected in the subsequent election of 1958, but the circumstances of that event (the support came as a result of an alliance with the provincial Union Nationale party, which was shortly to be decimated) meant that no firm party roots were developed in Quebec. Only when Brian Mulroney became leader were the Progressive Conservatives able to establish a solid base in Quebec, and this support has now more or less evaporated. It is hard to believe that a Stephen Harper–led Conservative Party can make major inroads in the province.

The New Democratic Party made gains in the 2004 election. It almost doubled its popular vote, to 16 percent, the best showing since 1988. Its new leader, Jack Layton, gained more attention than did the two previous leaders, putting the NDP in a position last occupied during the Ed Broadbent years (1979 to 1988) when the party challenged for power in a more credible way. But despite the eternal optimism of the party, it is hard to put too positive a spin on the results. The party's seat gain was minimal (six seats) despite the popular vote increase. The circumstances of the 2004 election — general discontent with the Liberals and the limited willingness of those wanting change to immediately trust the Conservatives — were particularly favourable to the party. With a telegenic new leader and the possibility of picking up voters from the Red Tory ranks of the defunct Progressive Conservative Party as well as disenchanted Liberal voters looking for a safe haven, the NDP should have done better. This was particularly true since the election, as the one before it, was dominated by discussion of the nation's social policy agenda, long the special preserve of the NDP. Medicare was pioneered in Saskatchewan under the party, which has championed it ever since. Much of the current debate over health care centred on the recommendations of a Royal Commission headed by Roy Romanow, a prominent New Democrat and former premier of Saskatchewan.

The NDP narrowly missed out on holding the balance of power in the current Parliament, a status that would have allowed them more control over the policy agenda and an opportunity to improve their credibility and visibility. Had the NDP extracted a promise from the Liberals to hold a national referendum on introducing elements of proportional representation into the electoral system, their position might have been secured for the foreseeable future. As it is, the party is in a position to lose support to both the Conservatives and the Liberals in different regions of the country if a consensus develops that minority government is undesirable.

A good argument can be made that the Green Party was one of the big winners of the 2004 election. Even though the party did not manage to elect a single member, it could boast a substantial proportional increase in its vote, now over 4 percent nationally. Changes to the party financing rules will mean that the party will receive funds for its operations during the interelection period and be able to retain a presence rather than disappear from the public consciousness until the next campaign. The Green Party's 2004 campaign centred on a more comprehensive issue agenda than previously (see Chapter Six), and in general they appeared to be taken more seriously by the news media than in the past. There was genuine sympathy for their demands to be included in the leaders' debates on the basis of their showings in the polls rather than their vote total in the previous election. Still, the party's main hope for growth appears to rest on a change in the electoral system to implement representation according to vote totals. The mixed proportional/single member electoral system in Germany, for example, allows the Greens to play an important role in government, and this model shines very brightly for the party.

Finally, the 2004 Canadian general election saw a further decline in the voting participation rate (see Chapter Twelve). On the face of it, the decline is quite small — less than one percentage point. But several aspects continue to prove worrisome to those concerned with maximizing citizen participation in contemporary democracy. As the chapters in this book show, the degree of competition showed a marked increase in several parts of the country, notably Ontario and British Columbia. Turnout was up in those two provinces, but not by much. The overall public climate of negativity toward politicians was not alleviated by the presence of new leaders in 2004, and in fact the negative nature of much of the campaign advertising may have exacerbated the public's disdain for politicians and all things political. The general level of political interest in 2004 did not seem to differ from that of previous elections, particularly among young people. Massive efforts were expended during the campaign to publicize the low voting rate among youth and exhort them to participate. While we do not yet have data that would allow comparative analysis of the participation of various age cohorts, the overall rate does not allow for optimism that youth were more energized by the 2004 campaign than they had been in 2000.

All of these developments outlined in this chapter place an enormous burden on the upcoming minority Parliament. The performance of the politicians in general, and of the individual parties and leaders, will make a substantial difference in the outcome, not only of the next election, but also of the relations of citizens to their government. To the extent that activity is constructive, issue related, and scandal-free, the public is likely to respond with increased attention and interest. If the new Parliament gains the reputation for inaction, bickering, negativity, and corruption, the consequences will be unfortunate, and not just for the Liberals.

NOTES

1 See Jon Pammett, "The Peoples' Verdict," in *The Canadian General Election of 2000,* ed. Jon H. Pammett and Christopher Dornan (Toronto: Dundurn Press, 2001), 303, for a summary of the results from all three previous elections.

2 Statistics for unemployment and other economic indicators are available at the Government of Canada Web site, http://canadaeconomy.gc.ca.

3 Harold D. Clarke, Jane Jenson, Lawrence LeDuc, and Jon H. Pammett, *Absent Mandate: Interpreting Change in Canadian Elections* (Toronto: Gage, 1991), 70–71.

4 Jon H. Pammett and Lawrence LeDuc, *Explaining the Turnout Decline in Recent Federal Elections: Evidence from a new Survey of Nonvoters* (Ottawa: Elections Canada, 2003).

CHAPTER TWO

Disaster and Recovery: *Paul Martin as Political Lazarus*[1]

by Stephen Clarkson

The 2004 election campaign was about succession, not success. How would Jack Layton, recently plucked from Toronto's City Hall by the New Democratic Party, lead it on the hustings? How would Stephen Harper make the transition from running the Alberta-based, right-wing Alliance Party to speaking for all Canadian conservatives after its merger with the PCs? Who would end up wearing the mantle as defender of Quebec's interests? And — the central issue for this chapter — how would Paul Martin manage the double-edged task of sustaining the Liberal Party of Canada's (LPC's) hegemony over federal politics while bringing it the renewal that he had promised during his determined campaign to oust Jean Chrétien from the Prime Minister's Office?

Renewal has seldom troubled new Liberal leaders. Five men have taken over the party leadership while their caucus faced the government from across the aisle in the House of Commons. Alexander Mackenzie (1873), Wilfrid Laurier (1887), Mackenzie King (1919), Lester Pearson (1958), and Jean Chrétien (1990) had ample opportunity to redefine their party while learning the ropes as Leader of the Official Opposition. Nor had the first two occasions when the Liberals changed leaders while in power proven problematic. Louis St. Laurent had carried on in 1948 as Mackenzie King's anointed successor and, embodying continuity rather than change, won two more majority governments before going down to defeat in 1957. Having won a highly competitive leadership race in 1968, Pierre Elliott Trudeau so incarnated fresh air in his personal style and philosophy while also winning his party's loyalty that he quickly turned Pearson's minority into a majority government without having to attack his predecessor in order to prove he was different. The transfer of power from Chrétien in 2003 took neither of these successes as its model.

Only the example of John Turner, who brought down the Liberal temple by shaking its pillars to the ground in 1984, proved irresistible to Paul Martin. Indeed, the parallels between the two aspirants were eerie. As former and successful ministers of finance who had left the cabinet following bitter personal breaks with their prime ministers, each had become the toast of the business community and the darling of the media. As dauphins-in-exile, each had rallied supporters who split the party into feuding camps. Once crowned leader following their prime minister's belated announcement of retirement, both swept into Ottawa as if the Opposition had just defeated the government. They purged incumbents connected to the old regime, which they disowned by announcing major restructurings. Then, supremely confident in their own electoral superiority, they rejected counsels of caution, preferring campaigning to governing. Unable to change their organizational approach while trying to please everyone, they blundered on the hustings, giving mixed ideological messages and managing thereby to enhance their opponents.

It was the difference in his Conservative opponent that saved Paul Martin from suffering Turner's fate. In 1984, Brian Mulroney had been the more "liberal" of the two leaders, more clearly offering the public continuity with the outgoing Trudeau record on bilingualism and social policies. Twenty years later, the Liberals' challenger came from the far right, not from the centre, thus allowing Martin to adopt the campaign strategy of his ousted nemesis, Chrétien. Like his predecessor, he could provide bland, left-leaning policy rhetoric while demonizing his opponent. With the media communicating deep concerns about Stephen Harper's social conservatism, the voters ultimately had second thoughts about dismissing the governing party, however unworthy of office it might have seemed.

To understand how Martin turned what was generally expected in the fall of 2003 to be the most boring of Canadian elections (because it would return the Liberals with an even larger majority) into one of the most exciting campaigns ever (in which their impending defeat was only averted on the weekend before the vote), we need:

- to show how the dynamic of Martin's ascent to power established the conditions for his near loss of it;
- to trace how his handling of the job of prime minister led him to call a premature election;
- to understand his campaign's near-disastrous organization, strategy, and platform;
- to review how the media first acted as enemy and then as ally to reinforce his message; and
- to establish how the campaign in the regions confirmed continuity rather than change in the Canadian party system as well as to reflect on what the results suggest about the continuing evolution of the Canadian party system.

PAUL MARTIN'S ASCENT TO POWER AND THE CONDITIONS FOR TROUBLE

Always close to his Liberal cabinet-minister father and namesake, who had unsuccessfully run for the party's leadership against both Pearson and Trudeau, Paul Martin Jr. went into politics to avenge these paternal failures by becoming prime minister himself. He had won the nomination in the safe Montreal riding of LaSalle-Émard in 1988[2] and, rookie though he may have been, was attractive enough as a successful, bilingual businessman that he would have won the party's leadership in 1990 had Jean Chrétien not already secured effective control over its organization following his own defeat by Turner in 1984.

Biding his time on the assumption that his turn would come in due course, Martin accepted Chrétien's assignment of co-authoring the party's winning platform in 1993 and went on to be the country's most successful finance minister. Even though he cut federal spending programs more drastically than had ever been tried before, he managed to remain the most popular member of the government, a reality that contributed to sustaining the prime minister's ambivalent animus against him. For his part, Chrétien was neither inclined to forget nor to forgive. He did not forget that, during a candidates' policy debate in 1990, Martin's supporters had shouted "*vendu*," implying he was a traitor to Quebec on the white-hot issue of the year, the Meech Lake Accord. And he did not forgive Martin's obvious ambition to succeed him. Nevertheless, Chrétien gave Martin such sustained support in his deficit-slashing mission that their prime minister–finance minister partnership proved the most productive in Canadian history. This volatile mix of political solidarity and personal antipathy remained stable during Chrétien's first ministry.

Following Chrétien's second majority election in 1997, Martin's advisers began to become impatient. At the party's 1998 convention they kept a low profile, not running insurgent candidates for the executive.[3] But the following year they launched a quiet campaign to take over the party organization. Starting at the riding level, John Webster and Michele Cadario started working with friendly MPs. In the summer, Martin organizer Karl Littler concluded from a study of Liberal Party membership rules that capturing riding presidencies was the key to establishing control. By September, these covert activists had taken over the party's Ontario executive at its provincial convention,[4] a pattern that was repeated over the next two years in all provinces outside Quebec. The Quebec wing remained under Alfonso Gagliano's patronage-fuelled control until the Martinites took it over in December 2002.[5]

By February 2000, one month before the party's looming convention, everything seemed to be falling in place for Paul Martin to realize his ambition, once the prime minister made his expected announcement of retirement. On March 10, just days before the delegates gathered in Ottawa, Martin's backers met at the Regal Constellation Hotel near the Toronto airport to review their situation.[6] When the press reported this gathering as a meeting of conspirators plotting against the party's leader, Chrétien reacted with typical spitefulness. Although Martin gained control of the LPC's national executive that month, Chrétien spiked their guns by pre-emptively calling another election, winning a third majority and postponing the inevitable showdown.

The pressure that was building up on Chrétien from the rebels within his caucus and the party's extra-parliamentary wing was exacerbated from the outside by the media's reports of polls suggesting strong public support for his replacement by his finance minister. Furthermore, his chief contender's grip on the party apparatus meant that his minions could skew the delegate-selection process to ensure their supporters would be elected in the ridings when convention delegates were being chosen. By 2002, the Alberta, B.C., Ontario, and Quebec wings had changed the rules for recruiting new members to the party. Riding presidents, who were now mostly in Martin's camp, would be given one hundred membership forms at a time, whereas others could only get five. In B.C., a further restriction favouring the Martin team required names of new party recruits to be submitted prior to getting the requisite forms. (Martin's rivals Sheila Copps, John Manley, and Allan Rock complained so vigorously about these rules' unfairness that they were modified in Ontario the following January, but complaints continued to be voiced that those opposed to Martin were not even receiving their five forms upon demand.)

Once it became clear that so many Martin delegates would converge on the Liberals' long-postponed convention in February 2003 that they would pass the party's constitutionally required resolution calling for a leadership convention (and in so doing indicate no confidence in their leader), Chrétien announced his intention to retire at a caucus meeting in Chicoutimi in August 2002.[7] But ever ornery, he declared he would hang on for eighteen more months, giving himself time to leave a more progressive legacy and keep Martin champing at the bit.

By this time, however, the prime minister had made the serious error of firing his finance minister. Whether or not Martin had engineered his own dismissal from cabinet,[8] his departure from the government on June 2, 2002, left him free to pursue his leadership campaign without being constrained by the norm of cabinet solidarity. With alacrity, he accepted high-profile speaking engagements around the country. He burnished his international bona fides by accepting the invitation of Secretary General of the United Nations Kofi Annan to co-chair, with former Mexican president Ernesto Zedillo, a study on how private enterprise might rescue the Third World from its poverty. He consulted with such public figures as Michael Ignatieff about the direction that Canadian foreign policy should take and commissioned papers from local policy analysts on the host of issues for which he needed to prepare positions.

The convention to choose the party's new leader — finally held in Toronto's Air Canada Centre on November 14, 2003 — was as bereft of surprise as any U.S. presidential convention whose outcome had been determined long in advance. Potential candidates John Manley and Allan Rock had already thrown in the towel, complaining of the rigged process and leaving a valiant Sheila Copps to deny Martin victory by acclamation.

After thirteen years of autocratic rule, the new prime minister's promise to do politics differently by reducing its "democratic deficit" was attractive to both activists and journalists. His charm (however wrinkled), his ideas (however focus-grouped), and his eloquence (however scripted) resonated with the general public's desire for change. On his left, the NDP presented no serious threat, as it languished at well under 20 percent despite having chosen the effervescent Jack Layton as its leader. Meanwhile, the Alliance party had just staged a reverse takeover of the Progressive Conservatives. The new Conservative Party of Canada (CPC) still had a bruising leadership campaign of its own to endure, so it was unlikely that Martin would have much to fear on his right. In sum, Martin's crown seemed to be fashioned of pure political gold. That this soon turned out to be mere dross had much to do with both the manner of its winning and the manner of its wearing.

A HYPERACTIVE PRIME MINISTER AND HIS PREMATURE ELECTION

In the cliché of the time — and Martin's highly programmed discourse was replete with clichés — the new prime minister hit the ground running. He appointed a new cabinet. He restructured the government. His caucus changed the standing orders of the House of Commons to allow for more free votes. He took legislative action to deliver on some of his commitments. The Governor General read his Speech from the Throne, and his minister of finance read a budget. He welcomed Kofi Annan in Ottawa to signal his support for enhanced international co-operation and he was welcomed by George Bush at the White House as a token of his determination to improve bilateral relations. And, of course, he staffed the Prime Minister's Office with the men and women who had brought him to it. Each of these facets of the prime minister's activities had its darker side.

The new cabinet sent out a message of renewal without assuring change would happen. It was no surprise that — beyond his leadership rivals Allan Rock, gone to the United Nations as Canada's ambassador, and John Manley, who had refused the Washington embassy — notable Chrétien supporters were out: David Collenette, Sheila Copps, Stéphane Dion, Elinor Caplan, Jane Stewart, Martin Cauchon, and Don Boudria. While these firings guaranteed deepened dismay from the party's defeated wing, the newly anointed could hardly hope to make their mark before a spring election. Pierre Pettigrew in Health quickly came to grief by stating the obvious, if politically incorrect, truth that part of the public health system was delivered through private practice. John Godfrey was named parliamentary secretary co-chairing a task force on Canadian cities. "Designed more for appearances than performance," wrote one commentator later, "that group ... made the machinery of government appear impossibly complex and hopelessly unmanageable.[9]

Martin significantly *restructured government* to create a new department, Public Safety and Emergency Preparedness Canada. He divided HRDC into two ministries, and separated Foreign Affairs from International Trade. These changes, which would have taken years to implement properly, were rushed through without proper consultation with the civil service, leaving bureaucrats stranded, not knowing how to adjust their work. Signalling his intention to improve Ottawa's relations with the Bush administration, he established a new secretariat to co-ordinate federal and provincial activities in Washington, created a special cabinet committee on Canadian-American relations, and appointed a parliamentary secretary to work with him on that issue. He set up new cabinet committees, several of which he intended to chair himself, such as the Cabinet Committee on Aboriginal Affairs and the Cabinet Committee on Security, Public Health and Emergencies. Each of these administrative changes had a rationale, as had been the case with John Turner's attempt to put his own imprint on government just before the 1984 election. They also demanded far more of his hands-on time than he seemed willing to spend during a pre-election period.

Legislative action, a Speech from the Throne, and the 2004 budget to keep some of his commitments were obviously worthy measures. But the relatively picayune nature of the actions in the House, the vagueness of the speech, and the small down payments that the 2004 budget made towards its more grandiose spending promises confirmed that Martin was not really planning to govern. It was his election campaign that this frenetic hyperactivity heralded.

There was nothing in the measures to revamp the *Prime Minister's Office* that necessarily spelled disaster. Unlike John Turner, who had not frequented the corridors of power for nine years when he became prime minister, Martin's year and a half sabbatical had been more like a busman's holiday, keeping him from getting rusty. Because he had been so focused on preparing for victory (unlike Turner, who had a big-time business lawyer's load to demand his attention), his extensive consultations had yielded coherent plans that he implemented immediately. Where Martin mimicked Turner to a fault was in the spirit his staff brought to their mission and the way he structured his relationship with them. It was natural for Martin to bring his own people to the PMO. Many of them had actually been at his side as political aides in the Department of Finance or virtually there through quarterbacking his covert mutiny from the offices of Earnscliffe, a prominent Ottawa lobby company. What was neither necessary nor politic was the way they ran the PMO and guided the PM. Like the Turnerites before them, they made no attempt to reach out to their rivals or their rivals' capable personnel; instead, they made them feel unwelcome. When Turner's people took over the PMO, they threw out the briefing books that had been prepared for the transition by Trudeau's principal secretary, Tom Axworthy. Unable to contain their triumphalism, Martin's people continued their vendetta by having all references to Chrétien wiped from the government's Web site the day they arrived.

Like Turner, Martin preferred a horizontal decision-making style. As minister of finance whose year-long job was the preparation of one complex budget, he had revelled in chairing lively debates animated by his political and bureaucratic staff. The transition to prime minister, who must constantly confront dozens of critical problems, did not move him to change this way of operating. Whereas Trudeau and Chrétien had started their days by meeting the clerk of the privy council (the bureaucratic head of the civil service) and the principal secretary (the head of his political staff), Martin, as Turner before him, began his work by meeting the clerk plus half a dozen from the PMO. These backroom boys and girls had much more recent political experience and were more closely connected to the federal government than Turner's had been, but with every opinion around the table seeming to have equal weight, Martin's behaviour continued to reflect their anti-Chrétien obsession. While they had Martin preach the gospel of democracy in public, they continued to practise the same centralized control from behind closed doors that had won him the ultimate prize. He talked about doing politics differently, but they kept power where it had always been: in the hands of the prime minister — and in their own. This management style was put to its first major test — and found terribly wanting — when political disaster struck on February 10, 2004.

There was little that was new in Auditor-General Sheila Fraser's report on the irregularities of the Chrétien government's Quebec sponsorship program. Monies unaccounted for and excessive rake-offs by communications firms profiting from their political connections had been detailed the previous autumn in her interim statement without eliciting much reaction. Instead of treating this new document as unfortunate history that needed further investigation and eventual discipline by a commission of inquiry (that would bury the problem at least until the election was over), Paul Martin turned it into an issue with which to prove that he represented that different kind of politics about which he had made so many speeches. With mad-as-hell outrage,[10] he mounted a frenetic media campaign, declaring on national television and radio his indignation at what had been revealed and his determination to punish the perpetrators. Although his caucus pleaded with him to stop keeping this scandal in the news by appropriating the issue (because the public was not distinguishing between the new and the old Liberals), Martin continued his cross-country campaign talking to media in British Columbia, Saskatchewan, and Manitoba. The unilingual anglophone staffers were no less eager to add fuel to the fire. With not-for-attribution phone calls to journalists, they eagerly contributed to a not-so-implicit blame-Chrétien campaign by talking about the program's "political direction."[11]

At the same time that a parliamentary committee chaired by a Conservative started hearings, Martin appointed an independent commission of inquiry. He then deepened the attack on Chrétien's administration by summarily removing without compensation from his ambassadorship in Denmark Alfonso Gagliano, the former minister in charge of the sponsorship program. Next, he fired Jean Pelletier, Chrétien's former principal secretary, currently the CEO of Via Rail, without obvious evidence of criminal behaviour, let alone due process. Acting as if an opposition party had come to power determined to vilify its defeated enemy, Team Martin managed in the process to raise doubts about its own integrity, given that its captain had been finance minister during the sponsorship program and that, as Chrétien's Quebec lieutenant, he could hardly have been unaware of what was happening. Unable to declare closure on their feud with the Chrétien camp, the Martinites exacerbated internal divisions within the party. And by so gratuitously vilifying the Chrétien record, they burned their own bridge to claiming credit for over ten years of government achievements, many of which were their own doing.

This dubious exercise in protesting their innocence boomeranged on the Martin team and created a more persuasive reason for voters to abandon the Liberals than any argument the newly elected leader of the Conservative Party of Canada could make. Within four weeks, support for the Liberal Party of Canada had fallen from 48 percent to 35 percent in the polls.[12] In the wake of this disaster, a consensus outside the PMO held that Martin should postpone his election plans, get on with the business of governing that had been laid out in the throne speech and budget, consolidate his identity as Canada's spokesman by attending summits on the international stage, and — not least important — give the public time to forget their anger over "Adscam." But the Martinites had long set their hearts on holding a quick election. The earliest date that was politically acceptable was April, lest the West protest it had been deprived of the five extra seats that redistribution would then give it. They *said* they needed a mandate to implement their demanding program. They *meant* they wanted an election to clear out the hostile Chrétienites from caucus and to elect new stars with whom they could replenish the cabinet. There was apparently to be no closure with his nemesis until Martin had won his own majority in Parliament.

Whereas Turner in June 1984 had been elected leader only eight months before having to call a new election, Martin had almost two years from when he was elevated. But his inner circle did not lack time as much as flexibility. Having decided on an early election, it seemed unable to realize it was no longer unbeatable. Consider these major problems:

- Unlike Martin, Harper had reached out to his contenders for the leadership, Belinda Stronach and Tony Clement, and was projecting a perhaps uncharismatic but certainly unscary image for his new party in Ontario, the one province that the Liberal party needed for its majority.

- Martin's honeymoon with the media had ended. Reporters were not giving the new prime minister any less cynical treatment than they had given the previous one.

- There would be little new policy for Martin to announce during the campaign to provide a positive message. He had spent the months since coming to the PMO making promises in every region and for every imaginable issue, such as giving hundreds of millions to support HIV/AIDS alleviation programs in Africa.

- Once campaigning started, the media would give equal time to the other parties, which would concentrate their attack on the

> incumbent Liberals. Martin would be constantly forced to defend such contradictions as the one between his pledge to create a more democratic politics and his actual record in manipulating the nominations of his own candidates.

However vulnerable to public criticism their management of the party's nomination process may have made them, it was its impact on internal party morale that should have caused them to pause in their electoral preparations. As with every party, the Liberals needed their rank and file to turn up at riding campaign offices and volunteer to canvass voters, put up signs, and carry out the myriad other chores required for a winning local campaign. But well-publicized example after well-publicized example of strong-arm tactics taking Liberal riding nominations out of the hands of the local constituency had shown that the Martin team's commitment to democratic practice was as instrumental as it was manipulative. Under amendments made to the party's constitution in 1992, the leader had the power to impose a candidate on a riding notwithstanding its own democratically expressed will. Also under Chrétien, the leader's provincial campaign chairs had acquired powers that allowed them to protect a sitting MP whom they wanted to keep, or favour a contender they wanted to win. As part of his advocacy for local democracy, Martin affirmed at an earlier stage that he would not automatically have incumbents protected unless they were strong, female, or from visible minorities. He would nevertheless appoint candidates with these qualities to make his team more representative of Canadian society's diversity.[13]

The application of these principles was strongly affected by the Martinites' continuing vendetta against their vanquished rivals. Most notoriously, Sheila Copps, who was not just a woman but the only Chrétien minister with hard-earned credibility in the cultural and anglo-nationalist communities, was exposed to a bitter fight for her nomination. Martin supporter Tony Valeri took this from her, thanks, it was widely reported, to dirty tricks. Nor did strength and ethnicity provide protection for male incumbents. Chrétien's minister of energy, Herb Dhaliwal, a Sikh, was shoved aside. Two substantial Chinese-Canadian candidates were frustrated by Martin's appointment of Bill Cunningham, his B.C.

organizer, as the party's candidate in Burnaby-Douglas. Buttressing the prime minister's power of appointment was his command of patronage. MP John Harvard was seduced by the promise of being appointed lieutenant-governor of Manitoba.[14] The MP for Brampton-Springdale was similarly bought off with the promise of an appointment.[15]

Even if Paul Martin did not get involved in a riding contest personally, his associates could generally manipulate the process to get the candidate they wanted. A Manley supporter, Andrew Kania, was displaced in favour of a glamorous female Asian, Ruby Dhalla, in the Brampton-Springdale riding.[16] Despite claiming its commitment to gender equality, the Martin team dissuaded a prominent woman from running in Ottawa South to favour the Ontario premier's brother, David McGuinty. In some cases, the PMO could get its way without manipulation. Where Martinites already controlled a riding association, they could produce an uncontested victory for their candidate without engendering more dissension. In such situations, more provocation was not needed to encourage non-Martin supporters to sit out the campaign. Thirty-six sitting MPs did not run again. Anger was so high in some cases that whole riding association executives moved to support another party.

Neither this rank-and-file alienation over present nominations nor public disaffection following the previous sponsorships scandal deterred the Martin machine. Although polls through April predicted the Liberals would achieve no more than a minority government, a blip suggesting they were back in majority territory momentarily gave them the figures they needed. On May 24 Paul Martin promptly announced that an election would be held in thirty-seven days. It would not be easy for him. His tacticians were untried. His platform was insipid. And the media were loath to extend him the benefit of the doubt any more.

ORGANIZATION, STRATEGY, AND TACTICS

The structural shape of the campaign had been devised months earlier, when polls commissioned and analyzed by Martin's chief strategist, David Herle, suggested that the future campaign should exploit his boss's extraordinary popularity. Perhaps deluded by the near unanimous delegate support they had bought for their leader's coronation at the Air Canada Centre with their $10-million organizational effort, the Martin group did what it could to differentiate itself from the party it had taken over. A new logo was designed, although it was barely discernible since Martin's face dominated the candidates' signs.

The campaign's organizers were talented and experienced. Mike Robinson had run the debate preparation for Turner. Terrie O'Leary had played an integral part in Chrétien's tour in 1993. Media spokesman Scott Reid had been politically involved through the 1990s. Along with other leading lights such as campaign co-chair John Webster, National Party Director Michele Cadario, Chief of Staff Tim Murphy, Communications Director Steve MacKinnon, and Ontario Director Karl Littler, the group was accustomed to collaborating, many having worked for Martin at Finance and all having done the recent leadership campaign together. Equally important, this triumph had left them in firm control of the party apparatus so that there were no tensions between the PMO and the campaign office as there had been under Turner.

But their various organizational assets had their darker side. Having successfully placed their man in the PMO through ruthlessly squeezing out his rivals and recruiting instant Liberals from ethnic groups, they were poorly equipped to rally the rest of the party faithful. And, having made their mark in Ottawa as high-profile lobbyists, they were unable to resist the lure of media fame themselves. In striking contrast to the discretion of Jean Chrétien's team — John Rae, Eddie Goldenberg, Gordon Ashworth — who kept themselves invisible as they managed the campaign, Martin's handlers eagerly joined the pundits on television or radio programs to spin their party's situation. But given its rapidly deteriorating conditions, their words were not always helpful to the cause. David Herle admitted to being "nervous" about running a national campaign for the first time, and conceded to making "rookie" mistakes in alienating the Chrétien wing of the party. He accepted full responsibility for "failing to reach out to those Liberals who remained faithful to former Prime Minister Jean Chrétien throughout last year's bitter leadership race."[17]

The deleterious impact on campaign morale of such poor judgment was aggravated by poor discipline elsewhere in the party. Hélène Scherrer, the Quebec campaign's co-chair, frankly expressed her dismay that Paul Martin was not politically adept: "I don't think [Martin is] a good politician, in the sense that he can't attack the others and be demagogic ... It's hard for him in an election campaign that is being fought below the belt. He is not good when it comes to playing that game ... He wants everybody to love him."[18] Scherrer's musing precipitated an admission one week later that the campaign's message was failing, and that a new strategy would have to be adopted to address Canadians' distrust of Martin.[19]

This self-destruction by the team leaders was aided by those it had alienated. Brian Tobin, the former Liberal minister of industry whom Finance Minister Martin had forced out of the race even before he officially declared his candidacy (by blocking the funding needed for a high-tech economic policy), told the press even before Week 1 was over that the Grits were heading for a minority.[20] MP Carolyn Parrish was quoted as calling the campaign a "comedy of errors."[21] And, in a presumed act of sabotage, someone helped connect a key journalist to a conference call organized so David Herle could give the straight goods to all the Ontario candidates. This covert access yielded a front-page story in the *Globe and Mail* blaring "Liberals are in a spiral," the words having come straight from no less authoritative a source than the campaign director's own lips. The report characterized the call as sounding "desperate," and revealed some MPs' discomfort with the negative ads that would begin airing later that day.[22]

Having also publicly admitted to failure in reaching out to the Chrétien camp, Herle supported two efforts to heal the rift. The first, hosted by Senator David Smith and party president Mike Eizenga in mid-April, provided leading disaffected Liberals with a chance to vent, but their advice — to postpone the election but specify a date for June 2005 — went unheeded. The second, three weeks later, was a forum Herle used to try to bring the party's factions together. When he told those in attendance he expected to win one hundred seats in Ontario, they realized they were being used so that he could spin the signal through the media that reconciliation had been achieved.

Detached from this organizational disarray in Ottawa but driven by its focus-grouped thinking, the leader launched his campaign, veering away from the continentalist right, where he had dug in as finance minister to satisfy the business community's demand for deficit reduction. No sooner was the writ issued than Paul Martin was on the nationalist left. Distancing himself from a U.S. model of society, he identified himself on Day 2 with that most Canadian of values, health care, and attempted to convey as much emotion over hospital waiting lists as he had over the sponsorship scandal — if with no greater success. It was no accident that Martin chose social policy for his first message. Months had gone into preparing its priority in his platform.

PLATFORM AS POSITIVE POLICY MESSAGE

Understanding the political impact of the Liberals' 2004 campaign requires us to distinguish the printed message from its messenger. The message was coherently if numbingly presented in the form of a traditional platform document. The messenger, Paul Martin, had considerable difficulty exciting the public with its contents on the campaign trail. *Moving Canada Forward: The Paul Martin Plan for Getting Things Done* was a document modelled on the Red Books produced in the three Chrétien campaigns, although in this case it was the product of the Martin leadership process whose extensive, pre-convention consultations generated a series of four connected documents.

First had come "Making History: The Politics of Achievement," the vague, committee-written, cliché-filled but comprehensive and politically flexible speech that Martin gave to the Air Canada crowd on November 14 after it had been warmed up by the excitement of hearing the rock star Bono. Whereas Bono had spoken from his capacious Irish heart about the specifics of Africa's HIV/AIDS crisis, Martin spoke in platitudes.[23] "Our foreign policy must always express the concerns of Canadians about the poor and underprivileged of the world," Martin read from his hortatory text. "This concern is shared by individuals of conscience the world over — like Bono — who have brought a new and welcome urgency to the plight of the people in the developing world. Because he cares. Because we care." This feel-good appeal to each constituency within the party made few commitments beyond suggesting that issue after issue was important, crucial, or urgent and that Canada had an historic opportunity to confront it. Though it contained few specific commitments, it did provide the framework for the later iterations of Martin's program.

Next came the greater specificity of the new government's Speech from the Throne (SFT). Whereas the convention speech contained two economic promises and seven concerning the democratic deficit, the SFT made forty-two, including $4 billion to be spent on the environment and $2 billion on health. Then Finance Minister Ralph Goodale's budget laid out the actual amounts that Parliament would be invited to spend on itemized programs. In some cases these amounts were extraordinarily small down payments: of the $5 billion promised for childcare, only $91 million would be spent in 2004 and $93 million in 2005. Of the $4 billion nominally committed to the environment, only $250 million would be spent in 2004 with a minuscule $10 million allocated for the following year.

Moving Canada Forward reworked these three statements, presenting a document similar in format and in style to earlier Red Books, which looked like corporate annual reports. Heavier in motherhood declamations about the importance of education or health or prosperity or peace than in hard policy content, it nevertheless managed to make forty-two promises that were printed in twenty-one coloured boxes and grouped in four main sections.

- "A Strong Start" reduced the seven promises from Martin's campaign text to one on eliminating the democratic deficit.

- "Strengthening our Social Foundations" provided a medley of admonitions and statements of good intent concerning such areas as hospital waiting lists, childcare (recycled from the 1993 Red Book), and the cities. Since all these fell under provincial jurisdiction, the text was replete with caveats about the negotiations and co-operation that would be needed with the provinces and/or the native nations.

- "Building a 21st Century Economy" reiterated the real action taken in the budget such as GST relief for the cities, but the rest of the text was notable mainly for its celebration of the Chrétien government's economic triumphs when Martin had been holding its purse strings.

- "Canada in the World: A Role of Pride and Influence" stood out for its vacuity. For all its claims to the country's unique international mission, it managed to mention neither the United Nations nor the United States. (Martin's convention speech had given a prominent role to improving relations with Washington.) Iraq was only mentioned in terms of reducing its debt.

The turgid, campaign-speak style and the many promises recycled from the Chrétien era deprived it of any sense of vision. Leaning to the right on fiscal prudence but to the left on social programs, it fitted the mould of the party's past ambivalent pitches. Worthy but weak in its sentiments, it should nevertheless have provided plenty of material for the leader to use on the road.

MARTIN AS MESSENGER

At first glance, it was a puzzle that Paul Martin, Ottawa's undisputed policy wonk, should appear so bereft of vision. The solution lay, in part, in his exhaustion from having spent much of his prime ministerial energy outside the capital promising goodies for every region. In doing so, he had seriously depleted his supply of policy ammunition. In part, it lay in his handling of the sponsorship scandal, which had brought him to an emotional precipice, as he faced the humiliation of jeopardizing the Liberal Party's dominant position that he had inherited from Chrétien. In part, his compulsive need to please all constituencies made it hard to determine what a re-elected Martin government would actually do. For instance, the platform took a multilateralist position, promising more money for the military to bolster its peacekeeping capacities, but his minister of defence, David Pratt, had made it very clear that Canada would support Washington's controversial National Missile Defense scheme, which was a first step towards Canada's forces integrating via an extended NORAD in Northcom, the Pentagon's newly integrated continental defence organization.

Worse, it was hard to credit his new, slightly anti-American stand. Having long sniped at Chrétien for not getting along with the Bush administration, and having made much of his own capacity to reconcile with the White House both in his convention speech and in reorganizing the government to integrate better with American security policy, he made a well-promoted trip to Washington to signal his pro-American bona fides. At the beginning of the campaign, however, here he was suddenly tweaking a feather from the eagle by asserting the superiority of Canada's social values.[24]

Martin might have managed the transmogrification from flinty-eyed neocon to warm-hearted liberal had he still been enjoying his honeymoon with the media. When heavy-handed, inaccessible, touchy Chrétien was in the PMO, the media had not portrayed Martin as disloyal, conniving, and heavy-handed himself (for example, in the party's delegate selection process) but as rebel with a cause. Now, the press gallery could easily have celebrated his Damascus, burbling about how this tough-minded business-executive-turned-politician had found his real ideological roots as son of the Paul Martin Sr. who had championed generous social programs in the 1950s and 1960s. But as soon as the media lost Chrétien to kick around and Martin had shown his political incompetence in the sponsorship scandal, he lost the journalists' respect.

It was the boys on the press bus whose eyes had turned flinty as they prominently reported Jack Layton's attacks on the contradictions between the prime minister's present promises and his past actions and relayed to the public Gilles Duceppe's sustained barrage over Martin's possible involvement with Adscam. Appropriating a role for itself as truth squad, for instance, the CBC on Day 3 responded to Martin's promise to fix the health care system by reminding its viewers that it was his 1995 budget that had caused most of the damage in the first place.[25] Anti-Martin commentary was not restricted to the public broadcaster. Although the Liberals scored high in "mentions" in the print media over the campaign — 80 percent of all articles referred to them — 22 percent of these were negative. (During the same period, 69 percent of all articles mentioned the Conservatives, but only 12 percent of these were negative.)[26] More important, the bulk of the negative coverage for Martin occurred in the first three weeks, when the Liberals' negative mentions exceeded those of all other parties.[27] In the campaign's opening phase, the Conservatives won what was known as the ballot box question, turning the election into a referendum on Liberal rule with their "Demand Better" slogan.

Paradoxically, the Martinites' disowning of Chrétien over Adscam prevented them from claiming ownership of Martin's great economic achievement as Chrétien's finance minister — eliminating the budgetary deficit and presiding over robust growth rates that improved Canada's economic position to the point where it was the only G7 country to have both fiscal and trade surpluses in 2002. This record was well presented in *Moving Canada Forward*, but Martin's attempt to assert it fell on deaf ears. His defence of health care cuts on the grounds that "if we had not taken the action that we did in 1995, we would be Argentina today"[28] had no resonance with reporters. Nothing positive that he tried seemed to work for him, whereas what others did worked against him. The storm of criticism that greeted Ontario Premier Dalton McGuinty over his broken promise not to raise taxes (his budget, which was unveiled just days before the federal campaign began, introduced a health care premium) rubbed off directly on his federal cousins. In Ontario, their support immediately fell to 33 percent,[29] and around the country their opponents gleefully charged that Martin's "fiberals"' could not be trusted to keep their new promises either.

Nor did the Liberals' negative campaign work any better. Their much ballyhooed attack on the Conservatives proved counterproductive. On Saturday, May 22, the day before the campaign was launched, full-page advertisements appeared in newspapers across the country with side-by-side photographs of both Paul Martin and Stephen Harper in business suits, managing to make the Conservative leader look just as respectable as the prime minister if considerably younger and certainly not scary.[30] Beyond the visual, the Liberals' negative campaign suffered from the same credibility gap as their positive message: it was disingenuous to allege Harper would endanger the country's social fabric by cutting taxes when this was exactly what Martin had done throughout the previous decade. Did the attack ads represent an implicit admission that the government had little record to defend? Were they aimed to divert attention from Adscam? The media raised these doubts while describing the pre-campaign television commercial that gave partial quotes from what Harper had said in the past and referred viewers to a Web site that would give them the full text. This multimedia ploy seemed ineffectual and was pulled within a week. The *Globe and Mail* called the early attack ads "unprecedented," and characterized them as a "last-ditch effort" to unite the fractured party.[31]

It was not necessary for the media to allege desperation on the Liberals' part. David Herle himself openly admitted as much on Day 19 (June 10), the day his most negative ad was released. "The Stephen Harper We Know" threw everything at the new leader: Iraq, abortion, environmental degradation, and separatism, all under the guise of Harper's supposed secret agenda. On Day 24 (June 15), "Conservative Economics" alleged Harper would introduce U.S.-style tax cuts and alter the country's social fabric. In an effort to show guilt by association, it invoked the records of former Ontario premier Mike Harris and former prime minister Brian Mulroney to suggest Harper would create a new fiscal deficit.[32]

Had Harper been a real Mulroney clone, Martin's fate would have been sealed. Not only was Mulroney in 1984 strongly identified with his province as a boy from Baie Comeau on Quebec's North shore but he had campaigned from the political centre, thereby making it impossible for Turner, the corporate lawyer from Bay Street, to polarize the election on a left-right basis. Fortunately for Martin, many members of Harper's Conservative caucus had impeccable credentials as social conservatives.

THE MEDIA: FROM ENEMY TO ALLY

Fortunately, too, for the new prime minister, the Conservative leader was declared by the pollsters to have the magic quality of momentum as early as Week 2,[33] inducing the fickle press corps to shift their baleful scrutiny to the one whose election now seemed likely. With the polls in Week 3 suggesting Harper would win at least a minority, reporters were no longer willing to give the free ride accorded him when he was just another opposition leader without serious prospects of victory.[34] This treatment was seen in both print and broadcast media. Negative mentions of Harper in the press, which had fallen dramatically from Weeks 1 to 3 (24 percent, 9 percent, 6 percent respectively), spiked to 15 percent in Week 4.[35] Television's about-face with the Conservatives was demonstrated by CTV in the final week of the campaign, when it showed almost no positive statements about the Conservatives.

The Conservative Party's fortunes moved in tandem with the kind of stories that appeared in the media. It was no coincidence that the Conservative momentum peaked in Week 3 when the networks' leading stories were about traditional Conservative strengths: justice at 21 percent and the economy/tax cuts/deficit at 18 percent of all statements made that week.[36] Week 5 saw a rebound in health care mentions (which played to the Liberals' strength) at 20 percent, up from 7 percent in Conservative-friendly Week 3. Most tellingly, mentions of government (leadership and ethics) plummeted to their lowest level of 1 percent in newspapers in Week 5,[37] demonstrating that the Conservatives had lost their battle for the ballot box question in that crucial final week of the campaign.

During the two televised all-party debates, the focus of attention was the incumbent prime minister, who was put on the defensive by the three other leaders' relentless attacks and seemed incapable of citing his own achievements along with those of the Chrétien government. Post-debate coverage described Martin's performance as that of a politician fighting for the survival of his party, and made the case that the election had become "one for the Conservatives to lose."[38] For his part, the Harper whom Canadians saw was decidedly unscary. He emerged calm, a bit dull, but unscathed from Martin's attack about the "black hole" of his budgetary planning or about his having wanted to send Canadian troops to join the U.S. war on Iraq: "Canadians were not wrong. You were wrong."[39] In stark contrast to the inflated expectations of Martin, the media's low expectations of Harper meant that he had "won" the debate simply by virtue of not having made any mistakes.

On June 12 (Day 21), the dean of the chattering caste, Jeffrey Simpson, signalled the crucial shift. Titled "A Conservative wolf in sheep's clothing," Simpson characterized Harper's openness to free votes on the issues of abortion and same-sex marriage as a "constitutional fraud, political sham, even a deceit" and cautioned readers that despite the Progressive Conservative and Canadian Alliance merger, the "Alliance dominates among candidates, organizers, and Mr. Harper's advisers (who are very, very right-wing)." Simpson went on to accuse Harper of "trying to bribe the Canadian electorate" into believing his party's "new" brand of economic conservatism that made both tax cuts and "huge amounts of spending" possible, despite all evidence of his puritan conservative economic tendencies. Even if he had relatively few readers on the *Globe and Mail's* op-ed page, Simpson was read by his colleagues, who proceeded to turn tough on Harper and, doing to him what they had done to Martin, watered the seeds of doubt already sown by the Liberals.

On Day 25 (June 16), articles reporting Harper's prediction he would win a majority[40] mocked him for presumptuously "measuring the curtains" at 24 Sussex Drive. His consultations on the transition into governance were also reported as premature, even though, as a leader with a strong chance of defeating the current government, it would have been irresponsible for him not to prepare for office. When on Day 26 (June 17) Premier Ralph Klein announced he was waiting until just after the federal election to bring in changes to Alberta's health care system that might violate the Canada Health Act, Martin was able to get four days' play in the national media for his claim that this proved the Conservatives had a "hidden agenda" after all.

With the press hounds baying, the CPC's most extreme candidates' well-known views on social issues were played up, giving Martin a chance to express his horror at the threat they posed to Canadian values. By Day 25 (June 16), the Conservatives had fallen back to being in a dead heat with the Liberals: 35 percent to 34 percent. On Day 27 (June 18), the media gave prominent play to a press release from Harper's war room that egregiously suggested Martin favoured child pornography. For the first time, in Week 4, Harper's negative mentions in the media exceeded those for Martin.[41] Stories on social issues exceeded those on economic issues, playing into the Liberals' fear campaign.

On Day 29 (June 20), it was bilingualism in Air Canada that was under threat.[42] The Liberals alleged that Harper would relax the airline's bilingualism requirements, citing a leaked pre-writ memo from the Conservative Party. On Day 34 (June 25), then-Conservative Justice Critic Randy White was reported to have said in an interview conducted months prior to the election that he was personally in favour of using the Charter's notwithstanding clause to override court rulings such as those pertaining to the definition of marriage.[43] By Week 5, when 40 percent of voters had still to make up their minds, the Liberals, though still in a virtual tie with the Conservatives, returned to promoting their platform, which seemed no longer to be falling on deaf ears.[44] Their final attack ad encapsulated all the fears they were trying to evoke. The buyer should beware. NDP voters should "think twice, vote once." And, to conclude, the slogan: "Choose your Canada."

If at the very end of the campaign the public forgot their fury at the Liberals and if former Tory voters in Ontario moved to Martin, it was less for what he stood for than for what he said Harper stood for. Poll-saturated coverage[45] had a discernible impact, not only on the way campaigns conducted themselves, but also on voter behaviour. This became especially apparent when polling numbers for the Conservatives began to rise, changing the way the media covered both Stephen Harper and Paul Martin, giving the former what ultimately proved to be a fatal sense of momentum, and the latter a boost to a scare campaign. Martin's "devil you know" plea was given more careful consideration. Stephen Harper's talk of Conservative consultations regarding a possible transition into governance meant that the prime minister could now warn that Canadians should be wary of the kind of change they would be voting for. Suddenly faced with the prospect of a Conservative majority, those voters leaning towards the NDP found themselves turning back to the Liberals, who still had the greatest chance of averting a Conservative government. Moderate voters in Ontario who were supporting the Conservatives as a protest against perceived Liberal abuses suddenly got cold feet when confronted with the possibility of a majority government harkening back to Harris/Mulroney days, with the likes of Randy White.

If the Liberals' negative commercials finally worked after their initial failure, it was thanks to the media's having switched from enemy to ally, helping convince Canadians that the Harper Conservatives lived up to their scary billing after all. The Liberal-paid advertisements bought them "earned media" through increased news stories commenting on social conservatism. Because voters typically distrust politicians but trust journalists, the earned media dulled criticism of Liberal attack ads. In Week 4, there was a discernible rise in coverage of the same-sex marriage and abortion issues — about one in every three campaign-related articles dealt with social issues, displacing health, taxes, and accountability.[46]

THE REGIONS: CONTINUITY IN THE PARTY SYSTEM

The struggle for the hearts and minds of the national press gallery was important, but not necessarily more important than what went on locally in each region.

Just over ten years after 1993's electoral earthquake seemed to have fragmented the Canadian party system along regional lines,[47] the Martin Liberals revealed that doing politics differently did not preclude such traditional governing-party behaviour as appointing MPs from each region to the cabinet, recruiting local stars, and making promises to fix local problems while maintaining a pan-Canadian thrust to their policy.

The Atlantic Provinces

Back in December 2003, Martin had brought Geoff Regan, the son of a former premier and federal cabinet minister, into his cabinet as minister of fisheries and made Newfoundlander John Efford minister of natural resources. With discontent running high among genuine Tories about their party's takeover from the Far West's far right, the Liberals were pleased to have induced MPs John Herron from New Brunswick and Scott Brison from Nova Scotia to cross the floor and to have appointed the latter parliamentary secretary to the prime minister responsible for Canadian-American relations. In Nova Scotia, they also recruited local stars Sheila Fougere, a municipal politician, and Mike Savage, son of another former premier. In Saint John, New Brunswick, it was president of Summa Strategies and legal counsel at Clark Drummie (a leading Atlantic Canada law firm), Paul Zed.

In the pre-writ months, Martin promised $400 million to clean up the environmental disaster of Sidney, Nova Scotia's tar ponds and $300 million for improving Prince Edward Island's harbours. One pan-Canadian policy with a distinctly regional tilt towards the Maritimes and Quebec was easing the eligibility criteria to give the seasonally unemployed easier access to employment insurance (EI). During the campaign itself, Martin promised a Liberal government would strengthen or withdraw from the North Atlantic Fishing Organization if abuses by Portuguese fishermen continued,[48] and undertook to give the provinces a greater share of the taxes generated by offshore oil and natural gas royalties.

Quebec

With its separatist Bloc Québécois in apparent decline, *la belle province* initially presented the Martinites with an attractive strategic challenge. From winning fifty-four seats and forming the Official Opposition in 1993, the Bloc had slipped to forty-four and then thirty-eight seats in the intervening elections. The Parti Québécois' defeat by the provincial Liberals in the 2003 election had put the Bloc on the defensive over the sensitive issue of separatism, forcing Gilles Duceppe to distance himself from the PQ's leader, Bernard Landry, keep the volatile former PQ premier Jacques Parizeau under wraps, and, in his platform, put Quebec's role in the world (a euphemism for sovereignty) in last place.

Then came Adscam, whose impact on the Liberals was far more devastating in Quebec than elsewhere. Not only did it show flagrant corruption within the federal government. Quebecers felt collectively insulted by Martin's unilingual anglophone handlers suggesting that the scandal was a function of the province's old-style patronage politics. References to Quebec's "tribal politics" and its "culture of corruption" were widely disseminated in francophone Canada as proof positive of the Liberals' hostility to Quebec. Even if the anger was more deeply felt among the elite than the general francophone public,[49] the Liberals' political support in the province fell ten percentage points (five times more than in the rest of Canada). It was not Harper but Gilles Duceppe as BQ leader who picked up this disaffected electorate, his double-entendre slogan, "*Un parti propre au Quebec*" subtly rubbing salt in the Liberals' wounds. Not only did the BQ belong to Quebec, its hands were clean.

In contrast, the Liberals' slogan — "*Tout droit d'abord*" — was that of the Martin family corporation, Canada Steamship Lines, whose use of offshore tax havens had landed the PM in considerable difficulty. His key organizational decision made things much worse. Having focused before the scandal on winning away soft federalist support from the Bloc, he had appointed as his lieutenant in charge of the Quebec campaign Jean Lapierre, a former Liberal who had abandoned the party in 1990 to become a founding member of the Bloc. Host of a talk-radio show for several years, Lapierre was not used to keeping his opinions to himself. He quickly alienated Quebec nationalists by pooh-poohing the importance of Adscam. Declaring Chrétien's anti-separatist Clarity Act "useless," he also managed to outrage the party's federalists, who were already smarting from the appointment of someone they considered a traitor.

With this context, none of the Liberals' traditional pre-writ tricks worked: not the change in EI for seasonal workers, nor $900,000 for a marine biology centre in Rimouski, nor $1.1 million for *Tourisme Outaouais*. Martin had banished Stéphane Dion from his cabinet and promoted backbenchers Irwin Cotler, Helene Scherrer, and Denis Paradis, but it was in vain that his reshuffled team of Quebec ministers tirelessly brought the message of these and other goodies to local communities. The former prime minister's supporters resentfully sat on their hands in the face of the Martin team's hostility. In a flagrantly gratuitous insult to the outgoing prime minister, his aide Stephen Hogue, who had been working since September 2003 to succeed Chrétien in the riding he had held for forty years, was told that St. Maurice-Champlain was reserved for a woman, Marie Eve Bilodeau, who turned out to be a Martin supporter.[50] Further assaults on their collective integrity came in the wake of Adscam with the firing without due process of Chrétien's long-time chief of staff, Jean Pelletier, from the presidency of Via Rail.

With the Liberals falling 20 percent behind the Bloc in the opening days of the campaign, Jean Lapierre was increasingly sidelined. After three weeks, Dion was brought back from political oblivion to connect the campaign with its alienated federalist core by warning of the danger represented by the Bloc. Together with Pierre Pettigrew, he published an open letter maintaining that a vote for the BQ would help bring to power Harper's Conservatives, whose values were inimical to those of Quebecers. Further shifting the Liberal message by replacing reconciliation for confrontation, the foreign minister, Bill Graham, was brought in from Toronto to affirm that the BQ shared the same values as the Liberals.

The ad campaign, as ever run separately from that in the rest of Canada, kept up the message that a vote for the Bloc would produce a Conservative government committed to cancelling women's rights to abortions and would leave Ottawa with no minister from Quebec.[51] The menacing style, which reminded Quebecers of threats made by Paul Martin during the 1995 referendum, was deemed a political disaster. New ads were more positive, suggesting that the Liberals would open the Canadian economy to Quebec business and claiming that they would fight in Ottawa for the social needs of a unique Quebec.

Ontario

The battleground where Harper's reconstituted party could credibly hope for its breakthrough to government also had the 106 seats that Martin needed if he was to rescue a minority from his self-made debacle. Vast in its geography and varied in its demography, Ontario presented several different political challenges to the Liberals. Most comfortable in the megalopolis of Toronto, the Liberals managed to attract some star candidates, most notably former Montreal Canadiens' goalie Ken Dryden, who was given the riding of former Chrétien cabinet minister Art Eggleton. Having put themselves on the wrong side of newly elected Mayor David Miller on the island airport issue, thanks in part to the antics of maverick MP Dennis Mills, they had difficulty capitalizing on Martin's previously announced commitment to increase federal financing for Canada's cities. On social questions, Foreign Affairs Minister Bill Graham championed the gay rights that the Martin team had finally, if reluctantly, brought itself to support.

In the broad, urbanizing semicircle around Toronto known for its telephone area code 905, the Liberals offered $1 billion to support the development of GO transit and nominated a goodly number of visible minority candidates. In the outer "blue belt" made up of the smaller cities and agricultural areas where the Conservatives were making their major gains, the party offered nothing specific, relying on the national campaign to save the situation and leaving their candidates to fend for themselves.[52] To the North, which had been taken for granted as a solidly red zone, Martin had to make visits later in the campaign to point out Harper's opposition to such regional development initiatives as FedNor and the Community Futures Program.

The McGuinty Liberals' provincial budget, delivered on May 18, only days before Martin announced the date of the election, served to exacerbate the general sense of mistrust of government. In response to the Ontario budget fallout, Martin initially defended McGuinty, arguing it was necessary to deal with what he considered the Harris social deficit and Eves fiscal deficit. But it became evident in that first week on the campaign trail that the five-percentage-point drop suffered by the Liberals between mid-May and June 1 was caused exclusively by the McGuinty budget.[53] By Day 9, Martin had begun to distance himself from McGuinty: "I believe it is very important for political leaders to keep their promises ... But don't over-promise, and then whatever you say you're going to do, do."[54] A variety of high-profile Liberals including Anne McLellan began to publicly accuse the McGuinty government of hurting federal Liberal support.[55] Ironically, McLellan and Martin were disavowing a provincial budget that the federal Liberals had helped to orchestrate as a symbol of federal co-operation to "save" the health care system. A highly publicized meeting between Ontario Health Minister George Smitherman and federal Health Minister Pierre Pettigrew had occurred less than a month before the budget was delivered, and only weeks after a meeting between McGuinty and Martin in Ottawa that specifically addressed health care.[56] The outcome of the Ontario budget fallout was that the federal Liberals were placed in the paradoxical position of having to denounce the outcome of their own pre-campaign tactics.

The West

Like John Turner before him, Paul Martin had come to the country's highest office having raised great expectations about how he would bring the West into a revivified Ottawa. His debut was promising, starting even before his elevation by meeting the premiers at the Grey Cup football game in Regina. He then brought Reg Alcock into his cabinet from Manitoba to be head of the Treasury Board, promoted Ralph Goodale from Saskatchewan to the government's number-two post of finance minister, and made Anne McLellan from Alberta deputy prime minister and minister in charge of his new Department of Public Safety and Emergency Preparedness, the next highest job in his government.

On the pre-writ policy front, Martin was no less prolific in his regionally focused promises than he had been elsewhere in the country: $1 billion for Alberta's beef industry to help it recover from the American embargo following the discovery of one mad cow in the province; a commitment to adjust the much-loathed gun registry; an International Centre for Infectious Disease for Winnipeg; more cash for Saskatoon's Synchrotron Institute. Having spent his ammunition, Martin had little more for the Prairies during the campaign apart from his pledge to give its cities the same new deal he was peddling in the rest of the country.

Although the Martin team worked hard on the recruitment front, their only major coup was persuading ex-mayor of Winnipeg Glen Murray to take the plunge. Strong-arm tactics to get their favourites nominated yielded the same bitterness within the ranks here as elsewhere in the country. Also as elsewhere, the plunge in Liberal ratings that followed Adscam drastically dashed their hopes of making any gains and forced them to struggle just to hold onto the few seats they had. British Columbia was the only province where there was a genuine three-way split, with each party hovering around 30 percent in the polls. Here the Liberals had a double message, attacking the Conservatives on the one hand and courting the NDP's supporters on the other. Stumbling as badly in B.C. as elsewhere by angering minority groups and party loyalists with their heavy-handed interventions in riding nominations, they nevertheless produced a so-called "dream team" by poaching three major figures from the NDP, including former premier Ujjal Dosanjh, and Keith Martin from the Conservatives, and parachuting a major business figure, David Emerson, into a safe seat.

The nature of all of these provincial campaigns suggests Canada has an evolving party system. The Liberals' behaviour in British Columbia provided strong evidence to support the thesis that, following the new partisan constellation introduced by 1993's electoral earthquake, federal politics had become radically regionalized.[57] Unique in anglophone Canada, *B.C. Agenda* was a separate provincial platform making special promises, including a crackdown on drug use and moving the headquarters for the federal tourism promotion department to Vancouver in anticipation of the Winter Olympics of 2008 at Whistler.[58] The B.C. campaign organization also produced its own commercial featuring its three former NDP candidates and pleading for support from the province's progressives.[59]

Further apparent evidence of political balkanization came on Day 33 (June 24), when the Liberals' last national attack ad, "The Harper We Know," spliced in, for B.C. eyes only, a reference to Kyoto, the global climate warming treaty from which the Conservatives would putatively withdraw if elected. The Grits practised regional differentiation elsewhere as well. For Saskatchewan, the ad attacking Harper for his debt-deepening promises substituted former Conservative premier Grant Devine for Mike Harris as bogeyman. But these last two actions could be given an alternative interpretation. While the Kyoto and Grant Devine mentions certainly added a regional reference, they were to commercials whose messages were nevertheless uniform across Canada.

A different regional element in the campaign was the last-minute fight that Martin picked over Alberta Premier Ralph Klein's expected further privatization of health care. Since few votes could be gained in Alberta by this manoeuvre, turning Klein into a scarecrow was an obvious case of mobilizing pro-medicare bias against Conservatives across the country. A parallel nationalization of a regional question could be seen in the Liberals' pitch in Quebec, where voting for the

Bloc was castigated as helping bring the Conservatives to power.[60] Beyond spelling out the national implications of voting for the BQ, the Liberals put a more positive, pan-Canadian spin on Quebec by celebrating its exemplary child care program, undertaking to use it as a model for the rest of Canada.[61]

THE CAMPAIGN'S RADICALLY NEW FINANCIAL FRAMEWORK

On May 18, 2004, just five days before the campaign was launched, the Supreme Court of Canada decisively resolved a twenty-year uncertainty concerning the capacity of wealthy groups from civil society to participate alongside or in competition with the national parties. Limits on what non-party groups could spend in advertising during federal elections had been successfully challenged by the National Citizens Coalition (NCC) in Alberta's courts in 1984. In 1997, the NCC, then being run by Stephen Harper, again successfully challenged in the Alberta courts an amendment to the Canada Elections Act (CEA) that would have constrained such "third-party" interventions. Third time, unlucky. When the NCC's appeal reached the Supreme Court, Justice Michel Bastarache read the majority ruling for the Court, which upheld Bill C-24's amendment that limited civil society organizations' spending to $3,000 per candidate for a total of $150,000 per election.[62]

A key element in Jean Chrétien's legacy, Bill C-24 was the most substantial change to the federal election financing system since the original major reform of 1974. It federalized Quebec's rigorous interdiction of corporate and labour-union political contributions, gave more incentives for individual contributions, required riding associations to register, applied spending limits to candidate nominations and party leadership campaigns, and increased the public subsidy for elections to 90 percent of their costs.[63] Although this analysis goes to press before the publication of the Liberal Party's financial data for 2004, the new CEA can already be seen to have had a significant impact. Whereas $12 million of the Liberal Party's $20 million budget from the federal election of 2000 had come from corporations,[64] this source had been closed down. In exchange, the party received a subsidy of approximately $9 million based on the new annual allowance of $1.75 per vote received.[65]

CONCLUSIONS

Surprising most observers who, on the strength of the poll results in Week 5, expected a photo finish, the Liberal Party received 822,000 more votes than the Conservatives on June 28. Their 37 percent of the vote won them 135 of the House of Commons' 308 seats: 22 of the Atlantic provinces' 32 seats, 21 of Quebec's 75, 75 of Ontario's 106, 6 of the Prairies' 56, and 8 of British Columbia's 36. The Bloc's sweep of 54 ridings outside Montréal and the CPC's 99 left the NDP just 19, not enough to hold the balance of power and extract proportional representation as its price for propping up the Liberals. With the electoral system intact and the Conservative Party restored as the only formation on the right, the prospects seemed good for the new two + two party system — two major parties of the centre and right coexisting with a weak left-wing NDP and a regional Bloc Québécois.

Thirty-four of the sixty-five women elected to the House of Commons were Liberals — a healthy share considering the dismal overall representation of females (21.1 percent of Parliament). The Liberal Party had the third largest percentage of female candidates to run in the election and the second highest success rate amongst the four. Martin awarded senior posts to women (nine in total for his new cabinet), notably Anne McLellan as deputy prime minister and minister of public safety and preparedness, Carolyn Bennett as minister of state (public health), and Judy Sgro as minister of citizenship and immigration.

In the end, enough voters had second thoughts to turn Paul Martin's succession story from that of a Judas to one of a Lazarus. According to a COMPAS/Global Television survey of voters having cast their ballots on election day, 40 percent decided who they would vote for in the previous week; 25 percent decided within twenty-four hours of the election.[66] At this last minute, mistrust of the Conservatives' putative hidden agenda trumped mistrust of the Liberals' corruption—largely in Ontario.

In virtually all post-campaign analysis, the minority government the Liberals won at the last moment was credited to the impact of their advertising. Though no explicit correlation between ads and electoral outcomes exists, the coexistence of the appetite for change with the re-election of that government can best be explained by the voters' overriding concern about the incumbent's rival. Since the Liberals' fear campaign had not initially triumphed, it appeared that the media's autonomous role in constructing the election as a decision about extreme social conservatism ultimately delivered the Liberal minority few thought possible. As a result, Paul Martin did not follow John Turner all the way down the road to self-destruction. Instead, he was put on a short leash by uncommitted voters relenting in their anger over Adscam and by Tory voters agreeing with Joe Clark's preference for the old Liberals over the new Conservatives.

The Liberals' decade of apparently unchallengeable hegemony had been shaken to the core. With the partisan succession resolved, the question became what kind of prime ministerial succession was Paul Martin going to make as leader of a minority government. Like John Turner before him, he had lost ground in both Quebec and the West, where he had failed to make his promised business-friendly breakthrough. Would he take his lead from Lester Pearson (1963–68) and, negotiating support for every issue with the opposition, produce a creative, highly productive government? Would he follow Pierre Trudeau's model (1972–74) and govern just long enough to regain his political balance, then provoke another election on his own terms? Or would he take his cue from Joe Clark (1979) and, running the PMO as if he had a majority, turn the provisional mandate received from the voters into a decisive defeat? Only time would tell how long and how well this revivified Lazarus would defy the grave he himself had dug.

NOTES

1 This text is based on research executed by Erik Bruveris, Dennis Laberge, John Mackay, Chris Pigott, and Annette Yuen, without whose hard work and collegial enthusiasm the analysis would not have been possible. Peter

Donolo, Akaash Maharaj, and Priya Suagh generously supported this research with their insights.

2 John Gray, *Paul Martin: The Power of Ambition* (Toronto: Key Porter, 2003), 89.

3 Susan Delacourt, *Juggernaut: Paul Martin's Campaign for Chretien's Crown* (Toronto: McClelland & Stewart, 2003), 118.

4 Ibid., 137–138.

5 Campbell Clark, "Rules have Martin rivals grumbling," *Globe and Mail,* January 25, 2003.

6 Gray, 189.

7 Lawrence Martin, *Iron Man: The Defiant Reign of Jean Chrétien* (Toronto: Viking, 2003), 387.

8 Delacourt, 24.

9 James Travers, "PM names players for key roles," *Toronto Star,* July 20, 2004, A17.

10 "I am mad as hell that some people did this.... This isn't a question of the Liberals' election. Liberals are mad ... I am very mad that some people may have enriched themselves, and I am very determined to get to the bottom of this and punish those who were involved." Jim Brown, "Martin 'mad as hell,'" *Globe and Mail,* February 15, 2004.

11 Paul Martin himself suggested there "had to be political direction" on February 12 (at an impromptu press conference following the release of Auditor General Sheila Fraser's report), but later back-pedalled that statement in an interview on *Primetime Politics* with Peter Van Dusen on June 7, 2004.

12 Jane Taber, "Liberals tell PM to ease up," *Globe and Mail,* February 19, 2004, A1.

13 Jane Taber, "Liberals move to ease nomination challenges," *Globe and Mail,* January 15, 2004, A4.

14 Graeme Smith, "How Winnipeg's mayor cleared Commons path," *Globe and Mail,* May 8, 2004, A5.

15 John Ibbitson, "Liberals take no prisoners," *Globe and Mail,* May 5, 2004, A4.

16 "Incumbent MPs not running in next election: 57," *The Hill Times,* May 24–30, 2004, 16.

17 Anne Dawson, "PM's adviser admits to making 'rookie' mistakes: Alienating Chrétien loyalists an error, says Martin's campaign manager," *Ottawa Citizen,* May 21, 2004, A4.

18 Warren Kinsella, "Latest Musings," June 4, 2004, http://www.warrenkinsella.com/musings.htm.

19 Daniel Leblanc and Rheal Seguin, "Attacks haven't allowed Martin to 'be himself,' Liberals feel," *Globe and Mail,* June 3, 2004, A4.

20 Brian Tobin during Question Period, broadcast by CTV on May 30, 2004.

21 "Liberal MP calls her party's campaign 'comedy of errors,'" CBC News Online, June 9, 2004, http://www.cbc.ca/stories/2004/06/09/canada/parrish_lib040609.

22 Jane Taber, "Liberals 'are in a spiral,' top Martin adviser says," *Globe and Mail,* June 10, 2004, A1.

23 Paul Martin, "Making History." Speech to Liberal Party of Canada leadership convention, Toronto, November 14, 2003.

24 On Day 2 of the campaign, Paul Martin drew a sharp distinction between Canada and the United States at a rally in Charlottetown, P.E.I.: "...you can't have a health care system like Canada's, you can't have social programs like Canada's with taxation levels like those in the United States."

25 Though Martin's $9-billion commitment to health care led the CBC's election coverage on May 25, 2004, it was followed immediately by a "Reality Check" that characterized his previous treatment of health care as finance minister as "scourging health care, not nurturing it."

26 Observatory for Media and Public Policy, McGill University, "2004 Federal Election Newspaper Content Analysis: Cumulative Results, from May 17th to June 25th 2004," June 25, 2004, http://www.ompp.mcgill.ca/pages/reports/CumulativeReport(June25).pdf.

27 Ibid.

28 Heather Scoffield and Campbell Clark, "Martin's big pledge: $9 billion for health," *Globe and Mail,* May 26, 2004, A6.

29 A Decima/Navigator Poll cited the Ontario budget as the key reason for this decline in voter support.

30 These ads appeared nationwide, with the caption "It's not which Canadian you choose. It's which Canada."

31 Jane Taber and Campbell Clark, "Liberals plan early ad attack on Harper," *Globe and Mail,* May 13, 2004.

32 Drew Fagan, "Liberals target Klein, Mulroney," *Globe and Mail,* June 18, 2004, A1.

33 Minority government coverage began two days before the writ even dropped and, fuelled by daily polls, began in earnest by Day 7 of the campaign

34 Observatory for Media and Public Policy, McGill University, "2004 Election Newspaper Content Analysis. Weekly Results, from May 17th to June 16th 2004."

35 Erin Research Inc., "Balance in Coverage of the 2004 Federal Election Campaign. Report 6, July 2, 2004 Content Analysis Conducted for CBC," 21.

36 Ibid., 31.

37 Observatory for Media and Public Policy, McGill University, "2004 Election Newspaper Content Analysis. Weekly Results, from May 17th to June 16th 2004," 3.

38 Don Martin, "Martin failed to land crucial knockout blow," *Calgary Herald,* June 16, 2004.

39 *Leaders Debate 2004*, broadcast on CBC, June 15, 2004.

40 The day after the English debate, headlines across the country reflected either Harper's comments on a transition of power or poll numbers that put him firmly in minority territory and seemed likely to rise from June 17, 2004.

41 Observatory for Media and Public Policy, McGill University, "2004 Election Newspaper Content Analysis. Weekly Results, from May 17th to June 16th 2004."

42 Liberal Party of Canada, "With the Liberals, Air Canada Will Remain Bilingual and Will Not Leave Montreal," June 20, 2004, http://www.liberal.ca.

43 Mark Hume, "For whistle blower, it got personal," *Globe and Mail,* July 12, 2004, A4.

44 Allan Woods, "Undecided voters handed victory to Grits," *National Post,* June 29, 2004, A4.

45 Horse-race stories led issues stories by a whopping 67 percent to 32 percent by the end of the campaign. (McGill, Observatory, "Weekly Results, from May 17th to June 16th 2004.")

46 Stuart Soroka, Antonioa Maioni, Ken Whyte, and Elizabeth Goodyear-Grant, "What will the important issues be?" *Globe and Mail,* June 15, 2004.

47 Kenneth R. Carty, William Cross, and Lisa Young, *Rebuilding Canadian Party Politics* (Vancouver: University of British Columbia Press, 2000).

48 John Ibbitson, "Politicos forcefully wag the cod," *Globe and Mail,* May 28, 2004, A4.

49 Patrick Fournier, Andre Blais, Joanna Everitt, Elisabeth Gidengil, and Neil Nevitte, "How the Liberals lost Quebec," *Globe and Mail,* July 21, 2004, A15.

50 Editorial, "Mr. Martin's cavalcade of instant nominations," *Globe and Mail,* May 13, 2004, A20.

51 This astonishing attack ad began airing June 10, 2004, in Week 3 of the campaign, which would turn out to be the strongest week of the campaign for the Conservative Party.

52 Gloria Galloway, “Ontario blue-belt may be grits' noose,” *Globe and Mail,* April 17, 2004, A7.

53 Drew Fagan, “Poll puts Martin's stumbling Liberals ahead by four points,” *Globe and Mail,* June 1, 2004, A1.

54 Paul Martin, Sault Ste. Marie, Ontario, May 31, 2004.

55 Richard Mackie, “Not our fault federal party lags, Ontario Liberals say,” *Globe and Mail,* June 3, 2004, A4.

56 Murray Campbell, “Ontario quarterbacking medicare change,” *Globe and Mail,* May 6, 2004, A7.

57 Carty et al.

58 Peter O'Neill, “B.C. Grits to set out a distinct agenda,” *Vancouver Sun,* June 7, 2004.

59 Liberal Party of Canada, “British Columbia and the NDP,” http://www.liberal.ca/ads_e.aspx.

60 On June 7 (only two weeks into the campaign), the Liberals launched their Quebec-targeted negative print ad that likened a vote for the Conservatives to one for separatism amidst talk that a Conservative minority would necessarily be propped up by the Bloc Québécois.

61 Les Whittington and Graham Fraser, “New spending, no deficit pledged,” *Toronto Star,* June 4, 2004, A6.

62 Kirk Makin and Brian Laghi, “Top court upholds spending limits,” *Globe and Mail,* May 19, 2004, A8.

63 William Cross, University of Toronto, March 30, 2004.

64 Elections Canada, http://www.elections.ca, accessed May 13, 2004.

65 Jane Taber, “Reports of Tory's political death premature,” *Globe and Mail,* June 30, 2004, A11.

66 Allan Woods, “Undecided voters handed victory to Grits,” *National Post,* June 29, 2004, A4.

CHAPTER THREE

New Conservatives, Old Realities: *The 2004 Election Campaign*

by Faron Ellis and Peter Woolstencroft[1]

Underlying the three consecutive Liberal majorities in the last elections of the twentieth century are two features of the Canadian party system: the fragmentation of the non-Liberal vote and the highly regionalized pattern of party competition. Both of these factors structured the events in the pre-election period and during the 2004 election campaign, especially for the Conservative Party, the successor to the Canadian Alliance and the Progressive Conservative parties following their merger in late 2003. After the 1993 election five parties held seats in the House of Commons. That the second and third largest parties — the Bloc Québécois and Reform — were new players, and two established parties — the New Democrats and Progressive Conservatives — were so reduced in numbers that they lost official party status were just two indicators that the Canadian party system was going through great changes.[2]

Historically, successful challenges to the Liberals by conservative political forces have been sporadic and episodic. Since the First World War, only Brian Mulroney had managed to win two consecutive Tory majority governments. But even his re-election in the tumultuous 1988 free trade election was followed by the historical pattern of a precipitous decline in public support and the near annihilation of the party as a parliamentary force in the 1993 general election. Even when voters were ready to turn the Liberals out of office, questions typically persisted as to whether the conservative side of the spectrum would be able to present voters with a platform cohesive enough to span the diverse regional and ideological divisions between constituent elements of the centre-right opposition. The formalization of these differences in two parties, the Reform/Alliance and the Progressive Conservatives, exacerbated the problem of challenging the Liberals. Contrary to the expectations of many — and certainly the hopes of Reform Party devotees — the PCs did not disappear, but rather reacquired and maintained official party status in the 1997 and 2000 elections. For many conservatives, the re-election of the Liberals seemed to be a certainty — "gritlock" would remain the norm as long as the Alliance and PCs were determined to wage an ongoing electoral war of attrition until one or the other disappeared.[3] After the 2000 election, one overriding question remained: would it be possible to establish a new nationally based challenge to the Liberals? Or would the PCs and the Alliance continue their separate journeys, effectively allowing the Liberals an unchallenged hold on government?

The regional dimension of electoral politics in the 1990s meant that the Liberals were competitive across much of the country but faced different opponents from region to region. In Atlantic Canada, the four provinces followed the traditional pattern of Tory-Grit rivalry, though the New Democratic Party was a substantial actor in Nova Scotia. In Quebec, the Bloc Québécois and the Liberals were the principal players, leaving Reform/Alliance, the New Democrats, and the PCs, including in 1997 when Quebec native Jean Charest led them, far behind. Liberals had a stranglehold on Ontario, winning almost all of the province's 103 seats. In the West, Reform/Alliance dominated Alberta and British Columbia, but the party system was more complex in Saskatchewan and Manitoba, where the Liberals, New Democrats, and Reform/Alliance were all competitive.

Having achieved in 1993 its first tactical objective of removing the PCs as a principal actor, Reform set out to consolidate its position by eliminating the PCs and galvanizing conservative forces under its brand. The Progressive Conservatives, however, refused to disappear. Under Jean Charest's leadership they surprised most observers with an electoral comeback in the 1997 election. Their 19 percent of the vote almost equalled Reform's totals, and winning twenty seats reconfirmed official parliamentary status on the PCs, somewhat blunting Reform's celebration of its sixty seats and new status as the Official Opposition. Charest's departure for Quebec politics, however, quickly raised anew questions about the viability of the Tories, concerns that were not alleviated by their leadership race of 1998. The contest attracted little interest from the media and the general public, though the party became the first national party to choose a leader on the basis of "one member, one vote." Joe Clark, former leader and prime minister, won the helm on the second ballot and immediately set his sights on rebuilding the PC Party independently from Reform. Furthermore, Clark's principal opponent was David Orchard, a vehement foe of the free trade agreements that had been the hallmark of the Mulroney government and opponent of any arrangement with Reform. Orchard was supported by about one-quarter of the party. Voices for finding rapprochement with Reform were few. Brian Pallister, the only candidate for the PC leadership interested in building ties between the two parties, ran poorly and soon drifted to the Alliance, winning a Manitoba seat for them in the 2000 election.

In spite of PC rebuffs, Preston Manning, the founder and first leader of the Reform Party, initiated a process in 1998 to unite the conservative opposition. The Canadian Reform Conservative Alliance Party (Alliance) was the result of Manning's desire to transform his western-based populist party into a national organization capable of unseating the Liberals. When the Progressive Conservatives refused to participate in their own demise,[4] and Manning boldly proceeded anyway, he succeeded in creating a new party but lost the leadership to Alberta Treasurer Stockwell Day. When Jean Chrétien called the 2000 election only months later, little appeared to have changed except the leadership of two still-separate parties.[5]

Despite the high regard many voters had for Clark, the Progressive Conservative 2000 campaign was sprightly enough to win only 12.2 percent of the popular vote and just twelve seats, the minimum required to maintain official party status.[6] The Alliance improved on Reform's 1997 results by capturing 25.5 percent of the vote and winning sixty-six seats. Most significantly, however, the party failed to unite the conservative vote in Ontario, where it managed to eke out only two wins. The Alliance made little headway in Quebec or Atlantic Canada, winning no seats east of Ontario, rendering its parliamentary caucus again almost exclusively western. Despite the Alliance's modest improvement on Reform's past efforts, Day's inability to effectively manage divisions within his party set off a series of events that would eventually see the Alliance and PCs merge into one party, just in time for the 2004 federal election.

THE ALLIANCE CAUCUS MELTDOWN

Alliance Leader Stockwell Day's leadership crisis started early in 2001 when he settled a defamation suit arising from his days as an Alberta MLA and member of Ralph Klein's provincial cabinet. In a 1999 letter to the *Red Deer Advocate* Day had questioned local lawyer and school board trustee Lorne Goddard's suitability to serve on the school board after Goddard had defended a convicted pedophile.[7] The affair cost Alberta taxpayers almost $800,000, reminded many of the problems Day experienced during the recent election campaign, and was just one of many upcoming controversies that would provide Day's opponents with ample ammunition to question both his leadership style and his competency for the job.

Day was also having difficulty managing the most raucous western elements in the Alliance coalition, inside and out of his caucus, while at the same time serving as leader of a federalist party attempting to expand outside its western base. When two of his MPs attended a meeting of the separatist Alberta Independence Party, and Day responded with a call for patience, he was pilloried by federal cabinet minister Stéphane Dion as being soft on separatism. Simultaneously, he was being forced to respond publicly to a variety of proposals emanating from westerners still smarting from their 2000 federal election rebuff by Central Canadian voters. Not least of these was an open letter published by six prominent Albertans, including Stephen Harper,[8] urging Alberta Premier Ralph Klein to adopt an "Alberta Agenda" by building a constitutional firewall around the province. Although the letter was directed at the Alberta premier, its authors' connections with the former Reform Party forced Day to attempt to reconcile his views with those of the "firewall six." To many it signified that those who had previously expended much effort in building the Reform and Alliance parties were no longer interested in pursuing their agendas in federal politics. Having turned their sights on provincial politics they appeared to be effectively pronouncing the Reform/Alliance experiment a failure.

Although Clark had been accusing Day of lacking the authority to conduct merger negotiations, once the PC management committee approved its "Consultations on the Future of the Progressive Conservative Party," and Day discovered that seven of his MPs had already been meeting with PC MPs to talk about cooperation, both Day and Clark granted teams of their respective MPs the authority to begin discussions on parliamentary cooperation. When twenty senior Alliance members held a special two-day summit on unity talks at Stornoway, and Day, Clark, and Bloc Québécois Leader Gilles Duceppe began to formally coordinate their parliamentary opposition to the government,[9] it appeared that some progress on unity was being made. The momentum prompted a cautious Clark, however, to hold a special caucus meeting and remind his MPs that no formal decisions could be made until after party members had been heard.

When it was revealed that two Alliance MPs had hired a spy to dig up dirt on the Liberals, and Day began a battle with a Quebec judge whom he accused of being in a potential conflict of interest, his handling of both situations again cast doubts on his leadership skills. This time, however, many senior Alliance party members were not willing to keep their criticisms behind closed doors. The deluge of critiques began when an Ontario riding association president accused Day, Alliance MPs, and members of the party's national council of being rank amateurs who were frittering away the party's credibility. He concluded that Day must resign. An exodus of talent from the organization ensued, including two former directors of communication, the party's director of research, its director of operations, and a press secretary.[10] Senior Ontario provincial Progressive Conservatives also jumped on the critical bandwagon, and by month's end, Day had a full-blown rebellion on his hands.

On April 23, 2001, Alliance Deputy Leader Deborah Grey and House leader Chuck Strahl resigned from their shadow cabinet positions. Citing frustrations over Day's handing of the series of internal crises, Alberta MP Art Hanger joined them and openly called for his leader's resignation. Dissention grew when Alliance MPs returned from the Easter break. B.C. MP Grant McNally resigned as deputy House leader, arguing that Day had failed to demonstrate a vision for the party. Another, Val Meredith, stated that the time had come for Day to step down. When long-time Manning organizer and Alliance national councillor Rick Anderson went public with his conclusions that the situation had deteriorated to the point where a significant number of Alliance MPs were considering sitting as independents or forming a breakaway caucus, it appeared that the one commonality the dissidents shared was their previous close association with the former Reform leader. For his part, Manning refused to quell the dissention, stating that he didn't think it was appropriate for a former leader to be commenting on or evaluating the present leader, and that no matter what happened with the Alliance leadership he was still planning on retiring from politics.

At the last weekly Alliance caucus meeting in April, Day endured a bruising four and one-half hours of debate and criticism by his divided parliamentarians. Through it all he adamantly maintained that he would not quit. Nor would he call an early leadership review, citing the party's scheduled mandatory review in one year's time at the party's general convention. He did, however, agree to return to caucus in one week with a strategic plan that would restore confidence in his leadership and give the party direction. He stripped Hanger of his defence critic portfolio and shuffled other assignments. He also managed to get the caucus to approve a "gag order" explicitly forbidding members from publicly criticizing the leader, an order Hanger violated just hours after the meeting.

Alliance rank and file soon became embroiled in the controversy when three riding associations passed motions asking Day for his resignation. At the same time, a cadre of former Manning aides and advisors worked behind the scenes with a group of fifteen Alliance MPs, including Grey and Strahl, to force Day out. When B.C. MP Gary Lunn broke the gag order and accused Day of "circling the wagons to protect himself," Day blamed others for his troubles, including Ottawa lobbyists, Manning's people, the media, and other MPs, whom he accused of joining in a conspiracy and attempted coup. As the Day forces began to fight back, party president Ken Kalopsis launched an investigation into the possible inappropriate use of the party's membership lists by the new "Grassroots for Day" forces. Rick Anderson emerged as the chief of the anti-Day forces when he again criticized the leader in a widely distributed e-mail that claimed Canadian voters were "not interested in [Day] as prime minister," had become "allergic to him," and thought the Alliance "made an awful mistake." Anderson went further, stating that he believed in the eyes of most "the leader has become a laughing stock." Day ally Alberta MP Jason Kenny immediately led a national council move to have Anderson punished. Dissidents countered by holding a meeting to plan strategy on how to deal with Day's threat to expel those who criticized his leadership.[11]

At the next weekly Alliance caucus meeting Day presented MPs with his forty-five-page, three-year strategic plan. It focused on improving external communications, giving MPs more responsibility, and raising the party's fortunes in the polls. Provisions would include more controlled media access to the leader, more fact-checking before going public on issues, and fewer and less open scrums and news conferences. Day left the meeting claiming unanimous caucus support for his plan. Art Hanger agreed immediately following the meeting but, just hours later, reiterated his call for Day to resign. Hanger was immediately suspended from the Alliance caucus and became the first of thirteen Alliance MPs to receive similar punishment or voluntarily remove themselves. Garry Lunn immediately chastised Day for disciplining Hanger, reissued his call for Day to resign, thereby breaching the new Alliance disciplinary code, and was immediately suspended. Lunn then advocated a mass defection of Alliance MPs as the only way to force Day to resign. He concluded that if twenty-eight Alliance rebels joined with the twelve sitting Tories in a loose coalition, they would outnumber the remaining Alliance caucus and the Bloc, thereby deserving status as Official Opposition.

Amidst the Alliance caucus chaos, PC Deputy Leader Peter MacKay and other Tories were holding meetings with disaffected Alliance MPs and officials, bypassing Day in the process. MacKay bluntly told reporters that he hadn't yet talked to Day, nor did he intend to, but would continue to communicate directly with Alliance members. Clark again cautioned his deputy that a PC Party membership-sanctioned process was still needed before consultations could go much further. Clark's caution did not stop seven Alliance MPs[12] from attending a Tory fundraising dinner in mid-May, at which Clark invited all interested Alliance members to join with him in rebuilding the Progressive Conservative Party. In doing so, Clark began to implement his strategy of talking unity but doing what he could to help the Alliance implode before reuniting the remnants of its support base under the PC banner.

Clark's strategy appeared to be sound when eight Alliance MPs held a news conference on May 15, 2001, to call for Day's resignation. They stated that Day had "exercised consistently bad judgment, dishonest communications and a lack of fidelity to [Alliance] principles" and that they did not want to be associated with such practices, and they requested a leadership review. They were immediately suspended from the Alliance caucus. Day remained defiant, demanding respect for the mandate given him by the party's grassroots. "Ten months ago, I was honored to receive the largest democratic leadership mandate in Canadian political history. Six months ago the Canadian Alliance received a democratic mandate from more than three million Canadians to be the Official Opposition in our nation. Eleven months from now, the members of our party will have the opportunity to democratically pass judgment on my leadership, a judgment I will fully respect."[13]

Amid threats of lawsuits between MPs and Day staff, crisis caucus meetings, and reports of internal plots and schemes, the remaining Alliance caucus attempted partial reconciliation by voting to suspend, but not expel, the dissident MPs. The party's national council then set out to restore order but only further inflamed the situation. They temporarily suspended Rick Anderson from their ranks, leading former Manning supporters Cliff Fryers and Nancy Branscombe to storm out of the meeting. Fryers charged that Day supporters were the "forces of darkness" and the Alliance leader the "worst abomination that you could possibly see in politics today." The national council also voted down a motion to have an immediate mail-in referendum on the issue of Day's leadership, and the crisis deepened.

By the end of May, another national councillor, Thompson MacDonald of Calgary, stepped forward to lead a leadership review Yes Committee to unseat Day at the party's next convention. Clark rejected Day's offer to hold joint policy forums aimed at cooperation, stating he planned to "go it alone" and wasn't interested in getting mixed up in the Alliance's problems. Then, on June 8, Reform's first MP, Deborah Grey, went public with her criticism of Day. Telling the Alliance leader that "the gig is up," she stated that she no longer had confidence in Day's ability to lead the party or ever become prime minister. She said she would be working for the Yes Committee but stopped short of demanding his resignation. Rather, she urged him to step aside immediately, being replaced by an interim leader until a leadership contest or a party-wide referendum could be held.

Day's leadership crisis and Clark's outright refusal to meet formally with the Alliance led a number of Alliance and PC members to decide to take matters into their own hands.[14] Both leaders were left out of a unity bid led by Chuck Strahl and Peter MacKay. Following a meeting between sixteen Tory MPs and senators and the Alliance caucus rebels, they decided to hold a series of summer summits aimed at creating a new party. Another round of bickering ensued, accompanied by threats of lawsuits, accusations of threatening e-mails, more calls for a leadership review (Alberta MPs Diane Ablonczy and Monte Solberg), and Alliance MPs meeting with the Tories without their leader's approval. Day attempted to regain some share of the unity agenda by announcing a proposal for a unity referendum among Alliance members. Should another new party be established, Day would contend for the leadership.[15] Clark flatly rejected the proposal.

On the weekend of his first anniversary as leader, Day found himself faced with further dissention when party co-treasurer Peter White threatened to release a letter from seven of the nine Alliance executive committee members demanding Day's resignation. Faced with no alternative, Day worked with Alliance officials to draft an attempted settlement with the dissidents. The offer included Day stepping aside and being replaced on an interim basis by deputy leader Grant Hill. The thirteen rebels would return to caucus after signing a loyalty oath, the current party president Ken Kalopsis would be replaced, and reconciliation committees for the caucus and national council would be established.[16] The dissidents balked at the terms, and when Day withdrew the offer White tendered his resignation. Even loyal Alliance MPs were now openly questioning Day's judgment, demanding to know why they weren't consulted about the resignation offer. Several decided to confront Day at an emergency caucus meeting scheduled for mid-July in Calgary. Amid media frenzy, Day emerged from the meeting to state that he would be asking the national council to schedule a leadership vote[17] and would be resigning as leader no later than ninety days prior to the vote.[18]

Most of the dissidents were not impressed, and twelve of them decided to form their own parliamentary caucus. They called themselves the Democratic Representative Caucus (DRC), and they planned to talk unity with the Tories and set up an association but not register themselves as a new party. In mid-August, the DRC and PC caucuses held meetings at Mont-Tremblant, Quebec, now with Manning's public endorsement. By early September the Alliance caucus leadership had its fill and issued an ultimatum to the rebels: either return to the Alliance caucus by Monday, September 10, 2001, or face having their suspensions turned into full expulsions. Four dissidents broke from the rebel DRC and returned to the Alliance main caucus. The remaining eight dissidents, including Strahl and Grey, formed a parliamentary coalition with the Progressive Conservatives, calling it the PC-DRC Coalition.[19] They petitioned House Speaker Peter Miliken for recognition, including extra budget allotments and more speaking time. Eventually, he granted the PC-DRC Coalition the right to sit together, elect their own caucus officers, and be represented on committees, but since they refused to form a party, he decided that he could not recognize them as a party, and therefore, despite their numbers, would sit fifth in parliamentary standings, still behind the thirteen-member NDP caucus.[20]

THE 2002 ALLIANCE LEADERSHIP CONTEST

In August of 2001, former Reform MP Stephen Harper announced that he would be leaving his job as president of the National Citizens' Coalition to seek the Alliance leadership. A dozen Alliance MPs immediately supported Harper, although his former boss, Deborah Grey, was not among them.[21] In fact, Grey launched a sustained attack on Harper, stating that he was not a populist and likely wasn't up to the demands of political life, especially the demands of leadership. But over the course of the next two years, the bilingual, forty-three-year-old, University of Calgary–educated economist would demonstrate otherwise. Harper had been organizing since June of 2001, and in a series of speeches and newspaper essays, often co-authored with his future campaign manager and fellow member of the "firewall six" Tom Flanagan, Harper outlined his assessment of the current state of conservative politics in Canada.[22] His message was clear: Canada was in need of a principled, small-c conservative party that would not retreat from taking a more ideological stance on policy issues, would not curry favour with Québécois nationalists, and, most importantly, would present Canadian voters with a professional political organization capable of earning enough trust to successfully compete for power.

Harper let it be known that he was suspicious of the current quest for mere strategic alliances and was particularly critical of Joe Clark and his red-Tory pragmatism. Harper said he would never negotiate a political merger with the PCs as long as Clark remained, but left the door open should the PCs change leaders.[23] He accused Clark of not being a true conservative and being more interested in luring Alliance dissidents into the Tory fold than in sincere negotiations for political unity on the right. Turning his attention to the DRC he launched what would become an important theme of both his successful leadership bids: the need to develop a disciplined, professional political organization. And finally, turning his attention to the more immediate task of defeating Day, he vowed not to let the religious right hijack the party or be beholden to any narrow special interest groups. He further committed that a Harper-led Alliance would not initiate legislation in moral areas, but he did give qualified support for referenda if the Alliance policy was clarified before the next election.

Alliance Deputy Leader Grant Hill, who had declined the job as interim leader,[24] joined Harper as a candidate. Hill, a southern Alberta medical doctor, was one of the original 1993 Reform MPs and had served the party in various capacities, including his most recent stint as deputy leader, a role he fulfilled admirably while defending Day during the dissident crisis.[25] Hill would campaign almost exclusively on achieving unity with the Progressive Conservatives. Calgary MP Diane Ablonczy entered the race as another pro-unity candidate.[26] Ablonczy had earlier flirted with the DRC rebels but made peace with Day prior to entering the leadership race. A lawyer, she was also another 1993 Reform MP, a fierce Manning loyalist who had served as Reform's first chairman. She would also campaign almost exclusively on a pro-unity platform. Day rounded out the field by choosing Montreal as his leadership launch pad. He claimed, somewhat curiously, that his experience in dealing with the rebellion was an asset, thereby making him the best candidate to expand the party beyond its western base. He touted the endorsement of a group of Quebec Tory youth who had abandoned Clark as evidence of his grassroots support. He blamed "backroom elites" for his troubles and urged the grassroots to "take back this party."[27]

The 2002 Alliance leadership contest, like most Alliance matters, opened with a debate over unity. Ablonczy immediately came under pressure from the Hill campaign to withdraw so as to not split the relatively small pro-merger vote. Day initially argued against full merger plans and accused Hill of being a danger to the party. In place of Hill's "unity at any price," Day offered his own "joint candidacy plan." Harper, not interested in discussing unity — a position reinforced when Joe Clark stated his plan to fight the next election as PC leader — began selling his leadership to Quebec federalists by explicitly casting aside the Québécois nationalist vote from his vision of the Alliance coalition.[28] He promoted his "professionalism" plank by lashing out at Day, calling his reign amateurish and damaging to the party as an institution. He also used his moratorium on discussing a merger with Clark as a wedge against Ablonczy and Hill, claiming he would take the party out of the hands of the spin doctors, lobbyists, and bagmen who got control of it during the United Alternative process. Nor did he shirk from promoting a thoroughly conservative economic policy.[29]

By mid-campaign, Day's membership recruitment tactics had become an issue. Of particular concern was the threat of being subsumed by Campaign Life, an anti-abortion lobby group backing Day. His campaign had been making open appeals to evangelicals, urging them to buy memberships and donate money, and, in the case of Campaign Life, to donate so the organization could buy bulk memberships, tactics that led to a party-issued censure. Day's campaign also sent e-mail ads to supporters urging them to sign up other people, potentially without their knowledge. When it was revealed that the Alliance membership had almost doubled to 123,312 by the February 28 cut-off, making a Day victory a possibility, an anybody-but-Day movement gained ground. Talks started between the Hill and Harper teams about the possibility of Hill stepping aside if Harper agreed to a party-wide referendum on merger. When the deal fell through and Hill remained in the race, he aided the Harper cause by aggressively criticizing Day, accusing him of poor judgment and shirking responsibility. Calling Day's leadership a "car crash," Hill openly questioned Day's character and accused him of blaming others for political blunders that were the result of his own errors. The strategy put Day on the defensive. His campaign responded by issuing a "zero-tolerance" position designed to alert members that should Day win, he was ready to get tough with dissenters. The threats alarmed party members and galvanized support for Harper.

On March 20, 2002, the party announced that Harper had won a clear first ballot victory.[30] Harper won majorities, or strong pluralities, in six of ten provinces, including Alberta, B.C., and Ontario. Day handily won Quebec and inched out Harper in Saskatchewan and Prince Edward Island. Reaction to the Harper victory was swift and previewed the strategy that would be employed against him in the 2004 federal election. The Liberals immediately seized on the firewall proposal, characterizing Harper as a regionally blinkered, right-wing ideologue who was out of step with the views of mainstream Canadians. Fearing his PC-DRC coalition may be in jeopardy, Clark said he was anxious to talk to Harper about cooperation. For his part, Harper set his sights on re-staffing the opposition leader's office, gaining a seat in the Commons, and addressing the Alliance's debt and revenue problems.[31] "My priority," stated the new leader, "is to rebuild this party, beginning now and getting it ready for the next election, with or without the Tories."[32]

Table 1:
2002 Canadian Alliance Leadership Contest Results by Province

	Harper	Day	Ablonczy	Hill
B.C.	62.7 %	31.7 %	3.3 %	2.4 %
Alta.	55.8	36.0	3.6	4.6
Sask.	47.3	49.2	1.6	1.9
Man.	52.1	41.8	2.5	3.5
Ont.	53.1	37.5	5.5	3.9
Que.	22.1	73.2	2.0	2.7
N.B.	49.4	45.0	2.9	2.7
N.S.	49.7	42.7	5.2	2.3
P.E.I.	44.8	49.4	1.1	4.6
Nfld.	41.7	41.7	11.1	5.6
Territories	61.5	26.9	6.7	4.8
Total	55.0	37.5	3.8	3.7

Source: Canadian Alliance

Harper built a transition team headed up by MP Scott Reid and former Reform MP Ray Speaker that included no Day backers. He immediately sacked a number of Day staffers, appointed Tom Flanagan his director of operations, and began building a team that would run both his Conservative Party leadership bid and the party's 2004 election campaign.[33] The Alliance nominated Harper to run in the Calgary South West by-election to replace Manning, which he easily won (72 percent) after the Liberals declined to offer up an opponent and PC challenger Jim Prentice withdrew citing the need for co-operation among conservatives. Harper assumed the duties as leader of the opposition to mixed reviews, including harsh criticism of his comments that a "culture of defeatism" is keeping Atlantic Canada dependent on federal transfers.[34]

PROGRESSIVE CONSERVATIVE 2003 LEADERSHIP CONTEST

With Harper moving the Alliance ahead of the Tories in public opinion polls, and the on-again, off-again merger/unity/cooperation discussions having completely broken down, Joe Clark moved to rescue his faltering PC-DRC Coalition and prepare for a leadership review of his own at the August 2002 Progressive Conservative convention. By mid-April, however, the PC-DRC coalition had collapsed[35] and Harper was appealing to disaffected conservatives in the PC Party, over the head of their leader.[36] Harper offered a unity package and placed an end-of-summer deadline for reaching agreement. Clark immediately rejected the offer, continuing to cling to his beliefs that the PC Party was the institution within which to unite conservatives and that he was best suited to become prime minister. After a series of senior Progressive Conservatives called on Clark to resign, he decided to avoid the mandatory leadership review and announced he would not be staying on to fight the next election. Harper immediately reminded PC delegates that his cooperation offer was still valid through the end of the summer. But despite repeated pleas from some senior Tories to stop their war with the Alliance, PC delegates overwhelmingly endorsed the party's "301 rule" (the commitment to run candidates in all constituencies) and soundly rejected the outcome of months of unity meetings, effectively shutting the door on electoral cooperation between the two parties.

Nova Scotia MP Peter MacKay and Calgary lawyer Jim Prentice entered the Tory leadership race first. As with the Alliance contest of the previous year, unity would define much of the campaign debate. Prentice campaigned on a pro-merger platform. MacKay offered a more modest cooperation scenario while maintaining that he would honour the 301 rule. Nova Scotia MP Scott Brison and 1998 leadership contender David Orchard rounded out the slate of candidates.[37] Orchard, who ran on a nationalist, anti-free trade platform, presented front-runner MacKay with his greatest challenge as delegate selection meetings geared up across the country. Orchard locked up approximately one-quarter of the constituency delegates to MacKay's approximately 40 percent. Prentice and Brison split the remaining first ballot support.

As delegates assembled for their convention, it became clear MacKay would need a substantial number of the ex-officio delegates to put his leadership bid over the top on the first ballot. When that didn't occur, a traditional convention atmosphere developed. After four gruelling ballots, MacKay emerged on top, but not before making a deal with Orchard after the third ballot to secure the victory. The deal, which neither candidate initially made public, included assurances from MacKay that there would be no merger, no joint candidates (the 301 rule remained effective), a review of the party's position on free trade, a policy emphasis on the environment, and some consideration for Orchard supporters in PC staffing decisions. The deal appeared to slam the door on any possible cooperation between the Alliance and the Tories.

Table 2: 2003 Progressive Conservative Leadership Convention

	1st Ballot		2nd Ballot		3rd Ballot		4th Ballot	
	Votes	**Percent**	**Votes**	**Percent**	**Votes**	**Percent**	**Votes**	**Percent**
MacKay	1,080	41.08	1,018	39.67	1,128	45.01	1,538	64.79
Prentice	478	18.18	466	18.16	761	30.37	836	35.21
Orchard	640	24.34	619	24.12	617	24.62	–	–
Brison	431	16.39	463	18.04	–	–	–	–
Chandler	0	0	–	–	–	–	–	–
Total	2,629		2,566		2,506		2,374	

Note: Delegates were committed to vote on the first ballot according to constituency delegate selection meeting results but were freed to vote their conscience on subsequent ballots.

Source: Progressive Conservative Party of Canada

THE ALLIANCE/ PROGRESSIVE CONSERVATIVE MERGER

Despite having signed the "Orchard deal," MacKay proposed to at least meet with Harper, who had been aggressively promoting a single slate of conservative candidates for the next election since the Alliance's disappointing third-place finish in the Perth-Middlesex by-election in May.[38] MacKay reacted to Harper's "common cause campaign" with muted enthusiasm, but enough that each leader appointed a team of negotiators to try to find some common ground. Former deputy prime minister Don Mazankowski, former Ontario premier William Davis, and MP Loyola Hearn led the Tory team. The Alliance negotiators were former Reform MP Ray Speaker, Ontario MP Scott Reid, and Senator Gerry St. Germain. Despite a Tory-Alliance parliamentary truce, any institutional merger still appeared out of sight as talks became bogged down a number of times, especially over the method of selecting a new leader. The Alliance had been insisting on a one-member, one-vote system, but MacKay, referring to the Alliance's much larger membership base, declared he wouldn't sign any merger agreement that would allow his party's fate to be determined by "the province of Alberta alone." MacKay had also become irritated by the frequent media leaks over merger talks, as he was having some difficulty controlling dissenting voices in the PC Party. But Harper doggedly persevered, and when negotiations appeared to have broken down for the last time, he authorized the Alliance delegation to accept the PC leadership selection process. On October 16, 2003, Harper and MacKay announced that they had reached an Agreement in Principle that would merge the two parties into the new Conservative Party of Canada.[39]

The merger agreement would treat each of the two existing parties as equals and would have the new party maintain all existing relationships with provincial Progressive Conservative parties. Upon ratification,[40] the new party would assume all of the assets and liabilities of the existing parties. A leadership convention was scheduled for March 19–20, 2004, just weeks prior to a possible federal election call. The agreement established nineteen founding principles but turned over detailed work on policy and organization to an interim council.[41] Clark and Orchard were outraged, while Manning and former prime minister Brian Mulroney pledged to work on behalf of the new party. The Alliance caucus overwhelmingly approved of the merger, as did the Alliance membership.[42]

Convincing some Progressive Conservatives would be a much tougher sell. Immediately, a group of two hundred prominent Tories, including Clark, former Newfoundland premier Brian Peckford, and current MPs Rick Borotsik and John Herron, attacked the deal as a betrayal of the history and principles of the Progressive Conservatives. Orchard filed legal action attempting to get a court injunction against the PC's planned "virtual ratification convention."[43] But Harper and MacKay, backed up by Mulroney and some big-name fundraisers, campaigned strongly for the deal and won over the PC membership in convincing fashion. Defections quickly followed. Joe Clark declared that he would not be part of the new party and would finish his political career as an independent.[44] PC MP John Herron crossed the floor to the Liberals, and Andre Bachand headed for retirement. Five PC senators also refused to join the new party's parliamentary caucus.[45] Nova Scotia MP and recent PC leadership contender Scott Brison defected to the Liberals, as did B.C. Alliance MP Keith Martin. By the time Parliament was dissolved, the new Conservative Party boasted 73 MPs to the Liberals' 168, the Bloc's 33, and the NDP's 14. There were 9 independent MPs, and 4 seats sat vacant.

CONSERVATIVE PARTY 2004 LEADERSHIP CONTEST

Stephen Harper was quick to signal his intention to seek the leadership of the new party. MacKay would decline to enter the race, and Harper would eventually face unknown conservative activist and billionaire Belinda Stronach, as well as former Ontario PC cabinet minister Tony Clement. In the immediate post-agreement period, however, the media focus revolved around those who would not end up contesting for the job. Former Ontario premier Mike Harris was the first of the rumoured front-runners to declare that he was not interested.[46] New Brunswick Premier Bernard Lord quickly followed, although he would continue to face considerable pressure to reconsider. By January, MacKay, DRC Leader Chuck Strahl, and former PC leadership candidate Jim Prentice had all decided against running. Each cited, among other factors, lack of finances and organizational support as reasons for their respective decisions.

Harper would this time emphasize his rather impressive track record as leader as his greatest asset.[47] In the course of just over two years he had soundly defeated Day for the Alliance leadership, put together a successful team of professionals, imposed some order and discipline on an often ill-tempered Alliance caucus, resolved the DRC dissident situation, and brought about a merger of the two parties that many predicted was impossible. Now he would attempt to add a more moderate image to the package by making himself much more accessible to the media and appearing at many more candidate functions than he had during the 2002 Alliance contest.

Stronach, the thirty-seven-year-old daughter of Magna auto parts magnate Frank Stronach, was a virtual unknown outside of elite conservative business and political circles, but had been supporting the latest round of unity talks. Although her personal wealth assured that financing would not be an issue, her lack of political experience and minimal profile presented problems for organizing a serious bid. She quickly recruited a blue-ribbon campaign team headed by veteran PC organizer John Laschinger and communications consultant Jaime Watt. Their strategy was to capitalize on Stronach's star power while attempting to turn her inexperience into a populist, anti-politician virtue.[48] But after an initial blitzkrieg of attention, her stiffness in front of the media and policy vagueness began to catch up with the campaign. Despite an earnest membership drive, the campaign fell well short of its organizational goals and couldn't overcome Harper's established momentum.

Tony Clement, former Ontario Progressive Conservative cabinet minister and long-time proponent of conservative unity, entered the contest with the intent of demonstrating that he had even more experience than Harper but didn't carry the Alliance leader's regional or ideological baggage. His campaign utilized three national co-chairs: former DRC leader Strahl, legendary PC stalwart John Crosbie, and former Alliance leadership contender Tom Long. Clement would focus on his strengths in Ontario, but with the two larger campaigns primarily responsible for the party's membership swelling from over 100,000 to better than 250,000, Clement would have difficulty carving out a distinct membership base.

After an often polite, agreeable campaign that left few deep wounds,[49] Harper soundly defeated his rivals on the first ballot. He swept the West and won a convincing majority of Ontario votes, but in a sign of weakness that the Liberals would exploit during the general election campaign, Harper lost to Stronach in Quebec and all of the Atlantic provinces. His win was convincing nonetheless, and Harper set out to establish his new party as a moderate and professional alternative to a government that Canadians could no longer trust. Ontario would be the focus. If the Conservatives could prove competency there, it was expected that other seats would follow, including a lucky win or two in Quebec.

Table 3: 2004 Conservative Leadership Contest Results by Province

	% of total points			Constituency wins		
	Harper	Stronach	Clement	Harper	Stronach	Clement
B.C.	79.9	13.7	6.4	36	0	0
Alta.	85.0	12.3	2.8	28	0	0
Sask.	81.5	14.9	3.6	14	0	0
Man.	73.5	21.4	5.1	14	0	0
Ont.	56.9	27.3	15.8	96	6	4
Que.	33.4	60.5	6.0	16*	56*	3
N.B.	46.1	49.2	5.1	6	4	0
N.S.	37.2	52.9	10.0	4	7	0
P.E.I.	21.3	68.0	10.3	0	4	0
Nfld.	33.0	52.7	14.6	0**	6**	0
Y.T.	62.0	32.0	6.0	1	0	0
N.W.T.	53.0	39.0	9.0	1	0	0
Nun.	28.0	56.0	17.0	0	1	0
Total	55.5	35.0	9.5	216	84	4

Source: Conservative Party of Canada. Membership numbers and number of voters not released.

Provincial totals may not add to 100 points due to rounding at the riding level.

* Harper and Stronach tied in three Quebec ridings.
** Harper and Stronach tied in one Newfoundland riding.

THE 2004 CAMPAIGN ORGANIZATION AND STRATEGY

The Conservative election campaign would be the best-financed[50] and most professional effort delivered by any of the conservative parties since at least the 1988 Mulroney victory. Tom Flanagan managed the campaign from Ottawa with a core staff he had been assembling since the Alliance leadership contest. Central to this group were senior policy advisor and fellow "firewall" author Ken Boessenkool; University of Western Ontario political scientist and executive director of the party Ian Brodie; Harper's chief of staff, Phil Murphy; Ray Novak, Harper's executive assistant since the Alliance leadership campaign; director of communications Jim Armour; press secretary Carolyn Stewart-Olsen; Doug Finley, director of field organization; and Mark Kihn, who had membership and fundraising responsibilities. The campaign was coordinated out of the Ottawa war room with Stewart-Olsen, Novak, and Armour accompanying Harper on the leader's tour. There were no formal provincial organizational structures, although each province and territory was assigned one or two provincial campaign co-chairs who served primarily as media spokespersons and fundraisers but were not active in strategy or organization. Two national campaign co-chairs were appointed, John Reynolds and Michael Fortier, with Reynolds ably standing in for the leader when Harper was unavailable to attend important media events.

The party's deputy director of communications, Yaroslav Baran, assisted Flanagan in managing the sixty-person war room that included fifteen full-time managers, four each in bookings and event organization, fifteen media people, and a dozen field organizers. The war room also utilized a dozen people to manage and operate their extensive computerized voter identification system. The Conservatives contracted Responsive Marketing Group Inc. of Toronto to conduct its telemarketing and get-out-the-vote (GOTV) strategies, while Dimitri Pantazoppoulos of Praxicus Public Strategies provided baseline polling and nightly tracking polls throughout the election.

Much of the GOTV efforts centred on what the party called its Blue List — a list of ridings considered winnable by the Conservatives, primarily but not exclusively located in Ontario. Originally an Alliance initiative, ridings were selected for inclusion on the list based on a number of criteria, including historical voting patterns, strength of the Conservative candidate and his or her opponents, and the potential for opposition votes splitting in the riding.[51] Incumbent MPs were not explicitly excluded from the list but most were expected to win on their own, or, as was the case for most of the Western candidates, to be in a position to carry out sophisticated GOTV strategies without being formally part of the war room's Blue List program.[52]

The Conservatives' national advertising budget was spent almost exclusively on TV, with only minor radio and no national print purchases. The party contracted with Watermark Advertising Design of Calgary to produce its English-language TV commercials and MediaVation of Montreal for its French-language ads. Only four English TV commercials were produced. Two focused on Harper while the other two attacked the Liberals' credibility. None was hard-hitting by most standards, and they were very mild in comparison to what the Liberals unleashed on Harper. Conservative strategists were aware of the message, if not the intensity, of the Liberals' attack plan well in advance of the election and were banking on it backfiring. They hoped to underscore the ballot question of trust by juxtaposing a calm, competent Harper with the record of Liberal corruption and arrogance. However, in comparison to the Liberal onslaught of negative ads, the Conservatives' low-key, sometimes whimsical message appeared to wane in impact by the end of the campaign. Interestingly, even as the ad wars increasingly appeared to be working in the Liberals' favour, the Conservatives stuck with their original ads, deciding against altering either their resources or their strategy to adapt to the campaign dynamics. The Conservatives also hosted a Web page featuring links to local campaigns, party policy documents, a media centre, and the leader's agenda and statements (see Chapter Seven).

A group of thirty Conservative staffers (including RCMP security) accompanied Harper on tour. Novak assumed the lead management role with assistance from Debbie Campbell, Boomer Throop, and Jonathan Denis of 3D Contact, who promoted the tour stops in local markets. The tour was supported by a chartered Air Canada campaign plane and six chartered Greyhound buses that travelled in teams of three, ostensibly one western team and one eastern, but at regular intervals both teams would be travelling in Ontario. Media were charged a standard fee for bookings with discounts for signing up for the full tour. The tour was designed to be national in scope, although Ontario-focused. Table 4 compares Harper's publicly reported tour events with those of Martin's throughout the course of the campaign with the exception of the two leaders' debates, commonly taken to mark the halfway point of the campaign.

Table 4: Number of Harper and Martin Campaign Events by Region and Campaign Period

CAMPAIGN TOTAL					
	West	**Ontario**	**Quebec**	**Atlantic**	**Total**
Martin	20	32	10	14	75
Harper	17	44	9	9	79
PRE-DEBATE EVENTS					
	West	**Ontario**	**Quebec**	**Atlantic**	**Total**
Martin	12	10	6	7	35
Harper	6	31	2	5	44
POST-DEBATE EVENTS					
	West	**Ontario**	**Quebec**	**Atlantic**	**Total**
Martin	8	21	4	7	40
Harper	11	13	7	4	35

Note: Martin lost three campaign days as a result of G-8 and D-Day commemoration commitments. Martin averaged 2.5 events over the course of the campaign and Harper averaged 2.4.

Overall, the Liberal and Conservative tours resembled each other. Both were structured by the strategic importance of Ontario, which attracted 41 percent of Martin's visits and 56 percent of Harper's. The Conservatives, despite their aspirations, knew that there was little to be gained by spending time in Quebec. The pre- and post-debate patterns are more puzzling. The Liberals spent more time in the western provinces in the pre-debate period than anywhere else, and the Conservatives gave an extraordinary amount of attention to Ontario (about 70 percent of their scheduled events). It appears that both parties — but especially the Conservatives — predicated their early campaign planning not on the idea of consolidating existing strengths but looking expansively for support elsewhere. The post-debate pattern reverses what happened in the first part of the campaign. While the Liberals increased their focus on Ontario, the Conservatives scheduled only about one-third of their events there. Instead, the Conservatives focused more of their attention on the West after the debate. On the final day Stephen Harper travelled from Edmonton to electoral districts in the centre of Alberta, an area considered to be a conservative heartland. His rhetoric was far removed from the policy document — and, indeed, the party's advertisements — that had been intended to define the Conservatives as "new." In particular, Harper's revival of the Reform refrain "The West Wants In" seemed to undercut the national messaging contained in the party's policy platform and advertisements.

THE CONSERVATIVE PLATFORM

Immediately after the merger, one of the most daunting challenges faced by the Conservatives was to cobble together a coherent policy platform in the limited time Martin would likely allow them before he called the election. Another challenge familiar to Reform and the Alliance also remained: how to build a platform that would simultaneously present Ontario and Atlantic voters with a moderate, competent image while not alienating its western support base. Lacking time for a full national policy convention, the Conservatives relied on Boessenkool to work with senior strategists, most notably Peter MacKay, to construct the policy platform. Building on the nineteen "founding principles" in the Agreement in Principle, and the Interim Council's "areas of agreement," the party, after three presentations by the policy group to the parliamentary caucus and approval from Harper, produced a forty-seven-page document under the slogan "Demanding Better." Its major themes were accountability and a cleaner government, a stronger economy achieved primarily through lower taxes, better health care, better communities, and a stronger Canada through better security. It was presented with a detailed spending plan and the party's founding principles attached.

The accountability plank was front and centre, allowing the Conservatives to attack the government for its record of "waste, mismanagement, and corruption," and in particular its gun registry, HRDC overspending, and the sponsorship scandal. More than any other, this plank was designed to drive the ballot questions of trust, accountability, and the need for change. Under the rubric of "better accountability" the party committed itself to expand the authority of the Auditor General, appoint an independent ethics commissioner, and reform election financing by banning corporate and union donations and eliminating public subsidization of parties.

Tax-cutting proposals emanated from the Conservatives' argument that Canada was one of the "highest taxed nations in the G-7." The central feature among a number of proposals was the cutting of taxes for all individuals and families. Most notably, the Conservatives planned to eliminate the 22 percent tax bracket, leaving all incomes below $70,000 to be taxed at the 16 percent rate. When combined with the annual indexing of the remaining brackets, they calculated a 25 percent tax savings for middle-income Canadians. Other commitments included a $2,000 per child deduction, reduction of Employment Insurance premiums, transfer of three cents of the federal gas tax to the provinces for infrastructure, introduction of a Registered Lifetime Savings Plan that would allow tax-free withdrawals, and control of government spending (but enhanced investments in research and development).

Sensing their potential vulnerability on the health file, the Conservatives introduced a health care plank designed to make them appear to be more similar to the Liberals than different. They committed to honour the terms of the 2003 Health Accord that was signed by Ottawa and the provinces. In particular, they dedicated themselves to working with the provinces to achieve a longer term plan for health care funding. Finally, the party proposed that the federal government would assume direct financing responsibility for catastrophic drug costs, a policy that seemed to run counter to the Conservative policy of supporting provincial autonomy. The "stronger Canada plank" encompassed a wide variety of matters, from increasing the funding of the Canadian military, instituting stiffer sentences for serious crimes, and eliminating loopholes for child pornographers to addressing financial problems associated with post-secondary education, responding to the needs of low- and fixed-income Canadians, and dealing with rising prices of gasoline, insurance, and utilities.

What was not mentioned in the policy platform was indicative of the party's attempt to present a moderate, competent, and safe choice for centrist voters. There was no mention of abortion, euthanasia, stem-cell research, family values, or multiculturalism. The discussion of same-sex marriage was included as a jurisdictional matter between Parliament and the courts, with the party advocating a free parliamentary vote to determine what constitutes a marriage. The free-vote position was yet another attempt by the party to modify, without abandoning, its populist western heritage, but it represented a similar populist trap for the Conservatives as it did for Reform. Although Harper would remain consistent with his arguments on social issues and parliamentary reform throughout the campaign, his main message — that he or his government did not plan to introduce legislation in one particular area or another during the next mandate but would not stand in the way of MPs introducing private member's motions and holding free votes — did not sufficiently inoculate him against accusations of harbouring a hidden agenda of social and moral conservatism. When various Conservative candidates, mostly with Reform or Alliance pasts, provided the Liberals with regular examples of what some free votes and private member's bills could deal with, many of the doubts the Conservatives were trying to remove from voters' minds were reinforced rather than removed.

Nevertheless, the Conservatives quickly produced a highly coherent policy manifesto, and did so with no public evidence of internal conflict. Further, according to party candidates and campaign managers, the campaign was well organized from the outset, with no sense that matters had not been properly tended to. The party logo and colours were attractive and widely used. Materials and resources were readily available. The war room was ready. Regional support desks were well staffed and quickly responded to concerns raised by local campaigns. By April, the campaign script was ready with set schedules for Harper's travel itinerary, policy statements, and releases. Events were booked to maximize media coverage and allow journalists filing time. One main message per day was deemed the best means of providing a controlled focus, although concessions were made to provide some variety to a hungry media machine that quickly grew tired of the tightly scripted tour's lack of spontaneity and absence of photo opportunities.

Candidate selection proceeded quickly following the legal registration of the new party. In a formal demonstration of Harper's insistence on professionalism, candidates were required to sign a pledge that they wouldn't criticize each other, the leader, or party policy.[53] With little rancour,[54] especially compared to the multiple controversies of the 2004 Liberal nomination process (see Chapter Two), the Conservatives nominated a full slate of 308 candidates. Thirty-six candidates were female, twenty were thirty years of age or younger, and many were visible minorities, including the first husband-and-wife team ever elected to the Canadian Parliament.[55] On the surface, the Conservative slate of candidates appeared national in scope. But the fundamental question of the core of the new Conservative Party turned, in part, on whether the merger was the coming together of two equal entities or little more than a takeover of the Progressive Conservatives by the Alliance.

In the West, the decade-long dominance of Reform/Alliance was demonstrated in the mix of western candidates. More than half of all Conservative candidates from the four western provinces were incumbent Alliance members seeking re-election (fifty-one of ninety-two total western candidates). In Alberta more than three-quarters of the Conservative candidates were incumbent Alliance MPs, many of whom were first elected as Reformers in 1993 or 1997. Notable exceptions included Calgary candidates Jim Prentice and former Progressive Conservative MP Lee Richardson. A reverse but much less pronounced situation existed in the Atlantic provinces where six of thirty-two Conservative candidates were incumbent Progressive Conservatives.

Table 5: Alliance Incumbents as a Percentage of Conservative Candidates in Western Provinces

	Number of Alliance Incumbents	Number of Conservative Candidates	Percent of Total
British Columbia	20	36	55.6
Alberta	21	28	75.0
Saskatchewan	7	14	50.0
Manitoba	3	14	21.4
Totals	51	92	55.4

With only two Alliance MPs elected in Ontario and one Progressive Conservative in Quebec in the 2000 election, incumbency is not a useful measure for examining the previous partisan history of the Conservatives' Central Canadian contingent. A more meaningful measure is whether or not candidates had previously run in a federal election for either party. In terms of party origins, slightly more candidates had PC backgrounds than Reform/Alliance (twenty-two of thirty-nine candidates with previous candidacies). Six of the ex-PCs in the two provinces had been candidates in both 1997 and 2000, while four Reform/Alliance candidates from both 1997 and 2000 were on the Conservative list in 2004. In terms of candidate recruitment, it appears as though the Conservatives drew from both its founding streams in Central Canada.

Table 6: 2004 Conservative Candidates with Previous Federal Reform/Alliance or Progressive Conservatives Candidacies (1997 and 2000), Ontario and Quebec

	Reform/Alliance	PC	Total	Total Seats	% of Total
Ontario	13	15	28	106	26.4
Quebec	4	7	11	75	14.7

Source: Centre for Election Studies, Department of Political Science, University of Waterloo

Note: Numbers do not include the four Conservative candidates who were previously members of the Ontario Progressive Conservative government.

THE CAMPAIGN DYNAMICS

As the campaign approached, the Conservatives engaged the Liberals in a preliminary ad battle in Atlantic Canada that foreshadowed the upcoming election war. The Liberals dredged up Harper's "culture of defeatism" comments about Atlantic Canada, the "firewall" letter, and other past statements in an effort to brand him an ideological extremist. But with the sponsorship scandal still raging, and Ontario voters in a foul mood after their provincial Liberal government's recent budget, polls indicated that the still-uncalled election race was shaping up to be a two-party contest and that the Liberals would face a legitimate challenge to their eleven-year lock on power.[56]

Once the prime minister called the election and presented his opening attack on Harper from the steps of Rideau Hall in a rather excited manner, Harper countered with imagery of "quiet competency," choosing a National Press Building room with a Canadian flag backdrop to launch his critique of the government's record of waste and mismanagement. He immediately left Ottawa for Quebec and the Maritimes, a move designed as much to assure Ontario voters of his party's new moderation on linguistic and regional issues as to win new Quebec converts. Hoping to demonstrate consistency, he defended the firewall principles and stuck with a modified version of his Atlantic dependency position. His swing through the region got a boost when one of Harper's previously harshest critics, John Crosbie, stated that his change of heart about Harper was leading him to consider a return to electoral politics under the new party's banner.[57] Harper's efforts to exorcise his party's predecessor's anti-bilingualism reputation suffered a reverse fate when Ontario MP Scott Reid, one of Harper's closest parliamentary advisors, began musing about restructuring the Official Languages Act. The comments were immediately pounced upon by opponents as evidence of the Conservatives' supposed hidden agenda, and Harper had to engage in damage control, stating that Reid was expressing personal opinions based on his vast knowledge of the subject, but not expressing party policy on the issue.[58] He finished off the first week of the campaign by travelling west, with stops in each of the four western provinces prior to returning to Ontario to begin week two.

Ontario would be the sole focus of the Conservatives' second week of campaigning. Harper announced a series of policy initiatives in the lead-up to the formal unveiling of the full platform at end of the week in Toronto. With polls increasingly predicting minority government scenarios, Harper would stick to familiar ground by rejecting any form of formal cooperation with the separatists. On abortion and other social issues, his delicate dance of assuring voters he had no plans to limit abortion access but would not formally clamp down on the democratic rights of people with other opinions was being spun by his opponents into more hidden agenda plans to strip Canadians of their cherished Charter rights. When Ontario MP Cheryl Gallant likened abortion to the recent terrorist beheading of an American captive, the 2004 Conservative campaign suffered from a familiar Reform dilemma: the impossibility of stifling 308 candidates (many of whom take seriously their ability to represent contrary views) for the entire thirty-six-day campaign.[59]

A populist trap, similar to that experienced by Day during the Alliance 2000 campaign, was now plaguing the 2004 Conservative campaign: the unknowns that are necessarily part of any populist platform. Free votes and other direct democracy decision-making mechanisms have built into them, by definition, a quality of the unknown. If the outcome is predetermined by policy, the direct decision-making mechanism becomes meaningless. Herein lies the populist trap: A new party with a new leader and a large number of unknown qualities cannot afford to compound the problem with formal policy expounding only more uncertainty. Populism often creates unknowns rather than resolves them, positively, in favour of their advocate. Except in extraordinary circumstances, the voters typically perfer the status quo to an unknown, possibly radical, extreme new party option. Hence the Liberal campaign theme of "our Canada" (known, comfortable, status quo) versus "Harper's Canada" (unknown, possibly extreme, changed). By mid-campaign, many voters, especially in Ontario, had yet to determine if their distaste for a tired-looking, possibly corrupt regime was greater than their concerns over not knowing enough about a still new and relatively untested western-led party.

As the leaders headed into the debates, Harper continued to present an image of competency and professionalism, especially in comparison to the increasingly frantic Liberal campaign.[60] The Conservatives spared no effort to prepare their leader for the televised debates,[61] but continued to exercise extreme control and discipline in an effort to minimize mistakes, ensure that the Liberal record remained the issue, and, as one staffer told reporters, not interrupt the enemy when they are shooting themselves. Harper performed admirably, if not strongly, in the French-language debate, generally succeeding in striking a statesmanlike pose and hammering home the ballot question by reminding Quebecers why they wanted change. In the English-language debate the following evening, Harper again performed well in a format more suited to his opponents' rhetorical styles than to his complicated and often subtle explanations of party policy. He nevertheless left the debates relatively unscathed over social issues, for the most part withstanding a barrage of attacks on his alleged lack of support for Canadians' Charter rights.

The post-debate phase of the campaign opened with Harper confidently declaring, "No Liberal seat is safe." He openly speculated about a Conservative majority government, and, in an effort to portray himself and his party as ready to govern, announced that he was building a transition team.[62] Put on the defensive when Martin attempted to link Harper with Alberta Premier Ralph Klein's potential future violations of the Canada Health Act, the Conservatives counter-attacked with an over-the-top news release questioning whether Martin supported child pornography. Although he ordered the release recalled to have the title changed, Harper did not disavow its intended message, repeating the charges. The incident was the only major stumble initiated by the war room, and it left the tour in relative disarray compared to the well-oiled machine of the first weeks. It was also a curious strategy to attempt damage control by drawing attention to a social issue that had more potential to reinforce their opponents' accusations of a hidden social conservative agenda than to drum up Conservative votes, especially in Ontario. To the Conservatives' credit, they immediately pulled Harper off the campaign trail to get their house in order before the multiplicity of negative events spiralled out of control. Sensing that the die had been cast and there was little more they could do to bring new support their way, the tour finished campaigning in Ontario by Thursday of the final week. Harper spent the last weekend of the contest shoring up support in safe Western Canada ridings (Kelowna and Red Deer) rather than chasing undecided votes in Ontario: the merits of this strategic decision will be debated for some time.[63]

CONCLUSIONS

Much as the elections of the past decade had done for Reform, the Alliance, and Progressive Conservatives, the 2004 results presented the new Conservative Party of Canada with a mixed bag of successes and failures. The most notable failure is that they didn't form a government. Not surprisingly,[64] in winning 29.6 percent of the national vote, they failed to win support equalling the combined Alliance and PC vote of the previous election (37.7 percent). But they did win more seats (ninety-nine) than the combined total of their predecessors (seventy-eight) and managed to hold the Liberals to a minority government, something many had considered impossible a mere six months earlier. In less than a year they accomplished an institutional merger,[65] and two months after being elected leader, Harper was fighting an election campaign with a generally well-prepared organization and policy platform. However, in light of the opportunity presented by Martin's unsure prime ministership, the unsteady Liberal campaign, and polls showing a majority of the electorate wanting change, the Conservatives only partially met the historic challenge of galvanizing centre-right opposition. In particular, they did not respond effectively to the severity of the Liberals' attacks or their own candidates' damaging corroborations.[66]

In the larger perspective, the new party put to rest one of the two distinguishing features of late twentieth century Canadian electoral politics — the fractured centre-right opposition. Although reconciling the two party cultures will remain a formidable task, including formalizing policy and sorting out the role of social conservatism in the coalition,[67] the merger should have ended, at least for the foreseeable future, the extraordinarily time- and resource-consuming unity efforts. At a minimum, the new stronger official opposition should be better equipped to concentrate on opposing the government instead of itself.

The new Conservatives were less successful, however, at ending the second late twentieth century feature of Canadian federal politics — the highly regionalized pattern of party competition. As Table 7 demonstrates, despite its twenty-four-seat Ontario breakthrough, the party's admittedly meagre efforts in Quebec produced correspondingly low voter interest, leaving that province the party's most daunting organizational challenge: how to break through the federalist-separatist dichotomy and build a social base of its own. The party also lost support in Atlantic Canada, losing three seats and polling less than either the old PC or Alliance parties in every province except New Brunswick. The Conservatives also lost ground in B.C., where they polled 13.2 percent less than did the Alliance in 2000 and won five fewer seats. Nevertheless, western MPs still dominate the new Conservative caucus, accounting for more than two-thirds (sixty-eight), with prairie MPs particularly over-represented (forty-six, accounting for almost half of the caucus). The strong western presence is both a blessing and a curse for Harper as he prepares for the next election. On one hand, the loyalty he commands within the western support base should forestall a repeat of the post-2000 election leadership problems his predecessor suffered. On the other hand, he continues to face the enduring challenge of finding the right mix of policies and positions to expand the party deeper into central and eastern regions without alienating the western core.[68] The challenge for Harper and the Conservative Party is similar to that faced by all centre-right Canadian opposition parties over the past half-century. They must reconcile the political restlessness of the West with the status quo orientation of Ontario and the culture of French nationalism in Quebec.

Table 7: 2004 Conservative Results Compared to Alliance and PC 2000 Results

	2000 ELECTION						2004 ELECTION			
	Alliance		PC		Combined		Conservative		Change vs. Combined 2000	
	% of vote	Seats	% of vote	Seats	% of vote	seats	% of vote	Seats	% of vote	Seats
B.C.	49.4	27	7.3	0	56.7	27	36.2	22	-20.5	-5
Alta.	58.9	23	13.5	1	72.4	24	61.6	26	-10.8	+2
Sask.	47.7	10	4.8	0	52.5	10	41.8	13	-10.7	+3
Man.	30.4	4	14.5	1	44.9	5	39.1	7	-5.8	+2
Ont.	23.6	2	14.4	0	38.0	2	31.5	24	-6.7	+22
Que.	6.2	0	5.6	1	11.8	1	8.8	0	-3.0	-1
N.B.	15.7	0	30.5	3	46.2	3	31.1	2	-15.1	-1
N.S.	9.6	0	29.1	4	38.7	4	28.0	3	-10.7	-1
P.E.I.	5.0	0	38.4	0	43.4	0	30.7	0	-12.7	0
Nfld.	3.9	0	34.5	2	38.4	2	32.3	2	-6.1	0
Y.T.	27.7	0	7.5	0	35.2	0	20.9	0	-14.3	0
N.W.T.	17.7	0	10.0	0	27.7	0	17.2	0	-10.5	0
Nun.	0	0	8.2	0	8.2	0	14.5	0	+6.3	0
Total	25.5	66	12.2	12	37.7	78	29.6	99	-8.1	+21

NOTES

1 The authors would like to express their gratitude to Alliance, Progressive Conservative, and Conservative candidates, officials, and members, as well as those not formally associated with the parties, for their time and consideration in consenting to be interviewed or this chapter.

2 R. Kenneth Carty, William Cross, and Lisa Young, *Rebuilding Canadian Party Politics* (Vancouver: UBC Press, 2000).

3 See Peter White and Adam Daifallah, *Gritlock: Are the Liberals in Forever?* (Toronto: Canadian Political Bookshelf, 2001).

4 In 1999 the Progressive Conservatives adopted what became known as the "301 rule," requiring it to run candidates in all of Canada's existing electoral districts, effectively barring electoral cooperation with Reform or the Alliance.

5 See Faron Ellis, *The Limits of Participation: Members, Activists and Leaders in Canada's Reform Party* (Calgary: University of Calgary Press, forthcoming, 2005).

6 Peter Woolstencroft, "Some Battles Won, War Lost: The Campaign of the Progressive Conservative Party," in *The Canadian General Election of 2000,* ed. Jon H. Pammett and Christopher Dornan (Toronto: Dundurn Press, 2001).

7 The settlement included $474,000 for Day's defense, a $60,000 settlement for Goddard plus his legal fees of $246,000 plus other court costs. Day eventually apologized to Goddard and agreed to personally pay the $60,000 in damages awarded. Later, the Alliance also had to account for and eventually return a $70,000 contribution from a lawyer associated with the firm that had defended Day in the Goddard case. In an unrelated but similarly mishandled situation, former Reform MP Jim Hart announced he had hired a lawyer to collect part of a $50,000 payment party officials had agreed to as compensation for giving up his B.C. seat for Day's 2000 by-election bid.

8 "Open letter to Ralph Klein," by Stephen Harper, president, National Citizens' Coalition, and former Reform MP; Tom Flanagan, professor of political science and former director of research, Reform Party of Canada; Ted Morton, professor of political science and Reform Party Alberta Senator-Elect: Rainer Knopff, professor of political science; Andrew Crooks, chairman, Canadian Taxpayers Federation; Ken Boessenkool, former policy advisor to Stockwell Day, Treasure of Alberta. *National Post,* January 26, 2001. See also Tom Flanagan, "Why Canada is a kleptocracy," *National Post,* February 6, 2001.

9 Stockwell Day, Gilles Duceppe, and Joe Clark, "The sullying of our nation's highest office," *National Post,* March 31, 2001.

10 Those who left included Press Secretary Renee Fairweather, Chief of Staff Ian Todd; Senior Adviser Rod Love; Hal Danchilla, Day's deputy

chief and campaign manager; communications directors Jim Armour and Phil von Finckenstein; Sean McAdam, the party's long-time question period coordinator; and Andrew Steck, the Alliance's political affairs coordinator. Severances totaling more than $240,000 were reportedly paid to the various resigning staffers. This in itself became another problematic issue.

11 One option available to them rested with the party constitution, which stated a leadership review could be held if 25 precent of the party's constituency associations voted to support the review. This would have required 74 of the party's 297 officially recognized constituency associations to approve the call for a review.

12 Alliance MPs Strahl, Lunn, Meredith, Monte Solberg, Jay Hill, Rahim Jaffer, and James Rajotte attended.

13 Day statement on Alliance caucus rebellion.

14 Peter G. White and Adam Daifallah, "Unbearable wrongness of Joe," *National Post,* June 8, 2001.

15 Stockwell Day, "One Conservative Party," speech to Empire Club, June 15, 2001.

16 Terms of Reconciliation, July 8, 2001.

17 The Alliance leader would be selected on a one-member, one-vote basis using a mail-in ballot. The winner needed to garner 50 precent plus one vote. If no candidate won on the first ballot a run-off ballot would be held between the two top candidates. Results of the first ballot would be released on March 20, 2002.

18 Statement of Stockwell Day, leader of the Canadian Alliance, July 17, 2001.

19 On December 14, 2001, the party's national council suspended the memberships of six former Alliance MPs, including Grey and Strahl. Inky Mark's membership had already lapsed, and Garry Lunn was seeking re-entry into the Alliance caucus.

20 News of the formal PC-DRC Coalition was splashed across the front pages of most Canadian daily newspapers the morning of September 11, 2001, the last time the Alliance and its leadership problems would make front-pages headlines for months.

21 Twenty-seven Alliance MPs would eventually support Harper in a campaign that raised $1.1 million from 9,500 donors.

22 See Tom Flanagan, "How to cooperate and beat the Liberals," *National Post,* June 14, 2001; Stephen Harper, "Building a bridge to the future," speech given to Canadian Institute of Plumbing and Heating in Charlottetown, June 27, 2001; Stephen Harper and Tom Flanagan, "Three tips for the CA: policy, policy and policy," *National Post,* June 20, 2001; Tom Flanagan, "Dissidence or destruction: Alliance rebels will have to choose,"

National Post, July 7, 2001; Tom Flanagan, "'Gritlock' is the least of conservative worries," *National Post,* January 4, 2002; Peter G. White, "The right can have purity — and power," *National Post,* January 9, 2002.

23 See Stephen Harper, "Appeasing the Tories has to stop," *National Post,* December 21, 2001.

24 Alliance House leader John Reynolds served as interim leader.

25 Alberta Premier Ralph Klein and five Alliance MPs backed Hill.

26 Diane Ablonczy, "A united right has to start with trust," *National Post,* February 21, 2002.

27 Day eventually received the backing of thirteen Alliance MPs.

28 Stephen Harper, "A vision of federalism for all Canadians," *National Post,* January 12, 2002.

29 Stephen Harper, "Get the state out of the economy," *National Post,* February 8, 2002.

30 Turnout was a healthy 71.1 percent.

31 At its May 2002 convention, the Alliance asked 115 constituency associations to lend the national party funds to internally finance its $2.3-million debt. By the end of the convention, $1.1 million had been pledged. By June, about 80 percent of needed funds had been raised.

32 Stephen Harper, "Alliance leadership acceptance speech," March 20, 2002. See also Stephen Harper, "The Rebirth of the Canadian Alliance: Address to the National Convention," Edmonton, April 6, 2002.

33 As late as September 2003, the Alliance organization was releasing new ads and a redesigned logo, demonstrating that it was preparing to contest the next federal election as a separate party.

34 See Stephen Harper and Rob Merrifield, "Health care funding — with strings," *National Post,* August 9, 2002; and Stephen Harper, "Canada must support its allies on Iraq," *National Post,* October 5, 2002.

35 DRC members Strahl, Grey, Hill, Meredith, McNally, and Pankiw asked to return to the Alliance caucus. Only Pankiw was refused readmission. Inky Mark did not seek readmittance but did run for the Conservatives in the 2004 election, handily winning his Dauphin-Swan River Manitoba riding.

36 Stephen Harper, "Open letter to federal Progressive Conservatives," May 1, 2002.

37 Conservative activist Craig Chandler also ran as a candidate but withdrew on the eve of the convention vote. He had secured only eight delegates.

38 Harper had made five trips to the riding during the by-election campaign, yet the Alliance finished a distant third (17.5 percent), only slightly ahead

of the NDP (15.3 percent) and far behind the Liberals (30.5 percent) and the winning PCs (33.8 percent).

39 See Stephen Harper, leader of the Canadian Alliance, and Peter MacKay, leader of the Progressive Conservative Party, "Agreement-in-principle on the establishment of the Conservative Party of Canada," Wednesday, October 15, 2003.

40 Ratification of the Agreement by both parties' members had to take place by December 12, 2003.

41 See "Update on the activities of the Interim Council of the Conservative Party of Canada," December 12, 2003; "Areas of Agreement: Conservative Party of Canada Partial Policy Statement," February 4, 2004; and "Conservative Party of Canada Electoral Districts Associations," December 2003.

42 On December 5, 2003, the Alliance announced the results of its party-wide mail-in referendum. The results indicated 95.9 percent of party members who participated voted in favor of the merger. Support did not drop below 90 percent in any province.

43 Beginning November 20, 2003, the Tories held four days of delegate selection meetings for a virtual convention to be held simultaneously in twenty locations on December 6, 2003. Approximately 90 percent of the delegates to that convention voted in favour of the merger.

44 A month prior to the election call Clark endorsed Paul Martin's Liberals over Harper's Conservatives, telling Canadians he was extremely worried about Harper and therefore would advocate going with "the devil you know." Conservatives across the country roundly criticized Clark. He also re-emerged in mid-campaign to help reinforce the "hidden agenda" theme by commenting that the spat of social conservative candidate missteps was vindicating his suspicions of the Harper-led Conservatives.

45 The five PC senators were Norman Atkins, Bill Doody, Lowell Murray, Jean-Claude Rivest, and Mira Spivak.

46 Statement by Michael D. Harris, Toronto, November 2, 2003.

47 Harper would eventually raise and spend \$2.67 million and spend the party-imposed limit of \$2.5 million. Tom Flanagan again served as campaign manager, and many of those who eventually served on the Conservative 2004 campaign team filled similar roles in Harper's Conservative leadership bid.

48 See Rod Love, "Team Belinda versus The Club," *Calgary Herald,* March 13, 2004.

49 Both Stronach and Clement would contest Ontario seats for the Conservatives. Stronach narrowly won her Newmarket-Aurora seat while Clement lost in Brampton West. Harper would appoint former PC leader MacKay as his deputy leader.

50 From a combination of the new party financing regulations (the Conservatives started 2004 with an $8.4-million grant), election expense rebates, and contributions throughout the year, the party expected to spend the $17.6-million legal limit on the campaign and end the year with no deficit.

51 In total, about sixty ridings were eventually included on the war room's Blue List.

52 JMCK Communications of Calgary conducted GOTV strategies for another twenty or so Conservative candidates not part of the Blue List program.

53 Harper had previously demonstrated a firm hand in denying controversial dissenter Jim Pankiw's request to re-enter caucus. Pankiw ran as an independent, garnering 20 percent of the vote compared to the winning Conservative candidate's 26.7 percent. Harper also threw Saskatchewan MP Larry Spencer out of caucus in early 2004 for advocating the recriminalization of homosexual acts. The ouster meant that Spencer could not run as a Conservative candidate. Spencer's independent candidacy attracted 4.9 percent of the vote, almost costing the Conservatives a seat they won by a margin of only 0.4 percent.

54 The party denied former Progressive Conservative Saskatchewan premier Grant Devine the opportunity to run as a Conservative candidate.

55 Twelve of the ninety-nine Conservatives elected in the 2004 election were female, and five were thirty years of age or younger. Gurmant Grewal retained his seat in Newton-North Delta while his wife, Nina Grewal, won the new B.C. riding of Fleetwood-Port Kells.

56 The Conservative campaign stumbled briefly when its policy platform was leaked a week prior to the election call and three weeks prior to its scheduled release, giving the Liberals considerable extra time to plan their "$50-billion black hole" challenge.

57 Crosbie eventually decided against another run for Parliament, but his endorsement energized the Conservatives' Atlantic campaign.

58 Reid immediately resigned his position as Conservative critic for official languages.

59 See Ellis, *The Limits of Participation.*

60 In the second week of the campaign, Liberal cabinet ministers Judy Sgro and John McCallum were sent on "commando raids" to Harper events. The stunts had the effect of making the governing party appear somewhat amateurish and desperate.

61 The Conservatives rented a television studio at Ottawa's Algonquin College, where Hill and Knowlton's Michael Coates prepared Harper.

62 Former Progressive Conservative leadership candidate and senior advisor to Brian Mulroney Hugh Segal would head the team.

63 But even in the West, the campaign continued to be dogged by social conservative controversy. Protesters showed up to an ill-advised public event in the Okanagan, and Alliance MP Randy White's equally ill-advised "to heck with the courts" comments when defending social conservatism garnered national media attention on the final weekend of the campaign.

64 See Neil Nevitte, Andre Blais, Elizabeth Gidengil, and Richard Nadeau, *Unsteady State: The 1997 Canadian Federal Election* (Don Mills: Oxford University Press, 2000) for an analysis of the unlikelihood of a merger capturing all of the Reform-PC vote after the 1997 election; and Faron Ellis, "The More Things Change…: The Alliance Campaign," in *The Canadian General Election of 2000*, ed. Jon H. Pammett and Christopher Dornan (Toronto: Dundurn Press, 2001), 59–89.

65 See Jean-François Godbout and Éric Bélanger, "Merger as a Means to (Re-)Gain Office for Right-Wing Federal Parties in Canada." Paper presented at the European Consortium for Political Research Joint Sessions of Workshops, Uppsala, April 2004.

66 By way of example, when Kitchener, Ontario, candidate Frank Luellau spoke about the unnaturalness of homosexuality, although Harper disassociated himself and the party from Luellau's views, the subsequent categorization of them as "personal" did not assuage questions about Conservative policy on rights issues. Furthermore, a visit to Kitchener-Waterloo was cancelled, ostensibly to avoid the potential bad optics of appearing in the same city as Luellau, denying the party exposure in an important media centre. The Conservatives lost all three Kitchener area ridings.

67 For a comprehensive analysis of the differing characteristics of the five major Canadian federal parties see William Cross and Lisa Young, "The Contours of Political Party Membership in Canada," *Party Politics,* Vol. 10, No. 4, July 2004, 427–444.

68 The party's 2005 policy convention, its first as a merged entity, will go a long way to determining how the party is branded in the next election.

CHAPTER FOUR

Jack Layton and the NDP:[1] *Gains But No Breakthrough*

by Alan Whitehorn

In the three elections from 1993 to 2000, the NDP averaged 8.8 percent of the votes and 4.8 percent of the seats, well below average (15.2 percent vote and 8.3 percent seats) since its founding in 1961. Following the electoral setback in the federal 2000 election (where the party received only 8.5 percent of the vote and won only thirteen seats),[2] Alexa McDonough chose to resign as leader. The subsequent leadership race in 2003 employed a direct ballot vote by all party members. The candidates included several NDP MPs (Bill Blaikie, Lorne Nystrom, Joe Comartin), prominent Quebecer Pierre Ducasse, and B.C. activist Bev Meslo. But it was Jack Layton, a university professor, long-time Toronto city councillor, and former president of the Federation of Canadian Municipalities, who won convincingly on the first ballot. As a left activist who had worked extensively with a diversity of social movements, Layton reflected a more urban and contemporary orientation, particularly in his commitment to environmentalism, feminism, and the peace movement. His candidacy and leadership were major factors in the NDP's rise in membership,[3] party income, and support in public polls — important developments for a fourth-place party. Nevertheless, as a new leader, Layton still needed to raise his profile across the country.

To a significant degree, the NDP's prospects in the 1990s had been affected by the growing discontent with several NDP provincial governments. The NDP federal vote in B.C. had dropped dramatically due to the backlash against the increasingly unpopular NDP provincial governments of Mike Harcourt, Glen Clark, and Ujjal Dosanjh. However, the new B.C. Liberal government revealed a remarkable ability to quickly alienate the electorate and thus provided hope that the federal NDP might regain some seats. Years of neo-conservative cutbacks in Ontario contributed to the election of the new Liberal provincial government of Dalton McGuinty but also gave rise to hope that the NDP could make gains federally. Brian Masse's federal by-election win in Windsor West in May 2002 provided credence for this view.

In Manitoba, Gary Doer's NDP government remained popular and gave hope that Manitoba could be fertile ground for the federal New Democrats. In Saskatchewan, historically the CCF-NDP heartland, the provincial NDP continued its long run of continuous electoral victories since 1991, but Lorne Calvert's government had only narrowly won in 2003 and had implemented an unpopular budget in the spring of 2004.[4] In Nova Scotia, the home of former federal leader Alexa McDonough, the provincial NDP was the official opposition, but it was uncertain whether McDonough's resignation as leader would adversely affect the party's prospects in the Atlantic region. In addition, mayoralty victories by left-wing candidates in Vancouver (Larry Campbell) and Toronto (David Miller) raised expectations for NDP gains in both those metropolitan centres.

The NDP had been formed in 1961 as a partnership of the Co-operative Commonwealth Federation (CCF) and the Canadian Labour Congress (CLC). The linkage between the trade union movement and the NDP has been pivotal in terms of organization, finances, and ideology. However, Parliament's passage of Bill C-24 in 2003 dramatically lessened the possibility of corporate and trade union donations to all political parties.[5] This change had an enormous financial and practical organizational impact on the federal NDP and its relationship with the CLC, its co-founding organization. The limit of $1,000 in donations (financial or services) per union and all of its local affiliates was a more draconian application than that applied to corporations and their subsidiaries. The state had, in effect, dictated the nature of the NDP's internal structure and workings and severed key financial bonds to the trade union movement.[6] How well the party would adjust in terms of finances and staffing would prove to be a key underlying story of the 2004 election campaign.

If the 1990s was marked by the ascendancy of neo-conservative and neo-liberal ideas,[7] there was reason to believe that the first decade of the twenty-first century would be more conducive to social democracy. The electorate's commitment to public health care, its growing concerns about the environment (e.g., safe drinking water and food supply), and increased apprehension about public safety fostered renewed emphasis on the key role of government. This boded well for social democrats and the NDP, but also perhaps for a resurgence of left liberalism.

Within the CCF-NDP, there have been periodic organized efforts to move the party in a more radical and militant direction. The New Politics Initiative (NPI), founded in 2001, endeavoured to push the NDP further left. With the selection of Layton as leader, the NPI had a leader that was more receptive to many of its positions and, accordingly, the NPI voted to disband on the eve of the election. Franz Hartmann, who had worked with Layton in Toronto, and was now serving as director of caucus campaigns, oversaw early efforts to mount an outreach campaign to different social movements. He focussed on six advocacy policy areas: democracy, peace/international development, sustainability, community investment, health, and diversity. Of particular note in the lead-up to the pre-election period were three campaigns showcased on the party's Web site. The pitch for proportional representation (PR), with its call for a more democratic and representative Parliament, echoed the arguments of the women's movement and others to make politics more inclusive. The "No to Star Wars" campaign fostered solidarity with the peace movement and tapped growing Canadian fears about American foreign policy. The "Fly Our Flag" campaign[8] simultaneously fostered a Canadian nationalist message and a populist critique of the tax avoidance tactics of the Paul Martin–owned Canada Steamship Lines.

While initially Layton and the NDP had gained a higher profile during the party's 2002–03 leadership race, the media increasingly shifted their attention away from the party, first to the Liberal Party's transferral of power from Jean Chrétien to Paul Martin and then to the merger of the Alliance and Progressive Conservative parties and the new Conservative Party's leadership race. Amidst these developments, the NDP needed to avoid losing visibility in the lead-up to the federal election. Accordingly, the NDP's strategy for the second phase of the pre-election campaign (the eleven weeks from September 13 to November 30, 2003) was to raise the leader's profile and project the image of a party with momentum as an alternative to the Liberals.[9] There was recognition of a regional component to NDP messaging, with the main opposition being Liberals in the East, Alliance in the West and the BQ in Quebec. The goal was to be above 20 percent in party support before the writs were issued.

An April 2004 Environics poll reported the NDP at 19 percent — double that of its 2000 election vote — and close to the 20 percent threshold and the historic high of the 1988 election. Regionally, Manitoba (32 percent) and B.C. (31 percent) showed the greatest promise, followed by Saskatchewan (27 percent) and Ontario (21 percent). Trailing were the Atlantic region (18 percent), Alberta (14 percent), and Quebec (8 percent).[10] Even better news followed, with the May 23 Compas poll showing the NDP at 20 percent.

To promote Layton's visibility and policy credentials, his new book, entitled *Speaking Out: Ideas That Work for Canadians*, was published on the eve of the election.[11] The chapter headings would resonate with key themes in the election campaign.

ELECTION ORGANIZATION AND COMMITTEE STRUCTURE

Between NDP conventions, the Federal Executive and Federal Council are the principal decision-making bodies of the party, but in the run up to and during an election several specialized committees are created. In May 2002, well before the new leader had been selected, a blue-ribbon election readiness committee (co-chaired by party veterans George Nakitsas, former chief of staff to Ed Broadbent in the 1980s and currently with the steelworkers union, and Angela Schira, secretary treasurer of the B.C. Federation of Labour) was established to assess past campaign performances. The ERC made recommendations in February 2003 to the new leader and the incoming election planning committee (EPC). Among the proposals of the insightful thirty-nine-page report were the need to be ready sooner and the need to run a truly national campaign, rather than a mere survival one, a campaign that would allow "for appropriate regional messaging and issues … [since the party] will be facing different opponents in different parts of the country." The report also cautioned against being caught in a single-issue campaign in which the party would be adversely affected by strategic voting. The committee forewarned of the potentially crippling consequences of the impending Bill C-24, which would in essence remove labour donations to the party. Accordingly, the committee strongly advised the party to "initiate an immediate fundraising appeal to labour prior to the passage of any restrictive legislation."[12]

The EPC was created in March, with its first teleconference meeting occurring in April and in-person meeting in May 2003. It involved about thirty to thirty-five members, along with key party staff. The EPC included representation from every province and territory and was composed of the leader, the party's federal officers, and a number of co-opts (including the EPC co-chairs Andre Foucault of the Communications, Energy and Paperworkers Union and Raj Sihota, director of outreach for the B.C. NDP caucus; parliamentary caucus representatives Dick Proctor and Libby Davies; CLC's NPAC representative Danny Mallett; campaign director Bruce Cox; Director of Communications Brad Lavigne; and platform co-coordinators Vicky Smallman and Bob Dewar). Staff members who were involved included the NDP's Heather Fraser, director of organization; Donne Flanagan, chief of staff; Jamey Heath, director of caucus communications and research; and Maureen Prebinski, director of caucus administration.

The EPC designed the strategic election plan, operating closely with its working group and platform committees and later the steering committee. The full EPC usually met once a month (increasing to every two weeks as the election neared), most often by teleconference call[13] to save time and money and allow greater representation from across the country. Given the size of the full EPC, a smaller working group committee (composed of top EPC planners, key federal staff from Ottawa, and, later, contracted polling and media consultants) met weekly before the writs were issued, while during the election the steering committee met daily to work out details of managing the ups and downs of the campaign. During the election, the full EPC convened by teleconference call three times (early, mid, and in the final stretches of the campaign. In practice, the steering committee, meeting each morning, collectively guided the campaign direction.

The election platform and communications committee (a sub-committee of the EPC), drawing upon past party conventions' resolutions and reports, drafted an integrated policy platform intended to maximize the party's electoral appeal. A draft of the sixty-four-page document entitled "Platform 2004: Jack Layton, NDP: New energy. A positive choice." was presented to the February federal council meeting on the eve of the election call.

During the actual campaign, a series of groups supervised and, where necessary, modified the election strategy. At the pinnacle of the decision-making hierarchy was the inner circle of campaign strategists on the campaign steering committee (the so-called war room), who met in person (or in the case of a few by teleconference) at the beginning of each day. They included the federal secretary, one of the EPC co-chairs, campaign director, assistant campaign director, assistant federal secretary, various section directors (communication, organization, the leader's tour, research, administration, finance), a representative from the labour movement, and the party's pollster and media consultant. The committee discussed modification to the leader's tour, daily tracking of polling results, focus group findings, ongoing testing of campaign slogans and phrasing, the final changes to the ads, when and how to replace the first round of ads with subsequent ones, and preparations for the leaders' debates. It heard reports on the various organizational activities. Co-ordination (and feedback) between the national headquarters and the leader's tour on the plane was achieved through the tour director's section, but also key discussions each day between Bruce Cox, the campaign director, and the lead political staff on the plane. In the end, all major campaign matters would need the campaign director's final approval.

ELECTION FINANCES

The 2004 federal election saw the implementation of the most sweeping election financing legislation since the mid-1970s. Much of the pre-election campaign period was covered under the old regulations, whereas post January 2004 fell under the aegis of Bill C-24. In the fall of 2003, the NDP and its labour allies realized that these would be the last few months that the state would allow trade unions to make significant financial donations to labour's party. Even more crucial, the trade union movement would no longer be permitted to guarantee the party's bank loans for future election campaigns. Encouraged by Layton and CEP union leaders, unions were asked to make one final historic donation. The party had long wished to have its own building once more, as possible collateral for future election loans. This one-time donation from many unions,[14] along with the CLC and the B.C. Federation of Labour, provided sufficient funds ($3.5 million) for the NDP to buy a three-storey building in downtown Ottawa.

As Paul Martin, the new prime minister, delayed the election call, inevitably the costs of the longer pre-election period rose. The initial amount was to be $716,891[15] for the 2003 period, while the amount in the first five months of 2004 was an additional $2.2 million (including $675,000 for media advertising, $225,000 for opinion research, and $100,000 for priority ridings).[16] In September 2003 the projected cost of the campaign was $8.8 million, but on the eve of the writs being issued the projected spending rose to almost $11.6 million. The 2004 campaign was planned to be more national than previously, and therefore more expensive than the campaigns of 1997 and 1993, and even more ambitious in spending than the 1988 campaign under Ed Broadbent's leadership.

Increasingly, the largest expense for a political party in modern elections is mass advertising. The NDP media budget for 2004 was set at $4.7 million, of which an unprecedented $4.2 million was for media ads and $345,000 for creative work and production. Echoing past practices, the largest amount of NDP advertising was allocated to the powerful medium of television.[17] In previous elections, one of the largest categories of expenses listed involved union labour releases (under the heading goods and services), but with the passage of Bill C-24, this practice was no longer permitted. The leader's tour now became the second largest portion of the campaign budget and was projected to cost $2.6 million (including $1.7 million for transportation, mostly for the plane). Without the donation of labour personnel, the NDP now had to hire more staff. Accordingly, the budget for organization rose sharply to $1.8 million (with the greatest amount for salaries at $800,000). Telephone call centres were projected to cost $450,000. In addition, $220,000 was earmarked for information technology (e.g., computers), and $5,000 for the Web site. Public opinion research costs were set at $436,000, followed by $471,000 for communications and the platform, $400,000 for direct mail (also $400,000 for donor special requests), and a modest contingency fund.

The state now became the key source of income for Canada's social democratic party. In terms of general annual revenues, government public financing provided $1,928,678 (versus a projected $2.6 million if the vote had occurred earlier) and was based on the 8.5 percent of the vote the party had earned in the 2000 general election. The NDP's near doubling of its vote to 15.7 percent meant that annual state revenues to the party would henceforth be about $3.7 million annually (2.1+ million votes x $1.75).

Turning to election income, the total projected was to almost match expenses at $10.4 million. The specific election reimbursements from the state were projected as follows by the NDP: the central rebate (covering 60 percent of permissible expenses) had been projected to account for about two-thirds of the NDP's election revenues at $6.4 million; the local riding rebate from the state (operational if 10 percent [instead of the previous 15 percent] of the vote is received) was estimated to provide an additional $2 million.[18] Under the new election financing legislation, apart from the state, individual donors were the other key source of funding. Direct mail requests for individual donations were projected at $1 million (but actually raised $2.3 million), while direct ask (telephone requests from larger donors) was projected to raise $560,000. To tide them over, the NDP sought a $9.5-million loan from the Citizens' Bank, an Internet/phone virtual e-bank set up by the B.C.–based VanCity Credit Union. As collateral, the NDP employed three major assets — the building in which its headquarters were now located and central and riding rebates to be provided by the state.

NDP INTERNAL POLLING

In 2004, polling was directed by the Toronto- and Vancouver-based Strategic Communications, led by Bob Penner, the son of prominent political scientist Norman Penner. The company had been involved in Layton's first ballot victory in the NDP leadership race, COPE's successful Vancouver municipal election, and the NDP's disappointing 2003 Ontario provincial campaign. The company, hired by the federal NDP in July 2003, commenced with focus group testing in a number of key cities, including Winnipeg, Vancouver, Toronto, Halifax, and Montreal,[19] during the summer and completed an important baseline survey of two thousand persons (conducted in about fifty ridings) in December. During the campaign itself, shorter surveys posed questions regarding party standings, the leaders, the mood for political change, the most effective messages, the viability of party commercials and literature, and the potential impact of emerging issues in the campaign (e.g., inheritance tax, homelessness, Clarity Act).

The December baseline survey, employing 170 questions in rotation, sought to profile the existing political landscape[20] when the Liberals were still riding high in the polls, but Martin, as the new prime minister, was potentially vulnerable regarding his corporate leanings. The Alliance and Progressive Conservatives were still engaged in their merger and had yet to select their new leader. Overall, in the baseline survey, the NDP polled in the upper teens to low twenties, depending on whether "undecided" voters were included in the calculations. The leader, widely perceived to be a major asset to the party, still lagged in name recognition, particularly outside of Toronto. Only about half of the respondents recognized the NDP leader and even fewer selected him as someone who would make the best PM.

Given the NDP's limited projected polling budget, the party had to be selective. While initially ninety ridings were polled in the early election period, the number was later reduced to about thirty (incumbent and top-tier ridings selected as most promising).[21] The surveys were based on a three-day rolling sample of about 150 persons per day. Towards the end of the campaign the sample rose to two hundred per day and involved ninety ridings. Over the campaign period, StratCom conducted about fifty riding polls (e.g., for the leader and Ed Broadbent's initial by-election campaign).

Health care was seen as the number one issue. In general, the perception of the party on issues such as medicare was positive, but its visibility had been low and it was perceived as inclined towards greater government spending (reinforcing the "tax and spend" stereotype). The primary target was soft Liberals. Given recent past federal elections and the 2003 Ontario election, party election planners were acutely aware that strategic vote-switching to the Liberals might occur once more if the Conservative Party looked as if it could win. This was a central theme the Liberals had employed in the past and could again in the future.[22]

During the actual campaign period, the party's internal polling of selected ridings found that NDP support ranged from 24 percent to 33 percent, while NDP candidate support was higher and ranged from 32 percent to 42 percent.[23] The public's name awareness of Layton would rise from 66 percent at the outset of the campaign in late May to 86 percent by mid-June, and preference for Layton as PM ranged from 16 percent to 25 percent. Interestingly, the support ranking was highest for the NDP candidate, followed by the party and its leader. Telephone call centres were used to monitor opinions and party identification and to try to persuade voters in targeted ridings. A number of regional telephone call centres were set up in Vancouver (StratCom), Regina (NDP), Toronto (StratCom), and Halifax (NDP).[24] Where gaps existed (Quebec and New Brunswick), the party improvised.

NDP STRATEGY AND NOMINATIONS

Echoing the recommendations of the election readiness committee, the 2004 campaign strategy was far more ambitious than in 2000 or 1997. The strategy sought to ensure the party was more visible, running a truly national campaign built around the new leader, Jack Layton, and offering a contrasting vision from the Liberals. Observing that all three opposition parties were in the low and high teens, there was a belief that any party, including the NDP, could break out of the pack. Accordingly, the publicly stated goals were to acquire more than 20 percent of the vote and win a record number of seats (more than the forty-three won in 1988) and, of course, to get the new leader elected in his home riding of Toronto-Danforth. He had not been able to win in two previous attempts in Toronto ridings in 1993 and 1997. On the eve of the election call, the NDP held fourteen seats. Twelve incumbents chose to run again, one less than expected with the dramatic news of Svend Robinson's non-candidacy because of pending legal problems. The social democratic NDP focused on winning over soft Liberal voters.[25] Amongst the key targeted socio-demographic groups were women,[26] young voters, unionists, and even soft Conservative voters (particularly those who might have recently moved from the Liberals) in NDP incumbent and priority ridings.

The NDP initially designated about forty targeted ridings. Fourteen of them were NDP incumbent ridings (with twelve MPs running again) and twenty-six were labelled "tier one," where 2000 voting results suggested a realistic voter base (usually over 20 percent). The largest number of primary targeted ridings was located in Ontario (eleven), followed by British Columbia (ten), Manitoba (six), Saskatchewan (five), Nova Scotia (four), the territories (two), and one each in New Brunswick and Quebec. It was projected that the largest growth in seats would be in Ontario and British Columbia. Twenty-four of the targeted ridings were found in the West, while sixteen were in the East. Of the twenty-six most promising potential new wins for the NDP, fifteen were to be taken from the Liberals, eight from the Conservatives, and one each from the BQ, an independent, and one new riding. All eight of the projected new victories over the Conservatives were to be from the West, while nine of the ten hoped-for victories over the Liberals were anticipated to be in Ontario.

Those planning the campaign were confronted with several image concerns. The first was that the new leader's profile needed to be increased outside of Toronto, particularly since this was to be a leader-based campaign.[27] Similarly, the party's visibility needed to be augmented, given that the by-election style of campaigns in 1997 and 2000 had adversely affected the party's prospects of being perceived as a major player in the long run. These were two primary goals of the pre-election campaign.

The NDP nominated candidates to run in all 308 ridings. With the growth in party membership in Quebec, there were fewer nominal campaigns in Quebec than in the recent past. In candidate selection, the NDP has been a strong advocate of affirmative action. It had the highest number and percentage of women nominated of any major party, but less than the party's stated goal of 50 percent. Amongst the nominated candidates, there were ninety-six women (31 percent), thirty-six youth, twenty-five visible minorities (including the high-profile Olivia Chow[28] and Monia Mazigh), fourteen lesbian, gay, or transgendered individuals, eight aboriginals, and two with disabilities for a total of 51 percent affirmative action candidates.[29] A significant number of the candidates (e.g., Peggy Nash, Sid Ryan, Father Des McGrath, Mike Bocking) had a union background.

NDP CAMPAIGN PLATFORM AND MAIN MESSAGE

The campaign platform document was a sixty-four-page booklet entitled "Platform 2004: Jack Layton, NDP" and sub-themed "New energy. A positive choice." Its drafting was under the general supervision of the party's election platform committee, chaired by Vicky Smallman and Bob Dewar, with key staffers Jamey Heath, Franz Hartmann, and Donne Flanagan. A draft of the platform was circulated to the party's federal executive and council in February, a few months before the election. While aspects of the themes were mentioned earlier in the leader's speeches and the section on the environment received a March pre-release, the final version was officially unveiled during the first week of the campaign, before the other major parties'.[30] Two thousand copies were printed, with fifteen hundred in English and five hundred in French (for candidates, riding campaign managers, and media), and the document was also posted on the party's Web site where it could be downloaded in its entirety or in sections. Echoing the format employed in recent Manitoba, Ontario, and Nova Scotia provincial NDP campaigns,[31] "Platform 2004" listed eight key commitments: 1) create opportunities and jobs in a green and prosperous economy; 2) improve public health care with innovation — not privatization; 3) invest in cities and communities through clean water, housing, and transit; 4) expand access to post-secondary education; 5) make life more affordable and secure — starting with protecting pensions, removing GST from family essentials, and expanding childcare; 6) strengthen Canada's independent voice for peace, human rights, and fair trade on the world stage; 7) restore integrity and accountability in government; and 8) balance the budget. The booklet was subdivided into five sections: a) building the country we want; b) building the planet we want; c) respecting who we are; d) protecting who we are; e) clear choices on how to get there.

The top three items — fostering jobs while protecting the environment (a co-operative labour and green message), public health care, and the role of cities — reflected the main thrust of the planned campaign, while the last plank was designed to give credibility to the party on financial matters and inoculate it against a tax and spend image. Overall, the platform was projected as positive, populist ("plan for today's Canadian families" versus "corporate tax breaks," p. 56), realistic, and practical. A "green and prosperous economy … where no one is left behind" became a key phrase in the campaign.

The typical structure of the platform document was to offer a detailed one-and-a-half-page presentation of the NDP's stance on an issue and then to briefly contrast these points to that of Paul Martin's Liberals, who were the prime target in the NDP's quest for more votes. Unfortunately, the platform did not seem to adequately address the rapidly changing political landscape in which the Liberals and Paul Martin had fallen so dramatically in popularity and the political right had united so swiftly into one new Conservative party. Amazingly, the platform document made no mention of the Conservative Party![32] The "Issue Sheets," a long list of thirty-two fact sheets on a variety of topics available in hard copy or on the party's Web site, were produced later and did include brief mention of Harper and the Conservative Party. Still, the coverage seemed too little. The public anger with the Liberal ad scandals was perhaps not stressed as much as it should have been. While the platform drafters anticipated that the section on the Middle East might prove controversial, in fact, the issue that evoked the most negative reaction from the electorate was the proposed inheritance tax for those receiving property valued at over $1 million. This backlash caught almost all NDP strategists by surprise and led to considerable discussion within the party's war room. In the end, the party stoically stayed the course, but the damage was done.

Several pamphlets were released over the course of the campaign. In the pre-election period brochures dealing with proportional representation, Star Wars, and student tuition and debt were issued (and could be downloaded). Special pamphlets were also produced for Ed Broadbent's by-election campaign (subsequently rolled into the general election) and Jack Layton's riding. Half a million copies of "Building the Alternative," the main pamphlet for the September 2003 pre-election campaign, were distributed. The pamphlet sought to introduce Layton, present the NDP's vision, and offer a critique of Martin's Liberals. In the first week of the campaign a bridge pamphlet[33] introduced the local candidate, criticized both the Liberals and Conservatives, and outlined some of the NDP's key positive planks. In the second and third weeks, a hybrid leaflet was produced that further profiled the local candidate, reiterated the NDP's eight key commitments, and gave space for regional campaign messages. Three million copies of the main central pamphlet, entitled "New Energy/Positive Choice," were issued during the final two weeks of the campaign, primarily in eighty key ridings. The leaflet outlined the NDP's eight commitments, criticized the Liberal's drift to big business, and warned of the Conservative party's "reckless cuts and privatization." Unlike the party platform drafted and released earlier, the central pamphlet, like the bridge and hybrid leaflets, attacked both the Liberals and the Conservatives.

ADVERTISING

The NDP's advertising was designed by Ron Johnson and Paul Degenstein of the B.C.–based Now Communications team, veterans of numerous NDP provincial and federal campaigns, working with Brad Levigne, the director of communications. The NDP's advertising budget was quite ambitious in 2004, growing from an initial estimate of $3 million to a final projection of $4.8 million — the biggest in the party's history. By contrast, the 2000 ad budget had been only $1.8 million.[34]

Whereas the 2000 election had focused on retaining ridings and was by nature more regional, the 2004 campaign projected growth and was more national in scope. Accordingly, TV time was bought on several networks and speciality channels (e.g., CTV Newsnet and aboriginal and multicultural channels). Over the last several decades, NDP federal campaigns have spent the largest portion of the advertising budget on TV ads, and this pattern was accentuated in 2004.

Table 1: NDP Advertising

Year	% TV	% radio	% print
2004	91	4	5
2000	54	40	5
1988	80	15	5

There were a total of thirteen English-language TV ads,[35] two during the pre-election period and eleven during the campaign. This may have been a record number for the federal NDP, although five of the ads were quite short at fifteen seconds in length and designed to be run with another in various combinations as a thirty-second placement. While the primary emphasis was on ads in English Canada, there were at least four French-language TV ads (unlike in 2000 when there had been none). The campaign also witnessed the first ever NDP ad in the Chinese language (in both Cantonese and Mandarin).

During the February and March 2004 pre-election period, there was a significant television buy, and two ads were aired. The first ad, "Layton," mostly in black and white, sought to introduce the new NDP leader and contrasted him to "Martin's corporate Liberals." The energetic Layton and the NDP offered a "positive alternative" with a strong commitment to public health and the environment. The ad made use of quotes from independent validators praising Layton. The video ran in both English and French in high-profile time slots during the Academy Awards and the hockey playoffs. The second ad, entitled "Meet Paul," noted that Martin was a "former shipping tycoon" who gave corporations tax cuts, whereas Layton fought for the "little guy, middle class and everyday families." The ad employed classic populist imagery.

Once the writs were issued, a number of ads emerged over the different phases of the five-week campaign. The opening ad, entitled "Ideas," running towards the end of the first week, was a positive presentation that echoed key planks of the party's platform, which had been released that week. The ad cautioned against privatization of health care, favoured tougher environmental laws, and sought to take the GST off family essentials and to make government more accountable. It closed with the clarion call "Together, we can build a green and prosperous Canada — where no one's left behind,"[36] a phrase that would be stressed throughout the campaign. In a format employed by all of the NDP ads, the video clip closed with the party's logo, Web site, and slogan, "New energy. A positive choice." The ad entitled "Both," airing briefly while Prime Minister Paul Martin was in the United States, cautioned that both Liberal Leader Paul Martin and Conservative Leader Stephen Harper wanted to move Canada closer to U.S. president George W. Bush. It warned about sacrificing our independence and values such as public health care.

The first of five fifteen-second ads was entitled "Liberals."[37] It advised Canadians to be skeptical about Liberal promises, given their past inadequate record on childcare, health care, and pollution. The next ad addressed the fact that increasingly the Canadian electorate was leaning towards political change. The ad "Harper" warned that the Conservatives favoured "reckless corporate tax cuts, expanded for-profit health care and weaker equality rights." Instead of the Conservatives' negative change, the NDP promised positive change. In seeking gains in both British Columbia and Ontario, two regional ads were crafted. "BC," running in weeks three and four, attempted to link Premier Gordon Campbell's cuts and privatization to Harper and the federal Conservatives. "Ontarians Know," running in weeks two to four, reminded viewers of the "damage of [Ontario] Conservatives' cuts and privatization" and the recent provincial Liberals' "broken promises." Whereas in the past the federal NDP had been adversely affected by unpopular NDP provincial governments, now NDP federal strategists hoped that both the Liberals and Conservatives would be vulnerable. The ad entitled "Affordable" was a positive statement of several planks (taking the GST off family essentials, doubling the child tax credit, and reducing tuition fees) from the NDP's platform.

The Quebec ads entitled "Pourquoi 1" and "Pourquoi 2" were in French and involved prominent NDP figure Pierre Ducasse and other Quebec candidates each reciting a feature of the party's platform planks. These ads ran during the entire campaign period in Quebec. Given that Olivia Chow, the NDP leader's wife, had a high profile in the Chinese-Canadian community, a Chinese language ad was designed to be aired in Vancouver and Toronto during the last two weeks of the campaign. Layton and Chow were both featured, while the messaging addressed community service, expediting recognition of international professional credentials, and government integrity. "Layton encore," which ran in week four, was an updated and slightly altered version of the pre-election "Layton" ad. The main change was to include Conservative Leader Harper with Liberal Leader Martin as a negative choice.

In the last week of the campaign, two final ads appeared and received extensive air time. The main message of "Don't Trust" was that Liberals were untrustworthy and the Conservatives planned a "hidden agenda and reckless tax cuts," and thus neither should be given a "blank cheque." In contrast, the NDP offered a positive choice regarding health care, education, and the environment and could "play a central role in Parliament." Much of the text was repeated in "Central Role," with the difference being that Layton spoke the closing lines, asking for the support that would give the NDP a "central role" in Parliament and promising to be "a powerful voice for you." The NDP TV ads showed the party's Web site address and a number of the ads were placed on the party's Web site.

The magnitude of the NDP's television buy in the 2004 campaign was the most competitive the party had undertaken in the last decade and a half. The leader was very much a key component of ads — a sign of his growing profile and perceived strength. As in recent past campaigns, the NDP's primary national target remained the Liberal Party, but as the Liberals slipped in popularity and the Conservative Party rose in the polls, NDP strategists did make later ads to include criticisms of the Conservatives as well as the Liberals. Did NDP strategists' fear of strategic voting, which played a role in 2000, result in the party's platform, TV ads, and pamphlets being initially skewed to critiquing the Liberal Party and not the political right? Given the regional variations of electoral prospects and rivals, several regional ads were created and given air time in their targeted region, but did they run soon enough?

INTERNET AND E-MAIL

Just as the mass medium of television transformed the dynamics of election campaigns in the 1960s, so too have the Internet and e-mail altered how campaigns communicate (see Chapter Seven). In the 2004 election the NDP Web site became an integral part of the campaign. In the pre-election period the structure of the Web site reflected a greater emphasis on the MPs, parliamentary activity, and party history. It also included a party members' interactive discussion forum ("Mouseland") and listings of pre-election Web campaigns (e.g., favouring PR and the very successful flyourflag.ca, with one hundred thousand hits by February 28, 2004). During the pre-election period, donations through the NDP's Web site were used to pay for newspaper ads opposing "Star Wars" missile defence in both the *Globe and Mail* and *La Presse*.

At the start of the 2004 campaign a new, more election-oriented, site was unveiled. The Web structure involved several major headings, and within each of these, options for subcategories: home, positive choice (the eight commitments and the party platform with more than sixty-four thousand downloads), Jack Layton (diary, speeches, articles, new book), news/media (news details, reality check, see our ads, what they are saying, campaign gallery, media kit), issues (Paul Martin's Liberals, Fact Sheets), E-campaigners (media watch, NDP news network), local candidates (ridings/individual candidate Web sites), get involved (join, donate, sign up) and contact. Visitors could download the party television ads. Interestingly, the video "Ed's Back," made by *This Hour Has 22 Minutes*, proved to be the most popular item, with more than seventy-three thousand downloads. Overall, the Web site was multi-purposed and touched on all aspects of the campaign.

Prior to the election, party members could sign up for an e-NDP news subscription, and more than twenty thousand people did. The party also commenced an internal daily e-memo ("Le Buzz") for campaign managers in the ridings and federal staff. Whereas recent campaigns had made substantial use of faxes to get various materials to ridings, now, given the increased level of computer literacy in campaign 2004, e-mail and the party Web site were used extensively with success.

The party reported that the NDP Web site generated about 410,000 visits and had received 29 million hits since it was launched ("Le Buzz," June 27, 2004). In the months leading up to the election increasing numbers of people joined the party through the Web site (595 in November, 741 in December, and 969 in January). In a party where membership recruitment has historically been through the provincial wings, the new technology enabled the federal party to process membership applications directly. Fundraising from the Web site was more successful than anticipated. Activists were also able to gather information about issues and the election through the Web sites of the CLC and its affiliate unions.

THE NDP CAMPAIGN AND THE LEADER'S TOUR

Over thirty-six days, the leader's tour[38] was perceived as a major vehicle for communicating the party's national election message. A major part of any leader's tour is designed to highlight a key issue or theme, with suitable photo ops. Usually in a federal election the party leader endeavours to travel to as many regions as possible in order to give the party the greatest media profile. Compared to 2000, the 2004 tour was more ambitious and endeavoured to be in all five regions as much as possible each week. Layton spent the greatest amount of time in Ontario, where the most Commons seats and the greatest gains were expected. It was also the region where much of the English media were centred, where the leaders' debates took place, and where the leader and his wife were both running as candidates. The tour spent the next largest amount of time in British Columbia (also where significant gains were projected), followed by Saskatchewan. The time allocated to Quebec, with one-quarter of Canada's population and where Layton was born, was substantially more than in 2000.

On May 22, the day before the writs were issued, Layton attended a major political rock concert ("Let's Jack It Up") in Toronto, reflecting the energy, youth, and hope of the campaign. Layton opened the first week of the thirty-six-day campaign (May 23 to 29) with press conference on Parliament Hill in Ottawa, flanked by his wife, Olivia Chow, Ed Broadbent, and Monia Mazigh. In his opening statement, Layton pointed out that the re-energized NDP was offering a positive and practical choice for a green and prosperous country that would leave no one behind, in contrast to the corporate drift of Martin's Liberals. Criticizing Harper on health care, Layton made a poignant personal reference to his own father's suffering under private health care and his son's asthma. In a characteristically energetic move, Layton promptly boarded the rented Airbus jet and flew across the continent to Vancouver's Chinatown to demonstrate the desire to include the West. While in Vancouver, the NDP announced a major part of its campaign message — eight key commitments. The hope was to give the party a publicity boost in the early phase of the campaign and keep it in the news.

The full platform was unveiled in Toronto and aired live on *Newsworld*, but the anticipated positive publicity from projected balanced budgets was clouded by the inheritance tax controversy. At the Wednesday evening nomination meeting for Olivia Chow, Layton got caught up in the emotion in the church hall and deviated from his script to accuse Paul Martin of being personally responsible through his economic policies for the increase in deaths caused by homelessness. Layton, having been profoundly affected by the death of one homeless person a block from his home several years earlier, had written a book on the topic.[39] The media reacted immediately to the charge by criticizing Layton, which became the focus of news commentary on the NDP for several days. A few days later in Sept-Îles, Quebec, Layton was asked a question about his position on the controversial Clarity Act. The former professor did not duck the question and, echoing the official party position, indicated he was opposed to the Act. However, the NDP parliamentary caucus had in the main supported the controversial legislation, and several prominent NDP MPs, including Blaikie, Nystrom, and McDonough, disagreed with their leader's view. In his comments Layton had reintroduced separatism as an election theme and, worse, was vulnerable to appearing soft on it. This charge was particularly important in English Canada, where virtually all of the NDP's electoral prospects were located. It was a rough and bumpy end to what had started out as a good first week and pre-election period. But no one could claim that the NDP was lacking visibility and media attention. At the end of the first week, NDP support ranged from 16 to 19 percent in the major public opinion polls[40] and it was amidst what seemed a three-party race in English Canada.

In week two (May 30 to June 5), Layton, the former president of the Federation of Canadian Municipalities, attended the FCM convention to talk about immediately providing municipalities with their portion of the federal gas tax and investing in cities regarding clean water, housing, and public transit. Elsewhere, reacting to the Conservative platform, Layton questioned the priorities of committing billions to aircraft carriers at the expense of public health care. Participating with Martin in CBC television's "Great Canadian Job Interview," Layton performed well, and Martin seemed to agree with the NDP in a number of policy areas — perhaps a sign the Liberals were trolling for NDP votes. At the end of the first two weeks, Layton's campaign had travelled to seventeen cities, making it, by many accounts, the most energetic of all the leaders' tours. At the end of the second week, two public polls had the NDP at 17 percent, with Layton in third place at just above 10 percent as best prime minister.

In week three (June 6 to 12), the election campaign paused for D-Day ceremonies to remember the many Canadians who had fought for democracy, perhaps a poignant reminder to vote in a free society. For the prime minister, it would be one of two international trips (the other the G-8 summit) amidst the domestic election campaign. With Liberal support declining, the Conservatives now became the target of more criticism by the NDP. Layton warned that the Conservatives would try to turn the clock back on social issues and were "intolerant and extreme on abortion," as suggested by Cheryl Gallant's comments. Layton drew parallels between Stephen Harper's proposed spending cuts and privatization and those enacted by Gordon Campbell's government in British Columbia. In comparing the Liberals and the Conservatives, Layton offered one of his most memorable lines of the campaign: "Liberals make promises and don't keep them; Conservatives make promises and we hope they don't keep them." It conveyed greater concern about the Conservative agenda. At the outset of the campaign, the media had sought to introduce the different parties. Now with public polls reporting NDP support ranging from 16 to 19 percent and seat projections in the low to mid-twenties (internal NDP polling suggested just over thirty seats), the media increasingly focused upon the two-party fight to form a government, at the expense of coverage on the NDP. As the prospect of a minority government arose, Layton declined to speculate on a possible NDP balancer role. The post-debate period would be another story.

The most important events of week four (June 13 to 19) were the French- and English-language leaders' debates. Three of the parties had new leaders who were inexperienced in such inter-party debates. The French-language debate immediately preceded the English one. While none of the leaders of the major parties in English Canada was Francophone, the NDP, for the first time since David Lewis, had a leader who had grown up in Quebec and was reasonably fluent in French. Layton opened with a positive message and expressed a hope to link with progressives in Quebec. In response to Martin's repeated attacks on the NDP as wanting to "increase taxes massively," Layton pointed out the huge tax breaks the Liberals had given to corporations and called upon the Liberals to halt the privatization of health care. While Harper condemned the NDP's position on NATO, NORAD, and NAFTA, Layton warned that the Conservatives wanted to cut programs too much. BQ Leader Gilles Duceppe questioned where the NDP stood on the Clarity Act and suggested the NDP was always asking the federal government to intervene, even when issues did not fall under federal jurisdiction. Post-debate accounts declared Duceppe had done best and Layton had come fourth in the eyes of Francophone viewers (Compas, June 16, 2004). To some, the NDP leader seemed too uninvolved in the French debate, though this was far less important than would be his placement in the English debate. His advisors encouraged him to be more assertive in the English debates, which were far more important for NDP electoral fortunes.

In the English-language debate, NDP strategists expected that Layton, the former university professor, would do well. Layton opened with an invitation for voters to give the NDP "a central role in the next

Parliament." He followed with criticism of the Liberal government's scandals and warned of the Conservative agenda and the need to protect public health care. During the debate, Layton reminded the audience that the NDP, not the Liberals, offered the best hope for a positive alternative to the Conservative agenda. Turning to foreign affairs, Layton criticized Martin's acquiescence to U.S. president Bush's "Star Wars" and the weaponization of space. To which Martin replied curtly: "Did your handlers tell you to not stop talking?" It would prove a cutting remark for Layton's image. Martin addressed the health care issue by making a solemn promise to reduce waiting times. In Layton's closing statement, he suggested that the NDP's eight commitments were an example of a positive choice. But it was the Francophone Duceppe who delivered the best blow to Martin with his penetrating questions about which of Martin's ministers were involved in the sponsorship scandal.

Post-debate assessment of the English debate suggested Harper overall did best and Layton came in third (Compas, June 16, 2004). Some commentators suggested that Layton had interrupted too much and was too aggressive. Had he gone after Harper enough? Overall, there was disappointment with his performance. Perhaps expectations had been too high for the new leader, who was the only one of the four not to have had parliamentary experience. In the post-debate period, with the NDP polling in the 16 to 20 percent range, Layton reiterated his plea for voters to give the NDP a central role and talked about the NDP winning as many as sixty seats. He presented the case that if you don't like the Liberals and are scared of the Conservatives, then the NDP is a positive alternative. New Democrats hoped both premises were solid foundations for building bridges for an NDP breakthrough.

Normally the day following the leaders' debates involves assessing the leaders' performances, but Alberta Premier Ralph Klein diverted the media's attention when he dropped a bombshell, informing them that an impending Alberta report would challenge the National Health Act. Warning against the ongoing drift to privatization, Layton signed a medicare protection pledge in Regina. But health care was temporarily eclipsed by another issue. In reaction to the Holly Jones murder story, Conservative Jason Kenny condemned the court's toleration of child pornography. The next day the Conservatives issued a press release stating that Martin supported child pornography. While Harper later withdrew the headline, he refused to apologize. It was yet another incident that reminded voters that the radical right wing of the Reform and Alliance parties had not been submerged in the new Conservative Party. NDP's concerns that citizens might vote strategically for the Liberals out of fear of the Conservatives seemed increasingly plausible. With the Liberals rebounding and a growing discussion of a possible minority government, Layton forcefully and bluntly characterized media speculation that the NDP would prop up a Conservative government as "bullshit." The endorsements by Greenpeace and the Sierra Club and Toronto Mayor David Miller's positive assessment of the NDP seemed lost in the headlines.

In the closing week of the campaign (June 20 to 27), the NDP had an ambitious plan to tour twenty-two cities in eight provinces. Layton spent Father's Day with his family in Toronto, where he also participated in White Ribbon Day — a program that he had pioneered to draw attention to the problem of violence against women. On Monday, Layton, speaking at the Toronto Board of Trade, promised a balanced budget, in contrast to the actual practices of Conservative governments (e.g., Mulroney's, Reagan's, and Bush's). Later that night Layton participated in an all-candidates meeting, one of the few times he, as leader, was able to spend much time in his home riding. Meanwhile, several prominent former B.C. NDP members, including Ujjal Dosanjh, warned that voting NDP would prop up a Conservative government. Martin suggested that the Liberals and NDP had differences but "share the same values." Layton rejected such a political embrace and critically noted the Liberals' cuts to health care and failure to reject "Star Wars." The "end game" plan for the Liberals included targeting NDP voters to shift their vote "strategically" to the Liberals to stop a Conservative victory. Reinforcing fears about the Conservatives, Randy White was quoted in a film documentary about the need to reassess the Charter of Rights and curb the power of the Supreme Court. Layton's endless energy was tested when the NDP leader embarked on "Super Friday," involving eight stops in Ontario over an eighteen-hour period, and this was followed by "Super Saturday," where he travelled to three western provinces before returning to his riding in Toronto the next day for the Gay Pride celebrations. Meanwhile, the Liberal party, in the final hours of campaign 2004, engaged in a phone blitz (including automated phone messages) targeting NDP supporters. Most public opinion polls had showed the NDP in the 17 to 18 percent range. Would their support be enough to win a record number of seats? Would there be a minority government in which the NDP would have a central role? Or would the NDP fall victim once more to strategic voting?

ELECTION RESULTS AND ANALYSIS

With just over 2.1 million votes (15.7 percent of those cast), the NDP 2004 campaign saw gains in both votes and seats compared to 2000. Campaign 2004 produced a vote just above the NDP average (15.2 percent) for the 1961–2000 period but below the goal of surpassing the 1988 NDP high of just over 20 percent.[41] Overall, the NDP's vote in the 2004 campaign went up in every province except Saskatchewan. No province gave the NDP a vote over 30 percent, but five provinces, along with the territories, saw the NDP vote over 20 percent. Nova Scotia led the way, followed by British Columbia, Manitoba, Saskatchewan, and New Brunswick. In Ontario, the NDP more than doubled its vote to just over 18 percent. Newfoundland and P.E.I. were also in the 10 to 20 percent range. The NDP vote was just below 10 percent in Alberta. Despite more than doubling its vote in Quebec, the vote still remained below 5 percent. Clearly, there is still need for substantial growth in the party's vote in the heartland provinces of Ontario and Quebec, where most of the seats are located.

Percent votes received provides a good preliminary indication of the number of ridings in which a party is competitive in either three-way or two-way races.[42] The results were as follows: 3 ridings where the NDP received over 50 percent of the vote (a factor affected by a multi-party system), 13 ridings in the 40 to 49 percent range, 29 between 30 and 39 percent, 47 between 20 and 29 percent, 103 ridings between 10 and 19 percent, and 113 ridings that were below 10 percent (far fewer than in 2000). The 92 ridings in which the NDP acquired more than 20 percent of the vote offer the greatest likelihood for future electoral gains; many of the 113 ridings in which the party's vote fell below 10 percent take on a symbolic importance for the party.[43] Within this category, all of the ridings (53) in which the NDP received less than 5 percent of the vote were found in Quebec. Clearly, a breakthrough in Quebec, a key rationale for the creation of the NDP in 1961, remains a distant hope.

Using a different indicator, party placement rankings, the data on first- (19) and second-place (51) finishes suggests that the NDP stands a good chance of future success in 70 ridings. This is a significant increase from only 39 in 2000 but is still far short of the NDP's appearing competitive enough to form the government or even the official opposition. The number of third-place finishes (168) indicates ridings in which the party has a reasonable chance of success if both the campaign and the local candidate are strong. Given that third place is the modal ranking for NDP candidates, it confirms the status of the NDP as a third party, at least in terms of votes. Most of the fourth-place (51) finishes and all of the fifth-place (19) finishes were in Quebec. Clearly, the NDP's future task in Quebec is the elementary need to establish a beachhead in that province.

With an almost doubling of the party's vote, the party did manage to win more seats, but only five more, significantly fewer than expected. As Alan Cairns, Fair Vote Canada, and the Law Reform Commission have documented,[44] the NDP, like its predecessor the CCF, suffers from under-representation and regional distortion in seat distribution under our current first-past-the-post (FPTP) electoral system. Prominent NDP politicians such as Ed Broadbent, Lorne Nystrom, and Jack Layton have been advocates of some form of proportional representation (PR). It seems plausible that the new minority Parliament might address this issue.

Except in Saskatchewan, all incumbent MPs were re-elected. A regional breakdown of candidates elected reveals five from B.C., four from Manitoba, seven from Ontario, one from New Brunswick, and two from Nova Scotia. Thus nine MPs are from the West and ten from the East (including Ontario).[45] The number of women in caucus (26 percent; five of nineteen) continues to be significant, and all four female incumbents were re-elected. In terms of party competition, of the seven new seats gained, three came from the Conservatives in B.C. and four from the Liberals in Ontario. The loss of two incumbents in Saskatchewan went to the Conservative Party. The loss of the Nova Scotia NDP seat went to a Liberal. Analyzing the fifteen ridings in which the NDP came close and were within 5 percent of the victor's vote, eight were seats won by the Conservatives (four in B.C., three in Saskatchewan, and one in Ontario), while seven were won by the Liberals (three in B.C., three in Ontario, and one in the Western Arctic). Ironically, the NDP platform had exclusively targeted the Liberal Party, but the NDP's primary party rival often differed in the East (Liberals) and the West (Conservatives).[46]

CONCLUSION

Coming out of Layton's first campaign as federal leader, a number of positive elements can be observed: the party's visibility and profile increased; more money was raised[47] (particularly important as funds from the labour movement would be restricted by the new party financing law); party membership rose and a significant number of the next generation of party activists were attracted to the NDP; the party's overall vote increased significantly; more NDP MPs were elected; the caucus is more diverse and includes several high-profile former federal leaders; and the leader won his own riding against a tough veteran MP and Layton is now a parliamentarian who can ask questions directly in the House of Commons. Given that it is a minority Parliament, the NDP is poised to play a key role, and the leader has a much higher national profile, having extensively canvassed the country in an election campaign. All of these developments suggest a solid foundation for the party in the next election (part of a so-called two-election strategy).

Jack Layton is well educated and articulate (author of two books) and shows a strong analytical perspective, ideal for debating in the House of Commons. His proficiency in French is the best of any NDP leader since David Lewis in the 1970s. Layton reflects a modern metropolitan perspective that even seems hip. He seems to possess inexhaustible energy and stamina, exhibits remarkable dedication and endless optimism — important traits in a world filled with too much apathy and cynicism. While Layton needs to continue evolving from political scientist to charismatic political communicator, he shows significant potential.

Nevertheless, several challenges confront the NDP in the first decade of the twenty-first century. Ideologically, the NDP continues to be vulnerable to Liberals who campaign on the left, despite having governed on the centre-right for years. This may be in part because voters fear the conservative and right-wing agenda and consequently engage in strategic voting. Or it may be because of an inability to find adequately powerful wedge issues between the social democratic NDP and the Liberal Party. Why, in recent elections, has the NDP not captured even more votes? Part of the answer can be seen in public opinion survey data. When respondents are asked which party best reflects their values and principles, the Liberals score the highest.[48] Similarly, the percent of voters indicating they would ever consider voting for the NDP has been consistently below half of the electorate (e.g., 35 percent in January 2003).[49] The health care issue was by far the top issue in the 2004 election, as in recent past campaigns, but increasingly, the electorate is skeptical about any party's, including the NDP's, ability to resolve the health care crisis.

If the NDP is befuddled by the Liberal party's ability to portray itself on the left, the NDP is increasingly challenged by the growing presence of the Green Party. The federal Green Party ran a full slate of candidates for the first time ever, achieved a record number and percent of votes, and raised an unprecedented amount of public funding. The Green Party attracts increasing numbers of activists and media attention and represents a growing conundrum for NDP candidates and strategists, particularly in B.C. and Ontario. Ignoring the Greens seems an inadequate and outdated strategy. More analysis will be needed to discern whether the Green Party's ideological challenge is from the left or from a different ideological dimension altogether.

Canada is a continental polity with a vast and varied geography. The NDP has belatedly recognized that strategically it cannot run a national campaign targeting a single political opponent, particularly given the different parties' seat distributions. In much of the West, the NDP's main challenge is to defeat a Conservative rival, while in the East it is the Liberals. However, the primary source from which to try to recruit new NDP votes remains soft Liberal Party supporters.

In all industrial polities, the number, power, and visibility of interest groups have risen, and, in comparison, parties seem to be in decline. The NDP was founded as a co-partnership of the old CCF and the CLC, and thus, the labour movement is a very special, even unique, interest group for the party. But Bill C-24 has driven a wedge into the party's relationship with the labour movement. What the labour movement can and cannot do during a campaign needs to be clarified, not only at the local level, but even on the national stage. In any case, labour's party needs to explore new ways to connect with its trade union members. Similarly, renewed connections need to be explored between the party and the women's movement, environmentalists, nationalists, and certain ethnic communities.

The future offers both opportunities and challenges for Canada's social democratic party. The NDP's overall election goals of achieving a record high number of votes and seats were ambitious. It was assumed that there would be an alignment of positive circumstances: an increasingly corporate leaning Liberal Party that would make it vulnerable on the left, the continuation of a divided and bickering right, and a re-energized NDP led by Jack Layton with his contemporary metropolitan persona and charisma that would be embraced by the increasingly urban Canadian public. The final NDP goal for election 2004 would prove to be a bridge too far. The breakthrough was not achieved, but with a minority Parliament, there may be another campaign sooner than usual and the NDP's future looks more promising than it has in the recent past.

NOTES

1 I am grateful to the many who kindly consented to post-election interviews and in particular members of the NDP's election planning committee and its steering group who allowed me to observe their deliberations. I also wish to thank NDP's Federal Secretary Chris Watson, Campaign Director Bruce Cox, the EPC co-chairs Andre Foucault and Raj Sihota, Senior Administrative Assistant Carmel Belanger, and the many others without whose generous assistance this chapter would not have been possible.

2 See Alan Whitehorn, "The 2000 NDP Campaign: Social Democracy at the Crossroads," in *The Canadian General Election of 2000,* ed. Jon Pammett and Christopher Dornan (Toronto: Dundurn Press, 2001).

3 Membership increased during the leadership race, and by February 2003 was reported to have surpassed the one hundred thousand mark. In a shift from the decentralist past practice of joining through the provincial party, individuals could now sign up directly through the national office's Web site.

4 J. Warnock, *Saskatchewan: The Roots of Discontent and Protest* (Montreal: Black Rose, 2004).

5 The magnitude of the impact of Bill C-24 draws comparisons to the Election Financing Legislation of 1974. See W.T. Stanbury, *Money In Politics: Financing Federal Parties and Candidates in Canada* (Toronto: Dundurn, 1991).

6 The legislation created a new system of financial proportional representation whereby each party would be rewarded by the state the amount of $1.75 per year for each vote.

7 See for example S. McBride and J. Shields, *Dismantling a Nation: Canada and the New World Order* (Halifax: Fernwood, 1993), and J. Laxer, *In Search of a New Left: Canadian Politics After the Neoconservative Assault* (Toronto: Viking, 1996).

8 This campaign also operated a Web site with the campaign's name.

9 The first phase was scheduled for May to September 2003.

10 "Pre-election Poll: NDP on the Move," NDP communiqué, April 23, 2004.

11 *Speaking Out: Ideas That Work for Canadians* (Toronto: Key Porter, 2004) was also translated and published in French as *Des idees pour les gens d'ici* (Laval: Guy Saint-Jean, 2004). Pierre Trudeau's *Federalism and the French Canadians* in 1968 and Brian Mulroney's *Where I Stand* in 1983/84 were examples of successful use of a leader's new book heading into the election campaign.

12 The committee also made a number of specific recommendations: the platform should take into account regional interests; the central platform should be a maximum of four to six items; the party should enhance the rapid response capacity of party headquarters given the twenty-four-hours news cycle; the party should ensure that all local campaign offices have e-mail access and compatible computer hardware and software; and the party should expand the party's central Web site services so that each riding campaign could download materials more quickly.

13 This was more frequently than in 2000.

14 The largest donations came from Communications, Energy and Paperworkers; Steelworkers; Canadian Autoworkers; United Food and Commercial Workers; National Union of Provincial and General Employees; Canadian Union of Public Employees; International Association of Machinists and Aerospace Workers; and Service Employees International Union.

15 ERC Report, February 2003.

16 Steering Committee, May 2004, and interview with Eric Hebert, assistant federal secretary.

17 A. Whitehorn, *Canadian Socialism: Essays on The CCF-NDP* (Toronto: Oxford University Press, 1992), 216; see also A. Whitehorn, "Alexa

McDonough and Atlantic Breakthrough for the New Democratic Party," in *The Canadian General Election of 1997,* ed. A. Frizzell and J. Pammett (Toronto: Dundurn Press, 1997) and Whitehorn, "The 2000 NDP Campaign: Social Democracy at the Crossroads."

18 Several MPs initially balked at continuing to have their local campaigns sign over their future election rebates to the national headquarters in return for services rendered, but in the end an agreement was negotiated that included the possibility of a minority Parliament.

19 Small focus groups (about seven to ten persons each) were conducted in different regions with groups separated by certain demographic categories (e.g., region, gender, vote intention, and age category) to explore images of the party, its policies, and its main platform to assess arguments for and against voting NDP, strategic voting, and to test the party ads.

20 One of the problems with the timing of the baseline survey was that the political landscape was undergoing major changes involving who was prime minister, the number of major parties, and the political leadership of the two largest parties.

21 The thirty ridings were composed of sixteen from the East and fourteen from the West.

22 The 2000 and 2004 election studies teams have questioned the extent of strategic voting. See E. Gidengil et al., "How the race was won," *Globe and Mail,* July 14, 2004; and A. Blais, et al., *Anatomy of a Liberal Victory: Making Sense of the Vote in the 2000 Canadian Election* (Peterborough: Broadview, 2002), 181–204. But for both the 2000 and 2004 NDP campaigns this issue was a major concern in the NDP's internal calculations and polling. The national election studies, by their nature, have sampled and tested hypotheses across the country. In contrast, the NDP, as a third- or fourth-place party, has surveyed in detail aspects of strategic voting in much smaller and germane samples of key ridings where it was competitive.

23 The power of sitting NDP MPs to attract voters in incumbent ridings was evident in that all but two from Saskatchewan were re-elected (N = 10/12).

24 Other computer/polling-based techniques employed included taped telephone messages sent to home phone numbers and "pol-cats" that systematically canvassed a poll in groups. The latter were effective at determining voter identification but less so in persuading voters.

25 ERC, December 18, 2003. Yet again, little attention was initially given to endeavouring to win over Conservative supporters, an issue that would become more important in the West as the campaign unfolded.

26 Academic research has found that women tend to favour spending on health and education (i.e., social issues), while men are more inclined to be concerned with debt and taxation levels (economic issues). See A. Blais et al., 137–155; N. Nevitte et al., *Unsteady State: The 1997 Canadian Federal Election* (Toronto: Oxford University Press, 2000), 110–115; and E. Gidengil,

"Economic Man and Social Woman? The Case of the Gender Gap in the Support of the Canada–US Free Trade Agreement," *Comparative Political Studies,* No. 28, 384–408.

27 Internal party polling data on leader recognition indicated steady growth from 10 to 12 percent in the summer of 2003, to 45 percent December, to 66 percent in May 2004, and finally to 86 percent by mid-June, during the campaign. As to the best person to be prime minister, Layton's numbers in the sampled ridings went from 16 percent in late May to 24 percent by mid-June 2004. Public domain polling for the entire country generally put Layton at a range from 9 to 13 percent (e.g., SES-CPAC campaign polls).

28 Layton's wife, Olivia Chow, a Toronto city councillor, was a high-profile member of the Chinese-Canadian community — an important asset in both Vancouver and Toronto.

29 NDP Communications Press Release, June 7, 2004.

30 This was designed to give the party a higher profile earlier in the campaign and maintain the party's visibility, but it did run the risk of losing momentum later in the campaign.

31 Doer's Five-Point Platform, Hampton's Six-Point Bookmark, and Dexter's Seven Key Commitments. Like the Nova Scotia provincial pledge, this last item was the federal NDP's promise of a balanced budget.

32 One major reason for this was the apprehension of driving voters to the Liberal Party as a way to stop voters' fear of the Conservative party. The document also ignored the Green Party.

33 The communications plan was to have three leaflets: a bridge leaflet (E36–E28), the key commitments leaflet (E28–E14), and the final leaflet (E14–E1). There were also translations of some material into other languages, most notably Punjabi, Arabic, Cantonese, and Mandarin.

34 Even earlier NDP election ad and media budgets were $1.9 million (1997), $3.28 million (1993), $3 million (1988), $1.8 million (1984), $1.8 million (1980), and $1.3 million (1979).

35 I am indebted to Brad Lavigne, director of communications, for his dedication in ensuring that I received copies of all advertising scripts and Aylwin Lo for invaluable computing counsel.

36 Interestingly, the closing line of the ad was reminiscent of the phrase "green and pleasant land" often employed at the end of speeches of Tommy Douglas where he quoted from a poem by William Blake. This poem was formally sung in celebrating the British Labour Party's 1945 victory.

37 The combination of "Liberals" / "B.C." ran in B.C. in weeks three and four. The combination of "Liberals" / "Harper" ran nationally at about the same time.

38 There was also a secondary tour of other party notables to help in key ridings.

39 Layton wrote *Homelessness: The Making and Unmaking of a Crisis* (Toronto: Penguin, 2000) and dedicated it to Eugene Upper, the person who had died a handful of steps from Layton's home.

40 CPAC, June 25, also the source for subsequent weekly ranges. The NDP's own internal polling of its top priority ridings averaged consistently higher.

41 See "Appendix" in Whitehorn, *Canadian Socialism,* 263–264.

42 I am grateful for the data provided by Heather Fraser, the NDP's director of organization, and her colleagues Brad Field and Tara Peel.

43 While seats are crucial to establish a party's parliamentary profile, party income is a key factor in organizational survival. Bill C-24 lowered the threshold for riding reimbursement from 15 percent to 10 percent of the vote. In 2004 the party qualified for financial reimbursement in about two-thirds of the ridings, a far better number than in the recent past. Still, the number of ridings in Canada that gave the NDP less than 10 percent in 2004 was 113.

44 For a review of the literature see H. Milner, "The Case for Proportional Representation in Canada" in *Party Politics in Canada,* 8th edition, ed. H. Thorburn and A. Whitehorn. Fair Vote Canada calculated that the ratio of NDP seats to votes was one seat per 111,000 votes, whereas the ratio for the other parliamentary parties was 40,000 for the Conservatives, 37,000 for the Liberals and 31,000 for the BQ. "Fair Vote Canada: Election Results Distorted," June 29, 2004.

45 For earlier data on the NDP see Whitehorn, *Canadian Socialism,* Chapter 1 and Appendix, and A. Whitehorn, "Alexa McDonough and NDP Gains in Atlantic Canada," in *Party Politics in Canada,* 8th edition, ed. H.G. Thorburn and A. Whitehorn (Toronto: Pearson Education/Prentice Hall, 2000).

46 See "Atlantic Breakthrough," 104, and "Social Democracy at the Crossroads," 131.

47 The party is far better off financially in the pre- and post-2004 election period than in 2000. There are several reasons for this: the party's vote, and therefore public financing, has increased; the party has more MPs and parliamentary staff; and the party headquarters is both paid for and generating revenue. Layton is a natural at fundraising.

48 See N. Nevitte et al., "Victory to the Middle Man," *Globe and Mail,* July 28, 2004; see also their *Anatomy of Victory,* 117–124, which noted that in the 2000 election Liberals predominated in voter identification, while the NDP was last amongst the major parties. See also their book *Unsteady State,* 116, on the 1997 election, which stated that the NDP is "so far from the median Canadian voters that should give party strategists pause."

49 Fifty-three percent replied either "no" or "never." Ekos, January 26, 2003.

CHAPTER FIVE

THE BLOC QUÉBÉCOIS:
The Dynamics of a Distinct Electorate

by Alain-G. Gagnon and Jacques Hérivault[1]

On the eve of the election call, the Bloc Québécois was probably the best prepared federal political party in Quebec. During the winter months and early spring of 2004, the Conservatives had merged the recently born Canadian Alliance with the Progressive Conservatives and held a leadership convention; they were still in the process of mobilizing ground troops and trying to come up with a viable electoral platform. Moreover, after the departure of Jean Charest, neither the Conservatives nor the Alliance had an organization worth mentioning in Quebec. The Liberals had just been through one of their most tumultuous periods, setting the stage for months of infighting, during their own leadership campaign to crown Paul Martin. This was followed by a purge of most of Jean Chrétien's supporters within the party, caucus, and government nominations, at a level rarely seen in Canadian political history. When combined with attempts to quell the furor over the sponsorship scandal, the Liberals were definitely ill-prepared for the campaign they had been so eager to call. The New Democrats, although better prepared than the Conservatives and Liberals, did not, and still do not, have a meaningful political organization in Quebec.

Even though Gilles Duceppe and the Bloc had experienced a major setback in the 2000 election, they could count on a well-organized party base throughout Quebec as well as the PQ organization. In addition, the party had spent a lot of energy recruiting members, holding party and riding conventions, and elaborating its electoral platform. One must not forget that the planned election call was strongly rumoured to be April 4, and that it was not until late February that it became clear that it would be postponed by Martin. The BQ had planned for an early spring election well ahead of time, and thus it was ready to get on the hustings whenever Martin's Liberals were ready to initiate the move.

As the results rolled in on election night, it became clear that what the polls had indicated throughout the campaign would be confirmed (see Figure 1). Quebec voters gave Duceppe and the Bloc an enviable score: fifty-four MPs out of a possible seventy-five, garnering no less than 48.8 percent of the popular vote. Duceppe came within a hair of outperforming Lucien Bouchard's impressive results of 1993 (fifty-four MPs and 49.3 percent). Paul Martin's Liberals were reduced to twenty-one MPs in Quebec, appealing to 33.9 percent of the popular vote, compared to 33 percent for Chrétien in 1993 (nineteen MPs) following the Meech Lake debacle and 30.3 percent for John Turner in 1988 (twelve MPs) at the time of the free trade debate. In Quebec, Martin's electoral appeal was even worse than that of Turner in 1984, when he obtained 35.4 percent (seventeen MPs) in the first federal election after Trudeau's repatriation of the constitution.

The Liberals, with dwindling majorities, held on to their bastions only on the island of Montreal and in the Outaouais region, except for the ridings of Denis Paradis in the Eastern Townships and Claude Drouin in the Beauce region, which were won respectively by majorities of 1,072 and 2,424 votes. Very close races were won by the Liberals in ridings that had been historical shoo-ins for them. In the Outaouais region, the Bloc came surprisingly close to winning Gatineau, coming within one thousand votes of the Liberal candidate. In Montreal, Pierre Pettigrew won the riding of Papineau by less than five hundred votes; Heleni Bakopanos in Ahuntsic won her riding by less than three hundred; and Liza Frulla almost went down to defeat in her Verdun riding (Jeanne-le-Ber), owing her victory to a judicial recount that gave her a meagre seventy vote majority. A couple of thousand more votes sprinkled here and there for the BQ and there would have been sixty sovereignist MPs heading to Ottawa.

Duceppe and the Bloc had a very good election night in terms of diversification of its caucus. Most notably, the newly elected Serge

Figure 1

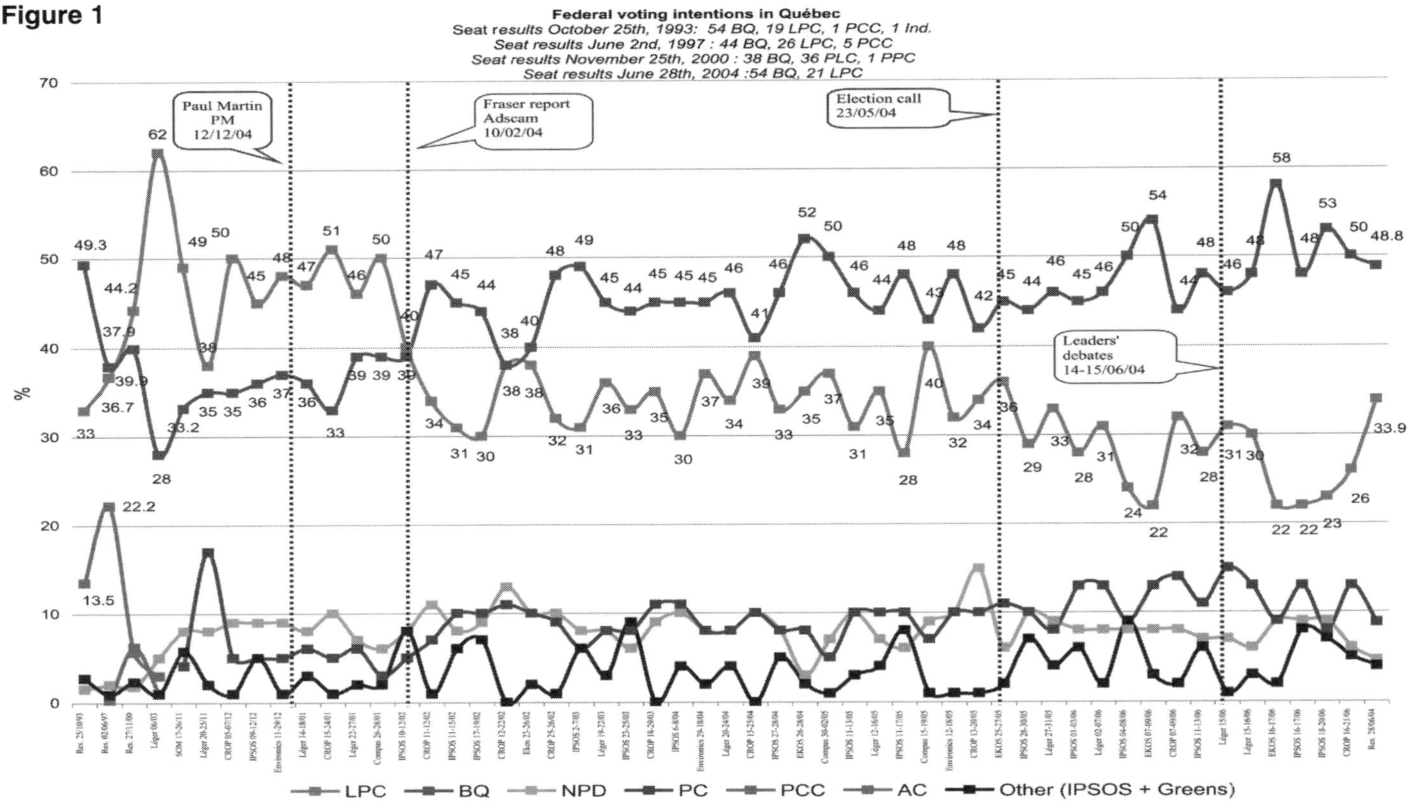
Federal voting intentions in Québec
Seat results October 25th, 1993: 54 BQ, 19 LPC, 1 PCC, 1 Ind.
Seat results June 2nd, 1997 : 44 BQ, 26 LPC, 5 PCC
Seat results November 25th, 2000 : 38 BQ, 36 PLC, 1 PPC
Seat results June 28th, 2004 :54 BQ, 21 LPC
Paul Martin PM 12/12/04
Fraser report Adscam 10/02/04
Election call 23/05/04
Leaders' debates 14-15/06/04
%
70
60
50
40
30
20
10
0
LPC
BQ
NPD
PC
PCC
AC
Other (IPSOS + Greens)

Ménard in Laval, ex-PQ minister of justice and public security, seems to represent an infusion of experience and maturity, and the election of Maka Kotto in Saint-Lambert and Meili Faille in Vaudreuil-Soulanges added a long desired presence of cultural communities to the BQ representation in Parliament.

Voter turnout declined, with only 59 percent of eligible voters going to the polls, the worst in a federal election in Quebec's modern times. Usually, low voter turnout is very bad news for the sovereignist movement, either in a Quebec election or a federal one, since its electoral base tends to be among the younger generation as well as francophones, two categories that tend to vote less than traditional Liberal voters. The latter stem disproportionately from older people who have a stronger sense of civic duty and, until recently it appears, from cultural communities in the greater Montreal region who also vote in very large numbers.

To get a better sense of the results obtained by the Bloc at this crucial election, this chapter will be divided into four sections. The first section will review recent events that have given meaning to the current Bloc successes. In the second section, we will closely examine the political strategy deployed by the BQ to undermine Paul Martin as well as present an account of the political impact of Auditor General Sheila Fraser's sponsorship report. Part III provides an in-depth analysis of the 2004 campaign and identifies key materials that explain the political mood at the time and its repercussions for the evolving Canadian party system. Finally, the fourth section casts some light on the changing political behaviour of second- and third-generation immigrants in Quebec and its consequences for party strategists.

ENTERING CANADA'S POLITICAL SCENE AND NAVIGATING WHITE WATERS, 1990–2003

It has been fourteen years since Quebec elected its first sovereignist Bloc Québécois MP in a federal by-election, current party leader Gilles Duceppe in the Montreal riding of Laurier-Sainte-Marie. At the time of that by-election, the Meech Lake Accord had entered the history books as a great constitutional failure. That particular context led to the 1993 federal election in which then Bloc Leader Lucien Bouchard pushed the party beyond expectations with 49.3 percent of the popular vote in Quebec, claiming fifty-four out of the seventy-five ridings, outperforming Preston Manning's Reform Party by two seats and becoming Canada's Official Opposition in the House of Commons. Canada had then a full-fledged separatist as leader of the opposition, giving a daily grilling to the prime minister of the time, Liberal Leader Jean Chrétien. From 1993 to 1996, the Bloc was a powerful force in Parliament, pointing out tirelessly that Quebec would not accept mere provincial status within the federation.

Things had changed, however, by the time of the narrow defeat of the referendum on sovereignty in 1995. Its founding leader, Lucien Bouchard, headed to Quebec City to become Quebec premier, and the federal sovereignist party entered into a period of turmoil. After a full year of infighting that led to the resignation of interim leader Michel Gauthier and a bitter leadership battle, the Liberals shrewdly called the 1997 federal election only a few weeks after Gilles Duceppe had been elected leader of the BQ. With so little time to prepare, the Bloc and Duceppe entered a general election with a fractious party, and their campaign was fraught with a series of mishaps and mistakes.

Throughout this transition period and the apparent absence of any desire by Quebec to plunge back into a debate about either sovereignty or the constitution, disaffection in Quebec toward the federal government persisted, further exacerbated by controversial remarks made by Jean Chrétien.[2] Although the Bloc lost ten ridings and 11.4 percent of the popular vote in 1997, the party came out on top with a majority of ridings in Quebec (forty-four MPs and 37.9 percent versus twenty-six MPs and 36.7 percent for the Liberals). It is also important to underline that many Bloc MPs benefited from a relatively strong performance on the part of the federal Conservatives, then led by Jean Charest, which garnered 22.2 percent of the vote in Quebec, thus dividing the federalist vote in many ridings (five Conservative MPs were elected). Even though a majority of Bloc MPs were elected in 1997, the party had to rebuild its organization and regain credibility. The Bloc Québécois spent the next three years consolidating its militant base with a series of forums on identity and globalization, as well as defending Quebec's interests in Ottawa and discussing the advantages of full-fledged sovereignty. On the political front, two issues were at the centre of the BQ's actions in the federal capital. First, unemployment insurance, where the federal reforms of the past years hurt Quebec workers — in particular seasonal labourers — and second, Jean Chrétien and Stéphane Dion's reference to the Supreme Court of Canada on Quebec secession, which led eventually to the adoption of the Clarity Act.

Before the November 2000 election was called, both the objectives of having a better organization and gaining credibility on salient issues appeared to have been met. The party was more unified than in 1997 and Gilles Duceppe's leadership was essentially unchallenged. The press started to recognize the Bloc's seriousness on major issues, thus giving the party better visibility and quality coverage. But one main thorn remained in the Bloc's side: Quebec's public opinion seemed to continue to shy away from sovereignty and constitutional issues, perhaps even more so than was the case in 1997. The party ran a very smooth and uneventful campaign in 2000, sticking to federal issues that caused discontent within the Quebec electorate and steering away from sovereignty issues. Not to be neglected, the departure of Jean Charest from the federal Conservatives in 1998 to lead the Quebec Liberals helped Jean Chrétien unify the federalist vote.

On election night, even though Duceppe's campaign did not experience one single glitch, the Bloc lost six additional MPs and saw Jean Chrétien win the Quebec popular vote (thirty-eight MPs and 39.9 percent for the BQ compared to thirty-six MPs and 44.2 percent for the Liberals). For the first time since the repatriation of the Canadian constitution in 1982, the Liberal Party of Canada obtained the largest share of votes in Quebec. Gilles Duceppe, and the sovereignist movement in general, took solace in the fact that the Bloc held on to a majority of Quebec seats and did slightly better than in 1997, garnering 2 percent more of the popular vote. However, the Bloc lost about eight thousand votes between 1997 and 2000. For all the efforts undertaken by Duceppe to rebuild the party since the departure of Lucien Bouchard to become Quebec premier, the future nevertheless looked very dim and the prospects for the Bloc very unappealing. The Bloc was set for a difficult period. With the sovereignty option hovering around 40 percent and sometimes even dipping below that psychological threshold, the Bloc appeared to no longer have the wind in its sails.

Early in the year 2001, a political bombshell would come to rest on the lap of Gilles Duceppe's Bloc and the Parti Québécois: Lucien Bouchard announced his resignation as premier of Quebec in the middle of a mandate obtained in 1998. In his resignation speech, the first reason mentioned was his incapacity to revive the sovereignist flame since he took office in 1996. Bouchard then went on to stress Quebecers' muted reaction to federal intrusions into Quebec's jurisdictions and to the adoption of the Clarity Bill in Ottawa as a sign that his efforts seemed to have been in vain. He concluded by stating that he could no longer perceive himself as the man of the hour and wished a new leader to emerge who could lead Quebec to sovereignty.[3] It became clear that Quebec's federal election results had been a watershed, with Jean Chrétien's Liberals improving even upon Lucien Bouchard's own showing of 1998.

As Bernard Landry took over from Bouchard as Quebec premier, trying desperately to shore up the PQ's political fortunes, Duceppe confronted many challenges both on substantive issues and within his own party. As a series of by-elections that the PQ had to call approached, the first signal of discomfort within BQ ranks came from the defection of MP Stéphan Tremblay, who announced in March 2002 that he would enter the race for the PQ candidacy in the riding of Lac-Saint-Jean, left vacant by ex-PQ minister Jacques Brassard.[4] Two months later, BQ MP Michel Bellehumeur did the same, explaining that he would run in the riding of Joliette that opened up due to the resignation of a PQ minister, Guy Chevrette.[5] Rumours of other Bloc MP's wanting to defect were rampant. The June 2002 by-elections were a disaster for the PQ, losing two strongholds to the then-promising ADQ and barely hanging on to the other, with Stéphan Tremblay winning a close call.[6]

Sovereignty continued to stay off the radar screen in Quebec, and the Bloc by then trailed the Liberals badly in the polls (see Figure 1). In August 2002, Jean Chrétien, after much hesitation, announced that he would be retiring in February 2004, giving himself an eighteen-month going away present in power. Freed of the normal constraints of politics, he put forward an ambitious activist agenda: adoption of the Kyoto accord, decriminalization of marijuana, legalization of same-sex marriages, radical reform to the federal party financing legislation — limiting corporate and union donations to political parties to $1,000 annually — and refusal to join George Bush's "Coalition of the Willing" in Iraq. All of these issues were the political bread and butter of the Bloc, having overall support in Quebec. Even though federal intrusions into Quebec's jurisdictions had not come to a halt and many basic issues still were unresolved between Ottawa and Quebec City — financing Quebec's ambitious universal daycare policy, social union, and fiscal imbalance between Ottawa and the provinces, for example — Chrétien's popularity rose to new heights (see Figure 1). With the prospect of Paul Martin, the most popular politician Quebec had seen in a very long time, soon becoming PM, Bloc MPs became uneasy and more vocal in their discontent.

The signing of an agreement between the Quebec government and the Innu nation on the Quebec North Shore became a lightning rod issue within the BQ caucus in August 2002 when Ghislain Lebel, BQ MP for Chambly, published a long letter in the Montreal Daily *La Presse*, accusing the Quebec Premier Bernard Landry of treason against the sovereignist movement and the Quebec nation because of his action.[7] Duceppe wanted to cut short the debate on this issue, fully supporting Landry in his quest for better and stronger relations between First Nations and the Quebec people. But many in the BQ caucus were wary of the content of the agreement, partly agreeing with Lebel's stance, a sentiment reinforced by the support for some of Lebel's criticism that came from former PQ leader Jacques Parizeau, which also contributed to additional dissent within PQ ranks.[8] Duceppe finally agreed to let the debate take place within the BQ caucus by inviting experts to explain the agreement, but maintained a hard line against Lebel's accusation of treason towards Landry, making a public apology on Lebel's part a condition for remaining within the caucus. Lebel chose to leave the caucus and decided to sit as an independent MP.[9]

A soothing balm came in December 2002, when the Bloc won the two federal by-elections that had to be called due to the departures of BQ MPs Tremblay and Bellehumeur, but this reprieve would not last very long. The beginning of 2003 signalled more turmoil. In January, BQ MP Pierre Brien announced he would be running under the banner of the ADQ in the upcoming Quebec general election.[10] Considering his right-leaning political views, his defection to the ADQ did not surprise those who followed Quebec politics closely. But what rattled the sovereignist movement was Brien's claim that Quebec sovereignty should no longer be a central issue for Quebecers — that its time had passed. More sovereignist defections to the ADQ would follow, reinforcing the idea that hopes for sovereignty were vanishing. Soon after Brien's move to the ADQ, another BQ MP, Antoine Dubé, decided to run for the PQ in the spring.[11] Again, rumours of other Bloc MPs' departures were swirling.

As if this weren't enough, Bloc MP Pierrette Venne decided she had had enough of Gilles Duceppe's leadership and contested it outright publicly, calling for a leadership convention and arguing that Duceppe could no longer exercise ascendance over his caucus.[12] The Bloc leader seemed to have no other choice but to expel her and have her sit as an independent MP, since she refused to support him or the

Table 1: Evolution of Quebec Representation in the House of Commons, 2000–2004

Party	Number of MPs elected in election 2000	Number of MPs on the eve of election 2004	Number of MPs elected on June 28, 2004
BQ	38	33	54
LPC	36	37	21
PCC	1	0	0
Independents	0	4*	0
Vacant	0	1**	0
Total	75	75	75

* The only Progressive Conservative elected in 2000 in Quebec, André Bachand (Richmond-Arthabaska), refused to sit as a Conservative after the merger between the Canadian Alliance and the Progressive Conservative Party. He became an independent and did not run in the 2004 election. Furthermore, Jean-Guy Carignan (Liberal, Québec-Est), excluded from the liberal caucus in October 2002 and thereafter reinstated, was excluded again in October 2003. Ghislain Lebel and Pierrette Venne were the other two independents and also did not run in the 2004 election.

** When Jean Chrétien resigned on December 12, 2003, the riding of St-Maurice was left vacant.

party program, to reaffirm his authority on the caucus and party.[13] Duceppe's firm action towards Venne had lukewarm success in reunifying a crumbling caucus. The Bloc and Duceppe had lost the advantage of being able to say it held a majority of Quebec seats in the House of Commons, with the Liberals occupying thirty-six and the BQ holding on to only thirty-four (see Table 1). The worst was yet to come.

March 12, 2003, was the day that Premier Landry called the Quebec provincial election. In the previous months, Quebec voters had proved themselves to be politically volatile, electing three candidates for Mario Dumont's ADQ in the June 2002 by-elections. Polls revealed that an ADQ government was a serious possibility during the spring and summer of that year,[14] shortly thereafter indicating that the next general election would be a close call due to a three-way race along with Jean Charest's Liberals. Finally, in the days leading up to the election call, the polls reverted back to showing a possible third mandate for the PQ.[15] The hopes of the sovereignist movement and the Bloc Québécois were once again high after more than two years of deceptions and uproar. The PQ lead in the polls eroded slowly throughout the campaign until just before the leaders' debate, when again it looked like the election would be a three-way race. Then came the *coup de grâce*. As he had done many times before, Jacques Parizeau came back to haunt Landry right in the middle of the debate. Referring to a press report that Parizeau had restated his controversial remarks pronounced on referendum night in 1995, Charest demanded that Landry disavow him on the spot. Landry refused to condemn Parizeau before hearing him out.[16] From that point on, Charest seemed in control, right up to election night on April 14, which saw Quebec Liberals seize power with 46 percent of the popular vote, leaving Landry the role of leader of the opposition with 33 percent — one of the lowest scores for the PQ since 1976 — and Dumont's ADQ at 18 percent, managing to get only four members elected to Quebec's National Assembly.

The fact that the sovereignists had lost power in Quebec for the first time in almost a decade with one of the poorest showings for the PQ in its thirty-five year history, combined with the Bloc holding only a minority of Quebec seats in the House of Commons, resulted in plenty of speculation about the demise of the sovereignist movement. This idea was reinforced in June by two federal by-elections that were lost to the Liberals, ridings held by the Bloc since 1993. Federalists in Quebec and in the rest of Canada were jubilant at the idea that Paul Martin, a well-known Liberal who polled well in Quebec and was expected to do much better than Jean Chrétien had, was on his way to replace him at the helm of the federal government. Just as Martin was to be sworn in as prime minister in December 2003, BQ MP Robert Lanctôt, sensing Quebec sovereignty's and the BQ's days were numbered, crossed the floor of the House to sit with the Liberals whom he had previously denounced.[17] The count for the Bloc and Duceppe was then thirty-three MPs, and polls were showing they would be wiped off the electoral map by the Martin juggernaut.[18]

A FEDERAL ELECTION IN THE OFFING

Just as prospects appeared most dire, the Bloc and Duceppe embarked on a concerted effort to put a dent in the political armour of Paul Martin. First, the BQ wanted to show that Martin was the one responsible for the fiscal imbalance between Quebec and Ottawa and to paint a broader picture of the misdeeds of the new prime minister when he was still minister of finance. To do so, the party published, between January and April 2004, three studies pertaining to federal finances written under the capable leadership of ex-Treasury Board PQ minister Jacques Léonard. Those studies dealt respectively with: a) the loss of control of federal finances, the report revealing that the federal government's basic operating expenses rose 39 percent over five years;[19] b) federal intrusions into provincial jurisdictions, stating that the government at that point spent more in provincial jurisdictions than in its own fields of competence;[20] and finally, c) federal transfers to the provinces, indicating that when all transfers since 1994 are taken into account, federal revenues went up by 45 percent, whereas the transfers inched up by only 1.9 percent.[21]

Second, in parallel with this strategy, the BQ wanted to discredit Martin as a good taxpayer and corporate citizen. Duceppe and the Bloc set out to associate Martin more closely with the activities of his holdings, Canada Steamship Lines (CSL) and affiliated companies, recently sold to his sons. They denounced the fact that CSL did not respect workers' rights and basic environmental standards, as well as operated under flags of convenience, thus depriving the federal treasury of $100 million in annual taxes that it would have received if the company's head office had been on Canadian soil.[22] This was in addition to the accusations made by the Bloc that Martin tailored a piece of legislation for the benefit of CSL while he was minister of finance.[23] To support these claims, the BQ published a book entitled *The Paul Martin Myth* under the pen of Bloc MP Louis Plamondon, summarizing what the party thought the new prime minister stood for: mismanagement, encroachment into provincial jurisdictions, and cozying up to Canadian corporate needs. The book was also aimed to link Martin to everything that was considered wrong during the Chrétien era.[24]

Finally, and not to be neglected, the new political party financing law put in place by Jean Chrétien[25] gave the Bloc a huge present in the form of public funding. As of January 2004, donations to federal political parties were limited to personal ones of up to $5,000 and corporate ones to a maximum of $1,000 per year. This was seen as a political victory for the BQ because until very recently it had strictly followed Quebec's political financing regulations of no corporate donations, even sparking an internal party debate about being on an equal financial footing with other federal parties, notably the Liberals, and leading to the adoption of an internal rule to allow corporate donations of up to $5,000. But the real gift to the BQ were the regulations within the new law about public financing of federal political parties. Registered parties that had done better than 2 percent overall and 5 percent in local ridings in the previous federal general election would receive $1.75 per elector who had voted for them. Due to the passing of this new law, Duceppe's Bloc received its biggest ever donation from the federal government, well before the election was called, an amount evaluated at $2.4 million. Combining this with its own financing campaign, its coffers were full to the brim.[26] The party would spend its biggest amount to date in a general election.

At the beginning of February 2004 things started to come around for the BQ. The party rose slightly in the polls, approaching the 40 percent threshold. This was still not enough to hope for a rescue from a humiliating defeat, since Paul Martin's Liberals were still ahead, hovering between 45 and 50 percent[27](see Figure 1). But the month of February would hold the key to a dramatic political reversal. On February 10, 2004, Sheila Fraser, Canada's Auditor General, released a scathing report on waste, mismanagement, and possible political misdealings in the federal Department of Public Works.[28] By establishing a federal program following the 1995 referendum to sponsor every festival and cultural activity in Quebec, Jean Chrétien's government funnelled huge amounts of money to Liberal-friendly advertising firms, which, in turn, could contribute to the well-being of the party.

This scandal had been brewing for quite some time. Strong rumours of a sponsorship program aimed at shoring up Canada's image in Quebec were circulating freely. Since 1995, the Bloc had put a lot of effort into denouncing covert federal activities to promote Canadian unity in Quebec. Every year, the BQ would criticize the one-sided financing of Canada Day festivities, with Quebec receiving more than 75 percent of the allotted budget for the whole country, again handled by well-known friends of the Liberal Party.[29] Data released by the Bloc's research staff put spending for Canadian unity in Quebec since 1995 at around half a billion dollars.[30] In 1996, Sheila Copps was responsible not just for the free distribution of Canadian flags but also for creating the Federal Information Bureau (this new program would end a long-running cooperation between the Quebec and Canadian governments on a single telephone number for information about government services to establish Ottawa's 1-800-O Canada! line), which would lead to an indirect and secret financing of the series "Le Canada du millénaire" on the French *Newsworld* of the CBC through known Liberal friends. When the news of this financing was made public, CBC executives terminated the series.[31]

At the time, the Liberals and Jean Chrétien benefited from the fact that the Alliance, the Progressive Conservatives, and the New Democrats did not appear interested in decrying such findings, apparently convinced that the electorate in the rest of Canada believed that this overspending in Quebec was necessary to save the country from breakup. They seemed to approve of Chrétien's strategy by turning a blind eye to it. But the attitude of the other parties in the House of Commons started to change when the amounts coming out of the public purse rose to new heights and it was revealed that political interference in the administrative process had been occurring. First, revelations contained within an internal audit of certain work training programs in the federal Human Resources Department showed that sponsorship spending was astronomical, reportedly reaching into the billions of dollars, involving friends of the Liberal Party, with the RCMP being called in to investigate cases of possible fraud.[32] Second, the situation was worsened by the nomination of Alfonso Gagliano (then responsible for the program that was going to spawn the sponsorship scandal) as Canadian ambassador to Denmark, as Jean Chrétien preemptively removed him from the political fire and scrutiny. Third, the Groupaction affair, made public in May 2002, put the sponsorship scandal on the political map with revelations of lost reports, contracts for no work done, and troubling relations between ministers and the heads of some Quebec advertising firms.[33]

The Auditor General of Canada, Sheila Fraser, was called upon to take a closer look at the sponsorship program in the Public Works Department, which led to the release of the now famous report on February 10, 2004, that was to provide key ammunition in the BQ campaign. Fraser herself stated that what she found was an unspeakable and blatant misappropriation of public funds.[34] The report was not only about a scandal confined to Public Works; it involved Crown corporations — Via Rail, the Business Development Bank of Canada (BDC), Canada Post, and even the RCMP — as intermediaries in the flow of money going to Liberal-friendly advertising firms in Quebec.[35]

Paul Martin, prime minister since December 2002, decided to take a very different approach than Chrétien towards the political scandal: he called back Gagliano from Denmark, fired Jean Pelletier, Jean Chrétien's chief of staff who was then Via Rail CEO, and Michel Vennat, CEO of the BDC, and suspended André Ouellet, CEO of Canada Post. Moreover, Martin agreed to fully cooperate with the Parliament's public accounts committee that would try to get to the bottom of the scandal and set up a public inquiry headed by Judge John H. Gomery. With hindsight, it seems that he made some strategic miscalculations. As Martin readily admitted that what happened was unacceptable, he maintained that he knew nothing of what was going on at Public Works, even though he was at the time finance minister, vice-president of the Treasury Board, and the most prominent Quebec minister in cabinet, blaming a small group of rogue bureaucrats at the department for the whole affair.[36] Seeing that the political fallout from the scandal could be enormous and that political ties above the bureaucrats' heads could not be ruled out, he changed his tune the next day, publicly laying veiled accusations that there existed a political direction to the whole affair, while maintaining his position that he knew nothing about it.[37]

Political fortunes of the federal Liberals in Quebec took a turn for the worst almost immediately after the publication of the Fraser report. In the rest of Canada, the Liberal Party took a nosedive of over ten points in the polls, putting them in a possible minority position, and, in Quebec, where the thought that the federal government could simply buy Quebecers' allegiance to the country added to the smell of cronyism, the Liberals tumbled by twenty points. Within a month, the Bloc Québécois went from political oblivion to the possibility of improving on Bouchard's remarkable showing of 1993[38] (see Figure 1). Everything was now smiling on Duceppe and the BQ, with the political inferno of the past three-and-a-half years behind them as the party got ready for the electoral fight to come.

THE BLOC PLATFORM AND ITS CAMPAIGN

As for every federal general election, the Bloc Québécois elaborated a very thorough and comprehensive electoral platform for the 2004 election.[39] Even though the BQ consciously does not run candidates elsewhere in Canada and therefore excludes itself from the possibility of forming or being a part of government, the party platform not only reflects its willingness to explain its defence of Quebec's interests in Ottawa and why Quebec should become a sovereign state but also provides a rigorous critique of every government portfolio and public department, including clear proposals to remedy the problems identified. Ironically, one could find in the BQ platform a complete government agenda.

Why does the Bloc choose to do such extensive research and put forward such a complete agenda for a country from which it seeks Quebec's departure? After the 1993 general election, Lucien Bouchard understood quite well that the Bloc, then the official opposition, could undermine Canada's political and democratic institutions and deliberately try to make it impossible for them to function properly. Of course, Canadians would not stand for this, nor would Quebecers, who would shun this type of behaviour. Consequently, during the 1993 campaign and after, Bouchard promised that the Bloc, even though it was seeking sovereignty for Quebec, would be a responsible political force in Parliament, not only criticizing government but also seriously trying to make it work by putting forth constructive ideas for both Quebec and Canada as a whole.[40] The Bloc, throughout all general elections since, has maintained this pledge.

The party's political discourse and platform are distinctly centre-left of the political spectrum. Of course, with sovereignty as its main objective, the BQ consists of a coalition of divergent political elements, attracting both right- and left-of-centre militants, as ex-MP Pierre Brien's move to the Quebec ADQ demonstrates. Were it not for its desire to attain sovereignty and its strict defence of Quebec's jurisdiction, the Bloc could theoretically be equated with the centralizing federal New Democrats, although its whole caucus would not be able to sustain such a political banner, as some MPs would probably feel more comfortable with the Conservatives. Ideologically, the BQ mainly stands for balanced budgets, sound fiscal management of public funds, comprehensive and progressive social policies, multilateralism in external affairs, progressive curbs on globalization, and a foreign policy based on compassion. The party's platform, beyond sovereignty and defending Quebec's autonomy, stands for these basic points of view.

The Bloc wishes to be in tune with how the Quebec electorate sees itself, how it wishes to be governed, and how the public purse should be shared. On defending Quebec's interests, Duceppe and his party echo the basic issues that are largely consensual among the Quebec people: eliminating the fiscal imbalance between Ottawa and the provinces, re-establishing federal fiscal transfers to the provinces in the health care system without any strings attached, and suggested compensation by the federal government for Quebec's progressive social policies such as its very popular daycare program. During the 2004 election, on general issues, the Bloc stood for strong environmental standards and sustainable development, and thus for a comprehensive implementation of the Kyoto accord; for major investments in social housing and greater accessibility to employment insurance benefits; against both armed intervention in Iraq and Canadian participation in the U.S. North American missile shield initiative; for reassessment by Parliament of international trade treaties; and in favour of Canada's commitment to make 0.7 percent of its gross domestic product available to foreign aid. On moral issues, the party has also adopted highly popular ideas in Quebec by promoting same-sex marriages and the decriminalization of marijuana. Duceppe's Bloc Québécois, with such a platform, was speaking to almost every issue concerning Quebecers and had all the ideological tools for success.

Musings about the date of the election call continued until the middle of May, as different dates for the election were spun continuously by the PMO and Liberal Party throughout the month of April. The Bloc did not wait for the election call to hit the hustings. In January 2004, the party launched its pre-campaign with the slogan "because we are different,"[41] touring Quebec extensively until the effective election call. Duceppe decided to launch his electoral campaign officially on May 15[42] even though Paul Martin would not visit the Governor General before May 23 to drop the writ. His tour bus was ready to go and his agenda full, one week before the Liberals would do the same, hitting the front pages of Quebec's dailies with the Bloc's remarkable campaign slogan "*Pour un parti propre au Québec*."[43] This slogan was a play on words, "*propre*" in French and in this context meaning both "clean" and "Quebec specific," thus summarizing the Bloc's objective of campaigning on the sponsorship scandal, suggesting that the Liberals were in a sense "dirty" and not vigorously defending Quebec's interests in Ottawa. This first political salvo by the BQ sent the Liberals screaming that it was dirty politics.[44]

The first week of the campaign was punctuated by controversial comments by Jean Lapierre, a Martin supporter in the 1990 Liberal leadership race, a Bloc founder in the early 1990s, and now Paul Martin's Quebec lieutenant, who invoked the possibility of a Liberal minority only two days into the campaign.[45] Lapierre would become a lightning rod for everything that went wrong during the campaign for the Liberals in Quebec as well as in the rest of Canada. By the second week of the campaign the Bloc, because of polls showing that a minority government was a distinct possibility and that Duceppe would sweep Quebec, was confronted continuously with questions about how the party would act if it held the balance of power. Its answer was clear: what is good for Quebec we will vote for, what is not, we will oppose.[46] Not much else was brought up, save for political infighting in the Quebec wing of the Liberal Party as most of the people close to Jean Chrétien were left on the sidelines. Martin and Lapierre even had to call a truce between the two factions to unify the party and hope for better fortunes in the weeks to come.[47] The campaign rolled along, and Duceppe went from event to event without much controversy, leading the media to dub his tour bus "the bubble" because nothing seemed to perturb the Bloc's campaign. However, journalists accused Duceppe of trying to avoid direct contact with ordinary citizens in order to maintain an apparently flawless performance.[48]

In essence, there were two campaigns taking place in Canada. In the rest of Canada, the health care system and moral values were at the core of the political battles. In Quebec, Duceppe's possible sweep and how the Bloc would manage the balance of power, the sponsorship scandal, and, on a minor scale, federal reinvestment in health care through transfer payments, seemed to be the only relevant issues.[49] Duceppe downplayed sovereignty by arguing that a federal election was not the moment to decide Quebec's future on this matter but never missed an occasion to remind his followers and Quebecers that he and his party were sovereignists, thus taking the only wedge issue out of the campaign.

The French leaders' debates yielded a clear winner, Gilles Duceppe,[50] while the English debate resulted in a strong rating for the sovereignist leader in the rest of Canada (See Chapter Eleven). By the luck of the draw, Duceppe got the first and final word in the French debate. He also came quite close to a knockout punch when he asked Martin how much money was left in the employment insurance fund, which is supposedly independent from government revenues, and Martin could not provide a satisfying answer, letting Duceppe answer for him: zero dollars, because the Liberals had used the $40-billion surplus to pay off the deficit.[51] In the English debate, the Bloc leader held his ground on the sponsorship scandal, asking Martin repeatedly what he knew and when he knew it, and getting no straight answer. His English performance led to a surprising appreciation in the rest of Canada, the Bloc even showing up in the polls in British Columbia, Manitoba, and Saskatchewan, and demand for interviews in the English media skyrocketed.[52]

For the Bloc, everything was going smoothly and election day could not come fast enough. The party was riding high in the polls, too high for Duceppe's liking, as he feared demobilization and voter abstention among his supporters who might perceive their vote as unnecessary (see Figure 1). Moreover, with his remarkable campaign and debate performances, Duceppe was even touted as a possible replacement for Landry as PQ leader.[53] The Liberals, on the other hand, were in a state of panic. Although Martin had looked past Stéphane Dion for a ministerial portfolio in December 2003, trying to signal a new era in federal-provincial relations,[54] he called upon him in the last days of the campaign to try somehow to get things going in Quebec. A press conference was called by Jean Lapierre, Stéphane Dion, and Pierre Pettigrew with the objective of warning Quebecers that if they voted for the BQ, it would be the first step towards another referendum.[55] It was quite ironic to see an ex-founder of the Bloc, the father of the Clarity Act, and Claude Ryan's old chief of staff on the same panel, considering their well-known distinct political views about Quebec's role in the federation.

The next day, controversial comments by PQ Leader Bernard Landry hit the front page of the *Globe and Mail* that seemed to confirm what the three Quebec Liberal candidates had to say. Landry was quoted as saying that the election of sixty Bloc MPs would hasten sovereignty, leading to a referendum in 2009.[56] This was counter to what Duceppe was saying all through the campaign, and the Liberals tried desperately to seize the occasion to gain momentum, but it was much too late with only a few days to go before the vote. With polls showing them leagues ahead, Duceppe and the BQ decided to campaign in some of Montreal's Liberal strongholds, convinced they could make inroads in these usually very difficult ridings.[57]

CHARTING NEW TERRITORY

So why did Duceppe and the Bloc do so well in Quebec? The still sketchy numbers point to two main reasons: an apathetic Liberal constituency and significant sovereignist inroads among an older and more diversified Quebec electorate. Sovereignists came out to vote in large numbers, as many Liberals seem to have stayed home. Considering the fact that the Bloc garnered almost 300,000 more votes than in 2000 and the Liberals lost almost 370,000 voters with a 5.1 percent drop in participation in general (see Tables 2 and 3), the BQ outperformed the Liberals in getting out their respective voting constituencies. Looking at the difference in the number of Bloc and Liberal voters since 1997 is even more telling (BQ +286,363 votes, LPC –182,688; see Table 2). These numbers show that the Bloc has closed its vote gap with its 1993 results by almost two-thirds. It is clear that old Liberal voters and potential new ones just did not make it to the voting booth, whereas the sovereignist electoral machine came within roughly 175,000 voters of equalling their 1993 showing in a dismal participation context (18.1 percent drop in voter turnout since 1993; see Table 3). Louis Massicotte's studies of voter turnout in each Quebec riding during federal elections, including 2004, point in the same direction, essentially demonstrating that contrary to 2000, sovereignist voters came out strongly and Liberal voters did not.[58]

One can put forth the hypothesis that the Bloc's success is partly due to a breakthrough among older voters as well as within communities of recent immigration. Some important evidence supports this claim. First, a poll was published a few days before the election stating that for the first time, Duceppe's party garnered a majority of voter intentions among voters fifty-five and older.[59] This is very surprising since this category of voters has demonstrated in the past that it has never favoured the BQ, the PQ, or Quebec sovereignty, even in the final days of the referendum campaign in 1995. No analysis of the results can clearly confirm this, since there are no ridings that contain a significant enough older population to verify this trend, but one could advance the idea that this is where the sponsorship scandal hurt the most. As the public health system and good management of the

Table 2: Number of Votes Obtained by Federal Parties in Quebec, 1993–2004

	1993	1997		2000		2004		Diff.
Party	Votes	Votes	Diff.	Votes	Diff.	Votes	Diff.	1997–2004
BQ	1,846,024	1,385,821	-460,203	1,377,727	-8,094	1,672,184	+294,457	+286,363
LPC	1,235,868	1,342,567	+106,699	1,529,642	+187,075	1,159,879	-369,763	-182,688
PC*	506,683	822,177	+315,494	405,027	-417,150	300,499	-104,528	-521,678
NDP	57,339	71,558	+14,219	63,611	-7,947	158,838	+95,227	+87,280

*PC = PCC + Reform for 1993 and 1997, PCC + AC for 2000.

Table 3: Voter Turnout in Quebec Federal Elections, 1993–2004

	Eligible voters	Valid votes	%	Diff.
1993	5,025,263	3,744,201	77.1	
1997	5,177,159	3,659,895	73.3	-3.8
2000	5,542,169	3,456,898	64.1	-9.2
2004	5,803,390	3,424,713	59.0	-5.1

public purse are major issues with older voters, seeing millions of dollars misspent and perhaps misappropriated to buy Quebec's adherence to the federation surely did not shore up Liberal fortunes here.[60]

Second, cultural communities in the greater Montreal region seem to hold the key to another shift in political views in Quebec. It has been a long-held theory that immigrants and cultural communities in Quebec do not support sovereignist parties and sovereignty, and as such vote massively for the Liberal Party, be it federal or its Quebec counterpart. They also leaned heavily to the "NO" side in the 1980 and 1995 referendums. But research done during the 1990s has slowly started to show that the situation is much more complex. Studies done by Nathalie Lavoie and Pierre Serré illustrate that second and third generations of immigrant communities to Quebec that were integrated in French due to Bill 101, the Quebec Charter of the French Language, which stipulates that they must be educated in French, adopt similar voting patterns as their "old stock" Québécois compatriots.[61] This is not to say that a majority of them support sovereignty or sovereignist parties, but their vote is certainly not monolithic, as most analysts have stated time and time again.

Polling has also slowly started to show a shift in voter intentions within these second and third generations within cultural communities, now dubbed "Children of Bill 101" in Quebec, indicating that those who were integrated in French have more positive feelings toward Quebec's French character, identity as a nation, and autonomy, and, in addition, that they tend to support sovereignty in larger numbers than their parents.[62] Immediately following the 2004 federal election, Pierre Serré felt his theory had been vindicated in view of the noted inroads obtained by the Bloc in some key Montreal ridings with a stronger concentration of cultural communities. He was cautious, however, about a major breakthrough during the campaign alone, noting that this shift was a long time in the making.[63] Incidentally, when holding their Quebec caucus in Brôme in mid-July, having had an opportunity to look at the numbers, Paul Martin's Liberals confirmed that second- and third-generation immigrant communities could no longer be taken for granted.[64]

The most probable explanation for this concrete shift in multicultural ridings in the greater Montreal region is a two-pronged one, a combination of abstention of older generations within cultural communities and a better showing for the Bloc Québécois with younger cadres. When analyzing the results in a sample of ridings with large proportions of cultural minorities in the greater Montreal region, one first notices that Liberal majorities have shrunk by an average of roughly ten thousand votes (see Table 4).[65] For these ridings to give way to such an important turnaround there must be some validity to the proposition of abstention and shift in political support within cultural communities. This would explain the very close calls that Pierre Pettigrew had in the riding of Papineau and Heleni Bakopanos had in Ahuntsic and the diminished majorities of Denis Coderre in Bourassa, Jean Lapierre in Outremont,[66] and Pablo Rodriguez in Honoré-Mercier.

All in all, the remarkable results obtained by Duceppe and the Bloc on June 28 go well beyond the simple fact of Quebec's anger at the Liberal Party of Canada due to the sponsorship scandal. It becomes clear that the Bloc's legitimate role in Ottawa[67] and its objectives of defending Quebec's interests and promoting sovereignty are generally well received by a large and now diversified Quebec electorate.

CONCLUSION

On June 29, 2004, one thing was striking from a Quebec point of view. Although Quebec sent fifty-four sovereignist MPs out of a possible seventy-five to the House of Commons and recent polling steadily reports that about 45 percent of Quebecers declare themselves sovereignists (some polls even putting that number as high as 50 percent[68]), no Canadian political leader wishes to acknowledge this enduring reality. As everyone tries to determine how Paul Martin will govern in his minority situation, very few in the rest of Canada, be it political leaders or political pundits, wish to assess the Bloc and the sovereignist movement as a whole in Quebec, save for strategic considerations. To our knowledge, only Jeffrey Simpson has questioned the federalist parties' dubious campaign strategy in Quebec.[69]

Canadians were told by the Liberal Party that all was well and safe with the Clarity Act and, until late in the election race, that Paul

Table 4: Evolution of Liberal Majorities in Multicultural Ridings in the Greater Montreal Region, 1997–2004

	1997		2000		2004			
Riding	**Party**	**Majority**	**Party**	**Majority**	**Party**	**Majority**	**Diff. 1997–2000**	**Diff. 2000–2004**
Ahuntsic	LPC	10,202	LPC	11,511	LPC	214	+1,309	-11,297
Bourassa	LPC	8,952	LPC	13,941	LPC	5,133	+4,989	-8,808
Brossard	LPC	7,334	LPC	10,048	LPC	2,559	+2,714	-7,489
Honoré-Mercier	LPC	7,631	LPC	13,379	LPC	2,762	+5,748	-10,617
Outremont	LPC	9,662	LPC	7,645	LPC	2,945	-2,018	-4,700
Papineau	LPC	12,177	LPC	12,176	LPC	468	-1	-11,708
St-Léonard	LPC	27,631	LPC	28,717	LPC	17,032	+1,086	-11,685
Vaudreuil-	LPC	6,102	LPC	8,705	BQ	3,062	+2,603	-11,767

Martin would sweep Quebec, setting to rest any problems on the constitutional front. Likewise, the Conservatives pacified Canadians with their argument about provincial rights but proved unable to get a decent electoral showing in Quebec (8.8 percent and no MPs). The NDP, as well, has been powerless to improve its fortunes with the Quebec electorate (4.6 percent and no MPs).

During the campaign, Quebec was brought up by the federalist parties only as a strategic concern. Paul Martin reiterated over and over that Quebecers should vote for him in order to prevent a Harper-led government. Harper mused continuously that Quebec needs a place at the Cabinet table without really stating why, and Jack Layton, who boldly took a fundamental stance on Quebec's unalienable rights and the Clarity Act, refused categorically to restate that position in front of the cameras. After the leaders' debates, on different news channels and in the morning papers, commentators went through the motions of identifying winners and losers, discussing momentum, but talked about Quebec and the Bloc only in terms of balance of power, saying nothing about what the election of fifty-four sovereignist MPs garnering 48.8 percent of the Quebec vote would really signify for Canada.

Gilles Duceppe stated unequivocally that he wants to defend Quebec's interests, promote Quebec sovereignty, and work on an equal footing with the rest of Canada. It seems no one was listening or even bothered to listen. Federalist leaders and the sovereignist leader seemed to be speaking past each other. Such an attitude in the rest of Canada rests largely on a false assumption: that the vote for the Bloc in this election boils down to a protest vote against the sponsorship scandal. This seems to be the way that commentators and even most Canadian politicians want to depict it, letting themselves off the hook of having to go a little deeper into the Quebec ethos.

As this chapter has illustrated, Quebecers *are* angry and frustrated about the scandal, and, of course, that reaction is partly the reason for the renewed political fortunes of the Bloc. But what is mainly forgotten in all the hubbub revolving around Adscam is that it stems directly from a political strategy that took for granted Quebecers' will to stay in the Canadian federation. Has Jean Chrétien's strategy really worked? If, after nine years, roughly 45 percent of Quebecers continue to consider sovereignty for Quebec a viable and realistic option, then it has become obvious that the Clarity Act and the will to put up the Canadian flag on every possible Quebec billboard, building, and festival are miserable failures. By refusing to see the Quebec question in this light, Conservatives and New Democrats confirm that they have no serious alternative to offer. They continue to think, convinced by the popularity of the Clarity Act in the rest of Canada, that abolishing the sponsorship program and catering to minimalist Quebec demands will be more than enough.

We appear to be now back to constitutional fundamentals. Because of a loss of appetite for anything that smacks of constitutional discussion, Quebec's refusal to sign the Canadian constitution in 1982 has become a Canadian non-event. Twenty-two years have gone by and many things have happened, but Quebecers are the ones who must continuously remind their Canadian partners that 1982, a "dangerous deed," as the late Canadian constitutionalist Donald Smiley had aptly depicted it, remains the litmus test to understanding the way Quebec sees its link to the Canadian federation. For federalist and sovereignist Quebecers, both political options remain closely affiliated with repatriation: on the one hand, Quebec federalists, even though they do not wish to bring the subject forward at the moment, cannot envisage signing the constitution before some basic criteria have been met. On the other hand, Quebec sovereignists have a very different understanding of how a signing ceremony would take place; it would entail the presence of two sovereign states. There is no other country among advanced liberal democracies that has such a flawed fundamental political contract, coupled with a federal political class that chooses to ignore the problem completely.

Following the most recent federal election of June 2004 a majority of sovereigntists occupy Quebec's seats in the federal Parliament for the fourth time in a row. All the Canadian federal parties have said over the past four elections is that they could understand Quebec's aspirations within the federal framework. Clearly this posturing has not been enough to gain Quebecers' trust back. These parties have also failed to examine their shortcomings with respect to Quebec over the years, and therefore have kept the rest of Canada blinded to one of its greatest challenges.

NOTES

1 The authors wish to thank Raffaele Iacovino, a research associate with the Canada Research Chair in Quebec and Canadian Studies at UQAM, for his thoughtful comments and insights on earlier versions.

2 Chantal Hébert, "Une majorité simple ne suffirait pas. Chrétien ne reconnaîtrait pas un OUI obtenu avec une majorité de 50% plus un," *La Presse,* May 26, 1997, A1.

3 Lucien Bouchard, "Bouchard: une décision mûrement réfléchie," *Le Droit,* January 12, 2001, 19 (excerpts of his resignation speech).

4 Raymond Giroux, "Stéphan Tremblay quitte le Bloc pour le PQ. D'autres députés pourraient le suivre," *Le Soleil,* March 15, 2002, A6.

5 Valérie Lesage, "Le bloquiste Bellehumeur confiant de relever le pari de Joliette," *Le Soleil,* May 8, 2002, A6.

6 Denis Lessard, Pascale Breton, et al., "La consécration de l'ADQ. Dumont rafle trois des quatre circonscriptions; Landry et Charest humiliés," *La Presse,* June 18, 2002, A1.

7 Joël-Denis Bellavance, "Un député bloquiste accuse le PQ de trahison," *La Presse,* August 9, 2002, A1.

8 Mario Cloutier and Emmanuel Tani-Moore, "Parizeau critique et l'entente avec les Innus et le député Lebel," *La Presse,* August 16, 2002, A1.

9 Manon Cornellier and Karine Fortin, "Lebel décroche. Pas question pour le député de faire ses excuses à Landry; il siégera comme indépendant," *Le Devoir,* August 16, 2002, A1.

10 Joël-Denis Bellavance, "Brien passe à l'ADQ. Une erreur, croit le Bloc," *La Presse,* January 14, 2003, A1.

11 Canadian Press, "Un autre député du Bloc passe au PQ," *La Presse,* February 28, 2003, A4.

12 Joël-Denis Bellavance, "Duceppe montré du doigt. Le départ de Pierre Brien crée un malaise au Bloc québécois," *La Presse,* December 17, 2002, A1.

13 Joël-Denis Bellavance, "Duceppe expulse Pierrette Venne. Quatre députés contestent la décision du chef bloquiste," *La Presse,* February 6, 2003, A1.

14 Denis Lessard, "L'effet Dumont persiste. Bon dernier, le PQ est menacé de disparaître," *La Presse,* August 24, 2002, A1.

15 Denis Lessard, "Le PQ part en tête. Les libéraux ont toutefois amorcé une lente remontée tandis que l'ADQ recule encore," *La Presse,* March 13, 2003, B1.

16 Karim Benessaieh and Mario Cloutier, "Parizeau au coeur du débat des chefs," *La Presse,* April 1, 2003, B1.

17 Joël-Denis Bellavance and Vincent Marissal, "Le bloquiste Robert Lanctôt s'en va rejoindre Paul Martin. Une 7e défection en 18 mois," *La Presse,* December 3, 2003, A3.

18 Vincent Marissal, "60 sièges pour Paul Martin?" *La Presse,* December 4, 2003, A1.

19 Bloc Québécois, Comité de révision des programmes fédéraux, "La perte de contrôle des dépenses de fonctionnement du gouvernement fédéral sous Paul Martin," January 2004, http://www2.bloc.org/2004/archivage/comite_leonard_volet_1.pdf.

20 Bloc Québécois, Comité de révision des programmes fédéraux, "Un siècle d'intrusions : les dépenses intrusives du gouvernement fédéral dans les champs de compétence du Québec et des provinces," March 2004, http://www2.bloc.org/2004/archivage/rapport_volet_ii_final.pdf.

21 Bloc Québécois, Comité de révision des programmes fédéraux, "L'étranglement financier du Québec par le gouvernement fédéral sous Paul Martin," April 2004, http://www2.bloc.org/2004/archivage/comite_leonard_volet_iii.pdf.

22 Sylvain Larocque, "CSL a évité de payer 100 millions au fisc canadien, selon le Bloc. Huit bateaux, qui appartenaient à Paul Martin, ont été incorporés dans des pays moins gourmands," *Le Devoir,* January 30, 2004, A3.

23 Gilles Toupin, "Le holding CSL à la Barbade. Martin soutient qu'il n'avait pas le choix," *La Presse,* February 6, 2004, A3.

24 Gilles Toupin, "Le Bloc tire à boulets rouges sur le nouveau chef libéral," *La Presse,* November 25, 2003, A4.

25 Gilles Toupin, "Les Communes adoptent la loi sur le financement des partis," *La Presse,* June 12, 2003, A6. See Elections Canada's Web site for all information pertaining to the new law: http://www.elections.ca.

26 Hélène Buzzetti, "Le Bloc quadruplera sa cagnotte. Le parti de Gilles Duceppe sort gagnant de la réforme du financement des partis politiques," *Le Devoir,* June 20, 2003, A1.

27 Pascale Breton, "Sondage CROP La Presse. La grogne s'amplifie envers le gouvernement Charest," *La Presse,* January 29, 2004, A4.

28 Joël-Denis Bellavance and Karim Benessaieh, "Le rapport Fraser. Gestion scandaleuse des commandites, dénonce la vérificatrice générale," *La Presse,* February 11, 2004, A1.

29 Canadian Press, "Fête du Canada. La manne au Québec," *Le Soleil,* June 11, 2000, A6.

30 Canadian Press, "Propagande fédérale," *La Presse,* May 16, 2001, A9.

31 Paul Cauchon, "RDI retire des ondes Le Canada du millénaire. La série de Robert-Guy Scully ne respecte pas la politique journalistique de la SRC," *Le Devoir,* May 12, 2000, A1. At the time this information became public, Alfonso Gagliano was responsible for implementing the program.

32 Joël-Denis Bellavance, "Fouillis au ministère de Jane Stewart: Les conservateurs sortent quelques fantômes. Le DRHC aurait subventionné des entreprises qui n'existent pas," *Le Devoir,* February 10, 2000, A4.

33 Joël-Denis Bellavance, "La GRC saisie de l'affaire Groupaction. Les hauts fonctionnaires ont contourné toutes les règles, conclut la vérificatrice générale," *La Presse,* May 9, 2002, A1.

34 Joël-Denis Bellavance and Karim Benessaieh, "Le rapport Fraser. Gestion scandaleuse des commandites, dénonce la vérificatrice générale," *La Presse,* February 11, 2004, A1.

35 Incidentally, these same Liberal-friendly Quebec advertising firms were used as go-betweens in the Bluenose II scandal in Nova Scotia; see Stephen Maher, "Bluenose contract probed; Public Works not sure what Quebec firm did with $2.3m," *The Chronicle-Herald,* March 9, 2004, B1.

36 Joël-Denis Bellavance, "Martin continue de plaider l'ignorance," *La Presse,* February 12, 2004, A1.

37 Joël-Denis Bellavance, "Martin agrandit 'le petit groupe de fonctionnaires.' Des abus dictés par des politiciens," *La Presse,* February 13, 2004, A1.

38 Gilles Toupin, "Encore plus bas. La popularité des libéraux de Paul Martin poursuit sa chute au Québec," *La Presse,* February 28, 2004, A8.

39 The complete BQ platform can be obtained at the party's Web site: http://www2.bloc.org/archivage/plate-forme_bq_2004.pdf. For a summary in English consult: http://www2.bloc.org/archivage/plate-forme_bq_english.pdf. A specific platform for Quebec's cultural communities was also put forth: http://www2.bloc.org/archivage/plate_forme_ethnoculturel.pdf.

40 Paul Cauchon, "À l'issue de la nette victoire du Bloc québécois. Bouchard propose un nouveau dialogue au Canada anglais et dit aux Québécois «à la prochaine»," *Le Devoir,* October 26, 1993, A5.

41 Geneviève Otis-Dionne, "Pré-campagne souverainiste. Le Bloc misera sur le caractère distinct du Québec," *Le Devoir,* January 26, 2004, A3.

42 Alec Castonguay, "Donné pour moribond il y a quelques mois à peine. Le Bloc québécois trépigne d'impatience. La récolte s'annonce bonne pour le parti de Gilles Duceppe," *Le Devoir,* May 15, 2004, B3.

43 Nathaëlle Morissette, "Le Bloc québécois lance sa campagne," *La Presse,* May 16, 2004, A7.

44 Kathleen Lévesque, "«Un parti propre au Québec». Le slogan du Bloc fait bondir le PLC," *Le Devoir,* May 17, A1.

45 André Duchesne, "Lapierre n'exclut pas un gouvernement minoritaire," *La Presse,* May 25, 2004, A11.

46 Karim Benessaieh, "Pas de compromis, promet Duceppe. Le Bloc ne se laisserait pas séduire par un gouvernement minoritaire conservateur," *La Presse,* June 2, 2004, A9.

47 Sam Dagher, "Martin appelle l'équipe Chrétien à la rescousse," *Le Devoir,* June 1, 2004, A1.

48 Karim Benessaieh, "La bulle increvable du Bloc," *La Presse,* May 30, 2004, A10.

49 This was true for Quebec's national media. Easier access to unemployment insurance was a big issue in Quebec's regions, especially in Gaspé and on the North Shore, where seasonal workers are hit hard by the strict rules. Due to Bloc insistence on this issue for many years and Liberal inaction, the Liberals had no chance of making this issue their own.

50 Denis Lessard, "Duceppe le plus convaincant," *La Presse,* June 15, 2004, A16.

51 Stéphane Paquet, "Combien y a-t-il dans la caisse?" *La Presse,* June 15, 2004, A16.

52 Alec Castonguay, "Duceppe superstar. Le chef bloquiste fait bonne impression, même au Canada anglais," *Le Devoir,* June 18, 2004, A3.

53 Nathaëlle Morissette and Mario Cloutier, "Solide comme le Bloc. Duceppe restera à Ottawa, pensent les observateurs," *La Presse,* June 30, 2004, A2.

54 Karim Benessaieh, "Le cabinet de Paul Martin. Pettigrew promet une 'nouvelle ère' de coopération avec les provinces," *La Presse,* December 13, 2003, B2.

55 Kathleen Lévesque, "Gare aux séparatistes! Les ténors libéraux lancent une mise en garde aux Québécois," *Le Devoir,* June 23, 2004, A3.

56 Réal Séguin and Daniel Leblanc, "Landry says Bloc sweep will hasten referendum," *The Globe and Mail,* June 23, 2004, A1.

57 Nathaëlle Morissette, "Le Bloc à l'assaut de forteresses libérales," *La Presse,* June 23, 2004, A19.

58 Louis Massicotte, "Les libéraux se sont-ils abstenus plus que les autres?" *Le Devoir,* July 3, 2004, B5.

59 Denis Lessard, "Élections 2004: vers un raz-de-marée bloquiste le 28 juin," *La Presse,* June 23, 2004, A1.

60 This theory is developed by several academics in André Blais, Joanna Everitt, et al., in "Coupés de la politique. Les jeunes votent moins parce qu'ils portent moins attention à l'actualité politique," *La Presse,* August 5, 2004, A14.

61 Nathalie Lavoie and Pierre Serré, "Du vote bloc au vote social: le cas des citoyens issus de l'immigration de Montréal, 1995-1996," *Canadian Journal of Political Science,* vol. 35, no. 1, 2002, 49–74. See also André Pratte, "Près du quart des «ethniques» auraient voté OUI. Deux jeunes chercheurs bousculent les analyses traditionnelles du vote des minorités," *La Presse,* February 24, 1996, A25.

62 Isabelle Beaulieu, "Plus on est jeune, plus on est nationaliste. Jusqu'à 16 % des jeunes non francophones se disent souverainistes," *Le Devoir,* June 23, 2000, A9.

63 Clairandrée Cauchy, "Une leçon pour le PLC? Signe des temps, le parti de Paul Martin devra maintenant courtiser les communautés culturelles," *Le Devoir,* July 17, 2004, B1.

64 Clairandrée Cauchy, "Le PLC passe en mode écoute au Québec," *Le Devoir,* July 10, 2004, A1.

65 For information about the ethnic and linguistic makeup of federal ridings see Statistic Canada's Web site at: http://www12.statcan.ca/english/census01/products/standard/fedprofile/SelectFED.cfm?R=FED03.

66 In the case of Outremont, one must take into account that the NDP had a very strong candidate, Omar Aktouf, who garnered 14 percent of the vote in the riding and seems to have done so with large support from the North African community in the Côte-des-Neiges district.

67 Sixty-one percent of Quebecers believe that the BQ's presence in federal politics is justified according to a spring 2004 CROP poll; see Denis Lessard, "Le scandale des commandites fait mal aux libéraux de Paul Martin," *La Presse,* April 1, 2004, A4.

68 Denis Lessard, "Élections 2004: vers un raz-de-marée bloquiste le 28 juin," *La Presse,* June 23, 2004, A1.

69 Jeffrey Simpson, "Why did they let the BQ skate through the campaign?" *The Globe and Mail,* June 25, 2004, A21.

CHAPTER SIX

The "Others": *A Quest for Credibility*

by Susan Harada

On a Saturday afternoon in June, as the second week of the election campaign drew to a close, a small group assembled on a busy street corner in Ottawa's Byward Market. Save for the single placard sitting on the sidewalk, propped up against the signpost, there was little reason that passersby would recognize the gathering as a Green Party of Canada campaign event. Although party leader Jim Harris, two local Ottawa candidates, and two party workers were there for what was billed as an hour of "mainstreeting," there was little effort on their part to do much handshaking. Shoppers and tourists wandered by without giving Harris and his group a second glance. Still, the party leader seemed in a buoyant mood — and for good reason. There, on the front page of the *Globe and Mail* that Harris clutched, were the results of a poll suggesting that not only did 6 percent of decided voters support the Greens nationally, but a seat projection based on the poll pointed to the possibility of the party winning two seats in British Columbia.[1] They were just two sentences in an article otherwise devoted to discussing the possible fate of the major parties, but their importance to the Greens was immeasurable. They gave credibility to what Harris and other party members had been saying since well before the election was called; the Green Party was poised to cross over to the mainstream from the land of the political "other." "We're trending upwards and predict we'll win over a million votes," Harris said. "We're going to win seats in this election, too, and actually from coast to coast. So it's a very exciting election for us."[2]

As it turned out, both the party and the pollster missed the predicted mark. The Greens failed to win a single seat, and slightly more than 580,000 Canadians voted for them. This was well up from the approximately 104,000 votes they captured in 2000, but nowhere near the million votes the party had talked about publicly. It can be said that the Green Party did make a breakthrough, however, in that it built itself, geographically, into a national party; it reached its primary goal of running a full slate of 308 candidates, compared to the 111 it ran four years ago.

In addition to the Greens, seven "smaller" parties ran in the 2004 election: the Christian Heritage Party, the Marijuana Party, the Progressive Canadian Party, the Marxist-Leninist Party of Canada, the Canadian Action Party, the Communist Party of Canada, and the Libertarian Party of Canada. Collectively, these seven parties ran 313 candidates who captured slightly more than 109,000 votes (0.8%). A number of other smaller parties did not participate: the Natural Law Party of Canada voluntarily deregistered; the National Alternative Party of Canada, The Ontario Party of Canada, and the Absolutely Absurd Party either lost or withdrew their registration eligibility.[3]

CHANGING ATTITUDES, CHANGING RULES

The smaller political parties in Canada have been referred to in a number of ways over the years: fringe, marginal, other. They are the parties that largely operate beneath the radar of the mainstream media and a majority of the Canadian public. In recent years, they have run the gamut from the Rhinoceros Party of Canada, which spoofed the political process, to the Natural Law Party of Canada, which promoted transcendental meditation and Yogic flying. Such parties have arguably done little to advance the cause of small parties in general; they can make it all too easy for voters and journalists to dismiss them as truly being "fringe." Shaking off that label in particular, in order to be taken seriously, was what the "other" parties that ran in the 2004 election were after. Each of them set their goals and worked toward attaining credibility in different ways.

For the Progressive Canadian Party, the election meant putting the diehard Tories who spurned the Alliance-Conservative merger back onto the political map with their own registered party. For the Libertarians, it meant winning the attention of Canadians — not necessarily their votes — long enough to promote the party's core principle of increased freedom and responsibility for individuals. For the Marijuana Party, it meant running in more ridings than the Bloc Québécois to demonstrate that it had the same level of candidate support for its main issue as Bloc members had for theirs.

However they measured it, in the days leading up to the dropping of the writ, each of the parties pegged attaining credibility as a crucial element of their campaigns. With that in hand, went the reasoning, there existed the possibility of wider, *serious* coverage in the mainstream media, and therefore a greater chance that they would not be dismissed so lightly when voters encountered their party names among the choices listed on ballots. It is not an unrealistic goal. The Reform Party of Canada, which went from outsider to official opposition within a decade, stands as the most recent example of what it is possible for a party with small beginnings to achieve.

The eight parties examined in this chapter entered into the 2004 campaign against a backdrop of change. It was to be the first election since a set of new rules governing political parties had come into effect, rules regulating party financing as well as the criteria for a party to attain registered status. Both changes can and will have a direct impact on the viability and sustainability of smaller political parties in Canada; both have already been subject to criticism from all sides.[4] The first change came with Bill C-24: An Act to amend the Canada Elections Act and the Income Tax Act (political financing). Among other things, the amendments prohibit contributions by corporations and unions to registered political parties; at the same time, public funding for political parties has been enhanced. Registered parties that win either 2 percent of the national vote or 5 percent of votes in ridings where the party runs candidates will receive $1.75 per vote annually, following each general election.[5]

Given the results of the 2000 election, none of the parties under discussion in this chapter stood to benefit from the legislation that came into force on January 1, 2004. There was, however, one significant change after the 2004 results were tallied: the Green Party managed to leapfrog over the 2 percent national threshold. With 4.3 percent of the popular vote, it will now receive approximately $1 million annually in public funding. The Greens were counting on that money going into the election; the party borrowed against its future income in order to raise the funds necessary to mount a professional national campaign.[6] The other parties did not fare so well. None of them surpassed 0.3 percent nationally and so none will benefit from the change in the rules. They were prepared for such a result: even before the election was called, a number of the smaller parties began talks with the aim of possibly joining forces to challenge the constitutionality of the 2 percent rule. They argue that the law discriminates against small and emerging parties by establishing a threshold that must be met in order for them to access public funds.[7] Christian Heritage Party Leader Ronald Gray is not alone when he states that the funding rules are simply "a formula for preserving the status quo."[8]

The line of reasoning that the establishment of a threshold is unconstitutional was also behind a court challenge that resulted in the second change in the rules just prior to the election. Bill C-3: An Act to amend the Canada Elections Act and the Income Tax Act wiped out previous conditions that political parties had to meet in order to become registered: after considerable debate, the number of candidates that parties were required to field in an election was set by Parliament at only one[9] — down from the previous requirement of fifty. At the same time, new obligations, such as signing up 250 members, were established.[10]

The change in the law was the direct result of a court action by Miguel Figueroa, the leader of the Communist Party of Canada; his court action was the direct result of the deregistration of his party and the liquidation of its assets after it failed to nominate fifty candidates in the 1993 general election. It took Figueroa ten years, but he successfully fought to strike down various sections of the election law. In 2000, new legislation allowed a registered party to keep its assets, even if it didn't meet the fifty-candidate requirement; in 2001, rules governing when a candidate's political affiliation could be listed on the ballot were relaxed; finally, in 2004, the fifty-candidate requirement for party registration was scrapped.

That last victory did not come easily; Figueroa pushed it right up to the Supreme Court of Canada. In June 2003, the Court ruled that the fifty-candidate threshold was unconstitutional but provided little guidance as to a remedy.[11] It gave Parliament a year — until June 27, 2004 — to amend the legislation, and the government pushed it right to the wire. By May 15, just eight days before the dropping of the writ, Bill C-3 finally made it through the Senate, received Royal Assent, and came into force. It happened just in time for Figueroa; the Communist Party ran only thirty-five candidates in the election. Had the old rules still been in place, the Communists would have lost their registered status once again. The Canadian Action Party, Libertarian Party, and Progressive Canadian Party benefited from C-3 as well. Each fielded fewer than fifty candidates, but thanks to the new law they still received registered status and related benefits such as the ability to issue tax receipts for contributions and to receive unspent election funds from candidates.[12]

Although some of Figueroa's electoral rivals in 2004 were also the beneficiaries of his court battles, he explained his decade-long quest this way: "We said all along this wasn't just an issue for our party, it was a basic democratic issue. The problem was the parties in power in Parliament have a mutual vested interest in not ensuring that the process is as inclusive as possible, that there's a level playing field. It's in their interests in fact to make it more and more difficult for other parties to compete with them or to challenge them or to become larger parties or more influential parties."[13]

In *Figueroa v. Canada*, the Supreme Court agreed that the contribution all parties make to Canadian political discourse is not dependent on their size:

> ...marginal or regional parties tend to raise issues not adopted by national parties. Political parties provide individual citizens with an opportunity to express an opinion on the policy and functioning of government. Each vote in support of a party increases the likelihood

> that its platform will be taken into account by those who implement policy, and votes for parties with fewer than 50 candidates are an integral component of a vital and dynamic democracy.[14]

There's still more to come with this particular legislation: the amendments have a sunset provision that will see them being revisited two years from now. It promises to be an interesting debate, given that attitudes toward the political process and the inclusion of more voices are shifting. That's evident not only in judgments such as *Figueroa v. Canada* but also in the growing public interest in examining electoral reform. A number of the political parties advocate moving to a system based on proportional representation. The issue will be discussed further a little later in this chapter; suffice to say at this point that there seems to be greater dissatisfaction with Canada's current first-past-the-post system, along with a desire to explore new ways of aligning the votes of the electorate with the resulting representation in the House of Commons.[15]

THE PARTIES ON THE CAMPAIGN TRAIL

The Green Party of Canada:[16] 580,816 votes (4.3 percent)

There is no question that members of the Green Party felt confident going into the campaign. That confidence was reflected in a comment made by a member of the campaign team; when contacted prior to the election call about this chapter, he objected — only half-jokingly — to the inclusion of the Greens in a discussion about political parties considered to be outside of the mainstream. In fact, how to deal with a party that was running a full slate of candidates and polling at approximately 6 percent nationally — what category to place it in — was a dilemma for the media. It came to a head when the Greens were shut out of the televised leaders' French and English debates by the broadcast consortium composed of CanWest Global, CBC/Radio-Canada, CTV, and TVA. According to consortium spokesperson Peter Kent, it used to be that parties had to have official status (twelve Parliamentary seats) in order to be invited in. He said the rules shifted when the parliamentary landscape did. Simply being a registered party with a seat in the House became the requirement, and, "if the Greens do get a seat in this election, they'll be in the next debate."[17]

Inclusion in the leaders' debates was a major goal for the Greens. The invitation alone would be the party's passport into the mainstream. The appearance of leader Jim Harris on the same stage as the major party leaders would be proof that it had arrived. Campaign Manager Wayne Crookes figured inclusion could top up the Greens' popular support by 2 to 4 percent. But although they lobbied hard, they were ready for rejection. In fact, they made the most of it: they produced broadcast ads to tell Canadians that "...a consortium of broadcasters is stifling the rights of 22 million voters by not including the Green Party of Canada in its televised debates."[18] They wrote to the CRTC; they launched an online petition on the party's Web site; they released text of what would have been Harris's opening statement; they appealed to other political parties and candidates to boycott any scheduled all-candidates meetings that didn't include all of those in the running. It can be argued that the Greens gained as much exposure and credibility by being excluded as they would have if their leader had actually been given a chance to speak. Public opinion, in the form of e-mails sent to the broadcast consortium, editorials and commentaries,[19] and a poll commissioned by the Greens,[20] largely came down on the side of including Harris in the debates. All in all, the party earned invaluable national coverage. According to Platform Chair Michael Pilling, that was not unexpected; the campaign team regarded the battle for inclusion as a win-win situation. "Either we win and we get on the debate, which most people thought was a bit of a long shot, or we win because we get the public sympathy at being excluded," he said. "Mainly we wanted to win over the public to this idea that the Green Party is a major mainstream party and our policies and ideas deserve to be heard."[21]

Certainly in other parts of the world, the Green Party is part of the mainstream; it has elected members internationally for years, and its first big breakthrough was in the Federal Republic of Germany in 1983.[22] In Canada, the party was formed in 1983 and first appeared on the federal ballot in 1984.[23] Although it has run in every federal election since then, it was at the provincial level that the Greens made their first substantial mark. The Green Party of British Columbia carved a space for itself during the 2001 provincial campaign. Though it failed to elect a single member, it came away with 12.4 percent of the popular vote.[24] More important for its future prospects, the party established credibility and was invited into the leaders' debate — a development that party strategists credit for the inroads made in B.C. What followed next was the Ontario election of 2003. Again, the provincial party failed to win a seat, but it ran 102 candidates out of a possible 103, and earned 2.8 percent of the popular vote (up from 0.7 percent in 1999).[25]

Along the way, the existence of the Green Party was slowly seeping into the Canadian consciousness. John Wright, the senior vice-president of the Ipsos-Reid Public Affairs polling firm, says the Greens began showing up on the public radar several years ago. That's when Canadians began naming — unprompted — the Greens as their party of choice when asked who they would vote for federally. When the number reached 3 percent, or approximately 720,000 people, the firm began what's called "prompting" for the Green Party in November 2002; in other words, it included the Green Party on the mainstream political party grocery list (Alliance, Bloc, Liberal, NDP, Progressive Conservative) in connection to the open-ended question, "What party would you vote for if there were an election held tomorrow?" By the time the writ was dropped in May 2004, the Greens were at 5 percent nationally in Ipsos-Reid polls.[26]

Did being named make a difference in the number of Canadians who claimed to be Green supporters? Another polling firm, Environics Research Group, did not prompt for the Greens, and measured support for the party at approximately 1 percent, in contrast to the higher number recorded by Ipsos-Reid.[27] According to Ipsos-Reid's Wright, "One could make the methodological argument ... that if you don't ask the question, then you may not remind people there is a party there to vote for. [But] I think at some point it's true that if you do tell people and give them a list of things you will end up with people saying 'yes' to something that they didn't know existed, like the Communist Party or something like that."[28] Ipsos-Reid didn't prompt for other smaller parties — they simply didn't match the 3 percent unprompted response the Greens initially generated. And whether or not the prompting had an impact on the Greens' numbers, the numbers definitely had an impact on their media coverage. The party attributes nearly 50 percent of the news coverage it received in the first three months of 2004 to its inclusion in Ipsos-Reid polls released prior to the election.[29]

Armed with their standing in the polls, and, for the first time, a sizeable budget,[30] the Greens set out to run a credible, national campaign. The party Web site was bilingual, professionally presented and updated regularly.[31] Full-time staff numbered fifty. News releases were issued a few times a day, to call attention to the party's platform as well to publicize the leader's whereabouts and his take on the campaign issues of the day. Full-blown formal news conferences were held twice on Parliament Hill for the benefit of the parliamentary Press Gallery: the first time, to unveil the party platform; the second time, to discuss the party's exclusion from the leaders' debates.

The leader's tour was designed to remind Canadians that the Greens were a national party with candidates from coast to coast. Harris zigzagged across the country between west coast and east, spent the last few days in B.C. (where the party's hopes were highest), and wound up on election night in his own riding of Toronto-Danforth. Up against the NDP's Jack Layton and the high-profile Liberal incumbent Dennis Mills, it was no surprise that Harris finished a distant fourth. As a resident of the riding, however, he threw himself into the midst of the Layton versus Mills battle to underscore the party's belief that candidates should run where they live.[32] It was the first federal campaign as Green leader for the management consultant, author, and former Progressive Conservative. The choice of Harris as leader in 2003 symbolized the party's recognition that in order to join the mainstream, it had to reposition and rebrand itself. Party members acknowledge that the Greens have been perceived as an organizationally unstructured group of left-leaning "tree-huggers," focused almost exclusively on the environment and thereby appealing to a narrow segment of the population. In an effort to broaden their base and capitalize on a growing awareness and concern about environmental issues, the Greens fashioned a broad platform that tried to balance strong environmentalism[33] with fiscal conservatism. The message they wanted Canadians to absorb was that they were neither left nor right but could appeal across the spectrum. The other critical message was that no vote would be a wasted vote. To win over soft support — Canadians who liked their policies but who might not be inclined to vote for a party still far from the centre of power — the Greens reinforced the fact that every vote would be worth $1.75 and would "... allow Canadians who vote for the Green Party to help build a new political voice for Canada."[34]

The Green Party's campaign received a boost from mainstream media; the leader, numerous candidates, and the platform received wider coverage — nationally and locally —than ever before. At times the party had to lobby hard in order, for example, to be included on the Web sites of major news organizations. Nevertheless, there were some breakthroughs: a number of extended reports and interviews with the party leader aired on national radio and television; mid-campaign, after the debate dustup put the Greens in the spotlight, the *Globe and Mail* opted to create a new coverage category — somewhere between the major parties and the smaller ones — just for the Greens[35]; the *Ottawa Citizen* endorsed Green candidate David Chernushenko in Ottawa Centre, passing over the likes of NDP candidate Ed Broadbent to do so.[36]

The word "momentum" is overused at times when describing political parties, but it applies in the case of the Green Party. In spite of the fact that it has yet to elect a member of Parliament, it showed growth over the past few years and over the course of the campaign. Clearly the question is whether the Greens can build on that. There was recognition within the party that, with the campaign over, the real work had just begun, if the Greens were to stay visible and expand their membership. "We're just building our base, and the people who voted for us generally decided to vote for us fairly early in the campaign," said Michael Pilling. "Right now we have to set up a lean and efficient organization to be able to propel us forward." To that end the party set up a transition team tasked with preparing for the future. It planned consultations with its own members as well as with members of Green parties in other parts of the world. A summer national conference had been scheduled to deal with organizational matters such as the election of a new federal council. And barely a week after the 2004 election was over, the Greens had already started moving ahead with preparations to fine-tune their policies for the next one, in the form of Platform 2005.

Christian Heritage Party:[37] 40,283 votes (0.3 percent)

The Christian Heritage Party was back in business for the 2004 election. It lost its registered status in 2000 for failing to nominate the then-required fifty candidates and disappeared as a party entity from the ballots. Four years later, the party had built back up. It fielded sixty-two candidates and pulled in more of the popular vote than any of the other smaller parties (excluding the Greens). In spite of that, there was disappointment within the organization that it failed to elect a member of Parliament. Party leader Ronald Gray had been optimistic. For the first time, Christian Heritage had attracted supporters to stand as candidates in a number of urban ridings — not areas where the party has traditionally found support, and certainly not areas where it has even bothered to run significant campaigns. But internal indications were that this election might be different. In the Toronto riding of York West, for example, candidate Joseph Grubb relayed back to the party leadership that he was getting a positive response at the door. According to Gray, as Grubb informally surveyed people about their attitudes towards same-sex marriage, abortion, and governance according to Christian principles, he found strong support for the party's position on all three issues. Grubb finished fourth with 5.7 percent of the popular vote, ahead of the Green Party candidate.

The venture into urban ridings did not preclude the party from devoting time and resources to court its core constituency in rural areas of the country. A portion of the party's $140,000 budget was spent on a leader's tour: for three weeks, Gray travelled through Alberta, Saskatchewan, Manitoba, and southern Ontario to support candidates and speak at rallies. Christian Heritage's beliefs and approach to politics has always resonated deeply in southwestern Ontario in particular. "I think there are two factors that help us there. One is that it is a rural area. It's agricultural," Gray said. "The other is there's a fairly large proportion of the population descended from Dutch immigrants and particularly from the Dutch Calvinists who have a long tradition of bringing their faith into public life."

The desire to marry faith with public life was the driving force behind the forming of the party in 1986. It fought its first election in 1988, and the 102,533 votes it won is still its high-water mark. In the years following, the Christian vote increasingly went first to Reform and then to the Canadian Alliance. By 2000, the Christian Heritage Party was no longer officially on the ballots. But with the merger of the Alliance and the Progressive Conservatives, party hopes were high that it could attract candidates and lure back support. To this end, it presented a full platform that put forward its faith-based policies on issues ranging from national defence to resource management to the arts. The core campaign message, however, as summed up by Gray, was that it is "... strongly pro-life, pro-family and ... the only party that has so far published a plan for restraining judicial activism to protect the Constitution." Those issues erupted during the campaign, when several Conservatives, including leader Stephen Harper, became embroiled in a debate about abortion, same-sex marriage, and the role of the courts in such matters.[38] But Christian Heritage lacked the means and the media coverage to weigh in with its traditional views. All attention was focused on the Conservatives and their seemingly conflicting messages about where they stood on such issues. Watching from the sidelines, Gray saw Harper's handling of the eruptions result, in the end, in the Conservatives retaining a major portion of the support he felt could have come to him. "I think the new Conservative Party leader wanted to distance himself from the moral issues that are of primary concern for us, not only Christians but other people of faith who would potentially be our natural constituency," he said. "But they also didn't want to alienate those people, so they tried very hard not to say anything ... I think if they had been more clear [that] they don't want to raise and will not raise those moral issues, that might have helped us more than it did. But quite understandably they maintained some ambiguity in their stance. And that left a lot of our natural constituency still sort of hoping that they might represent them."

With a minority government in place, the Christian Heritage Party began looking to the future immediately after the campaign ended. Planning for the next election got underway, with a national convention scheduled for the fall of 2005. Although Gray planned to stay on as leader and run again, he did feel that stepping aside at some point could create a golden opportunity for a younger leader to attract more followers to the cause.

Marijuana Party:[39] 33,590 votes (0.3 percent)

The raison d'être for the Marijuana Party is in its name; if there is a single-issue party in Canada, this one is it. The party's campaign strategy was as straightforward as its name — run as many candidates as possible in order to get the attention and votes necessary to pressure mainstream political parties into moving the marijuana issue forward. To that end, when party leader Marc-Boris St-Maurice kicked off his party's campaign in Montreal with the slogan "Let's Roll," he reiterated that "This is a serious issue and it's a serious party that is addressing a serious issue in a serious nature.... We want to change the law, and government is where laws are enacted."[40]

The party failed, however, to match its inaugural electoral success of 2000. Running two fewer candidates in 2004 (down from seventy-three in 2000), its share of the popular vote dropped by half, going from some 66,000 votes in 2000 (0.5 percent) to just under 33,600 (0.3 percent). Other parties, namely the NDP and the Greens, took a large bite out of the Marijuana Party's base of support with their own marijuana policies. The Greens advocate the legalization and taxation of marijuana production and consumption. And although the NDP platform was vague, leader Jack Layton's comments favouring legalization in the fall of 2003[41] resulted in a schism in the Marijuana Party. There was internal debate about whether to continue on or whether to join forces with the NDP. Some marijuana activists ended up working with the NDP or even becoming candidates. The most significant defection was that of the party's principal patron, high-profile activist Marc Emery, who actively endorsed Layton and the NDP. "The purpose of the party is only to advance the cause. The cause is best advanced in Parliament by the people who are there," said Emery. "If the NDP hadn't had such a positive response I would say we would have supported the Green Party, which has also a clear legalization position. In other words we'll pick the horse which is most likely to deliver the results we're seeking right now in Parliament. And that would have to be the NDP."[42] St-Maurice, however, said he "... never thought it was a good idea to merge the Marijuana Party with the NDP or with any other party for that matter. It keeps a base of strength within the marijuana movement. It keeps it concentrated."

It was to provide a political centre for the movement that the Marijuana Party was formed in 2000, at a time when the issue received attention but little concrete political action. St-Maurice was among those who joined the battle against the rules governing medical and recreational use. He helped create a provincial marijuana party in Quebec in 1998 (Bloc Pot) and then the federal party two years later in hopes of uniting the efforts of activists across the country. It is difficult to gauge how successful the party has been in achieving that goal. According to Alan Young — law professor, criminal lawyer, and long-time marijuana activist — the movement is extremely fragmented, making it hard for the party to weave together a unified front. Young himself has been involved since the mid-1990s in pushing the issue forward on a parallel track, through the courts. "The litigation strategy was started ... because in my opinion the political channels were completely clogged," he said. "You had an issue for which governments on many occasions for many years have promised change and haven't come through with it."[43]

Propelled by a number of judicial decisions, the federal government had begun moving ahead on laws regulating medical marijuana. On the recreational use front, there were promises to decriminalize but little action and much uncertainty after a number of significant lower court rulings. In December 2003, the Supreme Court of Canada ruled that prohibiting the possession of marijuana for personal use is not unconstitutional and tossed the ball back into Parliament's court. The Liberals, first under Jean Chrétien (with Bill C-38 in May 2003) and then under Paul Martin (with Bill C-38 reintroduced as Bill C-10 in February 2004), introduced legislation aimed at decriminalizing possession of small amounts of the drug.[44] Bill C-10 died with the election call, although the Liberals have pledged to revive it.[45]

Even if revived, such legislation would not be regarded as a victory for a political party looking for legalization, not decriminalization. Thus the Marijuana Party entered into the campaign ready for battle. It had slightly more than $40,000 to spend: the bulk of it went toward candidates' deposits, although some was set aside for campaign materials and travel for the leader. With the absence of Marc Emery, money was hard to come by. St-Maurice took out a mortgage on his house in order to raise most of it. The party ran seventy-one candidates, a diverse group of mainly younger people with little or no political experience. They were clustered in Montreal, but also spread through Ottawa, Winnipeg, Toronto, Vancouver, and Edmonton. Some of those candidates were highly involved and ran active campaigns; others, according to St-Maurice, came forward mainly to help the party get its name on the ballot. The party leader himself took on Prime Minister Paul Martin in Lasalle-Emard, finishing sixth out of seven candidates with some 350 votes.

Overall, the election results were disappointing, but as St-Maurice sees it, "The desire for activism is directly proportional to the level of repression. As things get better for marijuana, you can see support for the Marijuana Party dropping somewhat." Post-election, he felt the party still had a mission to accomplish, and there were no plans to fold the organization. Still, at the time this chapter was written, he was musing about whether to step aside as leader to give someone else a chance to breathe new life into a cause and a party he said he still very much believes in.

Progressive Canadian Party:[46] 10,773 votes (0.1 percent)

As with the Marijuana Party, the significance of the Progressive Canadian Party's story rests in its name. It is, party members say, simply a *nom de guerre* for what is the continuation of their old party, the Progressive Conservatives. The quest to carry on began practically on the eve of the election with a group of more than two hundred Tories who refused to go along with the majority and align forces with the new Conservative Party. They first filed an application to register as the Progressive Conservative Party in January 2004. When Elections Canada rejected that name, they were forced to go with their second choice: the Progressive Canadian Party. They scored a small victory, however, in winning approval to have "PC Party" listed as the official short form name on ballots. Speaking shortly before the election call, Interim Secretary Al Gullon said Progressive Canadians are Progressive Canadians in name only — party members and candidates remain Progressive Conservatives. "We view ourselves as surviving members of an evil wind from the west. And so the candidates will ... campaign as

Progressive Conservatives." The party had one goal: to become registered in order to keep the name, the history, and the dreams of the Progressive Conservative Party alive. It appointed a leader, Ernie Schreiber of Ottawa, the former director of the PC riding association in Ottawa South. It also adopted a fully fleshed out platform. Ernie Schreiber, however, was leader in name only — and the platform was the one developed by Joe Clark and his Tories for the election in 2000.

The PC Party went into the 2004 campaign with no real leader, a four-year-old platform, little money, and only sixteen candidates (mainly in Ontario, but also in Nova Scotia and Alberta). There were no big names from the Progressive Conservatives of the past attached to the 2004 effort, with the exception of former PC cabinet minister Sinclair Stevens, who helped publicize campaign events in a number of ridings. There was no staff, no headquarters, no central campaign control or strategy to guide candidates. "I don't care personally whether they go to any meetings, whether they put out any brochures, whether they have a Web site, whether they go shaking hands at every variety store," said National Coordinator Joe Hueglin. "Our aim is to exist legally as a registered party. So therefore let us reach that goal and then we will concern ourselves about who will be the knight on the white horse leading the charge. That is, the leader."

Why go to such lengths, against such odds? About two weeks before the writ was dropped, Hueglin sketched out one very important reason from his point of view: he said it was necessary to have a party able to engage the Liberals from the political centre, in order to give voters an option. "The danger that I see," he observed presciently, "is that the Alliance-Conservative Party will be painted into the corner as being as far right as the NDP is left, which would leave the Liberals with the uncontested centre." In spite of what seemed like insurmountable odds, PC Party candidates persuaded more than ten thousand Canadians to vote for them. Holding on to even that amount of support is the next challenge. The party's goals include setting up an organizational infrastructure and developing communications and outreach to attract more members and candidates. That, however, takes money, and lack of money was the main reason some wondered, post-election, whether they should just give up the fight and walk away. The soul-searching began the moment the results were tallied, but in the end, party members decided overwhelmingly to carry on. A real leader? Members say that's not a priority at this point, certainly not as important as first establishing a viable party.

Marxist-Leninist Party of Canada:[47] 9,065 votes (0.1 percent)

There's been much talk about vote-splitting on the right, but it's also an issue for the smaller parties on the very left. Although it appears on the ballot as the Marxist-Leninist Party of Canada, the party's official name — which is also listed on its Web site — is the Communist Party of Canada (Marxist-Leninist). Some voter confusion between the Communist Party of Canada and the Marxist-Leninists has not been unusual over the years. Are they one and the same? If not, how do they differ? Those were the sorts of questions Louis Lang, both the party's public relations officer and a candidate in Ottawa Centre, heard during the campaign. "There were two of us, the Communist and myself, running in the same riding. It really doesn't make a whole lot of sense and on many issues we basically said the same thing," he said. "We could see just in our case how ridiculous it looked and how impractical it was. And a lot of people wanted to know what was going on … it would distract from the discussion that people [were] asking these questions about, 'why are these two parties running in the same riding against each other?'"

The answer to that question lies in the history of the parties. The Marxist-Leninist Party was formed in 1970, half a century after the Communist Party came into being in Canada. The anti-war student movement of the 1960s set the stage. According to Lang, the more settled style and substance of the older Communist Party did not satisfy the young activists, who went on to found their own party. The differences in approach and ideology were a reflection of the larger differences being played out on the international stage between the communism of China and the communism of the Soviet Union. Though the Communist Party of Canada, from the beginning, was aligned with the Soviets, Canada's Marxist-Leninist Party began its political life aligned with China.[48]

It is still the young — especially students — and the working class in mainly urban, industrialized areas who form the backbone of support for the Marxist-Leninists, according to Lang. Since the 1970s, the party has been officially represented on the ballot in seven general elections; in the latest election it ran seventy-six candidates, the majority of them in southern Ontario and Quebec, although candidates also ran in B.C., Alberta, and Nova Scotia. To help support those candidates, party leader Sandra Smith did some travelling through Montreal and Toronto, but the party's campaign was not leader-driven, in the sense that those who organized it preferred to highlight the party's stand on issues as opposed to personalities.

The party felt the Internet played a key role in its election effort: the main aspects of the Marxist-Leninist platform — its political analysis of issues ranging from health care to foreign policy to taxation — were debated extensively and posted on its Web site as background material. There were also regular communiqués outlining Marxist-Leninist views of issues raised by other parties during the campaign. For a smaller party with a limited budget, the Web site and electronic mailing lists provided fast and inexpensive ways to reach the largest number of people. Without the means to produce a significant amount of other types of election material, the Marxist-Leninists also relied on going door to door in hopes they could, at the very least, encourage voters to visit their Web site. Another key campaign strategy was focused on speaking to as many groups as possible, given that many of the party's candidates belonged to larger workplaces, educational institutions, and community groups. Candidates were also encouraged to participate in all-candidates debates, although in some cases the local debates were an echo of the national ones — often only the “major” parties were invited, and the “others” had to push, not always successfully, for an invitation.

Even after fielding eight fewer candidates in 2004 as compared to 2000, and winning about three thousand fewer votes, there is confidence internally that the next election will see the party's fortunes reverse. As well, some sort of official cooperation with the Communists remains on the Marxist-Leninists' agenda. They've sent out tentative feelers about such an arrangement in the past and say it will now be pursued again. "We think that people should participate in actions based on specific issues," Lang said. "There's no reason why we can't get together and even decide not to run against each other in various ridings." At this point, however, an outright merger isn't considered possible by either party. Although he feels the major differences between the Marxist-Leninists and the Communists now have more to do with procedure than political ideology, Lang said it's probably not practical at this point, given the numerous issues — mainly administrative — that would have to be ironed out. The Communists feel a little more strongly about it. Party leader Miguel Figueroa didn't rule out cooperation, but said the two parties have yet to move beyond their historical differences, especially in terms of the issues each party takes on and the way in which they put forward solutions.[49]

Canadian Action Party:[50] 8,930 votes (0.1 percent)

It was a painful year for the Canadian Action Party (CAP). There was next to no money in the party coffers, a skeletal organizational structure, and a shrunken membership list. Things seemed so dismal that just days into the campaign, new leader Connie Fogal identified survival as one of the party's major goals. It seemed a long way from CAP's more optimistic beginnings in 1997, when its founder, Paul Hellyer, decided a brand new party was needed in order to get Canada back onto a progressive economic track. CAP's cornerstones were two key policy issues that Hellyer firmly believed in: monetary reform linked to ensuring the sovereignty of the country's money supply, and the abrogation of NAFTA and a pledge to stay out of similar agreements in the future. Hellyer formed CAP after a long career as a federal politician. He served as a Liberal cabinet minister as well as a Progressive Conservative MP, was a significant force in the Liberal leadership race in 1968, and also ran for the leadership of the Progressive Conservatives in 1976.[51] Two decades after that last, unsuccessful bid, Hellyer took the leadership reins of CAP, and his new economic nationalist party debuted on the federal political scene during the 1997 election campaign. It fielded sixty-two candidates and won slightly more than seventeen thousand votes (0.1 percent) in its first electoral effort. It registered slight growth three years later, in 2000, with seventy-two candidates and approximately twenty-seven thousand votes (0.2 percent). In 2004, it managed to attract only forty-five candidates, and the number of Canadians who voted for the party dropped by more than 60 percent.[52]

CAP's troubles in 2004 began after efforts to merge with the federal NDP came to naught. According to Hellyer, one of CAP's main goals was "to change the face of Canadian politics."[53] He figured that the means to that end would be joining with the NDP[54] "to form the nucleus of a new, broadly based, mainline pro-Canada party." The hope was that with the NDP on side, perhaps the Greens and even the progressive Tories who didn't want to merge with the Alliance could be convinced to join in as well. Sporadic talks with the Greens over the years had gone nowhere, however, and, ultimately, the more serious talks with the NDP failed as well. As Hellyer saw it, "They didn't want to merge with a, I don't want to put words in their mouths, but really it was a small party that a lot of people never heard of. And they thought they had the wind in their back and they thought they were going to do great things on their own." By the time the NDP made it clear a merger wasn't going to happen, in early 2004, CAP was left with little time to shift gears and ready itself for the late spring campaign. Although Hellyer remained active with the party, he resigned as leader and Fogal took over in March 2004. She inherited a party whose members had been geared up for the creation of a new, unified political party; many of them, she said, had actually been encouraged to join the NDP in anticipation of a merger. When it became clear that it wouldn't happen — at least not in time for the 2004 campaign — she said a number of those members stayed with their newly adopted party, some as candidates.

Those who were left opted unanimously to carry on. With the party's support concentrated mainly in Ontario and B.C., Fogal kicked off the campaign in Toronto but spent most of her time on the West Coast, in her own riding of Vancouver Quadra. Even then, her campaigning was limited. With only one full-time and two part-time staff members at the party's Toronto headquarters, much of the organizational work fell on her shoulders. According to Fogal, the uphill struggle smaller parties such as hers usually face seemed even more difficult during this campaign; they were excluded from a number of all-candidates' meetings, especially in urban ridings on the West Coast. The principal argument against including CAP and the others, she said, was time — organizers told her that putting more than four or five candidates on stage would leave little time for anybody to speak. Still, Fogal persisted: she showed up at meetings, tried to ask questions of other candidates from the floor, and either handed out her literature to audience members or left stacks of brochures at the back of the room. Her persistence also paid off when she landed interviews on well-known radio programs such as CBC's *The House* and Rafe Maier's *Hotline Show*. For the most part, the party depended on its Web site and e-mail lists in order to disseminate information quickly and cheaply. Although Hellyer assisted by raising some money and making a personal donation to CAP, attracting substantial financial support was difficult. The day after the election, the party's headquarters were closed and operations relocated to Fogal's home. In short, the party that once had such high hopes of leading the creation of a brand new mainstream political movement was left scrambling for its own survival both during and after the 2004 campaign.

Why go on? As Fogal put it, to win credibility for CAP's ideas, "… to be a pressure point, to have the potential to keep the pressure on, to influence those other parties who supposedly are on our wavelength … to drive them to take the stronger stand that we believe needs to be taken." Whether it can continue running on conviction alone is another question. Without money, it will be difficult to carry on. Still, the political will is there, if the financial way can be found. The party's dream of unifying a number of existing, like-minded parties to create a new, broadly based political alternative has not been abandoned. In the meantime, Fogal has taken a lesson from the Green Party and figures that fielding 308 candidates will be the surest route to credibility, and hence, national exposure for CAP's ideas. If the party finds the means to hold together for the next election, that will be its goal.

Communist Party of Canada:[55] *4,568 votes (0.03 percent)*

By week two, the Communists knew it was shaping up to be a difficult campaign. They were hearing rumblings, even from those who might have traditionally supported them (especially from within the trade union movement) that strategic voting may be in order. As the campaign wore on, that sort of feedback intensified. "It was a very highly polarized election campaign. I think to some extent that was used by the Liberals in order to increase the trepidation of a great number of Canadians about the impact of the election," said party leader Miguel Figueroa. He figured the Communists lost support, as people decided to deploy their votes elsewhere, "either to vote for the NDP ... or in some cases to vote Liberal in order to block the Tories. And that had an impact on the small parties except for the Green Party." As a smaller party with no extra money to adjust their campaign and advertising strategy, the Communists had to settle for adjusting their expectations. Not that their expectations had been unrealistically high. The campaign wasn't aimed at getting a Communist Party member elected: the goal was to present credible ideas situated on the left of the political spectrum to as many Canadians as possible. "Historically, we influence a lot more people than is reflected in our votes," Figueroa said. "A lot of people who are influenced by what we have to say end up saying 'Well, I agree with you guys but I can't vote for you because you're too far left. So I'll vote for the next best thing.' But that still moves people's thinking to the left." To that end, the party hoped to field at least fifty candidates who could help spread the word, but they attracted only thirty-five, and the overall number of Canadians who voted for them dropped by almost half, from the eighty-seven hundred who supported them in 2000.

There were bright spots, however, in the long weeks of campaigning. Figueroa travelled through B.C., Alberta, Manitoba, Ontario, and Quebec to help candidates drum up support. He characterized the response they got on the ground throughout the country as mainly positive. The interest that was demonstrated on-line also gave them hope. In 2000, the party's Web site recorded 150,000 hits over the course of the campaign; in May and June of 2004, that number reached 3.5 million. Even allowing for repeat visits, that translates into a great many Canadians browsing the site — the party's main vehicle for disseminating information about its platform. The platform itself touched on a wide mixture of policy issues — from health care to Aboriginal rights to a new deal for cities — and presented, in detail, the Communist Party's solutions.

What comes next is further development of policy and the continuation of the Communists' long-term project of building the party. They've identified three key areas in which to focus: strengthening their work within the labour movement and drafting a specific labour program; disseminating ideological information more widely through education, publishing, and writing; and doing more work with young people by working toward, for example, a pan-Canadian organization for young Communists. Those within the organization take the long view when it comes to the electoral fortunes of a party that has participated in more than a dozen federal elections since it was formed in the 1920s: according to Stuart Ryan, who ran in Ottawa Centre, the Communists have been around for decades and still believe they have something important to say about the future of the country.

Libertarian Party:[56] 1,964 votes (0.01 percent)

The Libertarians made a comeback of sorts in 2004. Although it was deregistered in 1997 and remained in political limbo for the 2000 election, the party regained its registered status just in time for the dropping of the writ in May. But by then, what had been a relatively thriving entity back in the 1970s when it was founded — with about three thousand members across the country — had shrunk to a bare-bones organization with one hundred registered members. Only eight candidates were put forward: in Quebec (one), Ontario (two) and B.C. (five). Even party leader Jean-Serge Brisson did not run; newly elected as a councillor in Russell Township in Ontario in November 2003, Brisson felt both his credibility and that of his party's would be damaged if he ran federally so soon after winning a municipal seat.

The Libertarian budget for election 2004 was minimal (about $8,000), as was any sort of central campaign strategy or candidate control. With no full-time staff to speak of, Brisson took care of the media enquiries, the production of the free-time broadcast ads, and the paperwork. Burnaby-Douglas candidate Adam Desaulniers joined the party just as the election was called. He said being deregistered for seven years had had an enormous impact on the organization: he was the only candidate, for example, with campaign literature and an active

Web site (even the party's Web site was not used as a key election communication tool).

Overall, the campaign goal was simple: re-establish a presence for next time and just spread the word. Libertarians operate from a core philosophy of individual freedom and responsibility coupled with minimal government, and so the platform hasn't changed much from year to year. "The general idea is that the more freedom you allow an individual to have, the more prosperous they can become, providing that person understands that their freedom ends where the other person's begins and vice versa," Brisson said. "Marriage, unions, economy, how you want to earn a living, all these things — providing you do not interfere in your neighbour's freedom of action — then you yourself should be able to act as you see fit." It is a philosophy that has adherents throughout the United States,[57] and, notably, Libertarians have been elected in Costa Rica. But electing a member of Parliament in Canada was not even remotely part of the campaign game plan of a party whose own leader refers to it as "fringe," in the sense that not too many Canadians know about it. "The reason why we're running is to bring about a change in the mindset of people," Brisson said. "Show them that privatization, more freedom of the individual and less oppression by government, less interference by government in our everyday lives is preferable to oppression and too much interference."

It's difficult for the Libertarians to spread the word about their ideas while operating from so small a base. With registered status once again, Brisson figured there would be opportunities for growth. In Desaulniers' view, however, growth will come only with the rebranding of the party and the injection of new blood into a core membership that has not kept up with changing times as effectively as it could have. He felt that what was required was an overhaul of the organization and a shift in terms of dealing with the various factions of libertarianism that exist. Whether that will happen remains to be seen. At the time this chapter was written, Desaulniers planned to create a new, updated Libertarian Web site. The aim? To tap into a natural constituency of mainly younger people the party feels is out there — people who may hold libertarian values without realizing there is a political party that can speak for them.

SMALL PARTIES, BIGGER VOICE?

Canada's smaller parties are like a political barometer, a marker of what matters to different groups of Canadians at different points in time, whether it is those Canadians who work actively for the parties or those Canadians who vote for them. The presence of such parties on the ballot is an indication of both a healthy political system and a healthy desire to challenge the dominant parties and the structure that aids them in staying dominant. There are those, such as the Communists and the Greens, that are the Canadian expressions of international political movements. The links those parties have to a larger political presence in the world help inspire their efforts in Canada. There is the Marijuana Party and, to a much lesser extent, the Canadian Action Party, known chiefly for their focused and singular stand on a specific issue or issues (although CAP's pro-Canada platform does touch on a variety of issues, from health care to the arts). Finally, the Christian Heritage Party, and even the Libertarians, can be characterized by the faith or deep-seated attitude that informs the way they see the country and how it should be governed. Although it certainly can't be said that all of the smaller parties that ran in the election of 2004 were single-issue parties, many did largely grow and develop their policies from the seed of a single theme. For the Green Party, for example, it was environmental responsibility; for the Christian Heritage Party, it was the entwining of religion with politics; for the Canadian Action Party, it was Canadian economic sovereignty in an increasingly globalized world.

The themes that provide the foundation for their identities and the ideas that flesh out their policies are what sustain the parties discussed in this chapter. Without exception, those parties are in turn sustained by core members who deeply believe in what each of their parties espouse. Unlike those who belong to larger parties, where ambitions are more easily realized and power within more realistic grasp, members of smaller parties have little but their ideas and ideals to fuel them. Every election that they fight brings into sharp relief what they are up against in order to make a mark. The election of 2004 was no different. But at a time when participation rates in Canadian political life are declining across the board, they managed to find the membership and the means to struggle, in varying degrees, to overcome the long hours, the lack of substantial funds, the sparse media coverage, and the indifference on the part of a good many Canadians in order to take part in the electoral process. And they did it because they felt that what they had to say was worth putting forward on the national stage. From the Libertarians to the Marxist-Leninists, it comes down to that — a core of members (and, according to the parties, a growing number of *young* members) who believe they have some answers, some unique approaches to issues they don't believe the larger political parties can or will resolve in the best way without external pressure. For most of the smaller parties that means ultimately winning seats; they have hope, in their heart of hearts, that they will someday ride a wave of support into the House of Commons just as the Reform Party did. For others, it means simply being there, election after election, to let Canadians know there are different ways to think about how life could be ordered.

Whatever their long-term goals and their success in reaching them, such parties serve an important purpose; they define the crucial issues and values that lie just below the surface of Canadian politics. They are issues and values with support enough to ignite a new party, or to fan the flames of an older small party, or to be adopted by mainstream parties, but rarely enough to land representatives in Parliament. That latter point is especially so, given Canada's current electoral system. It is one of the reasons why a majority of the smaller parties have made proportional representation part of their official platforms. For such parties, it has to do with gaining credibility, playing a larger role in the process, and giving real voice to Canadians whose votes for the political "others" seem to disappear into a big black hole at the bottom of the ballot box. The Green Party, for example, believes proportional representation will encourage voter participation as well as enable "new parties and new ideas" to evolve.[58] Increasing numbers of Canadians seem to want electoral reform as well. In five provinces, processes to examine reforms to the current first-past-the-post system are either underway or set to begin. The Law Commission of Canada examined numerous options and concluded that a "mixed member proportional electoral system" would best serve Canada's needs. It recommended a continued dialogue that would allow citizens as well as political players to have a significant role in determining how to shape a system for the future.[59]

Any type of electoral reform dialogue needs to start somewhere, however, and the Green Party, for one, isn't counting on the federal politicians in power to lead the way. It began a process to challenge the constitutionality of the first-past-the-post system in the courts several years ago, under former leader Joan Russow. The plan now is to press forward with the challenge.[60] Certainly, the Supreme Court, in *Figueroa v. Canada*, made it clear how it sees its role, in terms of the issue of electoral systems:

> The *Charter* aside, the choice among electoral processes is, as LeBel J. states, a political one — and not one in which the Court should involve itself. But if Parliament interferes with the right of each citizen to play a meaningful role in that process, it must be able to point to a pressing and substantial objective that it seeks to advance. In the absence of compelling reason to assert that a particular outcome will result in better governance, there is no basis on which to conclude that legislation that seeks to obtain that outcome advances an objective that is sufficiently pressing and substantial to warrant interfering with the right of each citizen to play a meaningful role in the electoral process.[61]

Provincial initiatives currently underway will lend impetus to the reform enterprise. Any change initiated at the regional level could set the stage for national change and would certainly help focus a national debate about what kind of reform, if any, should be pursued. In terms of the smaller parties, would a different system enable even those without significant bases of support to be voted into Parliament? Would that be a desirable outcome, or should a line be drawn? If so, where? Would more voices in Parliament — and likely more minority governments — enhance, or hobble, the political process? Those are just a few of the questions that have been raised already. Many more remain to be asked and answered. As Heather MacIvor noted, "While the effect of any electoral reform should not be overstated, and cannot be fully predicted, the idea of MMP [mixed member plurality] has enough potential to warrant serious official investigation and public discussion."[62]

From the point of view of small and/or emerging parties, reform could level the playing field, in the sense that it would bestow on them some amount of credibility. Within a system that puts more weight onto accounting for the wishes of everyone who votes, there would exist a greater possibility that even smaller parties could very well elect one or two or ten members of Parliament, thereby influencing the direction of life in Canada, not just from the fringes, but from the inside. It would be up to those parties to stand or fall on their individual policies and appeal, but at the very least they wouldn't enter the political arena forced to fight preconceived perceptions that their voices — and the votes of those who support them — don't really count for much at all.

NOTES

1 D. Fagan, "32-31: Liberals cling to lead: poll," *The Globe and Mail,* June 5, 2004, A1.

2 Jim Harris, Leader, Green Party of Canada, interview by author, June 5, 2004, in Ottawa.

3 Elections Canada, "Registered Political Parties and Parties Eligible for Registration," July 6, 2004, http://www.elections.ca/content.asp?section=pol&document=index&dir=par&lang=e&textonly=false.

4 See, for example, D. Howell, "Public funding plan will be boon for Greens," *The Edmonton Journal,* June 7, 2004, A5; N. Kohler, "Definition of 'party' has critics edgy: Bill C-3: Legislation could have a big effect — but not on this vote," *National Post,* June 14, 2004, A4.

5 LEGIS Info, Library of Parliament, Bill C-24: An Act to amend the Canada Elections Act and the Income Tax Act (political financing), http://www.parl.gc.ca/LEGISINFO/index.asp?Lang=E&query=3292&Session=11&List=toc (accessed May 20, 2004).

6 Wayne Crookes, National Campaign Manager, Green Party of Canada, telephone interview by author, May 17, 2004.

7 Peter Rosenthal, Lawyer, Roach Schwartz & Associates, telephone interview by author, May 14, 2004.

8 Ronald Gray, Leader, Christian Heritage Party, telephone interview by author, June 25, 2004.

9 For transcripts of debate in the House of Commons and the Senate surrounding setting the threshold at one, see: "Major Speeches in Parliament," http://www.parl.gc.ca/LEGISINFO/index.asp?Lang=E&Chamber=N&StartList=A&EndList=Z&Session=12&Type=0&Scope=I&query=4101&List=toc-2. Also see debate surrounding Bill C-51, the predecessor to Bill C-3, http://www.parl.gc.ca/LEGISINFO/index.asp?Lang=E&Chamber=C&StartList=2&EndList=200&Session=11&Type=0&Scope=I&query=3768&List=toc-2.

10 Bill C-3: An Act to amend the Canada Elections Act and the Income Tax Act, http://www.parl.gc.ca/LEGISINFO/index.asp?Lang=E&query=4101&Session=12&List=toc (accessed May 24, 2004).

11 For analysis of the Court's decision, see: H. MacIvor, "The Charter of Rights and Party Politics: The Impact of the Supreme Court Ruling in *Figueroa v. Canada (Attorney General)." Choices,* 10, no. 4, 2004. Montreal IRPP.

12 For a summary of benefits and obligations under Bill C-3: An Act to amend the Canada Elections Act and the Income Tax Act, see "New Law For Registering Political Parties," http://www.elections.ca/content.asp?section=gen&document=ec90538&dir=bkg&lang=e&textonly=false.

13 Miguel Figueroa, Leader, Communist Party of Canada, telephone interview by author, May 10, 2004.

14 *Figueroa v. Canada (Attorney General),* 2003 SCC 37.

15 See, for example, the report of the Law Commission of Canada, *Voting Counts: Electoral Reform for Canada.*

16 In addition to those cited directly in this chapter, I would like to thank the many other Green Party members and candidates who provided information and interviews before, during, and after the campaign. Also see the party Web site at http://www.greenparty.ca/.

17 Peter Kent, Deputy Editor, Global Television News, telephone interview by author, June 25, 2004.

18 Green Party of Canada, "Green Party TV Ad Breaks Silence" (Media Release), June 5, 2004.

19 See, for example: Editorial, "Green with envy and rightly so," *The Ottawa Citizen,* June 4, 2004, A16; Editorial, "Greens deserve a chance," *Montreal Gazette,* June 4, 2004, A22; Opinion, "Expand the franchise: Green Party has proven its credibility and deserves a place in the TV debates," *Calgary Herald,* June 4, 2004, A16; Desbarats, "Don't fence Greens out of the TV leaders' debate," *The Globe and Mail,* June 10, 2004, A23.

20 According to a poll commissioned by the Green Party of Canada, 76 percent of those surveyed thought the Green Party should be included in the leaders' debates. The poll was conducted by Oraclepoll Research between

May 27 and May 31, 2004. Five hundred Canadians eighteen years of age and older were interviewed. The margin of error for the survey is +/- 4.4 percent, 19/20 times.

21 Michael Pilling, Platform Chair, Green Party of Canada, telephone interview by author, July 5, 2004.

22 For an account of the emergence of the Green Party internationally, see, for example: Gerd Langguth, *The Green Factor in German Politics: From Protest Movement to Political Party* (Boulder, Colorado: Westview Press, 1984); Margit Mayer and John Ely, eds., *The German Greens: Paradox Between Movement and Party* (Philadelphia: Temple University Press, 1998).

23 See Joan Russow, "The Politics of Exclusion: The Campaign of the Green Party," in *The Canadian General Election of 2000,* ed. J.H. Pammet and C. Dornan (Toronto: Dundurn Press, 2001), 49–163.

24 Elections BC, "Report of the Chief Electoral Officer: 37th Provincial General Election May 16, 2001," http://www.elections.bc.ca/elections/ceofin2001.pdf (accessed May 2004).

25 Elections Ontario, "2003 General Election," http://www.electionsontario.on.ca/results/index.jsp (accessed May 2004).

26 "Into The Election Window," Ipsos-Reid/CTV/*Globe and Mail,* May 20, 2004. Available at: http://www.ipsos-na.com/news/pressrelease.cfm?id=2241.

27 Donna Dasko of Environics Research Group was interviewed by CBC journalist Susan Ormiston during a television report about the Green Party, broadcast on CBC's *The National* on June 2, 2004.

28 John Wright, Senior Vice-President, Ipsos-Reid Public Affairs, telephone interview by author, May 10, 2004.

29 Wayne Crookes, National Campaign Manager, Green Party of Canada, telephone interview by author, July 14, 2004.

30 According to party officials' estimates, the Green Party spent between $480,000 and $600,000 on its campaign.

31 For an account of the role the Internet played for all parties in the 2004 election, see Chapter Seven: "parties@canada: The Internet and the 2004 Cyber-Campaign," by Tamara A. Small.

32 Green Party Leader Jim Harris, interviewed by CBC Radio host Anna Maria Tremonti on *The Current,* May 3, 2004.

33 On environmental policies, the Green Party was rated second to the NDP by Greenpeace Canada and the Sierra Club of Canada. See "Sierra Club of Canada Revises Grade in Light of Conservative Reply to Questionnaire," June 22, 2004, http://www.sierraclub.ca/national/media/item.shtml?x=677;

and "Greenpeace reports on how to 'Vote Earth.'" Answers to the Greenpeace Election 2004 Questionnaire can be found at http://action.web.ca/home/gpc/alerts.shtml?x=59712 (accessed June 13, 2004). See Green Party response: "Harris Challenges Layton to Environment Debate" (Media Release), June 18, 2004, http://www.greenparty.ca/index.php?module=article&view=268.

34 Green Party of Canada, "Proportional Financing First Step to Reform: Green Party" (Media Release), June 24, 2004.

35 E. Greenspon, "Covering election's shifting tides," *The Globe and Mail,* June 12, 2004, A2.

36 Editorial, "Ottawa Centre: A Green breakthrough," *The Ottawa Citizen,* June 22, 2004, B4.

37 Ronald Gray, Leader, Christian Heritage Party, telephone interviews by author, May 7, June 25, July 13, 2004. Also see party Web site at http://www.chp.ca/.

38 See, for example, B. Lahgi, "Social issues hijack Harper's agenda: he wants to talk taxes, but questions about abortion, gay marriage and capital punishment just keep coming," *The Globe and Mail,* June 4, 2004, A10; A. Dawson, "Tories may use Constitution to ban gay marriage, Harper says: Notwithstanding clause allows override of Charter; Harper would withdraw question on issue before top court, allow vote in Parliament," *The Ottawa Citizen,* June 3, 2004, B1; A. Dawson and R. Fife, "Harper campaign veers right, gay marriage fight. Harper says he'd allow free vote on abortions," *Montreal Gazette,* June 4, 2004, A12.

39 Marc-Boris St-Maurice, Leader, Marijuana Party, telephone interviews by author, June 26, July 5, July 16, July 19, 2004; Hugo St-Onge, Leader, Bloc Pot, telephone interviews by author, April 29, June 25, 2004. Also see party Web site at http://www.marijuanaparty.com/index.en.php3.

40 Canadian Press, "Marijuana Party seeks support from grassroots," *The Star Phoenix,* June 2, 2004, A9.

41 See, for example: Pot-TV, "Jack Layton, Leader of the NDP, on Canada's Cannabis Laws!" http://www.pot-tv.net/archive/shows/pottvshowse-2271.html (accessed July 16, 2004); T. Reeb, "Marijuana 'wonderful,' should be legal Layton says: NDP leader 'blowing smoke to make a point,' his predecessor says," *National Post,* November 8, 2003, A5.

42 Marc Emery, telephone interview by author, July 19, 2004.

43 Alan Young, telephone interview by author, July 16, 2004.

44 C-10, An Act to amend the Contraventions Act and the Controlled Drugs and Substances Act, http://www.parl.gc.ca/LEGISINFO/index.asp?Lang=E&Chamber=C&StartList=2&EndList=200&Session=12&Type=0&Scope=I&query=4105&List=toc.

45 The Liberal government introduced Bill C-17: An Act to amend the Contraventions Act and the Controlled Drugs and Substances Act and to make consequential amendments to other Acts on November 1, 2004.

46 Al Gullon, Interim Secretary, Progressive Canadian Party, telephone interview by author, May 12, 2004; Joe Hueglin, National Coordinator, Progressive Canadian Party, telephone interviews by author, May 12, June 25, July 5, 2004. Also see party Web site at http://www.pcparty.org/.

47 Louis Lang, Public Relations Officer, Marxist-Leninist Party of Canada, telephone interviews by author, May 25, May 26, July 7, 2004; Enver Villamizar, Windsor West candidate, telephone interview by author, July 21, 2004. Also see party Web site at http://www.cpcml.ca/.

48 For an account of the history of Communism in Canada, see, for example: Ivan Avakumovic, *The Communist Party in Canada: A History* (Toronto: McClelland and Stewart Limited, 1975). See also: Lynn Ratliffe, "Canada," in *Yearbook on International Communist Affairs,* ed. Richard F. Staar and Margit N. Grigory (Stanford, California: Hoover Institution Press, 1990 and 1991).

49 Miguel Figueroa, Leader, Communist Party of Canada, telephone interview by author, July 8, 2004.

50 Connie Fogal, Leader, Canadian Action Party, telephone interviews by author, May 25, 2004 and July 5, 2004; Marc Bombois, West Vancouver-Sunshine Coast candidate, telephone interview by author, July 21, 2004; Paul Hellyer, founder and former leader, Canadian Action Party, telephone interview by author, August 20, 2004. Also see the party's Web site at http://www.canadianactionparty.ca/.

51 For accounts of Hellyer's role in the 1968 and 1976 leadership races, see, for example: Donald Peacock, *Journey to Power: The Story of a Canadian Election* (Toronto: The Ryerson Press, 1968); John Sawatsky, *Mulroney: The Politics of Ambition* (Toronto: Macfarlane, Walter & Ross, 1991); Martin Sullivan, *Mandate '68: The Year of Pierre Elliott Trudeau* (Toronto: Doubleday Canada Limited, 1968).

52 Information on past elections is available from Elections Canada at http://www.elections.ca/intro.asp?section=pas&document=index&lang=e&textonly=false.

53 For an account of the reasoning behind a merger, see Paul Hellyer, *Goodbye Canada* (Toronto: Chimo Media Inc., 2001).

54 See, for example: B. Curry, "Paul Hellyer the latest to be wooed by NDP: 'I think Mr. Layton's got a lot on the ball and he's going to stir things up,' ex-Cabinet Minister says: Former Liberal, Conservative," *National Post,* January 22, 2004, A4.

55 Miguel Figueroa, Leader, Communist Party of Canada, telephone interviews by author, May 10 and July 8, 2004; Stuart Ryan, Ottawa Centre

candidate, telephone interview by author, July 20, 2004. Also see the party's Web site at http://www.communist-party.ca/.

56 Jean-Serge Brisson, Leader, Libertarian Party of Canada, telephone interviews by author, May 20 and July 5, 2004; Adam Desaulniers, Burnaby-Douglas candidate, telephone interviews by author, July 20 and July 28, 2004. Also see the party's Web site at http://www.libertarian.ca/ and Desaulniers' site at http://adamdesaulniers.com/.

57 For an account of Libertarianism in the United States, see, for example: Joseph M. Hazlett II, *The Libertarian Party and Other Minor Political Parties in the United States* (Jefferson, North Carolina: McFarland & Company Inc., 1992).

58 See Green Party of Canada platform, available at http://www.greenparty.ca/platform2004/en/policies.php?p=41. Proportional representation (PR) is not in the official platform of the Progressive Canadian Party. The party has had no official discussions about PR as yet. The Libertarians, according to their leader, are wary of any initiative that may enlarge government. The Marxist-Leninists, according to Enver Villamizar, support PR but believe it is just one element of an electoral system that needs a complete overhaul in order to further empower Canadians politically.

59 Law Commission of Canada, *Voting Counts: Electoral Reform for Canada,* xviii.

60 Peter Rosenthal, Lawyer, Roach Schwartz & Associates, telephone interviews by author, May 14 and June 25, 2004.

61 *Figueroa v. Canada (Attorney General),* 2003 SCC 37, paragraph 81.

62 H. MacIvor, "Proportional and Semi-Proportional Electoral Systems: Their Potential Effects on Canadian Politics," Advisory Committee of Registered Political Parties, Elections Canada, Ottawa, April 1999.

CHAPTER SEVEN

parties@canada:
The Internet and the 2004 Cyber-Campaign

by Tamara A. Small

> *He said Albertans should build firewalls around Alberta.*
>
> *Then he proposed that Albertans withdraw from the Canada Pension Plan.*
>
> *Further he suggested, "each province should raise its own revenue for healthcare."*
>
> *Sound like a leader for all of Canada?*
>
> *For the whole quote, its source and context visit StephenHarperSaid.ca*[1]

In the weeks before the 2004 federal election was called, five Liberal Party television ads were aired targeting Conservative Party Leader Stephen Harper. The ads, featuring white text on a black screen, cited contentious quotations made by Harper on issues ranging from immigration to Iraq. Equally importantly, the ads ended by encouraging viewers to log on to the Web site StephenHarperSaid.ca for more information and further quotes made by the Conservative leader. Within days, the Conservative Party responded in kind by launching a similar Internet site. TeamMartinSaid.ca focused on quotes made by not only Prime Minster Paul Martin but also members of Liberal caucus. While the Internet has played a role in Canadian election campaigns since 1997, these two sites marked a significant moment in Internet-based politics in Canada. Attack television ads have become commonplace, but never before had Canadian political parties engaged to such an extent in a war of words on-line. This cyber-war was reminiscent of the e-buttal[2] sites used during the 2000 U.S. presidential debate between George Bush and Al Gore. Both of the campaigns launched Web sites that conducted real-time fact-checking during the debate. Within seconds of a point being made, an e-buttal would be posted on the rival campaign's site.

The Canadian Federal Election of 2000 was said to be "the nation's first Internet election."[3] This was the first election in which the majority of Canadians had access to the technology. Moreover, both major and minor political parties had established Internet sites. The general sentiment was that the Internet had not altered the campaign in 2000. In comparison to the sites of U.S. presidential candidates, one media commentator described the Canadian party sites as lacking "pizzazz."[4] The sites failed to take advantage of the full potential of the medium, especially in terms of interactivity. Also in 2000, very few local candidates used the Internet for campaigning. One-third of NDP and Liberal candidates had established campaign Web sites in 2000.[5] Attallah and Burton describe the 2000 cyber-campaign: "On the whole ... the parties' online offerings were lacklustre, suggesting that they accept the reality of the new medium and the need to meet a bare minimum, but they have not fully thought through its true political utility or value."[6]

Much has changed in the cyber-campaigning landscape since the 2000 election. One of the big American political stories of 2004 was Howard Dean's use of the Internet in his bid for the Democratic presidential nomination. Through his Web site, Dean raised more money than any other Democratic candidate. The Internet was also used to organize the thousands of volunteers through Meetup.com.[7] Even though Dean did poorly in the primaries, he will be remembered as the "small-state governor who, with the help of Meetup.com and hundreds of bloggers ... elbowed his way into serious contention for his party's presidential nomination."[8] Closer to home, it seemed as though the lessons of the Dean campaign were not lost on former Magna International CEO Belinda Stronach when she ran for the leadership of the Conservative Party in 2004 (see Chapter Three). Using many of Dean's techniques including a blog,[9] belinda.ca was very popular; in its first week her site had 12.8 million hits.[10] As well, the number of people surfing the Web continued to grow in Canada. In fact, 64 percent of Canadian households use the Internet regularly. This represents a 13 percent increase since 2000. Today, most Canadians access the Internet from home (55 percent) and subscribe to the Internet using a high-speed connection (65 percent).[11] Using the Internet is now a part of daily life for most Canadians.

Given the growing recognition of the importance of the Internet in political campaigns worldwide, it would appear that the launch of StephenHarperSaid.ca and TeamMartinSaid.ca in the pre-campaign period indicated a new willingness on the part of political parties in Canada to engage this technology for campaigning. This chapter examines the 2004 cyber-campaign: How did Canadian political parties present themselves on-line? To what extent did the parties take advantage of the Internet's unique features for campaigning? The 2004 cyber-campaign witnessed a definite progression in the use of the Internet by Canadian parties. Voters that visited party Internet sites were exposed to an abundance of substantive information. There were also many instances of the parties using their Web sites to facilitate engagement with voters.

Election campaigns involve many different political participants, including parties, their candidates, interest groups, the media, and individual citizens. All of these groups, to some extent, used the Internet during the campaign. Many national media organizations, for instance, developed special subsections of their sites that served as election information portals. This chapter focuses on the use of the Internet by political parties. The Web sites of the Liberal Party, Conservative Party, NDP, Bloc Québécois, and Green Party were tracked during the pre-campaign and writ period.[12] A content analysis, both qualitative and quantitative, of these sites was conducted over the thirty-six-day campaign. The qualitative portion included a daily monitoring of each of the sites. A coding scheme developed by Internet politics scholars Rachel Gibson and Stephen Ward was the basis of the quantitative portion.[13] Specifically designed for the systematic analysis of campaign Web sites, this framework allows for the understanding of the functions and effectiveness of campaign Web sites. This coding scheme has been embraced within the literature and has been the basis of several international research projects on cyber-campaigning.

It is important to stress that this type of analysis focuses on what Pippa Norris calls the "supply" side of party Web sites. Supply research typically employs some form of content analysis to determine the structure and content of the sites. This is opposed to the "demand" side, which examines how the online public responds to such Web sites. Demand research typically employs survey data on how the public uses party Web sites and is concerned with such questions as, "Do party Web sites reach party supporters and political activists or undedicated voters among the general public?" and "Do party Web sites increase public participation (voting, donating, volunteering) in the political process?"[14] It should also be noted that this analysis does not make any claims about the internal or intra-party uses of the Internet. In a large country such as Canada, parties make use of Intranet Web sites and internal e-mail. Both are effective and efficient ways to provide information about the campaign to all ridings, party activists, and regional party organizations (see Chapter Four). This chapter looks exclusively at the campaigning styles of parties in their attempt to reach out to voters through the (external) sites on the World Wide Web.

ON-LINE POLITICS: CHARACTERISTICS & PERSPECTIVES

The Internet has been described as the most revolutionary technology since the printing press. Since the mid-1990s there has been much speculation as to whether the Internet will change politics. There are many reasons to believe that it will be transformative. First, history has shown that the introduction of new communication technologies has substantially affected the functioning of politics. Television, for instance, has had a dramatic affect on politics. From the leaders' tours to the televised debates, television is the battleground on which campaigns are fought in Canada. However, the Internet is very different from older communications media, being distinguished from its predecessors by the following characteristics:[15]

- Interactivity: The interactive capability of the Internet is considered its greatest strength. The Internet allows for direct and instantaneous feedback between the sender and receiver.
- Information: The Internet is a storehouse of information. It allows for quick and inexpensive transmission, sorting, and storage of information.
- Multimedia: The Internet brings together print and electronic communication methods into a single medium. This allows for a change in the form and style of messages.
- Narrowcasting: In contrast to broadcasting, narrowcast mediums allows for the targeting of niche segments of the population. The Internet can, in fact, target individual users.
- Decentralized and Unmediated: Both the sender and receiver have the utmost control when using the Internet. Senders have increased control over the content of messages and who receives them. Users have increased control over what messages are received and when.

The Internet, therefore, provides new opportunities for campaigners to conduct their traditional activities and for the development of new forms of campaigning that are Internet-exclusive.

There has been much theorizing on the question of whether the Internet will change politics. Early speculation described the Internet as a force to revitalize and revolutionize democratic politics. More recently, as a result of empirical research, commentators have been promoting a more tempered stance. Here we will look at two perspectives relevant to virtual parties and cyber-campaigning: the cyber-optimist perspective and the normalization hypothesis.

In Canada, as in other advanced nations, there has been a steady decline in public confidence in government and non-governmental institutions including political parties. Since the 1988 election, voter turnout in Canada has continued to decline, reaching an all-time low in 2004 (see Chapter Twelve). Canadians have been looking to interest groups as vehicles for change instead of to parties. It is this context in which the cyber-optimist sees the Internet transforming politics. The Internet, it is claimed, will "contribute to revitalizing the role of parties in representative democracy, facilitating communications between citizen and the state, and strengthening support for these institutions."[16] E-mail and political Web sites will provide citizens with unparalleled access to the political system. In addition to information flowing downwards, with the click of a mouse Internet users can quickly make inquiries or provide feedback. Discussion boards and blogs can be platforms for ongoing discussion between political leaders and citizens. Citizens have access, not only to parties, but also to other citizens, including other party members. The Internet would allow "virtual communities" to flourish, which would enable people, regardless of where they are located, to share interests and information and advance common political agendas.[17]

Another common promise relates to the unlimited information found on the Internet. Political Web sites would undoubtedly increase the information available to citizens. What is more, this information would be straight from the horse's mouth, unfiltered by the media. Not only would the information be more varied, but also citizens would have greater control over what information they receive. This, according to cyber-optimists, would be beneficial to democratic politics because a more knowledgeable citizen is a more active citizen. Another claim of cyber-optimists is the "equalization hypothesis." It is argued that the Internet has the capacity to broaden political competition and equalize the playing field. The relatively low costs, lack of editorial control, and non-hierarchical nature of the Internet provide smaller or fringe political actors with numerous opportunities that do not exist for them in the offline world.[18] On the Internet, a minor political party has same potential as a major one to reach citizens.

Many scholars of Internet politics have come to question the deterministic view of e-democracy presented by cyber-optimists. Richard Davis, for instance, asks how the additional cost, involvement, and time commitment incurred by on-line politics would make people more politically efficacious.[19] Empirical tests of the claims of cyber-optimists led to the development of the normalization hypothesis. The hypothesis states that "as the Internet develops, patterns of socioeconomic and political relationships on-line come to resemble those of the real world. Applied to political parties, this hypothesis implies that just as the major parties dominate the sphere of everyday domestic politics, so they come to dominate cyberspace."[20]

In rejecting the claims of optimists, normalizers agree that there will be changes to democratic politics because of the Internet, but they argue that it will not radically alter the state of political competition, nor will it drastically change citizen engagement levels. The on-line political world will resemble the off-line one. Public levels of political knowledge and interest will be reinforced, not altered, by the Internet. In essence, politics on the Internet will be "politics as usual."[21]

Normalizers argue that the Internet will not dramatically change or equalize the status of minor parties (or their candidates). This is because major parties have both the resources and motivation to get on-line. The sites of major parties will be easier to access, because "they are able to advertise their Web presence more successfully than the smaller parties."[22] Not only would major parties be more successful in attracting users to their sites in the first place, but they would also be more successful in retaining them. The Web sites of major political parties will likely be much more professional, technologically sophisticated, and maintained by full-time staff to ensure the freshness of the content, thereby giving users incentives to return, they claim.

Empirical support for normalization versus equalization has been mixed. American, British, and German data have lent credence to the normalization hypothesis. Alternatively, Japanese and Southern European data show an equalization of party competition. Unlike normalization versus equalization, there is much more consensus about the political information capacities of the Internet. Empirical studies show that campaign Web sites serve Internet users by conveying much more political information than they might otherwise have access to. Supporting the claims of cyber-optimists, there is evidence that the Internet is beneficial to campaigns in that it gives them a new tool for control over the dissemination of information, thus avoiding the filters of the conventional press.

LAUNCHING THE CYBER-CAMPAIGN

The 2004 cyber-campaign had begun long before the writ was dropped on May 23. In addition to StephenHarperSaid.ca and TeamMartinSaid.ca, all of the party Internet sites moved into election mode in the weeks before the call, providing nomination and candidate information. The Green Party of Canada was the first out of the gates. Its platform and riding information was up on the site weeks before the election call. After the Bloc Québécois launched its campaign on May 15, its unilingual site was redesigned to incorporate a number of election-related links, including the party platform, detailed candidate biographies, and voter information.

In the hours after the Governor General dissolved Parliament, there was a flurry of activity in cyberspace. The Liberal Party site reflected the launch of their campaign with three "Top Stories," including the "Statement by Prime Minister Paul Martin on the call of the general election" moments after the call. The NDP had the most dramatic cyber-launch, producing a new site rather than re-launching its old one. However, much of it was still under construction and was exceptionally slow while loading for the duration of the first day. Both the Greens and the Bloc would update their sites reflecting the election call. The Green Party posted press releases regarding its leader and campaign, and the Bloc uploaded a video of leader Gilles Duceppe. Also to promote the beginning of their cyber-campaign and generate support, the Liberals, NDP, and Green Party sent out e-mails to subscribers of their mailing lists.

Unlike the other major political parties, the Conservatives did not launch their cyber-campaign until the following day. The next morning, users awoke to find a new site asking Canadians to "Demand Better." The site was plagued with problems; either it was extremely slow while loading or visitors would receive an error message. These problems would last for several days. Both the Liberals and the Conservatives faced greater problems during the second week of the campaign when hackers attacked the two sites. Hackers had configured a computer or group of computers to barrage the sites, making it difficult for other users to access them.[23] The RCMP was called by the Conservative Party to investigate. From site redesigns to attack sites to the launch of brand new sites, it was clear all of the parties had made a significant investment in their on-line presences for this election campaign. These five sites would prove to be much more informative and engaging than the lacklustre ones of the previous election.

POINT, CLICK & INFORM

The Internet gives political parties unprecedented control over the dissemination of campaign information. It also increases the amount of choice available to users. From the earliest cyber-campaign in the United States in 1996, most commentators agree that information provision is the most important function served by campaign sites. Sites commonly offered biographic information about the candidates, press releases, speeches, news files, and lengthy campaign statements. The archival nature of Web sites allows Internet users to visit and revisit information.

The Canadian experience reveals similar results with regard to information dissemination. As Table 1 indicates, visitors were exposed to a lot of substantive information during this campaign, including party platforms, media releases, and event calendars.

Web sites were particularly useful for finding out where any of the parties stood on the issues. Party platform links were prominent on all five sites. As noted, both the BQ and the Greens uploaded their platforms before the election call. The other three uploaded their platforms in tandem with the off-line launches. The launching of the platforms demonstrated the integration of the Web site in the campaign. Shortly after their announcement on the campaign trail, the platforms would be available on-line. The platforms were very accessible for users, offered in several formats, including PDF and HTML.[24] The Green Party offered one- or three-page condensed versions of their platform for quick viewing. In a surprising move, the Bloc even added an English version of their platform during the campaign.

In addition to platforms, extensive links to policy and issue statements could be found on the Web sites. The "Issues" section of conservative.ca briefly outlined the Conservatives' stance on twenty key

Table 1: Information Features on Party Campaign Web Sites, 2004

	BQ	Cons	GP	Lib	NDP
Party history	X	X	X	X	X
Party structure	X				
Party officials	X			X	
Leader profile	X	X	X	X	X
Candidate contact	X	X	X	X	X
Candidate bio	X		X	X	
Campaign news	X	X	X	X	X
Media room	X	X	X	X	X
Party platform	X	X	X	X	X
Issues & policy	X	X	X	X	X
Party policy comparison			X		
Election speeches	X	X	X	X	X
Endorsements			X		
Campaign calendar	X	X	X	X	X
Campaign diary		X			X
Voting information	X			X	X
Riding information			X	X	
E-buttal site		X		X	
Campaign media coverage		X	X	X	
Contact information	X	X	X	X	X
Archive	X	X	X	X	X
Members only sections	X			X	

issues, such as the Definition of Marriage and Tax Relief. Almost forty detailed policy statements could be found in "Green Values." More than thirty PDF fact sheets were made available on ndp.ca. The Bloc Québécois site had six extensive issues pages. Focusing on issues such as the similarities between Paul Martin and former prime minister Jean Chrétien, and Canadian Steamship Lines, each page would provide fact sheets, the BQ's stance, and links to other related sites. Without a doubt, if Canadians wanted substantive information about the policy positions of the different parties, the Internet provided it.

Equally important, this information was unmediated; the parties were able to provide voters with their own insights and interpretations of the campaign.

Party Web sites were also helpful in searching for candidate and riding information. Users were able to search for their candidate by postal code on all of the sites. A clickable map of Canada was also available on the Green and Conservative Web sites. The amount of information given by the parties about their candidates varied. The Liberals, Greens, and Bloc provided photos, bios, and contact information, including URLs to candidate Web sites. The Conservatives provided only basic contact information, including e-mail and Web sites, if available. Instead of providing candidate information in-site, the NDP Web site hyperlinked to the sites of all of its candidates.[25]

As a dynamic space, the Web allows for the continual publication of new information. From their computer desks, Internet users could essentially be on the campaign trail, since the Web sites were frequently updated to reflect the events and messages of the campaign. A good portion of all of the home pages of the sites was dedicated to campaign news. Table 2 shows the total number of news stories found on home pages over the thirty-six-day campaign and the section where they could be found on each party's site.

Table 2: Homepage Campaign News Stories, 2004

	BQ	Cons	GP	Lib	NDP
Number	59	65	60	153	109
Home page Section	Manchettes	Press Release	Media Releases	Press Release	The Latest News
				Top Stories	Headlines
				Reality Checks	Reality Checks

Some sites updated their campaign news several times a day, reflecting the ebb and flow of events on the campaign trail. While new content and links were added to the sites over the campaign, the news section was essentially the main driver of change on these Web sites. Once removed from the home page, the news articles were archived elsewhere in the sites.

In many cases, the campaign news was in fact press or media releases. There is reason to suggest that this form of information was targeted towards the mass media rather than ordinary Canadians, as it was written in the traditional press release format. On the sites of the Conservatives, Liberals, and the Green Party, items like the phrase "For Immediate Release," press contact information, or the typical "-30-" that indicates the end of a press release were found. On more than one occasion, even the statement "UNDER EMBARGO UNTIL 10:00 am" was found on a press release on the Conservative Web site. Under an embargo, the media or newswire agrees not to release the information until a specified time. Many of these home page stories could also be found in the media rooms or the press sections of the sites.

Campaign Web sites are obviously directed towards a number of different audiences, including undecided voters and party supporters. It should not be surprising that the media would be a major target of these sites.[26] For practical purposes, the Internet serves as an efficient and inexpensive tool for the campaign to reach the press. Moreover, there is evidence that the Internet is "reshaping political journalism" by being an important research tool.[27] It may be the case that the parties were just making use of information created for other aspects of the campaign. It would be incorrect to argue that just because of the format this type of information would not be useful to citizens in informing them about the daily happenings on the campaign trail and the most up-to-date stance on campaign issues. Juliet Roper suggests that the posting of media releases allows interested people to freely assess the viewpoints of the parties for themselves without the mediation of the press.[28] But this does raise an interesting question about the purposes and functions of party Web sites during election campaigns.

In addition to the previously mentioned items, users had access to speeches, party histories, and information about where and how to vote.

Some of the parties would occasionally upload or hyperlink favourable media stories or quotes relating to their campaign. It should be evident that information provision was a major component of the 2004 cyber-campaign. Like advertisements and the debates, the Internet serves as a tool for a party to speak directly to voters about its policy and agenda without any of the media's spin. This is extremely beneficial for the smaller parties, like the Green Party, who receive less media coverage. Through Web sites they are still able to get their message out to voters.

Although the information provision function of election Web sites is often praised by observers, it is also the focus of criticism. Web sites that have been heavy on top-down information provision have been denounced as electronic brochures, "seldom more than static versions of the brochures that fill the mailbox."[29] One recent study by Hillwatch E-Service claimed that in comparison to American campaign sites, Canadian ones, in this election, were little more than "electronic lawn signs." "They inform but don't engage."[30] The following sections consider the engagement features of Canadian campaign Web sites. While it was not uniform across the parties, there was indeed much progress in the area of on-line engagement since the 2000 election. There were instances of the parties interacting with voters in cyberspace and encouraging cyber-involvement in their campaigns.

PARTIES AND VOTERS INTERACTING IN CYBERSPACE?

Interactivity has been touted as the Internet's most significant characteristic. As mentioned, it is a clear plank in the cyber-optimists perspective regarding citizen engagement. Given its significance, early researchers were surprised to find limited use of it in election campaigns. British and American data show that two-way interactive features, in the form of discussion groups or blogs, were practically non-existent on campaign sites. One commentator called the lack of innovation in citizen-to-citizen or citizen-to-campaign discussion the "most disappointing non-development."[31]

Table 3 shows the results of the content analysis of interactive features found on the sites of the five parties.

Table 3: Interactive Features on Party Campaign Web Sites, 2004

	BQ	Cons	GP	Lib	NDP
Feedback form	X	X		X	X
Mailto:			X		
E-mail newsletters	X	X	X	X	X
Comment on	X				
On-line games/gimmicks					
Guest book					
Opinion polls					
Q&A sessions with leaders	*	*			
Blog					
Discussion board			X		

* Both Gilles Duceppe and Jim Harris participated in a cyberpresse.ca on-line chat.[32]

Clearly, very few interactive features were implemented during the election campaign. All of the sites made it extremely easy for the public to contact the parties. Even though all of the parties have e-mail addresses, only the Green Party put them on the site as a mailto: link. Clicking on a mailto: link opens up the user's default e-mail program and allows them to send an e-mail to the party from their own account. The other parties opted, instead, for the contact form. Forms are popular in campaigns for several reasons. First, because the Internet transcends geography, requiring certain information on forms, such as a postal code or phone number, is a way of filtering out non-constituents.[33] Additionally, forms can be beneficial to campaigns in their attempt to enhance their off-line activities, including direct mail or telephone campaigns. While the BQ asked only for the visitor's e-mail address on their form, the following table indicates the information requested by the other three parties:

Table 4: Information Requested on On-line Forms, 2004

Cons	Lib[34]	NDP
First name	First Name	First Name
Last name	Last Name	Last Name
City	Address	E-mail
E-mail	City	Postal code
Telephone	Province	Phone
Postal Code	Postal Code	
	Telephone	
	Fax	
	E-mail	

Just as it was very easy for Internet users to contact the party, it was also very simple to have the party contact users via e-newsletters. This was a welcome addition to the cyber-campaign not seen in the 2000 election. All of the parties provided sign-up boxes on the home pages of their sites. The number and purpose of the e-newsletters varied a great detail. Every evening during the campaign, the Liberal Party sent their "Liberal Party Nightly Bulletin." This newsletter recapped the daily press releases, campaign stories, and the following day's itinerary for the prime minister. Occasionally, the party would e-mail links to Web polls found on different media sites. Over the entire campaign period, the Liberals e-mailed forty-one newsletters to their subscribers. The New Democrats sent seventeen editions of "E.NDP" over the campaign. The E.NDP included press releases, notices of new videos on the site, and photos from the campaign trail. They also encouraged subscribers to donate or volunteer by having hypertext links in the e-mail that were sent directly to ndp.ca. The Bloc Québécois sent out thirteen e-mails. Many of these were from the party's youth organization, Forum jeunesse du Bloc Québécois. They would often include information about upcoming campaign events and multimedia messages from the party leader. Fourteen e-newsletters were sent by the Green Party, mostly including campaign information and press releases. They also used this forum to inform and rally support around their exclusion from the debates (see Chapter Six). The Conservatives sent only five e-newsletters. Getting people involved in the campaign, through donating and volunteering, was the focus on the Conservative e-mails.

E-mail contact and e-newsletters are important, yet basic, types of interactivity. They constitute a very low threshold for interactivity, given that in both cases information moves in only one direction. There were, however, attempts during this campaign to move beyond partial interactivity. One such case was the "Réagissez!" link on the Bloc Québécois site. This link was located at the conclusion of the campaign stories that the party uploaded daily. Clicking on this link would open a new browser window that allowed visitors to type in a comment. It would also display the comments posted by other visitors. In some instances, users could react to comments made by others. The "Réagissez!" link was an extremely popular feature during the campaign. According to the BQ, more than a thousand comments were posted over the campaign. Interestingly, Gilles Duceppe's performance in the English-language debate inspired Canadians outside of Quebec to use this feature, posting comments in English. The most posts to a single story were directed towards Bloc Québécois' success on the election day. Eighty-eight users posted messages of congratulation starting at 10:07 on election night. According to the party, this feature allowed the Bloc Web site to be a place of exchange and reflection for citizens.[35]

The second case regards the Green Party's platform "Someday is Now," which was explained on the Web site:

> The Green Party does politics differently. We want to engage the public, our members and the opposition parties in a sincere debate about the future of Canada. Our definition of grassroots democracy includes bringing people — from all walks of life — together in discussion about the future.... Our platform evolves with input from members and citizens because that is how democracy should work.[36]

Users were given two ways to participate in the evolution of the platform. First there was the "Rank a Plank" system. Rank a Plank allowed users to click on a thumbs-up or thumbs-down icon for any plank of the platform. Midway through the campaign, the Greens had recorded more than fifty-seven thousand votes. According to the site, the party "re-opened discussion on the least popular planks and ... [were] taking new ideas into consideration."[37] The second way to get involved was through the "Living Platform." The Living Platform was a discussion area in which users could post comments on various aspects of the party policy. It "represents the developing consensus of what future party policies will be."[38] True to their commitment to doing politics differently, the Rank a Plank and Living Platform features were available not only to members of the party but to any visitor to the site.[39] The site also made it possible for users to comment on posts made by other users. For instance, near the end of the campaign the party uploaded a "Cross Party Policy Comparison Chart." More than half of the posts to the Chart were in response to comments made by other users. In some cases the original poster would also reply to the comments made. There was a give-and-take dynamic to some of the discussions. Through these different forums the Green Party, as with the BQ, went beyond the basic interactive features during this campaign; the Liberal, Conservative, and NDP Web sites did not.

There were some surprising omissions in this cyber-campaign. The first was daily poll questions on party Web sites. Daily polls have become an exceptionally popular interactive feature on on-line media sites. On-line polls are an easy way for campaigns to allow visitors to state their preference on a range of issues and interact with the site. Some polls on the sites of major on-line media register over a hundred thousand votes on given questions. To be fair, it should be noted that the BQ site ran two on-line polls in the early weeks of the campaign, but the link was removed on day ten. The Liberals also sent e-mails regarding media polls and had links to major media polls on their site. Given the apparent popularity of such polls, this was a missed interactive opportunity by Canadian parties.

Leader blogs were also omitted. Political blogs were made famous by Howard Dean. Dean's blog entries included personal statements, calls to action, volunteer and staff reports, and links to news stories. More importantly for citizen engagement, the site allowed visitors to give feedback. Political blogs put the people in touch with the campaign and with the candidate. The blog is a "spirited forum for political discussion … 24 hours a day, people from all across the country — and the world — are debating, organizing, arguing, joking, and bringing innovative ideas to our organization."[40] While there was a "Blog" link on conservative.ca, it was more of a campaign journal for Harper, missing the all-important comment feature. In fact, the blog was not even written in the first person, but was written about Harper by an anonymous staffer. Here is an excerpt from the June 4 blog called "Down on the Farm":

> Stephen Harper dropped in on Fred Reicheld's farm in Haldimand-Norfolk today to talk about the new Conservative government's agricultural policy. He seemed to win over the beef cattle, but the pigs weren't convinced. They're too attracted to the trough to give up their Liberal memberships, I guess.[41]

Periodically, Jack Layton would post messages on ndp.ca. Layton's statements were personal, and he claimed several were sent from his BlackBerry Wireless Handheld. However, visitors were not able to comment here, either. While the leaders may have missed a great interactive opportunity during this campaign, many media organizations, including the *Toronto Star*, had election blogs.

The desire to engage citizens through interactive features was not uniform across the parties. The BQ's "Réagissez!" and the Green Party's platform were both extremely interesting attempts to engage citizens in the election campaign. Considering that interactive elements were virtually ignored in 2000, this is an important development in the Canadian cyber-campaign. The popularity of these elements is a testament to the willingness of users to participate in a political dialogue when given the opportunity by a party Web site. These two cases provide some limited support to the cyber-optimist perspective, that cyberspace can create a venue in which citizens and parties can come together to discuss political and campaign issues. This may be a lesson for other parties in future election campaigns in this country.

CYBER-INVOLVEMENT

Resource generation and recruitment was not something discussed in the early theorizing about Internet politics by cyber-optimists. From the very first cyber-campaign in the United States in 1996, candidates began using their campaign Web sites for these purposes. While on-line resource generation and recruitment will not replace off-line activities, there are good reasons for parties and campaigns to also use their Web sites, as explained by the Institute for Politics, Democracy & the Internet:

> Once you have installed a system to solicit and process donations, the cost per "acquisition" … plummets toward the marginal cost of sending out an online message, which is, of course, zero. Second, online funds can be reported and banked in a heartbeat, meaning that donations can be turned around for expenditure in a very short amount of time. Third, Internet users can initiate donations with unparalleled ease.[42]

Howard Dean's campaign has arguably been the most successful case of on-line resource generation and recruitment in recent years. In American presidential politics, the Web has become an invaluable part of reaching out to voters.

As in the 2000 cyber-campaign, resource generation and recruitment were evident on the Internet sites of all five major Canadian political parties in 2004. Table 5 shows that with a few strokes of a keyboard, visitors to all of these sites could join the party, volunteer to help with the campaign, or donate money.

Table 5: Voter Involvement Features on Party Campaign Web Sites, 2004

	BQ	Cons	GP	Lib	NDP
Donation	X	X	X	X	X
Membership	X	X	X	X	X
Volunteer		X	X	X	X
E-postcards	X	X			
Send to a friend		X	X	X	
Promote action			X	X	X
Downloadables		X			X
Contribute to the site	X				
Merchandise			X		X

All of the Web sites employed a secure server for transactions. By encoding communications, a secure server guards against unauthorized access to credit card information. The importance of resource generation and recruitment is evident in the many hypertext links on the home pages of some of the parties. For instance, the Conservatives and Liberals had six and five such links on the home pages of their sites, respectively. Likewise, both parties dedicated a portion of their site to highlight the contributions made by volunteers to their campaign. With every page change on the Conservative site, a new "Volunteer Profile" would be displayed. The profile was composed of the volunteer's name, photo, and a brief quote of why he or she is supporting the party. The Liberal "Volunteer Profile" was composed of the volunteer's name, photo, and a brief biography. There were nineteen profiles on the site over the campaign.

In addition to on-line resource generation and recruitment, Table 5 shows that many of the parties had additional voter involvement links during this cyber-campaign. The 2000 election cycle in the United States gave rise to cyber-volunteering or "viral campaigning." The purpose of viral campaigning is to make it easy for supporters to pass along the campaign message to others. Much of this activity is conducted over the Internet, including sending electronic postcards or placing banner ads on personal Web sites. Commentators have argued that encouraging this type of behaviour through the Internet may have been one of the most important developments and tactical tools of the 2000 cyber-campaign, next to fundraising.[43] The use of viral campaigning techniques in this campaign is again evidence of the progression made by Canadian parties since the last election.

The Liberals, Conservatives, and BQ all used the "send to a friend" technique. The Institute for Politics, Democracy & the Internet recommends this technique because it raises the profile of the campaign by "word of mouse: Your message will reach people you haven't targeted in an environment conducive to your cause, in as much as Net users are more likely to read an email from a friend than from a political organization."[44]

The Conservatives' "Refer to a Friend" sent a text-based e-mail to the friend from the user, inviting the friend to check out the Web site and encouraging him or her to get involved in the campaign. As part of the "Forum jeunesse du Bloc Québécois" Web campaign, users could select one of five e-postcards to send to a friend. The graphic-based postcards encouraged people to vote and reinforced the message of the Bloc campaign. Additionally, any of the BQ articles (Manchettes) could be sent to a friend. On liberal.ca, users could send a page, a press release, and even a video clip. The text-based e-mail would provide a hyperlink to the item sent. Videos could also be sent from conservative.ca. Sending specific videos or stories allowed users to e-mail information they felt was particularly relevant to their friend.

The Liberal Party also encouraged visitors to "Be Heard" by the Canadian media, listing the phone numbers, e-mail addresses, and Web sites of media outlets across the country. The "Be Heard" page also provided URLs to all the major media daily polls. Several days before the leaders' debates, the link "Debat 2004 — Posez une question à Paul Martin" emerged on the Bloc Québécois site. The party provided a form that allowed the public to send leader Gilles Duceppe a question that he should ask the prime minister during the debates.

Although the promised "Send to a Friend" link never emerged on the NDP site, the party did use the site to engage in some notable voter involvement activities. On day twenty-four of the campaign, the party launched the NDP e-Campaign. The letter to potential e-campaigners from leader Jack Layton reads:

> The NDP e-Campaign is Canada's first online election community that puts you in charge of your own personal campaign to raise money and bring new voters to support Today's NDP in this election. We want to put you in control, helping us to deliver the message about the NDP to as many Canadians as possible during the next few weeks of this election. Join the NDP e-Campaign today and we'll start you off running your own personal online campaign to collect pledges and rally support for the NDP. Using simple web and email tools, you can create and send messages to your friends, family and colleagues, inviting them to join you in supporting the NDP in the coming election.[45]

This is another technique made popular by Howard Dean; he was able to create an army of hundreds of thousands of supporters to campaign on his behalf without direct organization from campaign headquarters. Sites like these provide supporters with the tools and information; it turns ordinary citizens into e-campaigners. Another on-line voter involvement feature offered by the New Democrats was "Web badges." In a show of support for the party, supporters could put an NDP.ca (or NPD.ca) banner on their own Web sites. The supporter would simply have to cut and paste the HTML code, provided by the NDP, into his or her own site code.

For much of the 2004 campaign, resource generation and recruitment were the only on-line voter links on greenparty.ca. The exclusion of leader Jim Harris from the election leaders' debates gave the party an incentive. On May 30, a new section, "Green Party Excluded from Leader's Debate" emerged on the home page.

In addition to the letter written by Harris to the broadcasting consortium, there were several ways for supporters to help. The site encouraged supporters to send an e-mail to the broadcasters by providing their e-mail addresses.[46] Supporters could print off a copy of three sample letters to be snail-mailed. The Green Party also encouraged supporters to sign an on-line petition. This petition was found on the Web site PetitionOnline.com. This site "provides free online hosting of public petitions for responsible public advocacy." The petition directed to the Canadian News Media contended that the Green Party had earned a spot in the election debates. Users could view signatures, sign the petition, provide comments, and send the petition to a friend. Through word of mouse, thousands of people were mobilized on this issue, and in the end there were more than thirteen thousand signatures on the on-line petition. The reaction to the exclusion of the Green Party from the debates demonstrated that the Internet could be used not only to mobilize political support but also to react quickly to campaign events. According to Cornfield and Seiger, "the Internet transforms the action-reaction dynamic defining events."[47] Within a few moments of an important event occurring, the Web can be used by the campaign in public relations. It can quickly get out messages to the public, supporters, and the press.

The basic voter involvement links — on-line resource generation and recruitment features — are very important to any campaign and are still noteworthy examples of political parties using the Internet as a high-tech means to achieve their traditional party functions. In 2004, however, Canadian parties made extensive efforts to move beyond the basics, incorporating tricks learned from other on-line campaigns, and we saw many new developments. The "send to a friend" and e-campaigning links seen in this election represent recognition of the benefit of providing on-line links for voters to get involved. Very easily and quickly Internet users became cyber-volunteers helping to spread the message and generate excitement on the behalf of the campaign. Cyber-optimists have argued the Internet can serve as a virtual bridge between citizens and their political institutions. Whether many Canadians took advantage of these opportunities is still uncertain. But the parties did take advantage of the technology to reach out to voters and engage them in the campaign.

SEEING & HEARING THE CYBER-CAMPAIGN

In addition to providing campaigns with new possibilities to communicate their message, multimedia is also useful in making the site more engaging for users. A dynamic site will assist in getting users to stop and investigate the site and hopefully return. The use of multimedia can be an exciting way to present campaign information to users. Despite this, there were few attempts to exploit the multimedia capabilities of the Internet in the 2000 federal election, which was surprising since they were used extensively in campaigns in other countries at the same time. American presidential candidates in 2000 and British political parties in 2001 uploaded their campaign ads and aired live webcasts via their sites. These campaigns also made use of fun cartoons and games on their sites. But while the use of multimedia by Canada's political parties did not conform to that of their international peers in the previous election, it was an important feature of 2004 cyber-campaign.

Table 6 demonstrates that all five parties made extensive use of multimedia features during this election. From campaign songs to political cartoons to audio/video, there was a lot to listen to and watch on-line during this campaign. A campaign photo gallery was one of the most popular features of party Web sites. Photos from campaign events from across the country would be uploaded to the sites on almost a daily basis. In addition to a photo gallery, there was a photo slide show called "Prime Minister's Tour" on the home page of the Liberal site, updated almost daily. Uniquely, the Bloc Québécois site even allowed visitors to submit photos or videos to the party to be posted on the site.[48]

The parties made their television advertisements available on the Web sites. As the ads were released over the national airwaves, they could also be found in cyberspace. Radio ads, too, could be found on

Table 6: Multimedia Features on Party Campaign Web Sites, 2004

	BQ	Cons	GP	Lib	NDP
Flashing icons/moving text		X		X	
Animation	X				
Photographs	X	X	X	X	X
Campaign photo gallery	X	X		X	X
Slideshow				X	
Campaign ads	X	X	X	X	X
Other audio		X	X		
Other video	X	X		X	X
Live Webcasts					

the sites of the Green Party and the NDP. In fact, visitors to ndp.ca could listen to the Aboriginal or Portuguese radio ads used during the campaign, as all of the party's multilingual ads were made available on-line. Given that some advertisements are targeted to different regions or language groups,[49] Web site visitors were able to see and hear ads not normally available to them.

In addition to the ads, there was extensive use of video on the campaign sites. On the home page of conservative.ca there was also the "Video of the Day." Changed sporadically over the campaign, these would feature Stephen Harper at different campaign events; one even showed Harper playing soccer with some children on a campaign break. There were twenty-three videos, some not related to the campaign, on the "Video Footage" page of liberal.ca. One video, called "Candidate Photos," featured the prime minister posing for photos with hundreds of Liberal candidates in just forty seconds. The Bloc Québécois made the most extensive use of multimedia, offering different photos and videos with their campaign articles. The video usually featured Gilles Duceppe giving speeches on the cyber-trail. There were more than twenty-five different videos on the home page alone over the campaign. The NDP uploaded some innovative multimedia over the campaign. First, there was the controversial rap music video "Ed's Back." The fifty-second video, produced for a *This Hour has 22 Minutes* segment, featured former NDP leader Ed Broadbent rapping about his return to federal politics. The producer of the video donated it to the NDP.[50] The Ottawa-Centre riding association of Conservative Party requested an Elections Canada investigation of the video for violating election contribution laws. According to the riding association, the video may have violated the contribution limits allowed by the Bill C-24 in that the market value of the video was over $1,000.[51] According to the NDP, they checked with Elections Canada before uploading the video to the site. The Broadbent campaign responded by challenging Conservative Mike Murphy to a "rap-off." Also, on day thirty-three of the campaign, the NDP released their Flash[52] movie "Isn't it time." The three-minute music and text-based video focused on Harper's hidden agenda, the Liberals' broken promises, and the NDP's positive choices. The E.NDP newsletter encouraged viral campaigning and the passing along of both videos. "Ed's Back" was one of the most popular features on the NDP site. At one point it was downloaded almost as many times as the NDP platform.[53]

There was clearly a progression in the use of multimedia features by Canadian political parties from the previous election. If the campaign sites of 2000 were static electronic brochures, the sites of 2004 moved beyond text-based communications and were far more dynamic. The sites of the Liberals and NDP made these dynamic features very accessible to users; videos could be downloaded in a number of popular file formats. One thing not seen in the Canadian campaigns was live webcasts of campaign events. This technique has been used in other campaigns as a way of reaching press, party activists, and supporters that could not attend campaign events. Despite this, there was much to see and hear on-line during the 2004 election. If multimedia serves as a method by which campaigners can make visiting Web sites a more interesting experience to users, then Canadian parties made great gains in this area.

CONCLUSION

If the 2000 cyber-campaign was lacklustre, with the parties lacking any real sense of the political value or utility of the Internet, it is clear that the cyber-campaign of 2004 was a definite improvement. As in 2000, the party Web sites offered visitors extensive, detailed, and timely information. But in addition to informing, there were some real attempts by the five parties to engage visitors on the Internet during this cyber-campaign. The Green Party's Living Platform, the NDP's e-campaigners, the viral campaigning of Liberals and Conservatives, and the Bloc Québécois' "Réagissez!" were all attempts to reach out to voters and engage citizens in their campaigns on-line. Whereas no party had an e-newsletter in 2000, all of them did during this campaign. Moreover, all of the parties made better use of the technology in terms of multimedia. The on-line campaigns of the five parties were clearly integrated with their off-line ones.

This in no way means that the parties' cyber-campaigns were without flaws. All of the sites were periodically plagued by problems. More than once, French-language information was posted on English-language sites. Hyperlinks occasionally opened to blank documents. Campaign Web sites also seem to have missed out on the light and jovial uses of the technology seen in other campaigns. And there were some missed opportunities for the parties in terms of the technology. Narrowcasting or targeting voters, a defining feature of the technology, was practically non-existent during this election. It has been argued that this capability would be useful to campaigners in targeting young voters, heavy Internet users, but only the Bloc Québécois made a concerted effort to reach out to young voters. Through the Forum jeunesse du Bloc Québécois, e-mail messages and e-postcards were directed at young Québécois. The site even launched an interesting multimedia site called "Le Capsule de George W. Net" for younger visitors.

It may be argued that Canadian parties did not go far enough in terms of interactivity. But it can be argued that this criticism is unwarranted; use of interactive features by Canadian campaign Web sites does seem to be consistent with cyber-campaigns elsewhere. For instance, even though British and Italian parties made it extremely easy for citizens to send e-mail directly through their Web sites, chat rooms and discussion groups were not typically found on campaign Web sites during their respective elections in 2001.[54] While the sites of American presidential contenders have tended to be highly interactive, lower level campaigns have not. One American researcher has concluded that two-way interactivity is not used because it is burdensome and the campaign risks losing control of the communications environment.[55] Given these reasons it is questionable if campaigns, in Canada or elsewhere, will fully embrace the interactive nature of the Internet. However, the lesson of the BQ and Green Party campaigns in this election does show that visitors will engage with the campaign if given the opportunity.

The use of the Internet by political parties is unlikely to have changed the outcome on June 28. Nonetheless we should not underestimate the importance of on-line campaigning in this country. The 2004 cyber-campaign was far from lacklustre. In the 2000 election, cyberspace was uncharted territory for political parties, and they did not make effective use of the technology. By 2004, the parties were much more proficient in their understanding of this new political space. The Internet was more integrated in the political strategy of political parties, and substantial developments were made in their on-line presences from the previous campaign. The Internet and related technology are constantly evolving, and it is hard to know where such new technologies will take Canada's political parties in future election campaigns. The party Web sites of the 2004 cyber-campaign were like electronic campaign offices. If Canadians were interested, the virtual door was always open.

NOTES

1 StephenHarperSaid.ca, "Albertans should build firewalls around Alberta," May 23, 2004, http://www.stephenharpersaid.ca.

2 E-buttal (electronic rebuttal) refers to using the Internet to instantly refute or challenge statements made by one's opponent.

3 Susan Bourette, "Campaigning in the age of the Internet a cyberletdown," *The Globe and Mail,* October 30, 2000, A.9.

4 Nicolas Van Praet, "American election Web sites have bite: Canadian parties' lack pizzazz, though," *The Gazette,* November 7, 2000, A15.

5 See A. Whitehorn and S. Clarkson in *The Canadian General Election of 2000,* ed. Jon H. Pammett and Christopher Doran (Toronto: Dundurn Press, 2001).

6 Paul Attallah and Angela Burton, "Television, the Internet and the Canadian Federal Election of 2000," in *The Canadian General Election of 2000,* 227–28.

7 "Meetup is an advanced technology platform and global network of local venues that helps people self-organize local group gatherings on the same day everywhere. Meetups take place in up to 651 cities in 61 countries at local cafés, restaurants, bookstores, and other local establishments." http://www.meetup.com/about/

8 Gary Wolf, "How the Internet Invented Howard Dean," *Wired.com,* January 2004, July 13, 2004, http://www.wired.com/wired/archive/12.01/dean.html.

9 A blog, short for *Web log,* serves as a publicly accessible personal journal for an individual. Typically updated daily, blogs often reflect the personality of the author. (http://www.webopedia.com)

10 http://belinda.ca

11 "Broadband: High-speed access to the Internet," *The Daily,* September 23, 2003, http://www.statcan.ca/Daily/English/030923/td030923.htm. "Household Internet Use Survey," *The Daily,* July 8, 2004, http://www.statcan.ca/Daily/English/040708/d040708a.htm.

12 With the exception of the Bloc Québécois, this study is based on the English-language versions of the sites. While the BQ site is unilingual, all of the others exist in both official languages. It should be noted that there existed some content differences between the English and French versions of the four party sites.

13 Rachel Gibson and Stephen Ward, "A Proposed Methodology for Studying the Function and Effectiveness of Party and Candidate Web Sites," *Social Science Computer Review,* 18.3 (2000).

14 For an example of supply and demand research see Pippa Norris, "Preaching to the Converted?: Pluralism, Participation and Party Websites," *Party Politics,* 9.1 (2003).

15 For a discussion on how the new media has been distinguished from older communications technologies, see Jeffery B. Abramson, F. Christopher Arterton, and Gary R. Orren, *The Electronic Commonwealth: The Impact of New Media Technologies on Democratic Politics* (New York: Basic Books, Inc., Publishers, 1988); and Rachel Gibson and Stephen Ward, "British party activity in cyberspace: new media, same impact?," in *Reinvigorating Democracy: British Politics and the Internet,* ed. Rachel Gibson and Stephen Ward (Aldershoot: Ashgate, 2000).

16 Pippa Norris, *Digital Divide: Civic Engagement, Information Poverty, and the Internet Worldwide* (Cambridge: Cambridge University Press 2001), 148.

17 Leslie David Simon, "Democracy and the Net: a Virtuous Circle?" in *Democracy and the Internet: Allies or Adversaries,* ed. Leslie David Simon, Javier Corrales, and Donald R. Wolfensberger (Washington: Woodrow Wilson Center Press, 2002).

18 Rachel Gibson, Paul Nixon and Stephen War, "Parties and the Internet: An Overview," in *Political Parties and the Internet: Net Gain,* ed. Rachel Gibson, Paul Nixon, and Stephen Ward (London: Routledge, 2003).

19 Richard Davis, *The Web of Politics: The Internet's Impact on the American Political System* (New York: Oxford University Press, 1999).

20 Michael Margolis, David Resnick. & Joel D. Wolf, "Party competition on the Internet in the United States and Britain," *Harvard Journal of Press/Politics.* 4.4 (1999): 26.

21 Michael Margolis and David Resnick, *Politics as Usual: The Cyberspace "Revolution"* (Thousand Oaks, CA: Sage Publishing Inc., 2000).

22 Carlo Cunha, Irene Martin, James Newell & Luis Ramiro, "Southern European parties and party systems, and the new ICTs," in *Political Parties and the Internet Net Gain,* ed. Rachel Gibson, Paul Nixon, and Stephen Ward (London: Routledge, 2003), 78.

23 Tonda MacChartles, "Hacker hit Liberal, Tory Web sites," *Toronto Star,* June 2, 2004.

24 PDF, short for Portable Document Format, is a file format that makes it possible to send formatted documents that will appear on the recipient's monitor or printer as they were intended to look. You need Adobe Acrobat Reader to view PDF documents. HTML, short for HyperText Markup Language, is the authoring language used to create documents on the World Wide Web.

25 Most NDP candidates used a standard template Web site created by the party. Information for candidates in Quebec was provided on the Web site of the Quebec section of the NDP, http://www.web.net/qcndp/en/. One-quarter of NDP candidates had their own personal campaign sites. All of these Web pages were linked to http://www.ndp.ca.

26 See Jonathan Rose and Tamara Small, "Engaging Citizens or Engaging the Press? An examination of the 2004 Conservative Leadership Campaign On-line," paper presented to Communication & Democracy: Technology & Citizen Engagement Conference, Fredericton, New Brunswick, August 4–6, 2004.

27 Institute for Politics, Democracy and the Internet, "The Virtual Trail: Political Journalism on the Internet (Washington, DC: IPDI, 2002), July 1, 2004, http://www.ipdi.org.

28 Juliet Roper, "New Zealand political parties online: the World Wide Web as a tool for democratization or for political marketing?" in *The Politics of Cyberspace: A New Political Science Reader,* ed. Chris Toulouse and Timothy W. Luke (New York: Routledge, 1998).

29 Elizabeth Weise, "Not yet for the Net," *Media Studies Journal,* 14.1 (2000): 38.

30 Hillwatch E-Services, "Political Web Sites: Strategic Assets or Virtual Lawn Signs? Behind the Curve: Canadian vs. US Political Web Sites in the 2004 Electoral Cycle" (Ottawa, ON: Hillwatch Inc.). The article can be found on-line at: http://www.hillwatch.com/Publications/Research/Virtuallawnsigns.aspx.

31 Stephen Coleman, "Introduction," in *Elections in the Age of the Internet: Lessons from the United States,* ed. Stephen Coleman (London: Hansard Society, July 29, 2003), http://www.hansard-society.org.uk/ElectionsinThe AgeofInternet.pdf.

32 Cyberpresse.ca is an on-line news portal for the media company GESCA, which publishes *La Presse, Le Soleil, Le Droit, Le Quotidien, La Tribune, La Voix de l'est,* and *Le Nouvelliste.* Green Party Leader Jim Harris's cyberpresse.ca chat was on June 14, 2004. Gilles Duceppe, leader of the BQ, participated in a cyberpresse.ca chat on June 23, 2004.

33 Harold J. Jansen, "Is the Internet Politics as Usual or Democracy's Future? Candidate Campaign Web sites in the 2001 Alberta and British Columbia Provincial Elections," *The Innovation Journal,* 9.2 (2004), http://www.innovation.cc/.

34 Only first name, last name, phone number, and e-mail were required fields.

35 http://www.bloc.org/. Author's translation.

36 http://www.greenparty.ca/

37 ibid.

38 ibid.

39 In the Living Platform, visitors were able to view all pages and add comments. Members, however, had greater privileges, including a login to edit pages and the ability participate in the Members Only Forum.

40 Blogs for America, *Blog Tips,* July 14, 2004, http://www.blogforamerica.com/tips.html.

41 http://www.conservative.ca/.

42 Institute for Politics, *Democracy and the Internet. Online Campaigning 2002: A Primer.* (Washington, DC: IPDI, 2002), 18, July 14, 2004, http://www.ipdi.org/.

43 Don Lewicki and Tim Ziaukas, "The Digital Tea Leaves of Election 2000: The Internet and the Future of Presidential Politics," *First Monday,* 5.12 (2000). http://firstmonday.org/issues/issue5_12/lewicki/index.html.

44 Institute for Politics, *Democracy and the Internet. Online Campaigning 2002: A Primer.* (Washington, DC: IPDI), 14, July 14, 2004, http://www.ipdi.org/.

45 http://www.ndp.ca/.

46 The broadcasting consortium included CTV, CBC TV, Global TV, Radio-Canada, and TVA. The Green Party's site also encouraged supporter to file a complaint with CRTC, Canadian Association of Broadcasters, and Canadian Broadcast Standards Council. Contact information including phone, fax, and e-mail were provided.

47 Michael Cornfield and Jonah Seiger, "The Net and the Nomination," in *The Making of the Presidential Candidates 2004,* ed. William G. Mayer (Lanham: Rowman & Littlefield Publishers, Inc., 2004), 208.

48 Despite its being a unique feature, only one supporter submitted a photo to the site.

49 For a discussion of targeted campaign communication see R. Kenneth Carty, William Cross, and Lisa Young, *Rebuilding Canadian Party Politics* (Vancouver: UBC Press, 2000).

50 "Ed's Back" was produced by TV Factory for *This Hour has 22 Minutes.* TV Factory has a contract to produce segments for the show. The video never aired.

51 According to Bill C-24, contributions from individuals and corporations cannot exceed $1,000.

52 With Flash, users can draw their own animations or import other vector-based images. As long as browsers are equipped with the necessary plug-ins, Flash animations will look the same. Flash was known as FutureSplash until 1997, when Macromedia Inc. bought the company that developed it (http://www.webopedia.com/).

53 Steven Chase and Gloria Galloway, "Broadbent video goes 'viral' as NDP launches new ad push," *The Globe and Mail,* June 10, 2004.

54 See Rachel Gibson, James Newell, and Stephen Ward, "The New Technology: The First Internet Election?" in *The Italian General Election of 2001: Berlusconi's Victory,* ed. James Newell (Manchester: Manchester University Press, 2002); Rachel Gibson and Stephen Ward, "British party activity in cyberspace: new media, same impact?" in *Reinvigorating Democracy: British Politics and the Internet,* ed. Rachel Gibson and Stephen Ward (Aldershoot: Ashgate, 2000).

55 Jennifer Stromer-Galley, "On-line interaction and why candidates avoid it," *Journal of Communication* 50.4 (2000).

CHAPTER EIGHT

The Newspaper Campaign

by Christopher Waddell

"Predictable" best describes the coverage of Canada's thirty-eighth general election by the country's three major English-language daily newspapers. As circulation continues its slow but steady decline and pressure grows from television and the Internet as alternate news sources, the *Globe and Mail*, the *National Post*, and the *Toronto Star* replicated patterns from the past with little that could be described as innovative, exciting, or different from how they approached the federal election in 2000.

The core of their coverage followed the leaders' tours as always, and this time in English Canada there were only three leaders to pursue. The Canadian Alliance and Progressive Conservatives merged prior to the election creating the Conservative Party as a new, national alternative to the Liberals that turned into much more of an alternative during the campaign than many had assumed at its start. That race between the two parties dominated campaign coverage. By contrast, although the New Democratic Party seemed revitalized with its new leader, Jack Layton, it still received only about one-third of the coverage of either the Liberals or Conservatives. In Quebec the Bloc Québécois was perceived as the front-runner, but the readership of the three major papers didn't justify daily coverage of a party that the overwhelming majority of readers would not see on their ballots. On the other hand, the Green Party ran candidates in all 308 ridings, and from the outset of the campaign appeared destined to do better than it had in any previous federal election. That prospect, though, was not sufficient to entice newspapers to take any chances or abandon past precedents. The Green Party received what could be called only novelty coverage from the three papers and from the rest of the media in the country as well. That did not stop Canadians from supporting the Greens in surprising numbers; the party received 4.3 percent of the votes cast across the country, up from 0.8 percent in 2000 and 0.4 percent in 1997.

In general, newspaper coverage responded to campaign developments rather than attempting detailed or distinctive analysis of the issues or anything beyond the horse race of who was ahead and behind as framed by the opinion polls the newspapers commissioned and released regularly during the campaign. For instance, none of the three major newspapers — the *Globe and Mail*, the *National Post*, and the *Toronto Star* — did anything during the campaign on any potential issue that matched in content and resources the innovative approach of the *Globe and Mail's Report on Business* over the past two years in assessing and comparing the corporate governance performance of the boards of directors of Canada's publicly traded corporations.

Equally surprising, the three newspapers covered the campaign in strikingly similar fashion although they supported different parties. Soon after the May 23 election call, it became clear that the *Globe and Mail* was leaning heavily towards the Liberals, finally endorsing Paul Martin in remarkably qualified fashion on June 23 under the headline "The safe choice is to do no harm." The *National Post*, not surprisingly considering the paper's conservative background, was more blunt, telling its editorial page readers the same day, "On June 28, vote Conservative." There was of course never any doubt that the *Toronto Star* would, as always, back the Liberals as its June 26 editorial stated equally clearly, "Martin's Liberals best for Canada."

Despite their different political leanings, there were many more similarities than differences in the balance of issues covered in the three papers. Each allocated roughly the same percentage of its coverage to the same issues, also splitting coverage between news, editorials, and opinion in a roughly similar fashion. In an election campaign that contained its share of unexpected developments, including an apparent dramatic last weekend change of heart by many voters in Ontario, too much of the coverage contained too few surprises. In the end the papers largely missed the biggest surprise of all — the ease with which the Liberals won an election most commentators in the print and electronic media predicted would go late into the night before a winner could be determined, with voters in British Columbia likely casting the deciding ballots for the country.

This assessment of newspaper coverage during the campaign covers the Ottawa editions of the two national papers — the *Globe and Mail* and the *National Post* — plus Canada's largest newspaper, the *Toronto Star*. It does not include the local, Toronto-area coverage in the *Star* that concentrated on local riding races, profiles of individual constituencies, etc. The 1,688 stories collected from May 12 (twelve days before Prime Minister Paul Martin called the election) to June 29 (the day after the election) form the overall database. Each story was assigned one of five categories: news, editorials, columns, op-ed opinion, or features. A sub-group — the 1,334 stories the three papers published between May 23 and voting day June 28 inclusive — is the basis for conclusions about election coverage in those papers. The database can sort stories by any combination of the five categories mentioned above, by the publication in which the story appeared, the date published, the reporter or reporters, the page where it appeared, the dominant party mentioned if there was one, the major issue or issues covered in the story, and the region of the country covered by the story if there was a regional focus to a story. In some cases overviews that did not have a predominant issue, region, or political party as its focus were not placed in those more specific categories.

The 2000 campaign marked a change for newspaper coverage of federal elections as Christopher Dornan and Heather Pyman noted in their chapter "Facts and arguments" in *The Canadian General Election of 2000*. For the first time the *Globe and Mail* faced coast-to-coast competition as the *National Post* had arrived on the scene two years earlier as Canada's second national newspaper. From the start it had devoted considerable space to national politics, and the 2000 election was the *Post*'s chance to take on the established leader in newspaper coverage on grounds the *Globe* traditionally dominated.

Four years later, the newspaper world has changed completely. The *National Post* remains a presence but it is a substantially smaller and scaled down *Post* with less grandiose ambitions than in 2000. The change of ownership to CanWest Global from Conrad Black's Hollinger Corp. preceded sharp cuts in the *Post*'s reporting staff, particularly political reporting in Ottawa, matched by a smaller newspaper with less space for news than in Black's days. It was all designed to reduce losses at the paper, but it was like tying one hand behind its back when it came to competing with the *Globe*. Although the *Post* has been rebuilding slightly from the depths of the cuts, reduced staff and budgets still had a dramatic impact on its coverage of the 2004 campaign. The paper devoted significantly fewer reporting resources and less space in its daily and Saturday papers to election coverage than did the *Globe*. The *Post* printed approximately 25 percent fewer stories between May 23 and June 28 than appeared in the *Globe and Mail*. In fact the *Toronto Star* and the *Post* were almost equal in the number of stories each published during the campaign. That is a sharp decline from 2000, when the *Globe* published only about 10 percent more stories than the *Post* and both had about 30 percent more stories than appeared in the *Star*. While the competition between the two national papers changed dramatically between 2000 and 2004, the *Star* continued much as always tailoring its coverage to its large Toronto audience while still retaining a broader view than that of just a large local paper.

Newspaper coverage of this campaign continued trends Dornan and Pyman noted in 2000. Each of the three newspapers ran fewer stories in 2004 than four years earlier.

Table 1: Election Stories

	Globe	Post	Star
2000	764	710	522
2004	518	391	389

The decline is significant particularly as each campaign was thirty-six days long. Since 1984 the number of stories newspapers run during federal election campaigns has steadily declined, regardless of the competitiveness of individual elections. The *Globe* reversed that trend in 2000 in the midst of its circulation war with the *Post* by increasing the number of stories it ran from 1997. By 2004, the *Globe* was convinced it had won the war with the *Post*, so the pre-2000 pattern of less and less coverage re-emerged. Even so, *Globe* reporters and columnists wrote more stories about the campaign than the journalists at either of its large competitors.

It is not just the number of stories that has changed over the years. In addition to fewer stories, there has been a gradual but steady shift at all newspapers away from straight news reporting during campaigns. Who, what, where, when, and why play less and less of a role in more and more election stories. It has been replaced by comment and opinion primarily from each newspaper's own reporting staff as newspapers try to respond to twenty-four-hour cable news channels and the tremendous expansion of the Internet as a news source. Increasingly readers may be getting the basics from these instant media, but newspaper owners and newsroom managers argue papers can still be relevant by providing context and analysis that all-news television and the Internet too often lack. As the size of newspapers has not increased, devoting more space to columns meant less space for news stories. Some journalists at all three papers switched back and forth during the campaign between being reporters and commentators/columnists. Some days they filed as reporters with just a byline in their paper. Other days they would be columnists with their picture accompanying their article as a way to flag to readers that they were reading more than just reporting. Whether readers noted the distinction is less clear, and the result is a blurring of the traditional difference between reporting and commenting.

For both the *Star* and the *Globe* the steady shift away from news to comment and columns stalled in this campaign as both produced slightly more news coverage as a percentage of their total coverage for their readers than they did in 2000. It was the right decision for a campaign where, unlike in 2000, the result was in doubt until the end. However, just as the amount of coverage stopped its steady decline in

2000 only to resume falling four years later, the shift away from news may also resume with the next election. All-news television and the Internet will presumably play an even larger role in delivering information immediately to viewers and readers in that campaign, leaving newspapers continuing to search for new ways to interest an audience the next morning with information from the previous day.

The *Post* did not mirror the slight growth in the share of news stories at the *Globe* and *Star*. Its proportion of comment and columns grew dramatically from the 2000 level.

Table 2: News/News Background (percent of total coverage)

	Globe	Post	Star
2000	45	60	53
2004	47	40	55

The sharp drop in space devoted to news in the *Post* reflected the reduction in the paper's staff and a smaller paper with less space available for news than in 2000. There also seemed to be a conscious decision at the *Post* not to try to match the *Globe* story for story. While the *Post* under previous ownership dedicated itself to beating the *Globe* on news, with this campaign it tried to build election readership through reader loyalty to its journalist personalities and their comments and opinions rather than comprehensive news coverage. Some days the coverage was so constrained it almost appeared the paper was saying to potential readers, choose the *Post* if you don't want a flood of election coverage but are interested only in an overview story or two about what happened the previous day plus daily comment on the campaign from columnists.

Consistent with its move away from news, the *Post* in 2004 devoted a significantly larger share of its coverage to columns and columnists as compared to 2000. For the *Globe* and the *Star*, the slight increase in news coverage meant a corresponding small decline in columns with their comment and opinion.

Table 3: Columns/News Analysis (percent of total coverage)

	Globe	Post	Star
2000	32	21	28
2004	28	30	33

Table 4: Editorials (percent of total coverage)

	Globe	Post	Star
2000	5	7	9
2004	6	8	6

Table 5: Op-Ed (percent of total coverage)

	Globe	Post	Star
2000	7	8	1
2004	4	9	2

There were some differences in the amount of coverage the three papers devoted to comment found in the more traditional locations on each paper's editorial and op-ed pages.

While the national newspaper war on the news front was not much of a contest, the *Globe* and *Post* did fight it out on the editorial pages. Each increased slightly the amount of coverage devoted to editorials this time, while editorials became a smaller percentage of the *Star's* overall campaign coverage.

The amount of op-ed space devoted to campaign issues did not change much in 2004 from 2000 except at the *Globe*. Op-ed pieces — opinion written by people outside the newspaper — occupied a smaller share of the *Globe's* coverage in this election than it has in the past. The *Globe's* op-ed page is the most influential in the country and plays an important role in any campaign, allowing outsiders to express opinions about campaign issues and all aspects of the election. In early 2004, prior to the campaign, the *Globe* reduced its op-ed space to one page a day from two pages, replacing one of its comment pages with a daily page on health issues. That is the logical explanation for the decline in op-ed pieces as a share of the paper's total coverage in this election compared to four years earlier. It is an unfortunate development for campaign coverage, as outsiders who may have sharply different perspectives than the paper's staff and editorial management now have less opportunity than in the past to have their voices heard nationally.

At the *Post* and the *Globe*, features played a much larger role in this campaign than before. At the *Globe* this included a daily campaign notebook that focused on personalities, daily reality checks that examined the accuracy of statements made by party leaders or included in their campaign platforms, plus profiles of candidates, voters, and some issues. The *Post* had some of the same features plus some more off-beat ones, including assessment of the clothing and haircuts of the leaders and stories on leaders' wives. The *Post* also presented a daily campaign humour column that ran on page two of its front section. The *Star* by contrast spent less time on features and more on its columns than it had four years earlier.

Table 6: News Background/Features (percent of total coverage)

	Globe	Post	Star
2000	6	6	8
2004	15	13	4

There was surprising similarity in how the papers allocated coverage to the major parties in this campaign, which contributed to an overall sense of sameness and uniformity among the three. The Liberals received more coverage in each of the papers than any other party. The overall percentage of stories devoted to the party seeking re-election ranged from a low of 42 percent in the *Globe* to a high of 46 percent in the *Post*. The Conservatives were second in all three papers, with a high of 36 percent of stories in the *Post* and a low of 34 percent in the *Globe*. The *Star* devoted slightly more coverage to the New Democratic Party — 14 percent of its overall coverage — than either the *Globe* at 13 percent or the *Post* at 12 percent, but again the uniformity of coverage was more striking than any differences among the three.

Differences appeared, though, in how the papers approached the Bloc Québécois and Quebec. The *Globe* allocated 9 percent of its overall coverage to the Bloc, while the *Star* and *Post* each gave the Quebec-only party between 5 percent and 6 percent of their overall campaign coverage. There is no necessity for newspaper coverage to mirror political party support, as campaign coverage must follow the ebb and flow of campaign developments, but newspapers in this election as in others spent more time with the two major parties and less on smaller parties. It is an approach that is more and more at odds with the stated interests of the public. Since 1988 Canadians have increased their interest in new and smaller parties and shown a growing willingness to vote for them and to advocate changes in the electoral system that would, through proportional representation, likely increase the number of parties in Parliament and further break down the dominance of the Liberals and Conservatives. There was no sign in this campaign that any of the three major newspapers recognized this change or considered it important enough to modify past coverage patterns to embrace the evolving voting trends of Canadians. Canadians' enthusiasm for a minority government is the clearest sign yet that it is time for newspapers to review and adjust their traditional beliefs about which parties are important and abandon their strategy of relegating smaller and new parties to the fringes of campaign coverage. That approach is clearly out of step with the views and voting choices of their readers.

The three newspapers apportioned not only coverage of the parties but also coverage of the different issues that emerged during the campaign with only marginal differences. The *Globe*, the *Star,* and the *Post* divided coverage of everything from social policy, abortion, health and medicare, federal-provincial relations, urban issues, defence, taxes, the economy and business, the sponsorship scandal, and Quebec sovereignty in roughly the same fashion. As with other aspects of their coverage, there were many more similarities than differences. This appeared to reflect the fact that coverage was overwhelmingly reactive. The papers would write about an issue when something happened but only when it happened, which again reinforced the lack of distinctiveness of any of the coverage. None of the papers took chances and none had sufficient innovative spirit, confidence, or independence of mind to decide that issues needed detailed treatment independent of and prior to being raised by the parties.

For instance, with candidate Web sites easily available, why didn't any of the papers examine the stated positions of each party's candidates to assemble a composite profile of possible party caucuses on the social issues that attracted considerable media attention during the campaign, such as same-sex marriage and abortion? Was it simply a matter of too much work when it was easier simply to highlight what a candidate had said in the past regardless of the importance of that candidate in the formulation of the party and leader's position on the issue? Why was there virtually nothing written about financing campaigns? Who contributed to the parties under the old rules before restrictions took effect on the size of corporate and union donations and how did that affect party positions on issues in this campaign? How difficult was it to raise money for this campaign without the large corporate and union donations that were banned starting in 2004? Did the different financing rules change how parties campaigned or limit the amount they raised independent of government support? On a different matter, why did the papers wait until very late in the campaign before providing readers with details about the key advisors around Conservative Leader Stephen Harper, whose campaign was obviously very successful and smoothly organized? These are just a sample of the ideas and issues newspapers did not address. Instead they clustered campaign coverage around the same themes and repeated the same tried and true approaches from previous federal elections.

While similarities dominated campaign coverage provided by the three papers, each paper made some distinctive coverage choices. At the *Globe and Mail*, the cross-country travels of columnist Roy MacGregor gave readers a daily look at individual communities and candidates and the issues they raised, offering a valuable counterpoint to the newspaper's focus on the national campaigns of the major parties. How the media covered the campaign received more attention at the *Globe* than at either the *Star* or the *Post*, as Hugh Winsor presented consistently distinctive combinations of news and analysis that raised important questions about the media themselves. The paper's daily reality check by reporter Jeff Sallot provided concise snapshots of party positions and comments from leaders and the degree to which they were stretching the truth on the campaign trail.

Consistent with the *National Post*'s conservative leanings, it ran a larger share of stories on abortion and defence than the other two papers. Also consistent with the *Post's* campaign coverage strategy, the columnists in its business section, *The Financial Post*, were writing opinion about the campaign more often than the columnists in its competition, the *Globe*'s *Report on Business*. In the main part of the paper, Andrew Coyne's column was regularly thoughtful and interesting, often taking an unexpected twist in assessing campaign developments. However, there was also a trivial nature to some of the *Post*'s coverage. Features such as "PM's barber 'a bit jealous': No comment on quality of Saskatoon haircut, though" on June 2; "Behind blue eyes, our next prime minister: Odds of sharing trait: 1 in 1,000" on May 27, noting that all party leaders had blue eyes; "Never mind ordinary people, what do the actors who play them think?" on June 5; "No colour spared from leaders' ties (even orange): Dress-up Diary" on May 29; and "Language theorist ranks the party leaders: Harper's frequent use of the word 'and' deemed a sign of competence" on June 15 were presumably designed to provide a counterbalance to the pages of grey and serious coverage in the *Globe*. It may have been a good idea in theory and worked in the days of the Hollinger *Post* when the paper included as much election overage as the *Globe*. In this election, considering how little campaign coverage the *Post* contained some days, the trivial or "entertaining" features often left the impression that the paper itself shouldn't be taken too seriously by readers interested in national politics and the election campaign.

The *Star*'s decision to concentrate a lot of campaign coverage on columns played to the newspaper's strength, as it had by far the most experienced group of journalists covering the campaign. Columns and occasional features by Chantal Hebert, Thomas Walkom, James Travers, and Graham Fraser were all essential reading for those interested in assessments of the campaign that provided context and perspective that can come only with covering several federal elections. The *Star*'s media columnist Antonia Zerbesias also commented regularly on how the media covered the campaign, although not with quite the same depth of political analysis and consistent attention as the *Globe*. Beyond that there were many more similarities than differences between the number of stories in the *Star* on specific issues and those in the other two papers. However, the *Star* did focus in its coverage more frequently than the *Globe* or *Post* on the horse race. It is also not surprising to any long-time reader of the paper that the *Star* printed a larger percentage of stories than the other two papers on two of its long-time hobby horses — urban issues and social policy matters including health care.

Here is a snapshot profile of how each of the papers balanced coverage about issues and the political parties.

The National Post

While the *Star* and the *Globe* each printed more columns about the Liberals than the Conservatives, the *Post* presented an equal number about each of the two parties over the duration of the campaign. That balance in party coverage among the *Post*'s columnists did not extend to the paper's news pages, where 38 percent of the *Post*'s news stories dealt with the Liberals and only 25 percent focused on the Conservatives. That was the widest gap in coverage of the two parties among the three papers. In its news coverage the *Post* had a larger percentage of stories than the other two papers on justice, defence, social policy, and business issues. Its columnists mirrored the paper's news coverage, writing more often than columnists at the other papers about social policy, which included abortion, while more than 40 percent of the columns in the paper during the campaign concentrated on analyzing the horse race and the state of the campaign.

As a minority government became first a possibility and then probable, much of the analysis of the campaign in all three papers concentrated on how the parties would coalesce to support a Liberal or Conservative government. It was all idle speculation, but that didn't stop it chewing up lots of news space in the last half of the campaign at each of the papers. Opinion polls received broad coverage in the *Post*, including the results of separate polls conducted in individual ridings where races were thought to be close or that featured star candidates. Editorially the paper commented on a wide selection of issues with no concentrated focus on one or two themes. Slightly more editorials were written about the Liberals, usually highlighting their shortcomings and failings, than about the Conservatives, who benefited from *Post* editorials that supported both the party's policies and leader Stephen Harper.

The Globe and Mail

Opinion polling was also a major focus for the *Globe* throughout the campaign. At times it seemed the paper was publishing full or partial results of a poll almost every second or third day. It conducted both national and regional polls but did not match the *Post* in going down to the individual riding level to sample public opinion. There was also a narrower gap at the *Globe* between the 35 percent of news stories that focused on the Liberals and the 28 percent that concentrated on the Conservatives. Additionally, the previously noted emphasis on individual communities and candidates by columnist Roy MacGregor added distinctiveness and extra depth. It also highlighted the *Globe*'s more national perspective, compared to the *Star* and *Post*, which was an important element of the paper's coverage.

As well the *Globe* paid much more attention on its editorial page than the other papers to the question of how to reverse low voter turnout, particularly among young people. Almost 10 percent of the *Globe's* campaign editorials dealt with the need for people to vote. However, those exhortations had no effect, as turnout was approximately 60.5 percent of eligible votes, about three percentage points lower than in 2000. Unlike the other two papers the *Globe* devoted an equal number of editorials to the Liberals and the Conservatives.

Toronto Star

The *Star*, like the others, adopted a scattergun approach, spreading its campaign news coverage widely rather than concentrating on only a few issues. Underlying that was a consistent examination of the campaign and the jockeying between parties in the race to see who would win or to figure out how a minority government might work. That consumed more news space than details or analysis of specific issues or policy proposals from the parties. The paper distinguished itself particularly in its handling of the televised leaders' debates. It assigned reporters to write individual stories each night about what each leader said in the French and English debates. It produced a good, concise summary devoid of the clichéd talk of knock-out punches and other silly metaphors.

The newspaper's columnists focused heavily on analyzing and assessing the daily ups and downs of the campaign. With the Liberals proclaiming a new deal for Canada's cities, the *Star* gave more attention to urban issues than the other two papers, while its traditional emphasis on social issues emerged on the editorial pages. It published more editorials on health care and the linked issue of federal-provincial relations than either the *Post* or the *Globe*.

From the start of the campaign, the *Star*'s editorial pages also left no doubt in readers' minds as to which party the newspaper supported. Over the thirty-six days, the *Star* ran twice as many editorials about the Conservatives as it did about the Liberals. The tone of those Conservative editorials was overwhelmingly negative, stressing time and again the threats the party posed to the *Star*'s perceptions of what counted as Canadian values. It was a classic example of the old-time partisanship that in the past Canadian newspapers featured much more obviously and consistently, most likely driven by the growing sense at the *Star* during the campaign that the unthinkable might happen and the Liberals could lose.

POLITICAL COVERAGE — THE BROADER CONTEXT

Newspaper coverage during the campaign also highlighted substantive questions about how reporters cover politics, the role of the media in today's political process, and the relationship between newspapers and their readers.

Media Self-Interest and Culture

One of the campaign's more interesting developments was the reaction to a June 10 *National Post* story headlined "Tories would slash CRTC role: Could harm industry: Would seek to give U.S. satellite services access to Canada." It stated that a Conservative government would drastically limit the powers of the Canadian Radio-television and Telecommunications Commission (CRTC) and begin negotiations with the United States to end the practice that currently bans U.S. satellite TV companies from selling their signals to Canadians, protecting the market for domestic satellite TV providers.

The CRTC's fate generated some media reaction, with the *Globe and Mail* and the *Toronto Star* each publishing five pieces by their columnists and on their op-ed pages. The common theme warned about the threats posed to Canadian culture and broadcasting by the possible scaling back of the CRTC.

In the era of conglomerate ownership of media in Canada, newspapers are no longer independent entities but subsidiaries of larger corporations that have links and direct financial interests, often across several sectors of the economy. Opponents of cross-ownership of newspapers and television stations by a single corporation (whether or not the paper and station are in the same market) argue that there are dangers posed by the same corporation owning newspapers, which are largely unregulated by government (beyond foreign ownership restrictions), and television and radio stations (or for that matter telecommunications networks), which are highly regulated by government. They believe a conglomerate might press its newspapers to tone down any criticism of the government of the day to avoid potential government retaliation against the newspaper's parent through the regulatory system, in this case the CRTC, by introducing barriers to licence renewals, increasing competition faced by the parent, or denying rate increases to the regulated subsidiaries of that parent company. In other words, might BCE Inc. try to tone down any criticism of the federal government in the *Globe and Mail* to prevent government retaliation against the company's telecommunications carrier Bell Canada or its satellite television distributor Bell ExpressVu? The same question could be asked about any limits placed by CanWest on the freedom of its newspapers to criticize the federal government when the CRTC controls the fate of the Global television network and CanWest's expanding group of radio stations.

In fact the owners of the three major newspapers covering the campaign all have major financial stakes in the future of the CRTC. In the case of BCE Inc., much of its corporate empire, which generates revenue of $19 billion per year, relies on regulation from the CRTC, not the open market. The financial and operating structure of the CTV television network, the ExpressVu satellite television distribution system, and Bell Canada's land-based and wireless telephone and data networks would all require huge restructuring if the CRTC were dramatically downsized.

CanWest Global would face similar restructuring but unlike BCE CanWest might look more favourably on a diminished CRTC. CanWest has advocated a loosening of foreign ownership restrictions on television networks and a relaxation of restrictions that currently limit the ability of pharmaceutical companies to advertise on television. That might happen with a less intrusive CRTC.

Even the *Toronto Star* is affected, as its parent Torstar Corp. tried unsuccessfully to win a television licence for the Toronto/southwestern Ontario market but was rejected in 2002 by the CRTC in a very controversial decision. Having failed to get into broadcasting on its first attempt, Torstar could easily be back before the CRTC seeking a licence in the near future.

Yet none of the papers acknowledged in any of their news coverage and columns written about the CRTC that the financial interests of their parent companies would be affected by an emasculation of the CRTC if the Conservatives formed a government. There is no evidence that the papers covered the issue *because of* the potential financial impact on their parent companies, but the newspapers should disclose such potential conflicts of interest to their readers, just as the papers readily disclose potential financial conflicts of interest that may involve politicians and bureaucrats.

It is even more important to apply this principle of disclosure on the editorial pages of the papers. Each paper took a stand in the final days of the campaign, telling its readers which party it believed they should support. The *Globe* and the *Star* endorsed the Liberals and the *National Post* endorsed the Conservatives. None of the papers noted in their editorials the implications on the financial future of their parent if a Conservative victory led to shrinking the CRTC.

In the business world, most brokerage houses and investment dealers now disclose whether they own any shares in companies their financial analysts recommend that individual investors buy or sell. In other words, the financial institutions are advising whether they might profit from individuals following the analyst's advice. That alerts the individual investor to the potential for conflict of interest in the buying or selling advice being offered. He or she can then determine how much credence to give to that recommendation and whether or not to comply. It is incumbent upon newspapers in their support for transparency and freedom of information to be equally open in disclosing their potential conflicts of interest when offering advice to readers. In this election all three failed that test of minimal disclosure and openness in their vote choice editorials.

Who Wants to Talk about Abortion?

At the start of the election campaign, no one identified abortion as a campaign issue. How it emerged and remained an issue in this campaign is an interesting case study both in how the media today approach politics and in how political parties take advantage of their understanding of how the media operate.

The original story on the abortion issue by the *Globe and Mail*'s Edmonton-based reporter Jill Mahoney appeared below the fold on page one of the June 1 paper under the headline "Tory critic wants new abortion rules." The sub-heading for the story read, "Urges mandatory third-party counselling." The story detailed some comments made by Conservative Member of Parliament and Health Critic Rob Merrifield on the issue of women receiving counselling before proceeding with abortions. But nowhere in the story is Mr. Merrifield quoted as saying that there should be new rules or mandatory third-party counselling for women. The first three paragraphs of the story were as follows:

> The Conservative Party's health critic is advocating a dramatic shift in abortion regulations by calling for third-party counselling for women who are considering terminating their pregnancies.
>
> In an interview yesterday, Rob Merrifield said independent counselling would be "valuable" for women contemplating abortion because "people who take part in it may only be seeing one side of it."
>
> "I would think that they [should] have all the information in front of them. I think [with] any procedure that's a valuable thing for them to have," said the Alberta MP, who is opposed to abortion.

The story quickly morphed into something different, thanks to instant communication: political parties that flood reporters with e-mail propaganda designed to distort the comments of their opponents and reporters who appear mesmerized by the electronic handouts and too often do little if any research beyond what they are given. Even though the details in the *Globe* story did not back up its inflammatory headline, reporters began challenging Conservative Leader Stephen Harper on a daily basis. They asked him to prove that the Conservatives did not have a secret plan either to force all women to undergo mandatory counselling before receiving abortions or to ban abortions outright if they formed a government, either through government action or a private member's bill proposed by a Conservative backbencher. (At no point did the *Globe* correct the record and indicate the headline was wrong.)

On June 3 *Globe* op-ed page columnist Margaret Wente reinforced the impression that the Conservatives would restrict abortions. "Mr. Merrifield thinks women who want abortions ought to be obliged to get independent counselling first, apparently because we can't be trusted to decide for ourselves," she wrote, repeating the conclusion from the story's headline although there is no quote in the June 1 story to support either of her statements about the beliefs of the Conservative MP.

This was an excellent illustration of how campaigns are now covered. Understaffed and facing the relentless pressure of hourly deadlines, many reporters and their editors have abandoned any pretense of what was once considered essential to journalism — placing quotes in context and providing readers with as much information about an issue as possible. It is now sufficient simply to report or even paraphrase whatever a politician says with no context or background about the response and in many cases without sufficient, or even any, explanation of the context and details of the question that generated the response. Then take whatever was said and demand a response from the party leader or other leaders and build a daily story with the hourly back and forth, never addressing the substance of the issue raised by the quotes or partial quotes or in this case that the headline did not support the facts the reporter presented to readers in the story.

The hidden agenda and private member's bill allegations continued until June 6 when *Globe* columnist John Ibbitson finally explained how difficult it would be for a private member's bill to become law. That was followed by an op-ed piece in the June 9 *Globe* that noted:

> Guidelines of the College of Physicians and Surgeons of Manitoba, adapted from those of the Society of Obstetricians and Gynecologists of Canada, state: "Every woman seeking abortion should receive supportive and compassionate counselling ... she must fully understand the nature and safety of the proposed procedure ... possible immediate and future side effects, as well as potential complications ..." and must be given "the necessary information to make an informed decision."

But it was another *Globe* columnist, Hugh Winsor, who explained on June 8, a week after the controversy began, how his colleagues were manipulated by the Liberal Party because the media "have been waiting for an issue to show that Mr. Harper and the Conservative Party are really still the old Reform Alliance party." Winsor wrote:

> So when Mr. Merrifield, whose opposition to abortion is well established, mused to a Globe and Mail reporter about the usefulness of counselling (not mandatory counselling, mind you), the media pounced. In the beginning, however, your understanding of the story may have depended on whether you were reading newspapers or watching television.
>
> In the television clips, Mr. Harper began: "I've been clear. A Conservative government led by me will not be tabling abortion legislation. I will not be sponsoring an abortion referendum. We will not be making changes to federal law. The matter of how these kinds of services are delivered is within provincial jurisdiction."
>
> On the surface, that would seem to kill the issue. All of the major parties have zealots. In Mr. Harper's case, he won the Canadian Alliance leadership by defeating them, since the anti-abortion, anti-gay coalitions were all backing former leader Stockwell Day.
>
> But the headline in The Globe and Mail the next day read, Harper stands by MP in abortion furor. What Mr. Harper said was that Mr. Merrifield was speaking for himself, not the party. The headline and the comments of all the critics were based on the fact Mr. Harper didn't immediately fire him as health critic.
>
> The Globe wasn't alone. Almost every major paper ran stories that Mr. Harper had been blind-sided by his party's right wing.
>
> So how did we get from counselling (Mr. Martin said almost the same thing to a high-school audience

> in Saskatoon) to an imperilled Charter, deemed to be the keystone to Canadian democracy?
>
> Answer: by a lot of hyperbole, which the media not only faithfully reported, but in many cases prompted. The abortion-counselling issue transmogrified into the same-sex marriage issue (many Liberal MPs, including parliamentary secretary Roger Gallaway, are openly opposed to the Liberal position) and then on to the role of Parliament dealing with MPs' private member's bills and the use of the notwithstanding clause.
>
> Mr. Harper said that as prime minister he couldn't and wouldn't stop MPs from introducing private member's bills, whatever their subject. Mr. Martin has said essentially the same thing. Both have said that as leaders of the government, they would not feel bound by free votes on non-government legislation.

The scare campaign the Liberals successfully employed to persuade voters that the Conservatives were too extreme for Canadians began with the ease with which newspapers, and the electronic media as well, were conscripted to do the Liberals' bidding on the abortion issue. The last-minute change of heart Ontario voters underwent in deciding the Conservatives were too extreme and choosing to back the Liberals despite their unhappiness with the party's performance in government had its genesis in the abortion controversy and how the media covered and sustained the issue.

Whose Voices Are Important in a Campaign?

The uproar created about abortion soon morphed into a continuing examination of statements made either in the past or during the campaign by selected candidates, either members of Parliament seeking reelection or those running for the first time, on abortion, gay rights, same-sex marriage, and other social issues, plus the role of the Charter of Rights and Freedoms.

In an election with 1,685 candidates running in 308 constituencies across the country, what criteria did newspapers use to determine when comments from an individual candidate should be noted nationally, let alone receive prominent display? There are several approaches possible. News organizations could decide that comments from cabinet ministers and front-bench MPs from all parties from the dissolved Parliament deserve to be widely reported during a campaign. Perhaps that list might also include "star" candidates recruited by each of the parties who would clearly play a key role in that party's caucus or in a government.

What about an ordinary backbencher seeking re-election or a candidate running for the first time who has not played an influential role in the party or has no links to the leader or those involved in the party's policy formulation? Are that candidate's comments worth national attention that by its very nature implies the individual's views are representative of a broader sample within the party or its candidates? The media should bring the candidate's comments to the attention of the people who can directly vote for that person. Beyond that, what is the standard that newspapers use to decide that an individual candidate's comments should be reported more widely and sometimes even made into national front-page news?

In this election, as Winsor suggested, the comments chosen for national attention by the newspapers were most frequently made by Conservative MPs or candidates who expressed views that seemed to reinforce the perception that the new party was dominated by stereotypical extremist social conservatives from the defunct Reform Party. Frequently chosen for the media spotlight were candidates whose views diverged from the stated positions of Conservative Party Leader Stephen Harper. Liberal and New Democratic Party candidates who opposed their party's policies or the views of its leaders on social issues did not receive the same degree of media prominence.

In an era when more and more coverage concentrates on the game of who said what, how outrageous it might be, and how others react, newspapers need to tell their readers what criteria they will use to determine when a candidate's comments deserve national attention. Without any obvious criteria, the papers leave themselves open to charges of editorializing on their news pages in support of the party endorsed on the paper's editorial page.

When Good Polls Go Bad

Newspapers and opinion polling have walked hand in hand through many federal election campaigns, and it was no different in 2004. Opinion polls can enhance coverage in a variety of ways. They can highlight regional differences in what voters believe are the campaign's major issues. They can provide insights into how voters compare party leaders, can suggest how strongly voters hold their opinions, and of course estimate how the public would vote if an election were held the day the poll was conducted, as well as what issues and impressions are driving those vote choices. Watching how these responses change during a campaign can indicate how the election will turn out. It can also provide clues as to why parties change strategy and leaders change their focus and messages during a campaign. Of course each poll is a snapshot of how people responded at the time they were questioned, but the prevalence of surveys and the degree to which they have often been very close to the election's results means they are frequently viewed as "scientific" predictions of the future rather than reflections of a moment in time.

Newspapers have done nothing in their competition for readers to discourage that interpretation of the accuracy of polls and in 2004 tried to take it to another level only to have it backfire badly. In this campaign each of the three papers had its polling partner and featured prominently its own poll results. Just as with other aspects of campaign coverage, there was surprisingly little difference between the three papers in how they handled polls and polling results. The *Globe and Mail* had twenty-two headlines that included either the word "poll" or "survey." On one-third of the days the *Globe* published during the campaign — ten out of thirty-one — a front page headline contained the word "poll. " It was little different at the *National Post*, which had nineteen headlines during the campaign that included "poll' or "survey." On eight of the thirty-one days the *Post* published, its front page contained a headline that included "poll." The *Star* had nineteen headlines during the campaign that included "poll" or "survey." The newspapers reported polling results reached from small sample sizes that increased the likelihood of errors, regional breakdowns of polls with large margins of error, and individual poll results that were often methodologically not comparable to polls that had been reported previously.

All these shortcomings can undermine the quality of the polls and the reporting done about them. It was taking the next step, though, that caused the real problem for newspapers. The controversy arose because newspapers went beyond the sort of polling they had reported in previous campaigns.

This time they all played the seat projection game. By mid-campaign most coverage assumed the result would be a minority government. That made it irresistible to project seat totals for each party, as that could indicate who might win and by how much, and which party or parties might hold the balance of power in a minority parliament. The seat projection game became the newspaper equivalent of the contest between television networks to be the first to call the winner on election night.

Most seat projection models compare the results from any poll within a geographic region with the party-by-party results of the previous election on a riding-by-riding basis within that geographic region. It works like this. Take a poll and calculate the difference in each party's support from the support it received in the region in the last election. Then apply that party difference to the party's last election result in each constituency to project who would win that constituency this time around. For instance, if the New Democratic Party was five percentage points higher in an early May poll in Metro Toronto than the support the party received in Toronto in the last election, while the Liberals were seven percentage points lower and the Conservatives unchanged, the model would add five percentage points to the NDP share of vote in each Toronto riding last time while subtracting seven from the Liberal vote in each riding while not changing the Conservative vote share in each riding. Then see which party would be in first place in each riding to project the winning party.

The best seat projections come from looking at the difference between the results of a current poll and the last election results within as small a geographic region as possible. Applying the difference on a riding-by-riding basis between party standings in a poll of Metro Toronto residents and the party results in last election in each Metro Toronto riding will produce a more accurate projection of which party might win the constituency in this election than applying the results of a poll of all Ontario residents to Metro Toronto ridings to determine possible differences between last time and this election, as Ontario results may not reflect fairly the voting intentions of Toronto residents.

But there is a crucial calculation that risks undermining any predictions of which party will win each riding. Seat projections are based on the difference between party standings in a current opinion poll and party results in the last election on a riding-by-riding basis. In the months prior to the 2004 election, the Canadian Alliance and Progressive Conservative parties merged to create a new party, the Conservative Party of Canada. That created a problem for any seat projection model, as there is no previous election result for the Conservative Party against which to compare its current standing in any opinion poll.

None of the newspapers clarified how their projection models handled this difficulty. Did they simply add the Alliance and Progressive Conservative results in each riding from the 2000 election to create a Conservative base level of support for their seat projection models for this campaign? The assumption about the level of support to assign the new party in each riding in the 2000 election even though it didn't run in that campaign was fundamental to projecting the number of seats it might win in 2004. Yet that was little more than a guess on the part of the pollsters making the seat projections, sharply reducing the likelihood that any projection would be close to the final result.

All the newspapers played their seat projections as glimpses into the election-day future based on specific poll results, but none of them explained the degree to which their seat projections were based on guesswork about the Conservatives. That weak link, combined with massive shifting of voter intentions in Ontario in the campaign's final days, undercut the final polls released by the *Globe* and the *National Post* and their seat projections based on those polls. The *Globe* headlined its June 25 front page story by Drew Fagan "DEAD HEAT: With the election three days away, a new poll shows the main parties neck-and-neck. The implication: a deeply fractured Parliament." The *Post* featured on its front page the same day a Robert Fife story: "Liberals edge into seat lead: Seat projections, National Post poll have parties in dead heat." Only the *Toronto Star*, with polling conducted by Ekos Research, caught the dramatic last-minute shifting sands, prophetically headlining its June 26 story by reporter Susan Delacourt "Poll: Liberals 8 seats ahead: Martin projected to win minority: Shift in Ontario ridings called key."

Although there was considerable post-election criticism of the papers' use of seat projections, ironically in the next election they may be more accurate. The 2004 results provide a base level of Conservative support in constituencies from which to calculate the impact of changing voter support on a riding-by-riding basis. However, the 2004 experience seems likely to leave doubts about the legitimacy of projections in the minds of readers for some time to come.

Cheerleaders for Voter Turnout

Newspapers joined the electronic media in jumping on the turnout bandwagon, becoming cheerleaders for voting, particularly encouraging those under thirty to get involved and turn out on election day. The *Globe and Mail* led the way with three editorials focusing on the issue. While its concern was legitimate, it is hard to explain why the paper thought its schoolmarmish approach to the issue would be effective, with a May 27 editorial hectoring young people to "Grow Up and Vote."

The *Globe* also ran a series of features on the mental anguish suffered by twenty-three-year-old University of Toronto student and Saskatchewan native Chandler Powell as he debated whether or not to vote. Poking fun at this approach, the *National Post* cleverly replied by finding five people across the country also named Chandler, all of whom said they would vote and were critical of the *Globe*'s Chandler. Additionally, the *Post* ran one editorial advocating voting, while the *Star* avoided the subject on its editorial pages, concentrating instead on more news stories and columns than either the *Globe* or *Post* about low turnout, the alienation of young people from the political system, and the importance of those under thirty voting. In the end newspaper advocacy did not achieve the desired result, as the turnout was the lowest recorded for a Canadian federal election since the nineteenth century.

CONCLUSIONS

Jean Chrétien's year-and-a-half goodbye, followed by Paul Martin's six months of indecision about whether to call an election before the summer of 2004, left voters going to the polls as children were finishing school and families were contemplating summer vacations. Unlike 1997 and 2000, this was a campaign full of uncertainty with the unexpected possibility emerging partway through that the Liberals just might be defeated. Even given that, newspapers presented their readers with few coverage surprises. The tone and content of their papers were overwhelmingly set and occasionally manipulated by the political parties. Rarely, if ever, did leaders or parties have to respond to independent analysis of an issue done by one of the three major papers that injected a new or surprising element into the campaign.

Even in one of the rare examples that did, when the *Globe and Mail* reported on June 10 that Liberal campaign chairman David Herle told candidates, "We are in a spiral right now that we have to arrest," the paper told its readers only part of the story. Although Jane Taber reported direct quotes of Herle's comments in a conference telephone call the previous day, the story did not explain how the reporter obtained the quotes, leaving open the question of their accuracy. It only emerged later that Ms. Taber was in fact listening on her telephone, having been given the number to dial in as one of several hundred people on a conference call. In the interest of fully informing its readers, the *Globe* should have reported that Ms. Taber listened to the call to help readers assess the accuracy of the information in the story, as it would normally be impossible for a reporter to obtain such details.

It was also a campaign that left unanswered questions that newspapers, despite their involvement with polling, seemed not to have considered. For instance, what was the source of the voter rage against the Liberals early in the campaign? Is it really a sufficient explanation to say voters were upset about the sponsorship scandal and in Ontario by a reversal by Liberal Premier Dalton McGuinty of a pledge made in the previous year's election not to raise taxes? It seems difficult to accept that the depth of the dissatisfaction and desire for change expressed by voters so frequently and so vehemently early in the campaign was solely the product of the publicity around the sponsorship issue. The twists and turns of the campaign cry out for an explanation of what caused of the depth of this voter dissatisfaction and desire for change and why it was underestimated if even perceived at all.

The battle between Jean Chrétien and Paul Martin dominated political reporting in the two years prior to this election campaign. That battle was fought largely through unnamed sources that were willing to provide reporters with unsubstantiated allegations and rumours about their rivals in exchange for anonymity, a trade-off journalists should rarely, if ever, make. In much of Canadian political reporting by the spring of 2004, that sort of trade-off had become virtually standard operating procedure. Both factions within the Liberal party engaged in the practice, and the planting of stories continued after Martin won the leadership, as his purge of all Chrétien influences in the party did not end with his victory.

Not only the Liberals but all the political parties realized that reporters have become addicted to these "leaks" that are really carefully crafted strategic handouts. They were designed to obtain public relations advantages by exploiting the lack of diligence by many reporters, who would run with the stories provided to them on a platter, simply regurgitating them in their publications, asking not enough questions in the process. It is a short step from there to a campaign in which reporters and editors waited for events to take place or information to be forwarded to them on their Blackberry instant e-mail receivers from party headquarters rather than imaginatively taking the initiative themselves. The number of stories that mentioned the party war rooms suggests reporters became infatuated with the back and forth of insider misinformation, leaving readers and voters out of the loop, as their concerns were not those of the group playing the daily e-mail game. No one can argue that this political party–generated e-mail noise made newspaper coverage either more complete or more comprehensive.

Instead it was a successful diversionary tactic by the parties to keep reporters busy and when possible to sling mud against their opponents. The journalists and news organizations would all be much wiser and readers much better served if the papers did not provide their e-mail addresses to the parties for the next campaign.

Newspaper coverage of the 2004 campaign in the *Globe*, the *Star*, and the *Post* spent too much time following and not enough time leading. Newspapers reported some of what was said by politicians some of the time, and spent an increasingly large amount of space commenting and offering opinions about what was said. They did far too little enterprise reporting, too rarely trying to find the stories behind the obvious, and equally rarely substantively challenging the statements and polices that came from party leaders and were contained in their campaign platforms. In general the coverage showed limited imagination. Instead of taking the risks of being controversial that flow from ambitious and distinctive approaches and ideas that might produce head-turning successes or equally visible failures, the papers preferred the comfort of being safe, cautious, and predictable. In that respect the overall coverage of the election campaign was a fair but discouraging reflection of the current state of Canada's newspapers.

CHAPTER NINE

Television and the Canadian Federal Election of 2004

by Paul Attallah

Television occupies a peculiar place in election coverage. On the one hand, it is the indispensable medium of mass address without which modern democracy might well be unsustainable. Millions attend to it for the bulk of their election news. On the other hand, it is routinely assailed for the distortions and depredations it visits upon democracy. Its reporting is shallow, it is preoccupied with image, and it systematically fails to deal with issues substantively.

In fact, television and politics have benefited enormously from each other. The following pages examine the relationship between television and elections, particularly as they played themselves out in the Canadian federal election of 2004.

TV CRITICISM AND BUSES

The most curious phenomenon of the 2004 election was the decision by the three English-language networks (CBC, CTV, and Global) to outfit buses that would travel to lesser known parts of the country, collecting the views of so-called "ordinary Canadians." Buses were first used by CNN in the 2000 U.S. presidential election and their informational value remains an open question.

The use of buses is part of television's overall response to the criticisms usually levelled against its election coverage. The criticisms are well known and revolve around the suspicion that television privileges image over substance, triviality over depth, and emotion over rationality. Hence, television has been accused of reducing candidates' statements to sound bites, of concentrating on the electoral horse race rather than on substantive policy issues, of relying unduly on public opinion polls, and of emphasizing the personalities of politicians, especially of leaders, rather than their platforms or proposals.

Additionally, many believe that these shifts — broadly from issue to image — have themselves been hastened by news competition. As more all-news channels come on line, the rush for the scoop, for product differentiation, for the audience hook, etc., has become frenetic.

Television's standard retort — that these changes are driven by audience preference and not by internal structures, the quest for profit, or innate evil — now falls on deaf ears. Consequently, television has begun to incorporate within itself the criticisms of its activities.

The incorporation manifests itself as television's growing self-reflexivity. Barely a newscast occurs nowadays without accompanying commentary on how the newscast was delivered and constructed. Self-reflexivity is also evident in public affairs programs whose object is television or the media, such as *Inside Media* (Newsworld) or *I on Media* (I-Channel). Furthermore, it has long been a staple of such comedy programs as *Monday Report* (CBC) and *This Hour Has 22 Minutes* (CBC) which take the behaviour of television news itself as their object and presume considerable sophistication on the part of the audience about televisual forms.

Consequently, television coverage of the 2004 election was shadowed by an awareness of the criticisms of television election coverage itself. The networks vowed, therefore, to concentrate on "issues." The CBC declared that it would undertake no opinion polls of its own in order to concentrate on "issues"; the networks would launch buses across the country to discover "issues"; the coverage itself would be subject to scrutiny to ensure that it dealt with "issues."

Overall, with a few exceptions, the effort was successful. Regular newscasts were studded with reports emanating from the buses, but the networks also devoted special news events to "town hall meetings," profiles of candidates, and even public opinion polls.

The turn to buses was merely the most visible aspect of the overall attempt to move away from sound-bite, horse-race, and image/personality coverage. But the buses themselves were more public relations than public service. They provided novel footage, but in a campaign that proved highly competitive, and in which party leaders urged Canadians to vote strategically, they were not a wise choice. The most sophisticated means at our disposal for knowing what people think, and upon which politicians rely heavily, is public opinion polling. The observations of bus reporting are highly anecdotal and particularistic. They are unlikely to have informed the electoral strategies of the parties or the decisions of fellow citizens. The buses, then, were essentially a narcissistic indulgence for the networks to foreground their own sincerity, and they represent one of the bad ways of responding to television criticism.

However, the buses might make us reflect a little more carefully on the standard criticisms themselves, for they rest upon curious assumptions. The complaint that television does a disservice by focusing on image and personality, by highlighting opinion polls, by competing for scoops, etc., is based in the belief that in the old days — *before television* — politics and elections were treated seriously. Furthermore, it also presumes that television viewers (a) lack other sources of information and are therefore totally beholden to television, and (b) are too unsophisticated to know when they are being manipulated.

In other words, these assumptions assert that (a) television really is worse than what came before, that (b) we have no alternative sources of information, and that (c) we are fundamentally unsophisticated. Their true function is not to describe reality but to justify the attitudes of those who decry television.

While we do live in a media-saturated society, that fact alone has made us extremely adept at dealing with images and the media. The modern audience is the most media-savvy and image-literate in history. We do ourselves no favours by assuming the lack of sophistication of our contemporaries or by appealing to a fictional past. Indeed, we only demonstrate our naivety.

Of course, manipulation, dissembling, lying, and spinning are always possible. But the contemporary television audience is unusually sophisticated in its knowledge of the forms and history of television itself and is quite merciless in its awareness of and scorn for those strategies. It is certainly unwise to cast aside all caution on the pretext that the modern audience is sophisticated and sees through manipulation. But it is equally unwise to assume that television always produces noxious outcomes. The relationship between what television does and what those who use it intend it to do is infinitely more complex than "television effects" can begin to imagine.

THE ADVERTISING CAMPAIGN

The advertising campaign passed through two distinct phases that were driven by events in the election itself. But campaign advertising never *simply* capitalizes on campaign developments. It also constitutes one of the rare opportunities a party has to speak in its own voice without external intervention. The ads are uninterrupted by journalists, angry protests, inconvenient mishaps, or overenthusiastic supporters. They stage the world as the parties wish it to be and they stage the parties as they see themselves. They are the most utopian moment of any election campaign.

Naturally, campaign ads also need to be accessible to a majority of voters. Consequently, they draw heavily on the existing world of advertising imagery and tend not to introduce technical innovations or novel formats. Instead, they plant themselves firmly within the mainstream of contemporary advertising practices. They adopt the standard thirty- or sixty-second format, use slogans and catch phrases, run in heavy rotation, and use current production practices in order to achieve the look and feel of other ads. Indeed, most political campaign ads most closely resemble corporate advertising of the type associated with large industries such as aeronautics or insurance. They often sell no product in particular but seek rather to promote a diffuse feeling of goodwill towards an institution.

Finally, the ads also reflect the parties' budgets. Hence, the Liberals and Conservatives clearly had more ads and ran them in heavier rotation than the NDP. Likewise, the Bloc Québécois enjoyed comparatively large resources since it limited its campaign to Quebec. Furthermore, the big parties utterly eclipsed smaller parties such as the Green Party, the Marijuana Party, and the Communist Party. The smaller parties were generally confined to print advertising — often nothing more elaborate than party leaflets or lawn signs — or to whatever attention they could goad out of the media.

The most striking campaign slogan belonged to the Bloc Québécois. Its catch phrase — "*un parti propre au Québec*" — punned nicely on two meanings of *propre*: "Quebec's own party" and "a clean party in Quebec." It reminded Quebecers of the Liberal ad scandal and of the Bloc's dedication to "defend the interests of Quebec." However, the party's advertising campaign sought and received virtually no attention outside Quebec.

The Liberal, Conservative, and NDP advertising strategies changed abruptly halfway through the campaign. In phase one, no party could tell how the campaign would develop, and so their campaigns were fairly predictable.

The Liberal campaign consisted of a series of thirty-second spots on themes such as health care, education, the environment, and Canadian values. Each of these focused on Paul Martin. In some, Martin, wearing a loosely knotted tie (no jacket), spoke to a small group of politely nodding adults while a camera tracked elegantly around the group. In others, Martin, dressed comfortably and looking relaxed (no jacket or tie) mused about Canadian values, the environment, or the importance of a broad social vision. He was often photographed against lakes or forests.

These ads showed him to his best advantage, self-assured and trustworthy. They built upon and projected the notion of Paul Martin as the sure and steady finance minister, fully in control of his portfolio, supremely qualified for the task, and eminently reliable. The unspoken strategy was to focus on the respected leader rather than on the troubled party.

With their gently floating handheld camerawork and frequent use of jump cuts, the ads appeared to draw upon the visual style of music videos as it has been incorporated into television programming over the past decade. The style is frequently associated with the notion of being slightly hip and essentially forward-looking.

Simultaneously, the Conservative Party unveiled a series of ads focusing on Stephen Harper. In these thirty-second spots, Harper, looking very relaxed and comfortable (tie, no jacket), essentially introduced himself. Each short segment ended with the catch phrase "My name is Stephen Harper." Clearly, the goal was to introduce the new leader of a party formed only months before to an electorate that had no strong sense of him.

The Conservative strategy sought to affirm that the new party was neither the old Reform nor the old Progressive Conservative Party but an entirely new entity. It focused, therefore, on the new leader. Further, it sought to dispel any lingering suspicion that it harboured a hidden agenda by underscoring the frank though somewhat flat personality of the leader. The style of the ads, with their slight forward tracking, suggested strongly the qualities of forthright but unspectacular reliability.

The NDP unveiled an ad campaign that attempted to balance a focus on the new leader, Jack Layton, and on its "new ideas." As a result, the ads were relentlessly upbeat and emphatically urban. Layton (open collar or jacket, no tie) was featured in a number of shots, virtually all in bustling cityscapes, meeting and greeting various people, looking and nodding seriously, dipping a hand into a body of water, and smiling directly into the camera. The strategy was two-pronged: to introduce a new and energetic leader and to focus attention on its policy initiatives. The style of the ads was frankly cinematic and they looked very expensive. The NDP also released ads of Layton speaking Cantonese and Mandarin.

When opinion polls indicated that the Conservatives were drawing neck and neck with the Liberals, and perhaps surpassing them, the advertising campaign entered its second phase of all-out attacks.

The attack phase was inaugurated by the NDP. At approximately the halfway point, the NDP appeared to have stagnated in the polls. To this was added the fear of strategic voting, in which NDP supporters might abandon the party in favour of the Liberals in order to stop the Conservatives. Indeed, Paul Martin was specifically urging NDP supporters to do precisely that. In an effort to stem a potential voter hemorrhage, the NDP launched a somewhat surprising attack on U.S. President George Bush. Specifically, it accused Harper of being too close to the United States and too similar to George Bush. It then went on to claim that there was no essential difference between the Liberals and the Conservatives.

The NDP wanted to stop strategic voting. Those who supported strategic voting argued that a vote for the NDP was wasted because it would split many ridings, thereby allowing the Conservatives to win. The NDP's response was to argue that the truly wasted vote was for the Liberals, who merely represented a watered-down Conservative platform. The means of establishing this argument was to attack the United States. In the words of the ad itself: "Both Paul Martin and Stephen Harper want to bring Canada closer to George Bush, but Jack Layton thinks we can be good neighbours while still maintaining our values and independence."

There has long been a strand of anti-Americanism in Canada, especially on the left. Such an attack would, therefore, prove popular within the party. Furthermore, given the American war in Iraq and George Bush's divisive public image, it was also likely to resonate broadly with other voters as well.

Having established that alignment with the U.S. was bad, it was then necessary to demonstrate that Harper would bring Canada closer to the U.S. Harper had contributed directly to that perception by supporting the invasion of Iraq, writing an infamous letter to the *Wall Street Journal* and appearing on Fox News. The party then had to argue that there was no essential difference between Liberals and Conservatives. The NDP ads could hardly have been more pointed. They specifically and repeatedly portrayed Harper and Martin together, espousing similar policies, undertaking similar actions, making similar statements, and so on.

However, the attack on George Bush left the NDP open to two counter-charges. First, anti-Americanism is hardly a noble sentiment or one that would make effective foreign policy. Hence, it threw doubt on the NDP's judgment and readiness to govern. Second, it was obviously an emotional appeal, undermining the NDP's claim to be running a "campaign of ideas." As a result, the overt reference to George Bush was dropped but the invidious comparison of Liberals and Conservatives continued unabated. It was probably the most effective strategy for the NDP.

The anti-Americanism of the NDP ads made a slightly subtler appearance in the Liberal attack upon the Conservatives. In the second phase of the campaign, the Liberals, confronted with the same poll results as the NDP, abandoned their relatively positive initial campaign, which had foregrounded Paul Martin and his reliability, in favour of a series of attack ads that did not even mention the party or Paul Martin. The Liberal attack ads were all about the Conservatives, Stephen Harper, and the assault on fundamental Canadian values. The most notorious — and likely most effective of these ads — is worth reproducing in full.

> (Female narrator; deliberate diction; ominous music.)
>
> Stephen Harper would have sent our troops to Iraq (stock footage of tanks and soldiers crossing desert).
>
> He'd spend billions on tanks and aircraft carriers (stock footage of ship at sea), weaken our gun laws (close-up of gun pointed at camera), scrap the Kyoto Accord (stock footage of industrial pollution).
>
> He'd sacrifice Canadian-style healthcare for U.S.–style tax cuts (close-up of oxygen mask descending onto camera, cut to doctors wheeling patient on gurney).
>
> He won't protect a woman's right to choose (desperate teenager rocking on floor).
>
> And he's prepared to work with the Bloc Québécois (pan over Gilles Duceppe).
>
> Stephen Harper says that when he's through with Canada (zoom out on flag), we won't recognize it.
>
> You know what? (Flag begins to blur and disintegrate.) He's right. (Fade to black.)

As a piece of rhetoric, this was highly effective. It was both upsetting and frightening and became the object of discussion for days afterwards. Significantly, the Liberal Party and Paul Martin entirely disappeared. In their stead was an unrelenting attack on the Conservatives incorporating the theme of anti-Americanism, the fear of a hidden agenda, an association with violence (gun control, soldiers, tanks, warship), an attack upon individual liberties (a woman's right to choose), a reference to the permanent bogeyman of Canadian politics (the Bloc Québécois), and the spectre of social decay (health care versus tax cuts). This single ad condensed every phobic object of the Canadian political imaginary. It was the purest attack ad of the campaign. But it was hardly the only one.

Another Liberal ad specifically associated Harper with the economic policies of former prime minister Brian Mulroney and former Ontario premier Mike Harris, two figures it judged the audience would viscerally dislike. Another ad contrasted "the Stephen Harper we know" with the one we knew nothing about in order to underscore his "hidden agenda."

The Conservatives also went on the offensive with ads that focused relentlessly on images of Liberal waste and mismanagement. The ads focused on the general theme of anonymous people — presumably meant to be Ottawa mandarins — casually crumpling large sums of money which they threw into trash cans which were subsequently emptied by shrugging cleaning ladies and carried off by garbage trucks. In the words of one ad: "When does the government decide it's time to become accountable? After ten years? After they've proven just how reckless they can be with our money?"

The ads were simple, straightforward, and intended to arouse anger over the very casualness of the waste portrayed. It was a good tactic for the Conservative Party.

However, it is clear that these ads raise not only different issues but also issues of varying complexity. For example, the accusation that one's opponent fails to respect the constitution is of a different order from the accusation that one's opponent wastes money. The constitutional argument is not easily disposed of one way or the other. Furthermore, to respond to it — even in order to condemn the constitution — requires the development of a general orientation towards society, its disposition, and its institutions. Behind the constitutional argument, therefore, is an engagement with the voter as a reflective, rational citizen. The constitutional argument engages the public at the level of what may conventionally be called core values.

The money argument, on the other hand, is certainly more pointed and also likelier to provoke anger. But it's also easier to answer and to satisfy. Indeed, the anger induced may have little or no long-term carry-over as new issues wax and wane. In contrast, a fundamental orientation to values is likely to express a long-term predisposition and colour judgments across a broad range of issues.

It may be useful to bear these ideas in mind when turning to the perennial questions asked of all electoral advertising: are the ads effective and do negative attack ads really work? The only reasonable answer is that advertising does work but only to the same extent as any other persuasive discourse. We should also ask: do face-to-face arguments work? Does advice from parents work? Do religious sermons work?

Television advertising does not come with irresistible influence built in. Like every other persuasive strategy, television advertising only ever operates within a context made up of audiences who may be more or less receptive, more or less ironic, more or less sophisticated, etc. It works within a context made up of all other contending claims, some of which may be directly contradictory, some mildly supportive, others utterly unrelated, etc. It works within the context of the audience's familiarity with these other claims, their mode of operation, the sorts of outcomes they have generated, the types of people who seem to be persuaded by them, and so on. It works within the context of the life history of audience members, of their judgments about events elsewhere or in other realms of life, etc.

Hence, for some people, under some circumstances, some ads will be highly effective. For the same people, under other circumstances, the same ads may be highly ineffective. We can make judgments only on specific cases and try to inform our judgments by knowledge of the context.

In the election of 2004, we clearly observe cases in which some ads were highly effective and other ads were quite ineffective, and in which the effectiveness of ads varied over the course of the campaign. Hence, it is very likely that the NDP ads were highly effective within the party's core support but relatively ineffective beyond it; or more specifically, that their effectiveness beyond the core decreased as the campaign progressed and as voters received information from other sources, such as opinion polls.

Likewise, the Conservative ads appeared to be highly successful in the first half of the campaign and played an important role in humanizing the image of Stephen Harper. However, as voters received information from other sources, such as opinion polls, contradictory advertising, and statements emanating from within the Conservative party itself, the effectiveness of the ads tended to decrease. Naturally, among core supporters of the party it is likely that any ad would have been well received.

The Liberal ads appeared to be relatively ineffective during the first half of the campaign and were unpersuasive compared to other sources of information, such as the performance of the prime minister, daily news reports, opinion polls, contradictory advertising, and so on. However, with the switch to negative ads, the effectiveness of the advertising campaign appeared to increase. The negative ads, however, coincided with other sources of information such as opinion polls, the behaviour of other leaders, daily news reports, voter reflection, and so on.

The only unambiguous case of sustained advertising effectiveness occurs with the Bloc Québécois, where an unvarying message combined with opinion polls, contradictory campaigns, daily news events, etc., to produce a high level of convergence. But this is the exception rather than the rule.

Consequently, all ads work when they are inserted appropriately into the context in which their effects are intended. That context will necessarily consist of audience predispositions, familiarity with the universe of advertising itself, attitudes towards the immediate campaign and more distant events and issues, life experiences, the progress of the campaign, alternate sources of information, and so on.

The desire to see ads as effective is the failure to grasp communication in its entirety.

THE LEADERS' DEBATES

Traditionally, the high point of television's election coverage occurs with the leaders' debates. The anticipation that attaches to them is entirely justified. This is the only opportunity for most voters to see the leaders up close and to form a relatively independent judgment, free of journalistic interpretation or political spin. Furthermore, if attention to image is a prerequisite of modern politics, then the debates are an acid test of image management. Additionally, the antagonistic nature of the debates always holds the promise of an unanticipated outcome: a knockout punch, an unintended revelation, a glimpse of someone's true nature.

Finally, the leaders themselves attach overwhelming importance to the debates. Not only do they draw the largest audience of the entire campaign, not only are they preceded by oceans of speculation and followed by waves of interpretation, they are also the only occasion on which the leaders stand side by side and confront each other face to face. The debates personalize confrontation and highlight differences in personal style or interpersonal animosities.

For these very reasons, the debates are heavily stage-managed. The parties try precisely to avoid the potential knockout, the slip of the tongue, the spontaneous outburst. Consequently, the leaders rehearse intensively for the debates. They prepare debate books that contain not only their party's positions on the issues but also indications on how best to parry an offensive or to launch a counter-attack. The result is that a knockout blow is rarely landed, and most debates end up revolving around the questions of who lost, who won, or who did or did not meet expectations.

Furthermore, the debates are rarely the very first or last event in a campaign. They usually occur around its midpoint, within the context of "events up till then." They are, therefore, telling for how leaders explain away or capitalize on campaign developments and for how they try to seize control of issues or to redefine the campaign.

In 2004, there were two debates, one in French and one in English. Three questions were important going into them: (1) would Paul Martin be able to stem the precipitous decline of the Liberal Party; (2) would Stephen Harper be revealed as "demonic" because of his hidden agenda; and (3) would Jack Layton be as impressive as the advance publicity claimed? The French-language debate was enlivened by two additional factors: (a) for the first time, all the candidates spoke at least tolerable French, and (b) Gilles Duceppe's Bloc Québécois was surging in the polls.

It is fair to say that no decisive victory was scored by any leader in either debate. However, the French-language debate was clearly dominated by Gilles Duceppe even though, as virtually every commentator has observed, Mr. Duceppe lacks both charisma and charm. Nonetheless, if there was a winner, it was he. His style was forceful and accusatorial, but, more importantly, he demonstrated a mastery of issues that his opponents did not match.

Stephen Harper spoke surprisingly good French, though his facility was obviously limited. However, he neither alienated anyone nor was revealed to harbour a hidden agenda. On the contrary, he came across as both disconcertingly moderate and slightly bland.

Jack Layton spoke a more populist French and also managed to alienate no one. He specifically attempted to link his party's program to progressive impulses within Quebec. However, his ease in the language was also somewhat limited and, as a result, both he and Harper tended to remain on topic, closer to the zone of linguistic comfort, and slightly restricted in their engagements.

Paul Martin spoke the slightly rusty French of someone who had once been conversant in the language but who had had few opportunities to speak it. Nonetheless, he was fully at ease despite being the singular focus of most of the attacks.

In French, then, all the leaders gave good accounts of themselves but none did better or worse than might have been expected. They left the debate as they had entered it, ascending, descending, or stagnant.

The English debate followed a similar pattern. It was preceded by a brief squabble over the inclusion of the Green Party, which ultimately wasn't included in the debate, and over the democratic behaviour of "unelected TV producers." The squabble highlighted one of the enduring problems of Canadian leaders' debates. The debates are obviously modelled on U.S. presidential debates. The American debates, however, are organized by independent bodies, such as the League of Women Voters, and merely covered by the media. The Canadian debates, however, are organized directly by the television networks themselves. This leads to situations such as the one involving the Green Party. If the League of Women Voters chooses not to invite the Green Party, that is hardly a reflection on the television networks. But if the networks themselves refuse to invite the Green Party and then proceed to cover the debate, the obvious question is raised of the fairness and impartiality of television. It also results in the fact that all the questioners are television personalities, thereby excluding the enormous range of citizens who are not television personalities but who may nonetheless have interesting questions to pose. The Canadian leaders' debates, therefore, belong to television in a way that the American debates do not.

Nonetheless, the great unknown in the English-language debate was Gilles Duceppe. Indeed, many viewers had difficulty understanding why Duceppe was even participating in the debate since his party contested no seats outside Quebec. At any rate, Duceppe, whose English is roughly equivalent to the French of either Harper or Layton, did not dominate the English-language debate, though he did demonstrate his accusatorial tone and mastery of issues. Paradoxically, the very fact that he had nothing to lose — or to gain — may have humanized him and given him greater comfort in English than might have been expected.

Stephen Harper probably emerged as the "winner" of the English-language debate, if only because he avoided any obvious error, resisted all attempts to paint him as devious or demonic, and projected a steady blandness that seemed utterly unthreatening. He did not feel constrained to remain unerringly on topic in this debate and therefore engaged effectively with his opponents. He projected both ease and competence though without flash or sizzle.

Jack Layton was also visibly more comfortable in English than in French and also engaged more freely with his opponents, although his strategy of painting both the Liberals and the Conservatives as versions of the same thing required him to remain more firmly on topic precisely in order to highlight the differences he claimed. His television presence is definitely characterized by a higher degree of energy and forcefulness than that of his opponents.

Paul Martin was also at ease, and the debate was an opportunity for him to stem the tide of Liberal decline. His performance was good but he remained the focus of attacks and found himself engaging in defensive responses as much as in affirmations of his own views. He did not lose the debate and certainly engaged his opponents comfortably but he was not as effective as necessary.

Again, the leaders left the debate as they had entered it.

The myth of the television debate is rooted in the U.S. experience. The first and most analyzed televised presidential debate occurred in 1960 between John F. Kennedy and Richard M. Nixon. The candidates met four times in September and October of that year, sometimes in the same studio, sometimes by video link. The viewership for each debate was staggering, never falling below 60 million. It is a part of the myth that Kennedy scored a knockout blow against Nixon, but that never happened. In fact, while television viewers generally thought that Kennedy had performed better, radio listeners generally felt that Nixon had won the debates.

Over the years, Kennedy's modest triumph (49.7 percent to 49.5 percent) has been attributed to the fact that he looked more fit and tanned than Nixon, that he did not have a five o'clock shadow, and that his suit stood out better against the stage background than Nixon's. Whatever the reason, there is little doubt that Kennedy became an iconic president after the election. Part of his success was due to the fact that he was the first U.S. president to look like a movie star and to be aware of that fact. His entourage included a personal photographer, Jacques Lowe, whose carefully controlled images of the president played a key role in shaping the Kennedy myth. Likewise, Kennedy granted filmmakers Robert Drew and Richard Leacock unprecedented access to his campaign apparatus, resulting in the classic documentary *Primary: On the Road to the Kennedy White House* (1960), which has itself become the model for many later campaign films.

Kennedy was a master of the media, intensely aware of his image and of its construction. He was extremely careful in what he revealed and concealed and in the images he allowed to circulate. He is the *locus classicus* of the argument that modern politics is all about image, but he also hearkens to a time when the image was still innocent, a time before spin, image management, photo ops, and manipulation. Such, at any rate, is the myth.

THE LEADERS' IMAGES

No current Canadian politician — perhaps no politician anywhere — possesses Kennedy's degree of media awareness. Besides, it's not clear that such awareness would be as effective now as in the 1960s precisely because we are more sophisticated in the ways of the media. Nonetheless, it has been obvious since at least the 1960s that we have entered the "age of the image." The phrase is borrowed from Daniel Boorstin, the Librarian of Congress, who used it in *The Image: A Guide to Pseudo-Events in America* (1961). The "age of the image" designates a cultural trend that far exceeds television but in which television plays a key role. It describes a state of society in which the image appears able to substitute itself for reality in such a way that we attend to it rather than to reality. Of course, human cultures have long attributed mythical power to images. Plato wanted to ban poets from the city because they put bad images into the minds of the young and, in explaining how reality was degraded, his "myth of the cave" refers explicitly to images — shadows cast on a wall — as poor and misleading substitutes for reality. Some cultures explicitly ban certain categories of representations, some condemn the adoration of false idols, some recommend the adoration of icons, and so on. Our own culture invests images — especially television images — with the mythical power to induce collective behaviour and warp young minds. As such, we hem them around with ratings systems and codes, warnings and injunctions, hopes and fears.

Whether images ever possessed the power attributed them cannot be resolved here. The fact is, though, that modern politics are image politics and no political leader is likely to be successful without also attending to his image, a truism curiously captured by Geoff Pevere (2004) in his *Toronto Star* column, "Electing the next national TV host."

In the election of 2004, the party leaders came to the public with distinct images. Equally significant, however, is the fact that their public images, like their advertising campaigns, stand firmly in the mainstream of contemporary televisual practice. The look, feel, and personalities of television are the *lingua franca* of modern image-making.

Hence, modern political leaders are much less concerned with their appearances in newspapers or in film or their sound on radio.

Television is the only important reference. Consequently, image-makers construct likeability, persuasiveness, trustworthiness, etc., as *television* would construct them. The images of the political leaders can, therefore, be understood relative to our experience of the world of television and to other images in it.

Jack Layton is the most telegenic of the four leaders. He projects well and brings a bubbly energy to the small screen. He is always interesting to watch, even (perhaps especially) if one disagrees with him. He seems fully at home on television and even looks like he could have a second career as a TV personality. His persona is clearly enlivened by a sense of performance.

That very fact, though, may also undermine his effectiveness. The ambiguity between high-minded zeal and simple showmanship is captured in his permanent smile and direct gaze to the camera. Both features may be slightly too emphatic, casting him in the role of the too-congenial television host, a sort of adamant Alex Trebek.

Nonetheless, in the context of the NDP's recent leadership, the key factor may not be his policy orientation but simply the fact that the camera loves him. Layton's image is almost certain to comfort the true believers if only because it draws attention to their cause and, in so doing, lends it credibility. But it may not be effective in reaching out beyond the party precisely because of its intensity.

Stephen Harper, on the other hand, draws on the clean-cut but blank look of almost any sitcom dad of the 1960s or 1970s. He looks like the youthful father of a brood of rambunctious kids, living in the suburbs with one of those unspecified jobs (ad exec, pilot, architect) that never prevents him from doing yardwork or helping the kids play football.

This very persona, however, embodied the "family values" that the party wished to promote, and his mere appearance on TV — slow, steady, and steadfastly unspectacular — seemed to resist all attempts at demonization. Indeed, the devastating blows against his party were struck not by his opponents but by his political allies who seemed determined to conform to the worst stereotypes of the Reform Party.

Paul Martin possessed the most complex television personality because it changed so much over the course of the campaign. Although he had long been in the public eye as a key cabinet minister, he had never been the focus of his government's efforts. Furthermore, the recency and messiness of his rise to power left the permanent temptation of comparing him to his predecessor, Jean Chrétien.

Martin came to the public with a legacy of enormous competence — the finance minister who had saved Canada — which was reflected in the relaxed sleekness of his pre-election appearances. The comfort of his demeanour, the easy set of his features, the readiness and sincerity of his smile all spoke of the successful executive well satisfied of his achievements. Once he came to power, though, the public discovered a second Paul Martin who became increasingly directionless as his interregnum and the campaign wore on. In one-on-one interviews, Martin could be quite effective, almost a university professor leading a seminar. In uncontrolled settings, however, such as scrums or when delivering speeches or taking questions from the public, he came across as agitated, unable to form complete sentences, and agreeing with everyone.

If Stephen Harper's blandness protected him against charges of demonization, Paul Martin's ineffectiveness cast doubt upon his competence. Hence, his displays of anger and outrage at the sponsorship scandal, and his promise to get to the bottom of things, not only put him in opposition to his own party, but also contrasted sharply with how one imagines Jean Chrétien might have handled the affair. One can easily imagine Chrétien brushing past a throng of reporters as an expression of indifference. Such brusqueness would have demonstrated control. Martin, on the other hand, identified with the most aggrieved member of the public and seemed, therefore, to identify with those people who understood the least about public life. Hence, rather than project prime ministerial authority, he projected disorientation and supplication.

If Layton is the congenial host, and Harper the sitcom dad, then Martin is every fictional television news anchor — from the Ted Knight of *Mary Tyler Moore* to the Kent Brockman of *The Simpsons* — assured and mellifluous in his studio delivery, bemused and befuddled in his off-camera life. He seemed caught in the gap between his image and his reality.

Gilles Duceppe, finally, was both the best- and least-known of the leaders, at least for English speakers. He was well known because his public image — an endlessly circulated photograph from the 2000 election of him wearing an extremely unflattering hairnet — had essentially been reduced to a stereotype. The stereotype had been allowed to proliferate by the virtual exclusion of the Bloc Québécois from any serious commentary in the English-language media. So while the stereotype was very well known, the actual positions of his party were utterly unknown. However, knowledge of those policies became increasingly crucial as the prospect of a minority government loomed ever larger.

The anglophone media's treatment of the Bloc Québécois is rooted in its overall apoplectic dismissal of sovereigntist politics *tout court*. It runs on the presumption that we know all about the Bloc's agenda, which is bad, and which can therefore be ignored or caricatured. Chantal Hébert, writing in the *Toronto Star* (2004), observed the same phenomenon in a column that noted, "So used is the bulk of the Canadian media establishment to ignoring the Bloc Québécois that many of its charter members struggled their way through Monday night's French debate in search of a decisive Harper/Martin confrontation." This attitude is surely a disservice to the public. It seems unwise to ignore the views of any segment of society simply out of spite or because we disagree with it, especially when that segment aspires to genuine political influence.

Nonetheless, Duceppe possesses a brittle personality. Although he is the son of one of Quebec's most celebrated actors, he also spent much of his youth in the small Maoist Parti communiste ouvrier marxiste-léniniste, an experience that appears to have marked him more than his acquaintance with Québécois theatre. He seems neither charming nor likeable and projects stern aloofness from behind a decidedly steely gaze. And yet, he revealed himself to be not entirely without wit or skill. His greatest asset is his ability to handle information and to be up-to-date on the latest files. However, one can barely imagine him having any career after, or before, politics. He projects a single-minded relentlessness to such an extent that his manner trumps his personality and eventually becomes his image.

ELECTIONS USE TELEVISION

Politicians have always used whatever means of public address were at their disposal, whether silver-tongued oratory, whistle-stop tours, screaming headlines, or radio. Nowadays, television is the ubiquitous tool of election campaigning. The obvious point of mass media is to reach everyone quickly in order to make oneself well known. Indeed, the state of well-knowness, or fame, is the logical byproduct of access to a mass media system. And since images can travel anywhere, virtually any constellation of hopes, attitudes, values, ideas, behaviours, etc., can be attached to them. This is the source of their alleged power. It hardly matters whether the image is the likeness of an emperor struck on a coin, of a sovereign on a stamp, or of a president in a televised press conference. The wide dissemination of an image produces fame. Therefore, attention to the construction of the image is also attention to the meanings one wishes to instill in the public.

Television is the most useful mass medium for achieving this end because it reaches the largest number of people most efficiently. However, it possesses certain characteristics that anyone seeking fame must learn to use. In this respect, then, television does establish an equivalence between politics and all other fame-oriented activities. When it is accused of turning politics into entertainment, it is actually only making its methods available to anyone who would use them. It might just as usefully be accused of turning entertainment into politics.

First, television news is driven by deadlines and an insatiable appetite for content. A skilful tactician can use these facts to advantage, by routinizing appearances (press conferences), supplying content to deadline, speaking to the rhythms of television (sound bites), supplying visually interesting content (photo ops), taking over the difficult task of newsgathering itself (video news releases), etc.

Second, as already mentioned, television manufactures fame, or well-knowness. This is abundantly obvious in the current craze for reality TV, in which the most ordinary become, at least temporarily, the most extraordinary. A clever tactician can also use this aspect to advantage by gaining and maintaining access to television. Sometimes access is granted by simple fact of being in public life and therefore worthy of attention. Sometimes it is gained through stunts, outrageous comments, cultivating a pleasing personality, agreeing to any and all interviews, relentless glad-handing, the ability to show up whenever a camera is rolling, etc. There are many examples of politicians made famous by television and much forgotten afterwards. The enduring fame of politicians is increasingly linked to the enduring circulation of their images.

Television's ability to manufacture fame, though, is complex. It breeds not only fame but also familiarity. It can make ordinary people famous but it can also make famous people ordinary. The point here is not that politicians are rendered famous only because they have television exposure, although exposure obviously helps. It is, rather, that the price of television fame is the relentless pressure to seem ordinary. This can be illustrated by considering the opportunities and obstacles that television presents.

The most important political opportunity is obviously the ability to address an entire nation-state and to exercise genuine influence over the shape of social affairs. With that opportunity, however, goes a level of public scrutiny that many could not bear and some find highly distasteful. Such scrutiny, though, may itself be a contributor to fame, and is almost certainly part of the conversation of democracy. Other opportunities may include the exclusion of one's opponents or the sheer intoxication that often accompanies fame.

The obstacles are more interesting. Since television breeds familiarity, it can also breed exhaustion with an image that has simply become too familiar. But just as some actors have long careers, there is no easy way to know which political image will lose public favour. The deep suspicion, of course, is that political credibility now rests on a likeable image and that as images are easier to manipulate, manipulation itself has become a more pervasive phenomenon.[1]

The greatest obstacle, though, is the implicit equivalence drawn by television between those who watch and those who are watched. If television breeds familiarity, then those who are on television, however great they may first have been, eventually acquire a patina of ordinariness. And if the famous are ordinary, then television holds out the perverse promise that those who are merely ordinary may somehow also become famous simply by being on television. This is a state of affairs foreseen by Andy Warhol in 1968 when he said (at the opening of an exhibition in Stockholm): "In the future, everybody will be world famous for fifteen minutes."

Television, therefore, can rob politicians of any shred of specialness and tends to induce a complex dialectic between the ordinary and the extraordinary. For example, virtually all American politicians now affect some version of a Southern drawl, because it is familiar and works well on television. Brilliant politicians hide their brilliance for fear of seeming too *un*-ordinary. Politicians reveal aspects of their private lives as though they were guests on *Oprah*.

In short, they are made to seem relentlessly and mercilessly like us, and therefore undeserving of any particular respect. Indeed, they become the objects of special opprobrium and suspicion. The familiarity that television breeds can turn to contempt and become a corrosive force in public life.

But it should be observed, at this point, that while the making ordinary of the famous certainly occurs *on* television, the process is not the exclusive by-product *of* television. Interest in the private lives of the famous is a long-standing phenomenon that far exceeds television. It is the case, however, that television has offered itself as an unusually propitious ground for the flourishing of that tradition.

Nonetheless, this is the arena of modern politics and is why all politics is now image politics. Television manufactures fame by circulating images of the famous. One of the main efforts of modern politics must therefore be to situate itself within the world of television by attending to the nature and quality of one's image.

TELEVISION USES ELECTIONS

In an age when many feel that there's nothing to watch, election coverage draws viewers like a magnet.[2] From television's point of view, the 2004 election could hardly have happened at a better time — the dead of summer when both ratings and ad sales are depressed. Any election enlivens ad sales because parties bid for available minutes.

Additionally, elections also constitute ready-made special events with high viewer appeal. Elections are good for business.

Election coverage can also serve as part of television's overall promotional strategy. It can be used to schedule new or underperforming shows around important events (to channel audiences and encourage sampling), to counterprogram a competitor, to create a good feeling about a network, or to establish a link between a network and serious, high-minded content.

The precise value of elections for television may be measured by an ad that appeared on page A10 of the *Globe and Mail* on June 29, 2004, the day after the election. The full-page, full-colour ad was placed by CTV. It did not invite readers to tune in to the network. It did not herald a new event or exceptional spectacular. It did not even tout an existing show. Instead, it concerned the previous night's election coverage. The ad said: "On Election Day, Canada Voted for CTV." And, under the stern gaze of its anchor and other personalities, it reproduced both Nielsen and BBM ratings, according to which CTV had drawn a larger audience than either CBC or Global.

Clearly, the ad builds on CTV's election coverage in order to suggest that the network is both serious and successful, and therefore worthy of further attention. This is hardly surprising, as Canadian networks are known primarily for their news rather than their entertainment.

Elections, therefore, let television associate itself with an objectively important event, thereby deflecting the perennial criticism that television is an entertainment medium aimed at the lowest common denominator. Against the charge of pandering, television can point to the high social value of its election coverage.

But election coverage affords television several other advantages as well. It uses election coverage not only to foreground its serious nature and public service but also to showcase its on-air personnel. Furthermore, elections have become notable for their technical wizardry: they are frequently used to introduce new graphics and special effects (which highlight the network's modernity), to coordinate a dizzying array of remote locations, to switch seamlessly from anchor desk to news analysis to leaders' headquarters. They are, in short, an opportunity to project the power of television, its ability not only to draw events and locations together but also to draw together a nation of viewers and to construct an imaginary map of democracy.

Television's election coverage, therefore, produces a uniquely *televisual* event. It turns the election and its myriad isolated and uncoordinated events into a single comprehensible narrative held together by the technical wizardry of the network and the stature of its on-air personnel. If ever our experience of elections and of politics was personal, individual, or visceral, lived on the ground and in the daily interchange with our fellow citizens, it is now a seamless experience whose existence depends entirely on television.

Hence, our experience of elections is televisual not merely in the sense that TV covers elections but in the sense that television stages the map of the country and of the leaders' movements, the representation of their relative strengths, the virtual space in which they meet and discuss — in short, the only site in which we see and hear them.

If television has any power, it is the ability (shared with all techniques of representation) to tell a compelling and authoritative narrative by staging the world around us. It is a power that first became apparent during the Kennedy funeral. That event marked an important shift in public opinion. Prior to it, most people claimed to trust newspapers the most. After it — and ever since — most people claim to trust television more than any other medium.

The importance of the Kennedy funeral, therefore, is twofold: (a) it marks the ascendance of television as dominant news medium, and (b) it was the first notable occasion on which television turned an event occurring independently of it into a spectacle comprehensible to all. Whether television actually intervened in the event and altered it or whether its mere presence caused the event's managers to play to the camera is a moot point. Nonetheless, television covered and edited the funeral, its various locations, its symbolism, etc., into a story that could be observed as a single, unfolding event. And within that event, it provided the opportunity for its one memorable image — John-John saluting the coffin — which was itself staged by the supremely media-savvy Jackie.

Television uses politics and politics uses television.

IN CONCLUSION

The 2004 election marked the first time that television was permitted to report results from across the country, irrespective of time zone. Hence, Atlantic Canada results could be viewed in B.C. as they were reported, several hours before the polls closed in B.C. Previously, television had been required to cover results on a rolling time zone basis so that knowledge of the results in one province would not affect voting in another.

Apparently, the cross-time-zone reporting had no impact. And this fact is interesting because, as with so many other details of television election coverage, it refers us to the presumed power of television.

Overall, television coverage of the 2004 federal election was good. It was not confined to election night alone but spanned the entire campaign with a display of resources and competence that, on balance, do credit to both television and democracy. Television again demonstrated its centrality to the process by staging the most important ads, the leaders' debates, town hall meetings, etc. It was the principal arena for leaders and parties to advance their programs and shape their images.

On balance, the images are not *caused* by television. Rather, politicians *use* television to shape their images to their advantage. It may be more prudent to conclude that television is a highly pervasive representational medium than to claim it as an all-powerful representational medium.

REFERENCES

Lysiane Gagnon, "Communism Taught Duceppe Discipline and Duty," *The Globe and Mail,* June 21, 2004.

Chantal Hébert, "Duceppe plays winning hand," *The Toronto Star,* June 18, 2004.

Geoff Pevere, "Electing the next national TV host," *The Toronto Star,* June 15, 2004.

Warhol, Joenig, Hulten, and Granath (eds.), *Andy Warhol (*Stockholm, 1968).

www.bbm.ca

NOTES

1 While likeable images have always been helpful, it seems untrue that manipulation is more pervasive now than in the past. We sentimentalize the past when we assume it to have been nobler than the present and forget the schemes, deceitful rhetoric, gerrymandering, vote rigging, election fraud, bribery, alcoholic liberality, intimidation, shenanigans, misrepresentation, and outright lies of our ancestors. Furthermore, these *undemocratic* behaviours all occurred without the benefit of television. Nor is manipulation peculiar to democracy, as the equally pre-television propaganda of both Fascism and Communism will attest. If anything, the techniques and extent of manipulation are better known now than ever before and more subject to scrutiny.

2 In its measurement of the weekly top twenty television shows, BBM reports that in the week of June 28 to July 4, 2004, the CBC election night coverage drew 1.612 million viewers, second only to *Canadian Idol* at 1.666 million. Additionally, other news shows ranked seventh, eighth, eleventh, fourteenth, and fifteenth, thereby occupying six of the twenty top spots. (See http://www.bbm.ca/en/home.html.)

CHAPTER TEN

Public Opinion Polling and the 2004 Election

by Michael Marzolini

Polls are always of interest to the public, and never more so than during an election. Most major media organizations employ a pollster to examine the views of the voters and report on the state of the election race. At the same time, the political parties retain their own pollsters, whose job is not just to measure public opinion but also to manage it and to provide strategic recommendations based on their findings. The measuring and interpretation of public opinion, by pollsters and the media, is not just one of the most important jobs in the world, it is a public trust. Opinions are the most precious things that most individuals own, and it is a duty of those who report and analyze these opinions never to misstate, exaggerate, diminish, or skew them.

Pollsters, at least in the media, had a relatively easy task to perform during the 1997 and 2000 election campaigns. Public opinion did not change substantially during the course of either of those campaigns, and so it was fairly easy to measure. There were no changes in the relative order of preference for any of the political parties from start to finish. In both elections Canada's media pollsters successfully tracked each shift of the electorate, and all the final polls accurately reflected the actual election results, within the margin of errors of their respective sample sizes.

The 2004 federal election, however, was quite different. Public opinion during the campaign was more volatile, and media pollsters had to scramble to keep up with the fast-moving and ever-changing intentions of the voters. While more media polling was conducted in this election than in any past campaign, and it was given far more prominence in the media coverage, the actual results were a surprise to the great majority of the public and to those in the media themselves. Each of the media pollsters, in their last poll of the campaign released the week before the Monday, June 28 vote, showed a very close race between the two parties. Each of them, to be fair, showed the Liberals with a very small lead over the Conservatives. The three largest, and hence most reliable surveys, conducted by Ipsos-Reid for the *Globe and Mail* and CTV (2,000 interviews), for the *Toronto Star* by Ekos (5,200 interviews), and for Sun Media by Leger Marketing (3,100 interviews), each accurate to within 2 percent, had the Liberals ahead by only one percentage point. A similar one-point margin was reflected in a small-scale survey (800 interviews) conducted for Canwest-Global by Compas. A slightly larger Liberal plurality (4 percent) was produced by SES for the Parliamentary Channel (1,000 interviews), but even this poll, the closest of any to the outcome, did not reflect the final vote results, even after adding the pollster's own margin of error to the findings.

Despite the fact that the Liberals had a very small lead in public support, the expectation was that it would be the Conservatives who would form a minority government — not the Liberals. This conclusion was the result of seat projections, provided by a number of pollsters and academics, whereby historical election data is "adjusted" by the results of public opinion polls to show the changes to the numbers of parliamentary seats that each party could anticipate. Most of these projections, due to the regional concentration of votes and relative efficiency of those votes in the first-past-the-post system, concluded that the Conservatives would win as many as thirty more seats than would the Liberals. The media's concentration on these seat projections, without studying the faulty methodology on which it was based, clouded public perception of the real meaning of the poll results.

The Liberal plurality on election day was in fact 7.1 percent, and this fact was a sore tribulation to the polling industry in the weeks to follow. On Global Television on election night, their pollster from Compas and a Wilfrid Laurier University professor who had made a name for himself projecting riding results from public opinion surveys disappeared from the on-air coverage once the results began diverging from their predictions. On CBC, anchor Peter Mansbridge and his panel grilled pollsters Donna Dasko of Environics Research and Allan Gregg of Strategic Counsel, neither of whom was conducting polls for broadcast at the time, on why their industry had "fouled up so badly." Their explanations were obscured by the sarcastic remarks and jokes from other panellists and humorist Rex Murphy. The next day each of the major newspapers launched angry attacks on the credibility of public opinion polling, though each had added in its own way to the dissemination and further analysis (much of it faulty) of its own polls during the course of the campaign. Pollsters scrambled to provide excuses and to explain the differences.

So were the media polls in fact wrong? Were the pollsters interviewing the right people? Have falling response rates driven by people's declining motivation to answer public opinion polls had an impact on the findings? Was the analysis wrong? Did the media give too much emphasis to polls in their election coverage and thereby create a monster? Or did Canadians change their mind in the last few days of the campaign?

Polls have been wrong before. In 1936, the *Literary Digest*, based on two million mailed survey responses, predicted that Republican Alf Landon would beat Democrat Franklin D. Roosevelt in the race for U.S. president. At the same time, George Gallup, using a much smaller sample, correctly identified Roosevelt as the winner. Why the difference? The *Literary Digest* polled only subscribers to their publication — a publication whose readership demographics skewed towards high-income Republicans. Gallup interviewed the general public, notwithstanding what reading matter they preferred, and achieved the more accurate results. Only twelve years later, the Gallup Organization reported a presidential victory for Republican Thomas Dewey, rather than Harry S. Truman. This greatly embarrassed the polling industry, and even to this day polling detractors, and many politicians, trot out the Gallup debacle to undermine the credibility of the polls they dislike. What happened? According to David McCullough, in his biography of Truman, "The polls were reasonably accurate up until mid-October, the point when Gallup completed his final survey of the campaign for the forecast that was released just before election day. The fault was not that the polls were imperfect, but that they were two weeks out of date." Much can change in two weeks, and many Canadian pollsters would argue it could also change in one week.

In 1992, MORI and many other U.K. pollsters predicted a Labour Party victory and were surprised by the strong Conservative Party victory. Again, the survey sample they chose was faulty — the British telephone company at the time charged each of their subscribers for telephone usage rather than a flat fee, forcing British pollsters to use face-to-face interviews rather than telephone methodology to conduct their interviews. In the geography of public opinion, each street may vote a different way or hold differing attitudes. The economics of door-to-door surveying leads to the selection of perhaps only one hundred streets or "cluster points" where perhaps ten interviews with like-minded people are conducted. A telephone survey of one thousand people, however, would usually have one thousand cluster points — no two people are interviewed in the same street or household. This provides a much more balanced and accurate survey. In 1992, British pollsters made the same mistake the *Literary Digest* had fifty-six years before: they interviewed the wrong people. Since that time, pollsters in both countries have moved to the more reliable telephone survey methodology, improving accuracy, and along with computerization, increasing the speed of reporting, which would have saved George Gallup some mortification.

There are a number of methodological challenges inherent in conducting a good election poll. Most pollsters have met some, but not all, of these challenges. There is much room for improvement. However, the pollsters cannot deal with all of these issues without the active collaboration of the competitive media organizations that they work for, who have demanded that pollsters stretch their analysis into unsafe territory, such as providing seat projections that have no scientific or statistical basis. These methodological challenges that both industries face are as follows:

DID POLLSTERS INTERVIEW THE RIGHT PEOPLE?

While some media pundits have flagged declining survey response rates as a possible reason for the polls not reflecting the outcome, this is mainly just an economic issue for the polling firms, significantly increasing data collection costs, but not impacting perceptibly on the quality of the data, which should still be accurate and projectable to the population as a whole. Far more important than this is the question that pollsters must ask themselves: "Are we interviewing the right people?" In the 2000 election, while the pollsters all caught the trend across Canada and predicted the outcome very accurately, they did very poorly in their analysis of the Quebec vote. Indeed, most failed to discover that the Liberals were ahead of the Bloc Québécois, and not the reverse. Of the eight polls released shortly before the vote, only one had the Liberals actually ahead, and only marginally, yet the Liberals won with a substantial plurality. So where did they go wrong? Their opinion polling in Quebec was technically correct; they built a sampling model of Quebec residents and duly and accurately reported the preferences of the public. What they failed to do was report the intentions of the *voting* public, which was quite different from the will of the entire population.

POLLARA's polls for the Liberal Party in that campaign excluded the likely non-voters from the sample and hence predicted, exactly, the election outcome. However, doing this involves building a very sophisticated sampling model, being able to take into account, for example, that senior citizens, who form 13 percent of the population in the province, actually cast 28 percent of the votes. Younger people in Quebec, being more sovereignist than federalist but seeing little opportunity for the sovereignist movement due to the politics of the time, sat on their hands in 2000, while federalists trooped to the ballot box. There are many other fluctuations by region, gender, age, and ethnicity that need to be understood when determining whom to interview.

During the 2004 election there was very little attempt, by any of the pollsters, to actually exclude the 40 percent of eligible Canadians who did not intend to vote. There are three reasons for this. The major one is cost. Most media organizations have an election-polling budget of less than $100,000, some only half of that. Polling organizations conduct election polls to get their name in the media and demonstrate expertise in public opinion, with hopes of winning the jackpot by predicting the actual election outcome. (Accuracy is considered good for business, which is why three pollsters conducted between two thousand and five thousand interviews for their last poll.) The pollsters' fees are only honoraria, which never cover their actual data collection and professional costs. Therefore they have little motivation to double their interviewing costs by excluding unlikely voters.

Second, when pollsters do attempt to exclude non-voters, they run into the problem, documented in POLLARA election surveys, that 70 percent of Canadians will tell them that they do intend to vote, though actual turnout history would suggest that as many as 20 percent are exaggerating these intentions. Even when attempting to exclude non-voters, there will be 20 percent too many non-voters participating in the survey, and that is a potential source of error in an election poll. Framing the question "Are you absolutely certain you will vote?" can cut this error by half (60 percent of Canadians are usually certain), but as long as voting is considered a civic duty, there will always be some Canadians assuring pollsters they will vote, though later declining to do so. Still, interviewing an additional 10 percent of non-voters is far more accurate than interviewing an additional 50 percent of the population that does not intend to vote. And finally, once pollsters have excluded non-voters from the sample, they are faced with a poll, unrepresentative of Canadians as a whole, that has widely fluctuating demographics — especially by age and ethnicity. Without an accurate model of anticipated turnout by each of those demographics, for the current and not past elections, who is to say that the pollster has interviewed a representative sample of voters, and not just the voters they were able to contact? In any normal survey, one can check the demographics and ensure a quota usually based on gender, age, and geography. Few pollsters can ascertain, without doing separate studies on turnout (which could change from week to week), the exact demographic proportions of the voting population. There are many opportunities for error, and many pollsters would not want to risk their credibility reporting such a survey.

ARE POLLSTERS ASKING THE RIGHT QUESTION?

Canada's pollsters are not perfect, but they have generally learned from each other and improved over time. They tend to argue methodology among themselves and discuss arcane issues of question wording, inter-item bias, timing, sampling, and analysis. As far back as 1993, much public debate took place between two pollsters, Environics and Angus Reid, on whether the party preference "horse-race" question should include the names of the party leaders. The issue at the beginning of the campaign was that the two ways of asking the question produced two completely different sets of results. This was an effect of having a popular political party (Liberals) led by an unpopular leader (Jean Chrétien) versus an unpopular party (the PCs) led by a very popular leader (Kim Campbell). Party vote had the Liberals ahead. Adding the leaders' names reversed the order of public preference. This issue was never settled, but the debate became moot once voters started paying more attention to the election campaign and the two sets of poll results converged together into one that was fairly consistent.

Question wording on the horse-race question is still an issue. And one of the current issues is whether, when naming the party choices, all the political parties should be named or just some. And, if some, which ones? In early 2003, the Green Party of Canada conducted a lobbying campaign that involved contacting each media and party pollster in Canada to urge them to give survey respondents the option of naming the Green Party as their choice. Previously, voters were given the option of Liberal, Conservative, NDP, BQ, or "Other." Only if the "other" category surged in popularity would pollsters try to determine which of the minor participants on the landscape was responsible. There was a view held by the Greens that not giving their party the mind-share inherent in being included in the question actually underestimated their popular appeal in the poll. The counter view, voiced by firms like POLLARA, was that by naming the Green Party along with the four major parties, the GPC would have *too much* mind-share, and that this prompting would exaggerate public support for the Green Party, as it would any of the other minor parties if they were named in the question.

When a pollster attempts to synthesize the ballot in a survey question, the ideal would be to lay out an actual ballot in front of each respondent, with the names of all parties and independents from which to choose. This is not possible to do over the telephone without confusing Canadians and hence losing accuracy. Presenting a lesser known party, such as the GPC, as an option, would increase their mind-share for the survey question only, not in real life, giving them the entire "none of the above" vote, which in reality would be shared by all the other minor parties and independent candidates. Granted, not prompting with the party name may underestimate support for each of these parties individually, but still accurately reflect the actual number of Canadians collectively supporting minor parties. Most Canadian pollsters accept this argument. Ipsos-Reid, on the other hand, started naming the Green Party in their vote question early this decade. At both the federal and provincial level, this firm consistently shows the Green Party higher than do other pollsters (as high as 7 percent during the 2004 election), almost double their actual 4 percent vote yield.

Other question-wording issues are also subject to debate. Again in the "horse-race" question, some pollsters like to use the phrase, "If an election were held today, which party's candidate would you vote for?" This is technically the correct question, because in each riding a voter is indeed voting for a candidate. However, only 10 to 20 percent of voters in any riding make their decision based on the appeal of a local candidate. The remainder is split between the appeal of the political parties and the appeal of the party leaders. Therefore arises the concern that this question produces findings unfairly biased toward the local candidate, while ignoring the two more important factors that influence vote choice.

ARE THE POLLSTERS TALKING TO ENOUGH PEOPLE?

Sample size is important when analyzing a poll, and during the 2004 election there were many instances of insufficient and unreliable sampling. The Canwest-Global polls produced by Compas were cheap and cheerful small sample surveys that were actually quite adequate in showing overall party preference across Canada. However, with a sample of only six hundred interviews, occasionally boosted to eight hundred, the margin of error for each of Canada's regions was too high to be reported with any degree of confidence. This did not stop the *National Post* or Global Television from reporting these regional results, an irresponsible practice that shocked many market research practitioners and the more savvy journalists.

A national poll can be accurate with almost any size sample over one thousand, which provides a margin of error of 3.2 percent, nineteen times out of twenty. Reporting regional results is risky, however, even with a sample of this size. Canada has many small regions in which the population has very different attitudes, values, and opinions. In this we have greater regional variation than does the United States. Yet, in any proportional sample of 1,000 people, only 40 people will be interviewed in Saskatchewan, and less than 150 in all of Atlantic Canada. And within Atlantic Canada, voting trends differ widely between P.E.I., New Brunswick, Nova Scotia, and Newfoundland. Survey results broken down into regions like this become little better than anecdotal media "street interviews." A better sample, used by top pollsters in Canada, is twelve hundred base interviews, chosen by population representation across the country, augmented by six hundred additional interviews in all eight smaller provinces, to bring the sample up to three hundred per province (accurate to within 6 percent for that province). It is still not ideal, and the over-sample must be weighted down to produce national results, but it provides the best results for the least effort. Canadian election campaigns are too important to disregard the views of each region, whether Ontario, Quebec, or Saskatchewan, separately. Mini-polls, such as the Canwest-Global/Compas studies, contribute very little to the understanding of Canada's diverse electorate.

This was also true with respect to the Canadian Parliamentary Channel's daily opinion tracking system conducted during the 2004 campaign by SES Research, a comparatively new firm that had polled for former PC leader Joe Clark. This was the second time that a news organization had tracked opinion on a daily basis (the first was CTV in 1988), but the first time that results were reported every single day of the campaign until close to the end. As an indicator of general trends, many in the media found it of interest, but the sample size, only two hundred interviews per day, with a three-day roll of six hundred, yielded nothing accurate or useful in the way of provincial standings. Moreover, CPAC's decision to report these numbers daily clouded the perceptions of many journalists trying to understand the election, producing erratic and misleading daily fluctuations that would have confused the keenest poll-watcher. A better decision for CPAC would have been to report the results once every three days, when enough old sample had been flushed and new interviews added to make the differences between reports relevant.

Once question wording, analysis, sampling, and all other issues are dealt with, it is true to say that bigger is better in terms of public opinion surveys. The more interviews conducted, the more accurate the results, and the better the reliability of the findings in each province. From this standpoint, the best polls of the 2004 election were conducted by Ipsos-Reid, which consistently had the largest samples, followed by Ekos, with slightly smaller samples up to election night when they set a record for the most interviews in any one poll. Environics, as well, never allowed their sample to fall below a fairly robust fourteen hundred interviews.

WAS THE POLL ANALYSIS AND MEDIA COVERAGE OF THE POLLS COMPETENT?

It has been said that Canada's media use polls much like a drunken man would use a lamppost: for support, rather than for illumination. Never has this been truer than during the 2004 election. During election campaigns the media rely and focus almost exclusively on party preference "horse-race" numbers and comparatively little on polls showing other attitudes and opinions toward policy options, directions for the country, the party leaders, Canada's future, and the foundations for electoral support. Many have argued that if the media and pollsters had spent more time on these foundation issues, they would have discovered near the end of the campaign that the momentum was with the Liberals, and that the Conservatives would not be forming a government. Indeed, almost every pollster provided a clue to the vulnerability of the Conservatives near election day. Even Compas, with their last small sample survey of the campaign, was still able to show that Canadians believed a Liberal-led government, either majority or minority, would be better for the country (41 percent) than a Conservative-led government would be (28 percent). This should have given pause to the interpretations of the 33 percent of Canadians who told Compas they intended to vote Conservative, but went largely unreported among the Canwest-Global media clients who commissioned the poll. The rest of the media, all of whom should have had some reason for suspecting that public opinion may have shifted in the six to seven days after their pollsters were in the field, also ignored most of the "extraneous" findings.

Indeed, it was common practice for most media organizations to quickly pass over everything in the poll except for the horse-race numbers, and possibly "Who would make the best prime minister?" and, near the end of the campaign, "Would you prefer a majority or minority, and who should form it?" All the pollsters but the CPAC/SES (who were strictly tracking horse-race numbers) responsibly collected much more than just this, including issue priorities, perceptions of momentum, leadership characteristics, and desire for change, but it was only filler to most of the media and rarely explored in-depth. To be fair to the media, much of the motivation to ignore anything but horse-race numbers was driven by the lack of dynamics of the campaign. Since health care was by far the most important salient issue, that fact was usually just reported once, and other issues ignored. There was no attempt by the media and their pollsters to explore the mindset of Canadians for any latent issues, which may be very important to the public yet overshadowed with all the discussion on health care. Political party pollsters do this constantly, searching for emerging issues that can be co-opted into overall strategy. The media could have done this too, thereby taking a leadership role in the campaign, but they did not take the opportunity.

There was little polling on policy options during the 2004 election. The reason? There really were not many policies put forward by the political parties that made any connection with the public. The Liberals were still in a state of trauma following the release of the Auditor General's report on sponsorship advertising in Quebec. Behaving like deer caught in the headlights, they put forward no significant platform items that had any resonance with Canadians. By week three of the campaign, they advanced the need for better health care and shorter waiting lists, considering this a wedge issue, but for that to be successful the Conservatives had to be in favour of longer waiting lists and further deterioration of the system. There was really no specific policy here for any pollster to poll on. Other Liberal policies were either further "motherhood" issues, such as improving childcare, or arcane and confusing proposals, such as the revenue-sharing formula with municipalities. The general public reacted to most of these policies with little more than a shrug.

The Conservative policies were in the same category. Their opening strategy was simple but effective, sticking close to the centre of the political spectrum, or at least to wherever the Liberals positioned themselves. Their policies were as similar to the Liberals as was possible, with the simple message, "You may not be keen on the Liberals, since the sponsorship advertising scandal shows they can't be trusted, but we know you're comfortable with their orientation of government and we're not going to change that. You don't want risk, and we don't represent risk. Most importantly, we're not the Liberals, and we're cleaner." The Conservatives' one intentional foray outside this box, promising to scrap the gun registry, was a risky position that has never been supported by public opinion, but the Conservatives were leading in the polls at the time of that announcement, and possibly they believed they could sacrifice some of their public support to keep their right-wing conservative principles.

As election campaigns go, 2004 was blander than most. Canadians had no strong opinions on any of the issues under discussion. There were no working wedge issues and no real policy option choices for the public to deliberate over. The Liberals simply staggered from one unfavourable opinion poll to another, with no coherent election strategy, watching their plurality fall from nine points to one point by the end of the first week of campaigning. By the second week of the campaign, with the two major parties basically tied, and the Liberals badly trailing the BQ in Quebec, the opinion polls *were* the issue of the campaign. They drove news. People were entranced by the slow but steady climb of the Conservatives. They watched this at first with satisfaction, as they were determined to refuse the Liberals a majority government. They were still angry at the Liberals for the sponsorship scandal and, though still wary of the Conservatives, were gaining comfort with Stephen Harper. For the first time since 1993, it appeared as if a horse race was taking place.

The Liberal implosion and Conservative gains caused far greater interest in public opinion polling than was usual. The media appetite for polls swelled overnight. The *Globe and Mail* and CTV requested extra polling from Ipsos-Reid to bridge the gap between their traditional weekly polls. They went from one per week to one every five days, then four days, with their last poll only three days after the one before. Polls done by other news organizations were cross-reported by their competitors, a practice that had not been followed even during the much more volatile 1988 free-trade election.

Even the political parties had a poll fixation, and the Liberal Party at least took the unprecedented steps of commissioning their own polls and spinning them publicly. One, conducted by Createc Plus and paid for by the Liberal Party, showed the Liberals well ahead in Quebec, though at the same time all the media polls showed them well behind the Bloc Québécois. Their pollster, David Herle of Earnscliffe Research, constantly shared his own polls with the media, stating that the Liberals were actually either ahead in support or, later, recovering their support, but that the numbers were always better than the media polls suggested. This was only the second time that a Canadian party pollster has ever spun polls directly to the public. Allan Gregg, polling for Joe Clark in 1980, and arm-twisted into giving an upbeat press conference, later wrote that he much regretted doing so and that risking his credibility and reputation in this way wasn't worth it. In his later career, engineering two majority governments for Brian Mulroney, he never did this again.

The Conservative pollster, Dimitri Pantazopoulos of Praxicus Strategies, who had polled for the Alliance during the 2000 campaign, did not speak to the media, but also did not appear to have much impact on his party's strategy. All the Conservative deviations from a middle-of-the-road agenda caused angst with a good part of the electorate, which increased as Conservative support grew. In a position to win an election by default, Stephen Harper would take more and more risks as the election campaign swung into the final weeks. His greatest mistake with public opinion was talking publicly about winning a majority government and claiming that he had the support to do it. This was very unpopular with voters, who wanted to punish the Liberals and limit them to a minority, but who wanted to restrict any potential Conservative government to a minority. The problems inherent in Harper's boast should have been immediately unearthed in their nightly poll tracking to ensure he would not say it again. However, Harper did repeat it, many times, in the last days of the campaign.

Harper's refusal to apologize for his remarks about Paul Martin endorsing child pornography should also have been explored by Conservative polling within hours, but he never took action to limit the damage, despite the widespread criticism. He also never took action to resolve the doubts Canadians had about his abortion policy. He addressed it but never shut the door decisively on the issue. Focus groups would have flagged his abortion explanations as "weasel words" within hours of his statement, and he might have made a better attempt. The Conservative campaign appeared to be flying blind in terms of managing public opinion. They might have been ahead in the polls, but they were making mistakes that limited the gains they could have been making.

The Liberals thought that they should be winning by default and were severely shocked by the trends of the first three weeks. Strategist David Herle advised all Liberal candidates by conference call that they were in a "downward spiral." Indeed, the Liberal internal polling numbers, which were not spun to the media, plunged even lower than the public ones. For the first time, the pollster had chosen not to conduct national polls, but rather to poll in only twenty-five key ridings. This provided only a partial picture of the country and ignored more than 90 percent of the voting public. Key ridings, moreover, are usually chosen because they are bellwether and hence more likely to lose and gain support than the average riding. The effects of the public opinion slide were exaggerated even more, giving the impression internally that things were much worse than they actually were.

Some retired Liberals, who had worked for former prime ministers Pearson, Trudeau, and Turner, wrote unsolicited missives to the campaign urging Paul Martin to talk about his record as finance minister, which he had ignored, feeling it referred too much to the past leadership and not his own. He was also advised to highlight national unity, which the experienced advisors felt would be in dire straits with a strong Bloc contingent in Quebec and a Conservative federal government. The Liberal campaign chairmen went as far as asking for advice from the pollsters at POLLARA, architects of three back-to-back Liberal victories. POLLARA prepared a strategy memo based on their private polling from the third week of the campaign. It urged the campaign to "drag out the dinosaurs" among the Conservative caucus, to highlight and explore their positions on social issues, like abortion, gay rights, immigration, bilingualism, and gun control. Of special significance was the "hidden agenda" abortion issue, which in the 2000 election had been the Achilles' heel of former leader Stockwell Day. It wouldn't have the same potential against Stephen Harper, wrote the pollsters, but it would serve to make the ballot question "Does Harper think like I do?" rather than "Should I punish the Liberals?"

Liberal strategy was slow to come together and might not have worked if the Conservatives had not self-destructed with Harper's comments on the child pornography issue, boasts about majority governments, and the constant lack of judgment shown by various Conservative candidates, some of whom promised private member's bills limiting abortion rights, using the notwithstanding clause to curtail gay and other minority rights as determined by the courts, changing the Official Language Act, ending Air Canada bilingualism, reintroducing the death penalty, stopping hate crimes legislation, and many other right-of-centre issues of questionable appeal to the electorate.

By the week after the leaders' debates, the Conservatives were still ahead by between three and five points, but the bucket was leaking. The lift they expected from Harper's strong debate performance provided only a couple of points before petering out, and there was no further trend toward increasing support. Conservative candidates were finally forbidden, in phone calls to campaign managers across Canada from the central campaign office, from speaking to the media or advancing any new issue or policy without their leader's approval. By this time, however, much of the damage was done. And to compound this, extremely negative Liberal advertising, demonizing Harper as having a secret agenda on abortion and comparing his "destructive" economic policies to those of Brian Mulroney and Mike Harris, were running constantly on television and radio.

With two weeks to go, Harper still had a small lead but lacked any further momentum. According to a POLLARA poll conducted across Ontario, with two weeks to the vote Toronto had completely deserted the Conservatives, though support was still high for them across the rest of Ontario. The media was on a gaffe-watch, playing gotcha politics with the Conservatives their target. All sensed a general unease with the Conservatives amongst the public, which increased with every mistake that Harper or his undisciplined team of candidates would make.

In the final week, all the media opinion pollsters showed a reversal of the previous trends. What had been a three- to five-point lead for the Conservatives was now a one-point lead for the Liberals. The question among the pollsters was, or should have been, "Is this a new trend, or just a partial recovery?" Clearly, it should have been the question among journalists as well, as they largely ignored the changes reflected in the polls and were hypnotized by the effort of trying to project the number of seats that each party would gain. These last polls, conducted a week to six days before Canadians actually went to the ballot boxes, were again treated like lampposts by the media. Most polls showed the Liberals one point ahead of the Conservatives, as opposed to being three points behind the Conservatives a week earlier (Ipsos-Reid), or two points behind (Ekos). Media coverage perhaps should have delivered the message "Liberals rebound" and then asked, "Will they go any further?" The actual message delivered said, "Too close to call, and we can't imagine it changing, but the poll results aren't all that important, because our seat projections show the Conservatives forming a minority government."

THE SEAT PROJECTIONS: VOODOO SCIENCE?

The *Toronto Star*, sitting on likely the largest scientific election poll ever conducted in Canada, 5,254 interviews by Ekos research, actually featured the seat projection and not the poll results in their headline of June 26, 2004. The headline and subhead both dealt with the seat projection, as did the first two paragraphs. The actual poll numbers were referred to only in the third paragraph, which was followed by twenty further paragraphs on the seat projection, the methodology involved, and how many seats each party would likely win in each province. Further stories embedded in that day's *Toronto Star* examined key ridings across Canada using the national poll to determine who would win and lose each seat. Such a dubious exercise would only have been valid if Ekos had used a sample of at least ninety thousand Canadians, and even then the results for each riding would have been accurate only to 6 percent.

The *Globe and Mail* and to a lesser extent CTV were not much better in their reporting of the Ipsos-Reid poll, which was, like the Ekos one, a very competent and likely accurate public opinion poll. They too ignored a deeper analysis of what the data actually meant, even though they had the best tracking data, which appeared, to anyone looking at the graphs on their Web site, to be clearly showing a Liberal trend upwards and Conservative trend downwards. Bizarrely, however, they were also preoccupied with riding projections. In the headline *Globe and Mail* story of June 25, the journalists and pollsters reported, "The Liberals and NDP appear unlikely to win enough seats to be capable of building a majority coalition between them, and the results point to the Conservatives having the best chance of winning the most seats of any party." Their expectation was between 115 and 119 Conservative seats, versus 99 to 103 for the Liberals.

The *Globe and Mail* and CTV were not alone in this view. It was echoed by Professor Barry Kay of Wilfrid Laurier University, who had made a cottage industry of seat projections with mixed results over many elections, but who this time, for Canwest-Global, predicted the Conservatives would take 115 seats to the Liberals' 108. (Ipsos-Reid was so annoyed that Kay was basing his projections partly on their surveys that mid-campaign they threatened him with a lawsuit if he did not cease and desist. Presumably they have now lost interest in pursuing this.) Leger Marketing and Sun Media also had the Conservatives ahead with more than one hundred seats, as did many armchair pundits, and a new firm called Electoral Engineering in Toronto, which claimed to specialize in seat projections.

The methodology of most seat projections is simple:

1. Start with a spreadsheet database of historical election results, in this case the riding-by-riding results for the 2000 election.

2. Divide the country into as many separate regions as possible, as long as the survey covers each of these regions with a sample of at least four hundred interviews (in fact, many seat projections used less than one hundred per region).

3. Use the changes in support within each region to adjust the results for each political party's candidate upwards and downwards by the percentage change.

This is a basic seat projection model. It has no statistical validity. It makes no allowance for the differences between a riding and an adjoining riding that may vote a totally different way. It assumes that each riding in a region is affected proportionally by the region's net change, which defies common sense. In most cases, the samples used in seat projections are too small to be accurate. Ipsos-Reid and the *Globe and Mail* had a seat projection model with thirty-three regions, into which they divided the two thousand interviews from their last poll. This produces regional variances based on the voting intentions of sixty-one people, which can have no accuracy at all, even when overlaid on historical election results.

However, the greatest error, the point where all seat projection models spun off into fantasy, concerns the historical election results themselves. In short, one cannot adjust historical election results for a political party that has no history. What were the pollsters and academics using as the basis for the 2000 Conservative vote, considering that the Conservative Party did not exist then? Did they combine the old PC and Alliance parties together, assuming that all the supporters of each would vote for the new party? This should have been improbable, considering that all pollsters had conducted surveys at the time of those parties' merger that found that the new Conservative Party could rely on almost all the former Alliance supporters but would split the former PC vote with the Liberals, and in some regions lose some votes to the NDP. It was unfathomable that successful public opinion analysts and learned academics would base their reputations, and those of their media clients, on a projected fictitious historical vote for a party that never existed.

Certainly, some might have ventured to create more sophisticated riding projection models that would project a historical Conservative vote consisting of perhaps 96 percent of former Alliance voters and 46 percent of former PC voters, but this would also be full of error. There are too many regional variations. For example, in Nova Scotia, PC voters leaned mainly toward the Liberal Party, with few backing the Conservatives. In Hamilton, PC voters actually split between the Liberals and NDP. In Toronto, a great majority went Liberal, while in Saskatchewan a small majority would go Conservative. There was absolutely no way to derive a historical core vote for the new Conservative Party.

Are all seat projections useless? No, and ironically, while they have been largely discredited by the 2004 election, some seat projections will actually have some validity during the next election. They can be very accurate, but never within any reportable margin of error, and no pollster or journalist should ever risk credibility or reputation providing them. On election eve in 1993, the POLLARA pollsters provided the Liberal Party with a seat projection that showed the Progressive Conservatives holding on to only two seats. That number was correct, but one of the seats identified as going PC was wrong, leading former prime minister Chrétien to joke with journalists that his pollster had a 50 percent margin of error. Accurate riding projections, within three seats, were also provided by the same pollsters for the elections of 1997 and 2000, and publicly to CTV News for the election of 1988. These more accurate riding projections resulted from two or three elections full of historical data, in a more sophisticated model than the media use. They took into account the sensitivity of each region to overall national change, overlaid regional changes based on large sample polls, weighted down the impact of these changes in more stable seats, and also reflected the voting behaviour in neighboring ridings. But most important, they had real historical election data to base the methodology upon.

In the upcoming 2006 or 2007 election, seat projections by pollsters and academics will once more be as useful as they were in past elections. The 2004 historical data will enable all pollsters, academics, and journalists to produce something of far greater credibility and integrity than they did this past election. It is doubtful, though, that any news organization in Canada will ever consider them better than a voodoo science in the future. And being with seat projection more of an art than a science, perhaps this is for the best.

THE LAST POLLS

All of the news media polls released during the last week of the 2004 election campaign showed the Liberals rebounding and the Conservatives falling. Moreover, the foundation of support for the Conservatives was seen to be crumbling. Fewer people wanted to see them form a government than said they would vote for them. This suggests that the Conservatives were further trending downward and would likely fall further. Impression ratings of Stephen Harper had once more fallen behind those of Paul Martin. Anger over the sponsorship scandal was wearing thin. Concern over Harper's supposed secret agenda, highlighted by the news media and by Liberal advertising, was causing much wavering. The number of undecided voters was down, but the number of voters who were "only leaning towards" their vote choice was still high. The Liberals did not look any better to Canadians than they had throughout the campaign, but the Conservatives looked a lot worse. It would be a vote based on who people did not like, rather than who they liked the best. These clues were contained in the opinion polls that were released but were obscured by the news media's preoccupation with horse-race numbers and smothered by their concentration on seat projections, which appeared to contradict the poll numbers themselves.

The last polls might have been released between June 24 and 26, with the election to be held on June 28, but the interviewing for these polls had been conducted between June 21 and 23. Interviewing takes time, and polls are not instantaneously tabulated and reported in a newspaper that needs time to be printed and delivered to its readers. So it was not unreasonable that many Canadians cited in these polls had been surveyed a full week before voting day. Besides, while the Canada Election Act had been changed to allow polls to be published up to the day before the vote (as opposed to the old law requiring a three-day blackout period), no news organization wished to tempt criticism by conducting a late poll for the Sunday newspapers.

Normally this time lag is not so important with final polls. It is assumed by the news organization that they will receive their poll the day after the interviews are completed and publish it the following day. It was also assumed in 2004, based on the previous three federal elections, that public opinion had largely settled by the final week and voter intention would not change. Unfortunately, none of the media pollsters analyzing the 2004 campaign had polled during the very volatile 1988 campaign, which would have proved the fallacy of this assumption. In 1988 a Liberal majority turned into a PC majority near the last week of the campaign, and responsible pollsters saw and understood the changing numbers, scrapped the oldest interviews from their poll, and back-ended as many interviews as possible near the end of the campaign. CTV, for example, reported its last poll of the campaign less than three hours after the final interview was completed, and did so with perfect accuracy. Public opinion can, and sometimes does, change in the last week of an election campaign. The media polls reported in this last week may have been accurate, but too old to reflect the election's outcome. How can we be sure?

The CBC provides some of the evidence. This news organization was the only major media outlet that did not conduct its own polls for broadcast during the election — a great source of frustration to many of its on-air personalities, who were strictly forbidden from reporting or commenting on polls during the election campaign. While this policy was sometimes abused, once when correspondent Keith Boag enthusiastically and at great length reported on the CPAC-SES tracking on-air, by and large there was little discussion of the polls on the CBC. But the CBC did have its own internal polling, conducted by Environics on election eve in five key ridings, meant to provide guidance to the deployment of news resources on election night. Each poll was in a tenuous Liberal seat that most pundits predicted would be lost to one of the opposition parties. However, the Environics polling, which was accurate in every riding, showed that the Liberals would hold at least four of the five. This may suggest why the CBC election desk personnel were not too surprised by the eventual "unexpected outcome."

The CBC, like any news organization or private individual in Canada, is by law prohibited from broadcasting a poll on election day. Yet other pollsters saw the same trend reflected not just in riding surveys but also in other national studies. Pollster Conrad Winn of Compas took the unusual and risky step of technically breaking the law in order to post his election-day tracking poll on his Web site by 10:00 p.m. Toronto time. It showed the Liberals leading the Conservatives by five points, closer to the actual seven-point plurality than the previous polls. A POLLARA poll conducted the weekend before the vote and provided to the office of the premier of Ontario on election day showed the Liberals leading the Conservatives, 35 percent to 29 percent, close to the final results. Like the Environics and Compas polls, it was not broadcast ahead of the vote. Final evidence that the change to the electoral landscape was last-minute could be found in POLLARA's post-election study, prepared for Carleton University and analyzed in Chapter Eleven of this volume. Of special note is the 25 percent of the electorate who say they made their vote decision "in the final days of the campaign."

Like George Gallup chasing the support for Thomas Dewey and finding that electoral support can fall apart in the final two weeks of a presidential campaign, so did Canada's media pollsters miss the boat by not polling late enough into the campaign. It could be argued that the polls might have been accurate within the period in which they were conducted, but within six to seven days after the first interviews had been conducted, the situation changed. Stephen Harper had made numerous mistakes in the last weeks of the campaign, and he was under pressure from the media and the other party campaigns. It was only a matter of time before this achieved traction. The public was experiencing cognitive dissonance. Initially pleased with their choice to support him and his seemingly middle-of-the-road party, they were now having doubts about both him and many of his candidates. These doubts coalesced into action between June 23, when the last polling interviews were conducted, and election day, June 28.

Canada's pollsters, though, have indeed lost credibility and reputation. Some of the criticisms levelled against them are justified. Polling is a learning experience, and new techniques must always be developed to chase the ever more elusive voter opinion. It would be hoped that next election all of Canada's media pollsters will finally make the effort to exclude likely non-voters from their surveys, interview enough people to analyze each region, determine the correct questions to ask, and try to understand more about Canadians' motivations and attitudes rather than just shallowly tracking the horse race. Riding projections, no matter how accurate they become in the future, will never be scientific and should never again be treated with much gravity by public opinion professionals.

Yet many of the pollsters' critics have also gone too far. Most of the polls released the week before the vote were in stark agreement with each other, with the same one-point Liberal plurality in each. However, the public's attitude towards the final polls is that if the actual results are not reflected, then the polls are wrong. Pollsters would argue that their polls were accurate when conducted, but they were conducted too early. There is much evidence behind this argument. Certainly the methodology for some of the polls could have been better, but the uniformity of results would suggest that there was indeed much last-minute voter movement. Still, in both politics and professional reputation, perception is reality. Pollsters will need time and hard work to restore much of their damaged credibility.

For many years it was illegal under the Canada Election Act to publish or broadcast a poll during the last seventy-two hours of a campaign. This law was struck down earlier this decade, before the 2004 election. Yet both before the blackout restrictions and afterwards, there was always an unwritten code of conduct, among pollsters and news organizations, that polls would never be published within that seventy-two-hour span. Both professions have always wished to avoid the charge that polls unduly influence elections, while some pollsters would prefer not to risk being wrong — reporting that "twentieth poll" that may exceed the statistical margin of error and losing credibility and reputation. But if public opinion is going to change in the last seventy-two hours of an election campaign, then pollsters should insist on polling during this period. News organizations should be prepared to publish polls until the eve of election day, as the law allows.

In 1998 the *Globe and Mail* led many other news organizations to the Supreme Court to strike down the seventy-two-hour poll ban. They considered the restriction an infringement on the right of the public to access information they want in a timely fashion and the right of publishers and pollsters to provide it. The Court agreed, but despite this victory, no pollster or media organization has ever published a poll later than forty-eight hours before the voting process begins. A right not exercised is a right soon lost, and if many Canadians decide to make their vote choice late, they should have the ability to understand where this choice is leading. Canada's media pollsters have a reputation for accuracy, which they have gained through fifty years of hard work and much time on the part of individual Canadians who answer their surveys. It is time they were allowed to show their abilities without being hampered by unwritten agreements based on archaic and superfluous blackout laws.

CHAPTER ELEVEN

Canadians Speak Out

by André Turcotte

Former British prime minister Harold Wilson once observed that in politics, a week is a long time and a year is an eternity. Few Canadian politicians understand this oft-quoted cliché better than Paul Martin. What was supposed to be a coronation turned into a near-death experience for him and Liberal candidates across the country. When Martin officially became Canada's twenty-first prime minister on December 12, 2003, pundits and political observers were agreeing on the inevitability of a fourth consecutive Liberal majority.[1] The newly minted prime minister was also clearly looking to the future. During the swearing-in ceremony, Paul Martin gave an outline of his ambitious agenda: "As prime minister, I look forward to the opportunity to rally Canadians toward a new sense of national purpose and around a new agenda of change and achievement.... We are going to change the way things work in Ottawa in order to re-engage Canadians in the political process and achieve demonstrable progress on our priorities."[2] At the time, Martin was blissfully unaware that he would bear the brunt of the forces of change he proposed to unleash.

Within less than six months, the Martin juggernaut came off the rails. The lingering divisions over the Chrétien-Martin leadership battles, the unification of the conservative forces, and the sponsorship scandal combined to seriously threaten Martin's pursuit of a mandate from the Canadian electorate. On May 21, 2004, two days before the election call, the *National Post* headlined, "Poll Predicts Minority." According to the COMPAS survey conducted with 1,579 Canadians between May 15 and 19, the Liberals were holding on to a slim advantage with 39 percent of voter support ahead of the surging Conservatives at 31 percent. The NDP came in third at 17 percent. On a regional basis, the Conservatives were ahead in B.C. with 40 percent of the decided vote, followed by the Liberals (32 percent) and the NDP (26 percent), as well as in Alberta (57 percent over 27 percent for the Liberals). The Liberals had a slight lead in Saskatchewan/Manitoba with 35 percent of support compared to 32 percent for the NDP and 27 percent for the Conservatives. In the battle of Ontario, the Liberals (42 percent) and Conservatives (39 percent) were almost neck and neck, while in Quebec, the Bloc (43 percent) and Liberals (40 percent) were in a similar dead heat. Atlantic Canada was the only region to unequivocally support the Liberals, with 50 percent of the decided vote, ahead of the Conservatives (26 percent) and the NDP (20 percent).[3] Martin's insurmountable lead had evaporated, and the Liberal troubles gave new life to the opposition parties.

For the recently formed Conservative Party of Canada, the realistic objectives were to reunite conservatives after the schism of 1993 and hopefully to hold the Liberals to a minority. The NDP had to regain the support of its traditional voters and increase its representation in the House of Commons. The Bloc Québécois had to reaffirm its raison d'être as the best defender of the interests of Quebecers in Ottawa. For the Liberals, holding on to power emerged as the only goal. The election results indicate that some parties were more successful than others in meeting their objectives.

On June 28, 2004, for the fourth consecutive election, Ontarians played the key role in re-electing a Liberal government. The Martin Liberals won 36.7 percent of the popular vote and 135 seats — 74 of those from Ontario. Nationally, the Liberal drop in popular support was substantial, down from 40.8 percent in 2000. However, the 2004 results were more similar to those of 1997 when the Chrétien Liberals received 38.4 percent of the popular vote. In the 2004 election, the Liberals improved on their 2000 vote results in eight of the ten provinces. But the two exceptions were crucial. Martin's electoral fortunes suffered in Quebec because of his handling of the sponsorship scandal and the resurgence of the Bloc. In Ontario, the sponsorship scandal and the

Alliance/PC merger both contributed to bringing Liberal support closer to its historical level. Unfortunately for Martin, perception is reality in politics and the 2004 election will be seen as a failure.

The Conservatives succeeded in preventing a fourth consecutive Liberal majority by electing ninety-nine candidates. This result constitutes clear electoral progress from the Alliance position after the 2000 election. However, the merger of the Alliance and Progressive Conservative Party ignited expectations that the unification of conservatives forces in Canada — a process that began with the United Alternative in 1998 — would create a viable alternative to Liberal dominance. Accordingly, the 2004 election should be analyzed in terms of the progress made in that direction. From that perspective, the Harper Conservatives failed to unite previous supporters of the Alliance and the Progressive Conservative Party. They received only 29.6 percent of the vote — a significant drop from the 37.7 percent of combined Alliance and PC support in 2000. Harper barely improved on the ill-fated performance of Stockwell Day in 2000 in terms of popular vote (25.5 percent) even with the added benefit of the Alliance-PC merger. As Table 1 shows, if we compare support for the Conservatives in 2004 with the combined Reform/Alliance and PC support in the previous three elections, we clearly see that the 2004 election was a setback for the conservative forces and that the institutional merger failed to receive partisan approval. Under Harper, the Conservatives have lost vote share in every province since the 2000 election. The most important erosion occurred in British Columbia, where their support dropped from 56.7 percent in 2000 to 36.2 percent. The Conservatives also lost support in their Alberta stronghold (down from 72.4 percent to 61.6 percent), and their Ontario showing in 2004 (31.5 percent) was worse than in 1993 (37.7) and 2000 (38.0). They remain irrelevant in Quebec (with only 8.8 percent in voter support) and have regressed in all four Atlantic provinces.

The two main election winners were Gilles Duceppe's Bloc and Jack Layton's NDP. Duceppe ran a smart campaign focused on Quebecers' resentment over the sponsorship scandal and was rewarded with a strong victory in that province. With 48.8 percent of the Quebec popular vote, Duceppe almost matched the Bloc's best showing in 1993, when they garnered 49.3 percent of the vote under Lucien Bouchard's leadership.

Table 1: The Vote, 1993–2004

	Liberal				"Conservative"				NDP				Bloc			
	'04	'00	'97	'93	'04	'00	'97	'93	'04	'00	'97	'93	'04	'00	'97	'93
Canada	36.7	40.8	38.4	41.3	29.6	37.7	38.3	34.7	15.7	8.5	11.1	6.9				
Nfld.	48.0	44.9	37.9	67.3	32.3	38.4	39.3	27.7	17.5	13.0	24.8	3.5				
P.E.I.	52.5	47.0	44.8	60.1	30.7	43.4	39.8	33.0	12.5	9.0	15.1	5.2				
N.S.	39.6	36.5	28.4	52.0	28.0	38.7	40.5	36.8	28.5	24.0	30.4	6.8				
N.B.	44.6	41.7	32.9	56.0	31.1	46.2	48.1	36.4	20.6	11.7	18.4	8.5				
Que.	33.9	44.2	36.7	33.3	8.8	11.8	22.5	13.5	4.6	1.8	2.0	1.5	48.8	39.9	37.9	49.3
Ont.	44.7	51.5	49.5	52.9	31.5	38.0	37.9	37.7	18.1	8.3	10.7	6.0				
Man.	33.2	32.5	34.3	45.0	39.1	44.9	41.5	34.3	23.5	20.9	23.2	16.7				
Sask.	27.2	20.7	24.7	32.1	41.8	52.5	43.8	38.5	23.4	26.2	30.9	26.6				
Alta.	22.0	20.9	24.0	25.1	61.6	72.4	69.0	66.9	9.5	5.4	5.7	4.1				
B.C.	28.6	27.7	28.8	28.1	36.2	56.7	49.3	49.9	26.6	11.3	18.2	15.5				

Source: Adapted from Elections Canada

The Bloc also succeeded in preventing the Conservatives from rebuilding the Mulroney coalition and in the process denied them any chance of forming government.

For his part, Jack Layton succeeded in reviving the NDP with its best showing since 1988. The NDP improved its standing in terms of both seats with nineteen (up from thirteen in 2000) and popular vote with 15.5 percent (up from 8.5 percent in 2000). He made inroads in popular support in every province except Saskatchewan. His most important gains came in British Columbia, where the NDP share in popular vote increased from 11.3 percent in 2000 to 26.6 percent. These gains occurred at the expense of the Conservative Party, which experienced a decline in support in that province. Arguably, Layton was able to attract to the NDP fold those B.C. populists who had supported Manning's Reform and appeared to reject Harper's elitist style of leadership. Layton also made important gains in Ontario (up to 18.1 percent from 8.3 in 2000) and in New Brunswick (from 11.7 percent to 20.6 percent). However, despite these relatively positive results, the NDP remains a marginal presence in the House of Commons.

The aim of this chapter is to put the results of the 2004 election in perspective by isolating the factors that have contributed to the outcome. The analysis is based on the results of a national survey conducted by POLLARA in the days immediately following the election. The findings from the POLLARA survey will allow us to look at the flow of the vote and the impact of issues, leaders, and parties as well as the campaign itself on voter choice. We will draw some general conclusions about the results and what the future may hold for Canadian politics.

THE FLOW OF THE VOTE

Unlike in previous elections, most notably in 1997 and 2000, the Liberal Party in 2004 was the least successful of the main parties at retaining its previous vote. As Table 2 indicates, only 59 percent of 2000 Liberal voters continued to support their party in 2004. This is lower than the 64 percent retention rate in 2000[4] and the 63 percent

Table 2: Vote Stability and Change, 2000–2004

2004 BEHAVIOUR	2000 BEHAVIOUR						
	Non-Voters	Liberals	Alliance	PC	NDP	BQ	Others
Did Not Vote	72%	8%	3%	9%	2%	3%	6%
Liberals	5	59	2	11	13	5	6
Cons.	9	13	88	68	12	3	29
NDP	7	14	2	9	63	5	12
BQ	2	3	-	2	2	80	6
Others	6	3	5	1	8	4	41
N =	217	322	42	101	67	65	17

Source: POLLARA Post-Election Survey

NOTE: Percentages add to 100 percent in columns

in 1997.[5] In contrast, both the Bloc Québécois (80 percent) and the NDP (63 percent) retained a solid percentage of those who voted for them in the previous election and performed better in maintaining their core support than in 2000.[6] The Conservatives were very successful at holding on to the support of core 2000 Alliance supporters (88 percent) but less so with 2000 PC voters (68 percent). It appears that the fears about the merger between the Alliance and PC Party were justified. When McKay and Harper hatched their backroom deal, the progressive wing of PC Party decried the agreement. Party stalwart and former leadership candidate Scott Brison even left the PCs and joined the Liberal Party caucus in protest. He felt there would be little room for socially progressive policies in the new Conservative Party. Joe Clark also came out publicly against the merger. The findings in Table 2 confirm that a significant segment of the traditional PC vote deserted the Conservative Party and turned to the Liberals and the NDP in almost equal numbers. It is also interesting to note that 2000 PC voters were more likely to stay home and not vote in 2004 than voters for the other parties.

Overall, our findings show that despite losing some of its 2000 support, the Liberals were able to prevent more significant erosion in overall support and remain in power by attracting 2000 PC and NDP supporters. The Bloc Québécois improved its standing by attracting disgruntled Liberal supporters. Gilles Duceppe and the Bloc Québécois successfully tapped into Quebecers' resentment over the sponsorship scandal by offering a party "*propre au Québec*," a clever slogan translating into a "clean" as well as "genuine" party for Quebec. For their part, the Conservatives were able to offset their loss amongst PC supporters by also attracting disgruntled 2000 Liberal voters. However, it is the NDP that was most responsible for denying the Liberals their fourth consecutive majority. Some 14 percent of 2000 Liberal voters switched to the NDP in 2004. Moreover, the composition of the NDP support is currently divided between core NDP voters and Liberal deserters. "Uniting the Left" may be the starting point for rebuilding the Liberal majority.

FACTORS IN THE VOTE DECISION

For three decades, election studies have been asking Canadians to identify the most important factors in influencing their vote choice. The question format first asks whether party leaders, local candidates "here in this constituency," or parties as a whole were most important in deciding who to support in the election. Then, a follow-up question queries whether the choice of leader or candidate was motivated by issues or by the personal qualities of the individuals, or, in the case of the parties, whether it was the party's general approach or specific issues that was most important. Table 3 summarizes the findings for the 2004 election as well as for each election since 1974. The table indicates in a set of parentheses the proportion of the leader, candidate, and party vote that was motivated by issues rather than personal qualities or the general approach of parties.

First, for the fifth consecutive election, at least 50 percent of Canadians identified "parties" as the most important factor influencing their vote choice. The resilience of this factor is significant and should send signals to Conservative strategists to instill some permanence in the vehicle they are presenting to the Canadian electorate. Arguably, the permutations from the right of the spectrum — from PC and Reform to the Alliance and DRC and finally the Conservative Party — have been destabilizing for their target electorate. This lack of stability can explain some of the decline in the percentage of Canadians who mentioned parties as their most determining factor. In 2004, one in two Canadians (50 percent) cited parties as the most important influence on their vote choice, down from 58 percent in 2000. This represents the lowest level of influence since the 1984 election. Party leaders came in second at 24 percent, up marginally from 2000 (22 percent) and at its highest level since 1984. For the second consecutive election, local candidates had the least impact on the final vote decision.

Table 3: Most Important Factors in Voting, 1974–2000

(Percent citing issue basis in parentheses)

Election	Party Leaders	Local Candidates	Party as a Whole
2004	24% (60)	20 (49)	50 (51)
2000	22% (60)	21 (58)	58 (46)
1997	20% (71)	22 (59)	58 (57)
1993	22% (62)	21 (52)	57 (54)
1988	20% (71)	27 (57)	53 (57)
1984	30% (56)	21 (46)	49 (37)
1980	36% (53)	20 (40)	44 (43)
1979	37% (54)	23 (43)	40 (45)
1974	33% (58)	27 (48)	40 (43)

Sources: 1974–84 Canadian National Election Studies; 1988 reinterview of 1984 CNES; 1993 Insight Canada Research post-election survey; 1997–2004 POLLARA Post-Election Surveys

The resurgence of party leaders as key factors in influencing vote choice is hardly surprising. In 2004, the main parties ran leader-centred campaigns, with Martin, Harper, and Layton crowding out the spotlight from other candidates. Duceppe ran a more low-key campaign, focusing on his appealing Quebec-first message. The coverage of the campaign has also become increasingly focused on the leaders as the main proponents of their parties' election message. Thus, voters were reacting to what they were exposed to through the media.

Increased attention to party leaders and their personal qualities in 2004 can also be explained by the fact that we had three new party leaders in this election. Since 1974, the issue stance of party leaders has been most important when the election was fought by well-known political leaders, notably in 1988 when Mulroney, Turner, and Broadbent fought over free trade and in 1997 when Chrétien, Manning, and Charest tried to give shape to the aftermath of the 1993 collapse of the PC Party. In contrast, the arrival of new leaders can initially shift the focus towards image over substance, such as in 1979 when Joe Clark ran in his first election as PC leader, 1984 and the appearance of Mulroney, Turner, and Broadbent, and to some degree in 2000 with Stockwell Day. We return to the impact of leadership on the election outcome later on in this chapter. What remains is the resilience of issues as the important determinant of party, leader, and local candidate evaluations in Canadian elections. Canadian voters continue to claim that what politicians are saying is still more important than how they look.

THE ISSUES

Health care, accountability, and corruption was what politicians were talking about in 2004 and what was on the mind of Canadians. On May 23, 2004, Martin's opening remarks of the campaign were a nationalistic warning that the Conservatives would make Canada look like the United States. He attempted to frame the key ballot-box question as a stark choice between a Liberal government that would invest billions of dollars a year in health care and social programs and protect Canadians from a Conservative government, and the aforementioned Conservatives, who would destroy all the Liberals' accomplishments. The Conservatives shot back that the Liberal goal was to distract from the corruption evident in the sponsorship scandal.[7] They tried to inoculate themselves on the health care issue by promising to outdo the Liberals by spending more money as well as creating a national drug plan. Their main objective was to avoid the issue and talk about the economy and corruption.

The party leaders were deliberately framing the electoral discourse around the issue priorities of the Canadian electorate. As Table 4 indicates, one-third of Canadians mentioned health care as the most important election issue; another 18 percent cited issues related to government trust and accountability, while 4 percent specifically mentioned the sponsorship scandal.

Table 4: Most Important Issues, 1993–2004

Issue	2004	2000	1997	1993
Health Care	32%	31%	8%	3%
Unemployment, Jobs	1	2	24	44
Economy	3	3	4	8
Deficit, Debt	4	6	10	18
Taxes	3	7	3	-
National Unity, Quebec Regionalism	1	3	13	4
Resources, Environment	2	2	1	-
Social Issues	1	4	2	1
Government, Trust, Parties' Accountability, Leaders	18	8	3	7
Sponsorship Scandal	4	-	-	-
Other	12	5	3	4
None, Don't Know	19	29	29	10

Sources: 1993 Insight Canada Research Post-election survey; 1997–2004 POLLARA Post-election surveys
Note: Percentages add to 100 percent in columns.

Noticeably immaterial in 2004 was the national unity issue. Only 1 percent of Canadians (5 percent of Quebecers) felt it was an important issue. This constitutes an important decline from 1997. Despite the electoral success of the Bloc Québécois, there was little difference between the issue priorities of Canadians outside Quebec and Quebecers themselves. Health care (25 percent) and issues related to government trust and accountability (20 percent) dominated the issue agenda in *la belle province*.

Economic issues such as debt and deficit (4 percent), taxes (3 percent), "the economy in general" (3 percent), and unemployment (1 percent) ranked far below in terms of issue priorities. Such findings represent a significant departure from the issue environment that had shaped past Canadian elections. As Pammett demonstrated,[8] Canadian federal elections have traditionally focused on economic issues.The 1974 election evokes memories of inflation and wage and price controls, while energy prices dominated the 1980 election. We also remember "jobs, jobs, jobs" in 1984, free trade in 1988, and jobs again in 1993. The deficit and unemployment were central issues in the 1997 election, but national unity and social issues were also preoccupying Canadians. In the last two elections, social issues in general and health care in particular have dominated the agenda. The emergence of social issues represents an important electoral development to the extent that these issues have become differentially associated with a particular party. In 2000, the surfacing of health care as the most important issue benefited the Liberals. The Liberals used their advantage as the party perceived by Canadians as being closest to their own views on health care to portray the Alliance as a party that would likely allow the creation of a parallel private health system. In many ways, the 2004 election was a repeat performance. As Table 5 demonstrates, the Martin Liberals retained their advantage over the other parties on health care. In fact, health care was the only remaining issue on which they could claim a clear advantage over the opposition parties. They used this beneficial positioning to attack Harper and the Conservatives' supposed hidden health care agenda.

The failure of the Conservative campaign to move the debate away from health care and to focus on economic issues hurt the party's electoral chances. Harper and his Conservatives were favourably positioned to deal with accountability. Strikingly, the Conservatives also emerged as closest to the views of Canadians in dealing with budget and taxes despite Martin's reputation and accomplishments as finance minister.

Table 5: Party Closest on Most Important Issue, 1993–2004

Social Issues (Including Health Care)

	Libs.	Cons.	PC	Reform/All	NDP	Bloc	Other	None
2004	37%	18	-	-	17	6	2	20
2000	33%	-	10	15	20	3	1	19
1997	31%	-	10	17	25	-	1	17
1993	40%	-	8	9	21	4	4	15

Taxes

	Libs.	Cons.	PC	Reform/All	NDP	Bloc	Other	None
2004	7%	58	-	-	20	1	1	10
2000	25%	-	4	50	1	1	1	18
1997	22%	-	27	30	6	-	1	14
1993	46%	-	18	9	18	-	-	9

The Deficit/Debt

	Libs.	Cons.	PC	Reform/All	NDP	Bloc	Other	None
2004	15%	43	-	-	10	19	1	12
2000	32%	-	13	29	1	7	4	14
1997	62%	-	8	19	2	3	1	6
1993	24%	-	21	29	4	4	1	17

Accountability

	Libs.	Cons.	PC	Reform/All	NDP	Bloc	Other	None
2004	18%	27	-	-	13	12	3	27

All Issues

	Libs.	Cons.	PC	Reform/All	NDP	Bloc	Other	None
2004	27%	26	-	-	16	9	2	20
2000	31%	-	10	23	13	4	2	18
1997	35%	-	14	20	14	2	2	14
1993	48%	-	9	13	4	6	2	18

Sources: 1993, Insight Canada Research post-election survey; 1997–2004 POLLARA Post-Election Surveys
NOTE: Percentage adds to 100 percent across rows.

Notwithstanding such favourable issue positioning for the Conservatives, the election campaign was fought on a different set of priorities, and voters responded to a different dynamic.

THE CAMPAIGN, THE LEADERS, AND THE FINAL OUTCOME

To better comprehend the outcome of the 2004 election, we also need to look at the interactions between the campaign, the leaders, and the vote. The impact of the campaign on voter preference is of particular interest, since one of the secondary stories of the 2004 election was the poor performance of pollsters (see Chapter Ten). All the major polling firms, IPSOS-Reid, EKOS, Environics, COMPAS, SES, and Léger Marketing were unable to predict the final election outcome. Most firms blamed an unusual last-minute change in voting behaviour for their debacle, but we will see that this can account for only part of their inability to predict the election result.

When looking at Table 6, we notice that the campaign itself played a more important role in shaping vote choice than in previous years. Specifically, while 50 percent of voters had already made up their minds by the time the election was called (down ten percentage points from 2000), about one-quarter (24 percent) waited for the campaign, presumably to find out more about the issues, leaders, and parties, before deciding which party to support. This is significantly higher than in 2000 (18 percent) and 1997 (16 percent). However, despite the pollsters' assertions, there was no unusual last-minute change in voter intention. About one in four Canadians (25 percent) made up their minds in the final days of the campaign. This is almost identical to the patterns in 2000, when 24 percent made up their minds in the final days, and in 1997 (23 percent). If pollsters were able to account for the late decision patterns in previous elections, 2004 should have been no different. A reflection on the role and prominence of polls in election coverage needs to be conducted with the onus on the pollsters to come up with a better explanation for their performance.

Table 6: 2004 Vote, By Time of Vote Decision

	Before Election Called	When Called	During Campaign	Final Days
	(42%; -5%)*	(8%; -5%)	(24%; +8%)	(25%; +1%)
Liberals	33%	32%	34%	40%
Conservatives	32	24	32	26
NDP	12	20	23	23
Bloc	19	17	7	5
Other	4	7	4	6
N =	318	54	164	24

* change from 2000 election

Turning our attention to the impact of campaign dynamics on vote choice, it appears that the Liberals regained their lead and secured their minority government in the final days of the campaign. They were able to reverse the mid-campaign vote patterns that were benefiting the Conservatives, who were capitalizing on a Liberal team in chaos. On June 10, the Liberal campaign appeared to be unravelling. Paul Martin's top political adviser, David Herle, was quoted — on the front page of the *Globe and Mail* — as saying that the Liberals were "in a spiral." His comments were made to a number of Liberal MPs in a conference call the day before and were leaked to the newspaper.[9] Instead of hurting the Liberals, this sense of desperation led Harper to commit his first and most important mistake of the campaign. Harper began to talk confidently about his chances to form government and even about the possibility of a majority government.[10] Harper's comments demonstrated a misjudgment of the public opinion climate. Voters were likely to be voting against the Liberals to punish them for the sponsorship scandal and their arrogance in power despite their misgivings towards the Conservatives. Harper gave the Liberal campaign the perfect opening for the rest of the campaign. From then on, Martin was able to force the electorate to focus on the consequences of registering their anger towards the Liberals. Their vote would no longer only send a message to the Liberals; it would elect Harper and the Conservatives, a prospect a majority of Ontarians, in particular, were not ready to contemplate.

The Liberals began to attack Harper and his past policy positions regarding taking Canadian troops into Iraq, heavy military spending, the Conservatives' "hidden agenda" on social issues, and especially their "secret agenda" to limit a woman's right to choose. Unbelievably, the Conservative campaign did not seem to have prepared an answer to the last two accusations, despite the fact that they were used effectively against Stockwell Day in 2000 and were bound to resurface in 2004. Harper denied having any plans to reopen the abortion debate *in his first term*. While Harper was busy trying to deflect attention away from the abortion issue, Conservative MP Cheryl Gallant likened abortion to a videotaped beheading of an American released the previous month by Iraqi terrorists.[11]

The two leaders' debates, held on June 14 in French and June 15 in English, gave Martin an opportunity to refocus his message on Harper. This is not to suggest that the debates had a direct and significant impact on the final outcome. As Table 7 indicates, the impact of the leadership debates was more about reinforcing voter intentions than conversion. Of the 18 percent of Canadians who thought Martin won the debates, 77 percent voted Liberal. This is almost identical to Chrétien's showing in 2000, when 75 percent of those who picked him as winner voted for the Liberals.[12] Similarly, 76 percent of those who chose Stephen Harper as debate winner supported the Conservatives on election day. In 2000, 74 percent of voters who chose Day voted for the Alliance.[13] One exception to the lack of impact of the debate on the final outcome pertains to Quebec. As we have seen, Quebecers shared the same issue priorities as the rest of Canada. Accordingly, the Bloc did not reap the electoral benefits of favourable positioning on specific Quebec issues such as national unity, as it was the case in 1993 and 1997. However, the Bloc reaped the benefits of a strong performance by Gilles Duceppe in the leaders' debates. Duceppe entered the debates as the most experienced performer and was declared victorious. This is the result of having 60 percent of Quebecers crowning him as winner, far ahead of Martin (12 percent), Harper (5 percent), and Layton (3 percent).

Nevertheless, Martin was able to use the debates to lay the groundwork for the closing weeks of the campaign. He repeatedly attacked Harper and put the Conservative leader on the defensive over whether he would use the notwithstanding clause if the Supreme Court struck down a law that would take away women's right to choose an abortion or to override equality rights of gays and lesbians.[14] The strategic objective was to further raise doubts in the minds of a key segment of the electorate — Ontarians — that the Conservative leader may hold different values and a Conservative government may not reflect the direction they want the country to follow.

Table 7: 2004 Vote by Perceived Debate Winner

	Martin (18%)	Harper (22%)	Layton (11%)	Duceppe (23%)
Liberals	77%	9%	35%	17%
Conservatives	16	76	15	10
NDP	6	9	44	19
Bloc	-	3	2	51
Other	1	3	4	3
N =	82	54	101	109

Note: The remaining 27 percent of respondents did not identify a debate winner.

Our findings suggest that the change in strategy positively impacted Liberal electoral fortunes. Before Harper's boastful comments about forming a majority, the Conservatives were running neck and neck with the Liberals and the outcome of the election was uncertain. But in the end, the Liberals emerged as clear last-minute winners; just in time to stay in power.

The final point to be made about the 2004 election pertains to leaders. As previously noted, we had three new party leaders in this election, and leadership played an important role in influencing vote choice. Back in early 2004, the Liberal strategy was to run their campaign on the personal appeal of Paul Martin. He had been a successful finance minister, becoming known for his part in slashing the national deficit "come hell or high water." His 1995 budget was hailed a milestone budget, one that re-established Canada's credibility with the international financial community.[15] For years, Martin had seemed unassailable. He had led a charmed and seemingly effortless political life with glowing performance reviews as finance minister and favourable media coverage. But as was to be expected, the media were much more aggressive with Martin as prime minister. Martin had problems adjusting, and his image was tarnished by his handling of the sponsorship scandal and his inability to meet the high expectations he had created.

The Conservatives also organized their campaign around their new leader. Stephen Harper stood in contrast to Martin, especially because of his youth. More importantly, he stood in sharp contrast to his predecessor. Unlike Day, Harper is actually bilingual, a policy wonk, and more substance than flash. But under the glare of an election campaign, Harper came across as aloof, elitist, and devoid of a sense of humour. He also made the mistake of surrounding himself with people with little experience in running a national campaign and even less patience with voters and the intricacies of popular democracy.[16] Jack Layton was also a newcomer on the federal scene after a successful career in Ontario municipal politics. His relatively good showing on election day must have come as a vindication considering that the day after the English debate he was described as "bobbing up and down like a wannabe marionette trying to get someone to take him seriously."[17]

Canadians had the opportunity to observe the new leaders and to pass judgment. The campaign did not leave them unscathed. In the POLLARA study, Canadians were asked to rate their impression of each party leader on a scale of one to ten where one is "not at all impressed" and ten is "very impressed." Overall, Martin received the highest rating at 5.1, ahead of Harper (4.6), Layton (4.6), and Duceppe (4.5). The first point to be made is the low ratings garnered by all leaders. Between 1974 and 1993, most leaders registered scores at least over the midpoint,[18] while in 2004 only Martin made it over that midpoint, and that just barely.

In comparative terms, impressions of Martin were slightly higher than Chrétien's after the 2000 election (4.8). Stephen Harper's ratings were identical to those of Stockwell Day in 2000 (4.6), suggesting that in terms of public perception, the Conservatives are not much better off with Harper than the Alliance was with Day in 2000.

Table 8: Leader Evaluations

	2004	2000
Chrétien	-	4.8
Martin	5.1	-
Day	-	4.6
Harper	4.6	-
McDonough	-	4.6
Layton	4.6	-
Duceppe	4.5	4.6

Source: 2000–2004 POLLARA Post-Election Surveys

Looking at leaders' evaluations from a regional perspective, we first see the extent to which Harper's appeal is regionally concentrated. Harper is the best-regarded leader in only one region — the Prairies. This is also the only region where he managed to improve on Stockwell Day's 2000 impression ratings. Everywhere else, Harper failed to outperform his forerunner in terms of overall impression. He comes in third behind Martin and Layton in B.C., Ontario, and Atlantic Canada and trails Martin and Duceppe in Quebec.

The regional results are also troubling for Martin and the Liberals. The Liberal Party continues to experience poor leadership ratings in their historical Quebec stronghold. As Table 9 shows, Martin did improve on Chrétien's ratings in Quebec but remain far behind Duceppe's. He also failed to improve on his predecessor in Ontario, the Prairies, and B.C.

Table 9: Regional Leader Evaluations

	B.C.		Prairies		Ontario		Quebec		Atlantic	
	2004	2000	2004	2000	2004	2000	2004	2000	2004	2000
Chrétien	-	5.0	-	4.9	-	5.6	-	3.8	-	5.4
Martin	4.8	-	4.9	-	5.3	-	4.6	-	5.8	-
Day	-	5.3	-	5.2	-	4.8	-	4.1	-	4.8
Harper	4.5	-	5.4	-	4.6	-	4.1	-	4.3	-
McDonough	-	4.1	-	4.3	-	4.7	-	3.6	-	5.3
Layton	5.0	-	4.8	-	4.7	-	4.1	-	5.1	-
Duceppe	-	-	-	-	-	-	6.1	6.0	-	-

Source: 2000–2004 POLLARA Post-Election Surveys

Previous studies have demonstrated that every party leader since 1968 has declined in public esteem from the benchmark established in their first election as leader, no matter how popular or unpopular the leader was at that juncture.[19] Unlike Trudeau or Mulroney, who both enjoyed high impression ratings when they burst onto the political scene only to steadily decline in public esteem over their years in office, Martin, Harper, and Layton come out of their first campaigns with low impression ratings and no room for a slow and steady decline.

CONCLUSION

With the Liberals remaining in power but in a minority position for the first time since 1972, the Canadian political landscape appears to be struggling with the conflicting forces of change and continuity. Despite their electoral victory, the Liberals no longer face the divided opposition that has guaranteed them a majority of seats in the House of Commons with low pluralities of the vote. They will have to concentrate on rebuilding their majority, and our analysis suggests they may want to look towards disgruntled Liberal, NDP, and former PC voters to do so.

Other new realities appeared in 2004. The election results indicate we are inching closer to a return to the pre-1993 party system. The Bloc Québécois is proving resilient, but the conservative schism seems settled. The Conservatives can once again depend on a single group of potential supporters. But forming government remains a distant goal. Despite the Alliance-PC merger, the Conservative performance was only marginally better than the Alliance's in 2000 in terms of popular vote. The new party has lost the support of a significant segment of former PC voters and currently relies on discontented Liberals who may or may not support them again in the next election. It also depends too much on a stagnant group of Reform/Alliance voters, unable to grow beyond that core. The Harper Conservatives are marginal in Quebec, and despite a scandal-plagued Liberal government, Harper was unable to unify, let alone increase, the conservative vote in Ontario. Regardless of their ninety-nine seats, Conservatives must address the fact that with only 29.6 percent of Canadians supporting them, they have not been so unpopular with Canadian voters in more than fifty years. One has to go back to the 1949 (29.7) and 1945 (27.4) federal elections to find such poor showings by a united conservative alternative to the Liberal Party.

For its part, the NDP is slowly leaving the political cellar. Its support remains low but it is resurging in its traditional B.C. stronghold and doing better in Ontario. After years of fighting to keep party status in the House of Commons, the NDP may now look forward to falling back into its cherished role of "conscience of Canada."

The results of the 2004 election shed light on some of the academic lessons of the 1997 and 2000 elections. In *The Anatomy of a Liberal Victory*, the authors asserted that if a merger between the Alliance and the PC were to occur, many supporters of both parties would rally to the Liberals rather than to another opposition party.[20] Specifically, their analysis suggested that in the event of a merger, about 30 percent of Alliance voters and more than 40 percent of Conservative voters would turn to the Liberals as their second choice, with the NDP gaining very little of that support.[21] This proved to be only partly right. As we discussed in Table 2, a significant proportion of PC supporters and some Alliance voters did not embrace the merger. However, there is little evidence that they simply flocked to the Liberals. While the Liberals attracted some of those disgruntled conservative voters, regional patterns were at work, with the NDP attracting discontented Alliance supporters in the West and disgruntled PC and Alliance supporters in Ontario.

The authors mentioned above also argue that under the existing electoral system, the Liberals seem poised to maintain their dominance of Canadian electoral politics.[22] Again, this turned out to be partly true. For the fourth consecutive election, the Liberals won at least a plurality of seats. With this victory, the current Liberal hold on power will be the longest since the King era. However, it appears increasingly obvious that the Conservatives are slowly re-establishing themselves as "heirs apparent."

The true lessons of 2004 will emerge only when the parties face each other again in the not so distant future. What is certain is that, after an election when 40 percent of Canadians were so uninterested in the process that they decided to stay home and not vote, Canadian voters will be subjected to a rematch sooner than most want.

NOTES

1 Drew Fagan, "How Martin came back from brink," *The Globe and Mail,* June 29, 2004, A1.

2 As reported on CTV December 12, 2003. See transcript "Paul Martin Sworn in as Prime Minister," http://ctv.ca/.

3 Robert Fife, "Poll predicts minority," *National Post,* May 21, 2004, A1 and A9.

4 Jon H. Pammett, "The People's Verdict," in *The Canadian General Election of 2000,* ed. Jon H. Pammett and Christopher Dornan (Toronto: Dundurn Press, 2001), 296.

5 Jon H. Pammett, "The Voters Decide" in *The Canadian General Election of 1997,* ed. Alan Frizzell and Jon H. Pammett (Toronto: Dundurn Press, 1997), 228.

6 See Pammett, "The People's Verdict," Table 1. The retention rate for the Bloc in 2000 was 67 percent; 56 percent for the NDP.

7 Heather Scoffield and Campbell Clark, "Martin waves the flag," *The Globe and Mail,* May 24, 2004, A1.

8 Pammett, "The People's Verdict," 300.

9 Jane Taber, "The Liberals are in a spiral, top Martin adviser says," *The Globe and Mail,* June 10, 2004, A1.

10 Jane Taber, "Confident Harper talks majority," *The Globe and Mail,* June 11, 2004, A1.

11 Jonathan Fowlie and Brian Laghi, "Harper tries to allay fears on abortion," *The Globe and Mail,* June 10, 2004, A1 and A7.

12 Pammett, "The People's Verdict," 308.

13 Ibid.

14 Heather Scoffield and Drew Fagan, "Debate exposes key differences on protecting minority rights," *The Globe and Mail,* June 16, 2004, A1.

15 This point was made in Edward Greenspon and Anthony Wilson-Smith, *Double Vision: The Inside Story of the Liberals in Power* (Toronto: Doubleday Canada Limited, 1996); Susan Delacourt, *Juggernaut: Paul Martin's Campaign for Chrétien's Crown* (Toronto: McClelland & Stewart Ltd., 2003); and John Gray, *Paul Martin: The Power of Ambition* (Toronto: Key Porter Books, 2003).

16 See John Ibbitson, "Educating Stephen Harper," *The Globe and Mail,* June 26, 2004, A4.

17 John Ibbitson, "Passionate and ruthless, Martin looks like he's fighting to survive," *The Globe and Mail,* June 16, 2004, A1.

18 See Harold D. Clarke et al., *Absent Mandate,* 3rd edition (Toronto: Gage Educational Publishing Company, 1996), 77.

19 See Harold D. Clarke et al., *Absent Mandate,* 2nd edition (Toronto: Gage Educational Publishing Company, 1991); and André Turcotte, "Fallen Heroes" in *The Canadian General Election of 2000,* ed. Pammett and Dornan (Toronto: Dundurn Press, 2001).

20 André Blais, Elisabeth Gidengil, Richard Nadeau, and Neil Nevitte, *Anatomy of a Liberal Victory: Making Sense of the Vote in the 2000 Canadian Election* (Peterborough: Broadview Press, Ltd., 2002), 201.

21 Ibid., 77.

22 Ibid., 204.

CHAPTER TWELVE

Behind the Turnout Decline

by Jon H. Pammett and Lawrence LeDuc

From an average of 75 percent turnout in federal elections since World War Two, a rate which appeared to be sustained as late as 1988, the percentage of registered Canadians voting in a federal election fell to 70 percent in 1993, 67 percent in 1997, and finally to a historic low of 61.2 percent in 2000. Voting turnout in many recent provincial elections has appeared to follow the same trend.[1] This sharp decline in voting participation also mirrors that found in a number of other countries.[2] Consequently, the issue of voter turnout, once a topic of interest to a small group of academics, has become an issue of concern to the wider scholarly community, the media, and attentive members of the general public. By the time of the 2004 federal election campaign, the phenomenon of declining turnout in elections was very much on the radar screen of the country's mass media. The generational aspects of the turnout decline, whereby young people appear to be turning away from the electoral process in large numbers, have accentuated the public concern. In 2004, virtually every media outlet in the country ran programs or series of programs on the reasons for the lack of engagement of the nation's youth. Elections Canada spent a record amount of money on advertising to try to ensure that information about the election was available to all, and also to encourage maximal participation. Hopes were high. Electoral competition was greater in 2004, with public opinion polls throughout the campaign showing a neck-and-neck race between the Liberals and the newly resurgent Conservatives. And yet, turnout in the 2004 federal election was 60.5 percent, a small decline from the 2000 election but a decline nevertheless (see Figure 1).

Several converging trends have contributed to this sustained pattern of turnout decline in Canada over the past decade. Generational replacement, an increasing regionalization of the party system, decreasing party competition, and increasing public apathy towards politics (particularly among the young) are all longer term trends that have worked in concert with each other in recent years (Pammett and LeDuc, 2004). The growth of regional political parties has decreased party competition in many constituencies, and decreased party competition has removed meaning from elections for many potential voters. In turn, the low turnout has helped, in some parts of the country, to perpetuate the existence and dominance of regional parties. The electoral system, with the advantage that it gives to parties that concentrate their votes regionally, has magnified these trends. Younger people, particularly those newly eligible to vote, have thus perceived a party situation where meaningful choices, even where they existed among party ideologies, did not have a realistic chance of achieving parliamentary representation.

In the 2004 election, some of these longer term trends may have partially offset each other. Many constituencies, particularly in

Figure 1: Canadian Federal Election Turnout 1945–2004

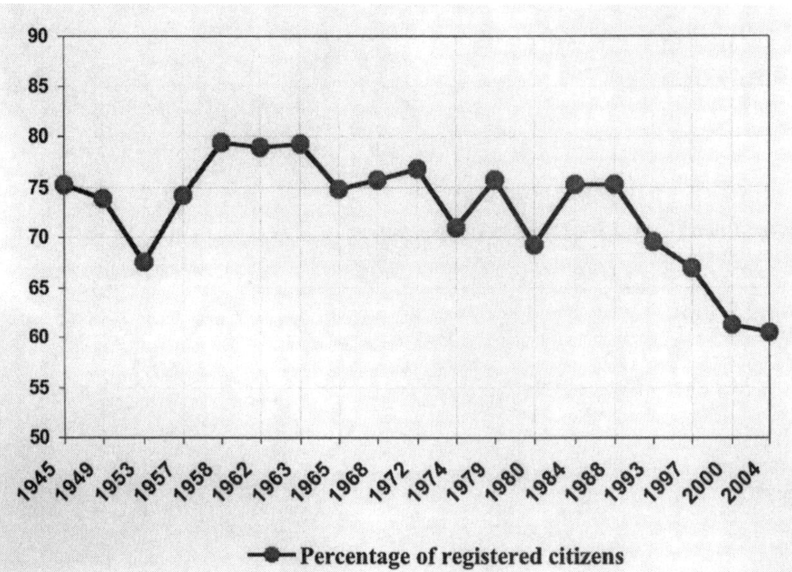

Ontario, were more competitive in 2004 than in the three previous elections. In the country as a whole, the election outcome remained in doubt until the final days. Yet, the low turnout in 2004 itself demonstrates that many of the forces that have been driving voting participation down in recent years nevertheless remained in place.

WHY SO MANY CANADIANS DON'T VOTE

In 2002, Elections Canada sponsored a national survey, designed by the authors, to examine the causes and correlates of nonvoting in federal elections. This survey was unique in that its design called for the collection of data from a much larger than usual group of nonvoters in the 2000 federal election.[3] It accomplished this by means of a short screening interview with a large number of respondents (5,637), followed by a longer interview with 960 reported nonvoters in the 2000 election and an equivalent number of reported voters. We will review some of the findings from this study in this chapter and also look at the reasons given by nonvoters in the 2004 POLLARA post-election survey reported in Chapter Eleven for their lack of participation in the 2004 election. Together, these two sources of evidence can provide some insights into the significant demographic and political trends that have brought about another historic low in voting participation.

Table 1 reports the answers to the open-ended question, "Voter turnout has been declining in recent Canadian federal elections. In your opinion, why is turnout going down?" It provides an initial overview of Canadians' general perception of the turnout situation and its causes, before they were asked any questions about their own behaviour, including whether they had voted or not.

TABLE 1: Reasons for the Turnout Decline, 2000 Election (Open-Ended; Multiple Responses)

Reasons Given	% of All Respondents	% of Nonvoters
Politicians and Political Institutions		
Politicians (negative public attitudes)	26.2	24.9
Government (negative public attitudes)	13.0	16.0
Candidates (negative public attitudes)	11.7	12.4
Political parties (negative public attitudes)	6.3	6.2
Issues (negative public attitudes)	5.5	4.2
Leaders (negative public attitudes)	3.3	2.3
Electoral system (negative public attitudes)	1.0	0.5
Election administration (problems)	1.0	1.2
	68.0	**67.7**
Meaninglessness		
Meaninglessness of participation	15.7	14.5
Lack of competition	14.0	8.6
Regional discontent	2.8	1.8
	32.5	**24.9**
Public Apathy		
Apathy and disinterest	22.7	24.2
Turned attention elsewhere	5.1	5.8
Lack of knowledge, information	4.3	5.0
Cynicism	4.0	3.4
Youth not voting	3.1	1.9
	39.2	**40.3**
Other	3.1	5.0
Do not know	1.4	2.5
N =	4,659	848

Note: In Table 1, category totals should be regarded as approximate, since respondents could give more than one response in the same category.

The majority of Canadians attributes the turnout decline to *negative public attitudes to the performance of the politicians and political institutions involved in federal politics*. Over two-thirds (68 percent) gave an answer in this category. The objects of perceived public displeasure run the complete gamut of personnel and institutions, but the most prominently mentioned were "politicians" and "the government," general terms that indicate the broad nature of the attitudes people ascribe to others. There is a widespread perception that politicians are untrustworthy, selfish, unaccountable, lack credibility, are insincere, etc. Similarly, the government, sometimes with a capital "G" and sometimes without, belies the people's trust and accomplishes little. Candidates are mentioned frequently because the question asked specifically about the turnout decline, thereby placing it in the election context. As one might expect, they are perceived to have the same faults as "politicians." Political parties are singled out as well, because some attributed the lowered voting rate to the difficulties people might have in finding any good choices or in distinguishing between the parties that do exist. And some said that potential voters have difficulty relating to the issues brought forward by the parties at election time, or sometimes that the policies proposed are misguided.

In addition to the negativity, there is a widespread feeling that *political participation is meaningless*. A number of these responses are captured specifically in the second section of Table 1, but such feelings may lie behind some of the other responses as well. Those classified under the "meaninglessness" heading commented on the lack of choice in elections, that their votes would not change anything. "It's always the same thing over and over," said some. Others referred to the situation of single-party dominance, whereby it seemed that there was no realistic hope of an alternative government, or the lack of competition in the local constituency context.

The final major category in Table 1 identifies those responses that blamed *public apathy and lack of interest* for the decline in voting. We are faced with a situation where people just do not care, do not pay attention, are lazy, or do not find the political scene exciting enough. A variation of this explanation is that people see nonvoters as simply interested in other things, giving political participation a low priority.

Table 2: Main Reasons for Not Voting in 2000 and 2004 Federal Elections (Open-Ended)

Reason Given	2000	2004
Disinterest		
Not interested; didn't care; apathy	23.2	16.0
Vote meaningless; not count; election result forgone conclusion	7.8	6.0
Forgot; unaware	2.2	2.1
Too complicated; confusing	0.4	0.8
	33.6	**24.9**
Negativity		
No appealing candidates/parties/issues	12.6	8.0
Lack of faith/confidence in candidates/parties/ leaders, regional discontent	11.4	7.3
Lack of information about candidates/parties/issues	3.3	1.6
	27.3	**16.9**
Personal/Administrative		
Too busy with work/school/family	13.7	18.4
Away from riding/province/country	10.3	15.5
Registration or moving related problems	6.7	8.5
Illness, health issues	2.9	11.1
Didn't know where or when; polling station problems; transportation	3.3	3.2
Religious reasons	1.5	1.7
	38.4	**58.4**
N =	1,036	117

Source: 2000 data from Elections Canada survey; 2004 from Pollara post election survey

Notes: Data is weighted. First response only from 2000. Category of "Other; unclassifiable; none" reasons removed.

Or perhaps it is because those choosing not to vote have not bothered to get the information required to cast a meaningful vote. Some cited attitudes of cynicism, disillusionment, discouragement, frustration, and hopelessness. Some specifically targeted young people as responsible for the voting decline.

Let us compare Table 1 with the open-ended reasons given by nonvoters in 2000 and 2004 for not going to the polls (Table 2). These reasons can be classified into three broad types, which are mentioned to roughly equal degrees by nonvoters. These overall types of reasons we call *disinterest, negativity, and personal/administrative*. The largest single group of responses in the first of these categories was from those who simply weren't interested in the election (or politics more generally), didn't care it was being held, and did not want to vote. For others in this category, however, it was the meaninglessness of the voting that counted, as they reasoned that their vote would not matter or make a difference and that the election result was a foregone conclusion.

We have classified responses as expressing negativity rather than simple disinterest if they indicated a lack of confidence in any of the electoral contestants, candidates, parties, leaders, or said that they could find none them appealing enough to vote for. Some of these respondents also said they did not find the issue discussion engaging, or they did not have enough information about the issues or other political factors to make a choice. A few of these respondents expressed grievances against the federal level of one sort or another or stated they weren't interested in federal politics.

The third category, personal/administrative, has a variety of forms, including illness, absence from the constituency, registration problems, and being "too busy." We have classified such reasons as "too busy" and "away" as personal/administrative reasons because closed-ended measures of these reasons are associated with other personal or administrative reasons rather than those measuring disinterest. However, undoubtedly, some of those who said they were too busy to vote were simply rationalizing a lower level of political interest. It is interesting to note that the survey of reasons for nonvoting in the 2004 election produces substantially more people who cited these personal or administrative reasons for staying away from the polls. Those who state they did not vote because they were too busy, because they were away (the election was held in the summer), were ill, or encountered registration problems were even more numerous than in the previous election.

There are a number of apparent differences between tables 1 and 2. While two-thirds of the general public thinks the turnout decline is being produced by negative public attitudes towards politicians, candidates, parties, leaders, political issues, etc., less than one-third of nonvoters cite such negative attitudes as reasons for not casting a ballot. Slightly more important are reasons of apathy and disinterest, a category of reason cited by many fewer people in Table 1 than the category of negativity. And finally, the whole category of personal or administrative reasons, which more than one-third of the nonvoters in 2000 and more than one-half in 2004 cited as important to their decision not to participate, is basically absent from the general characterization of the evaluation given for the nonvoting trend in general.

We can only speculate as to why negativity is so frequently identified as the main causal agent for public distancing from the electoral process (Table 1). For one thing, it is an easy explanation in that it essentially places the blame on others, namely the politicians, for people's unwillingness to participate. "It's not our fault," people seem to be saying — "It's the poor choices of parties and issues and the poor quality of the politicians and leaders that we are being given." Another reason for the popularity of the negativity explanation for the turnout decline is that its acceptance makes it possible to downplay the seriousness of the phenomenon and to believe that the solution might be a new set of party leaders, a new Pierre Trudeau, perhaps, that would rekindle the spirits of a discontented public and revive electoral participation. But the decline is strongly related to generational and age factors, with younger age groups voting at extremely low levels (only about 25 percent of those under 25 years of age voted in the 2000 Canadian federal election), and the factors that younger nonvoters cite for not voting are even less related to negative opinions of political leadership than are those of older nonvoters.

RECENT TRENDS IN FEDERAL POLITICS

Declining voting participation is only one of several major shifts in the Canadian political environment that have taken place over the past decade. Also important is the *decreased level of competitiveness* in the Canadian party system, which has been in evidence in each of the last four elections. Canada has become, in many respects, a one party dominant political system in which, even in 2004, the Liberal Party faced little serious competition in the race to form a national government. Unlike citizens of many other countries, Canadians have only a single vote, which must be cast for a local candidate at the constituency level. In many single-member constituencies, the winning candidate, often the incumbent, is elected by a large plurality. In the 2000 federal election, the mean margin of victory for the winning candidate overall was 23.8 percent. In ridings won by the governing Liberal Party, the average was a slightly higher 24.6 percent, and in those won by the Canadian Alliance in 2000 the average margin was 32.0 percent. While there was considerable variation in this regard between particular constituencies, the fact remains that Canadian federal politics in recent years has become increasingly uncompetitive.[4] As the public has become more aware over time of this major change in the Canadian political landscape, many have increasingly come to believe that voting in federal elections is no longer a meaningful political act. In the survey that we conducted for Elections Canada following the 2000 election, which forms the database for part of the analysis in this chapter, large majorities of respondents stated that their vote could make "little or no difference" in the country as a whole (69 percent) or even at the constituency level (57 percent). Clearly, the reduced level of competitiveness in the Canadian political system has gradually become salient to many potential voters.[5]

Another factor, which is also connected to the longer term pattern of turnout decline, is the *increased regionalization* of Canadian politics at the federal level. The Bloc Québécois, which first came to prominence by winning fifty-four of Quebec's seventy-five parliamentary seats in 1993, has continued to hold a substantial number of those seats in 1997 (forty-four seats), 2000 (thirty-eight seats), and

2004 (fifty-four seats once again). But the Bloc is a party that fields candidates only in Quebec. Thus, its very existence has made Canadian politics more regional than it had been prior to 1993. However, increased regionalization of the party system is not due to the presence of the Bloc alone. The Conservative Party of Canada together with its predecessor parties — the Reform Party and the Canadian Alliance — won the majority of its parliamentary seats in the western provinces. Although the new party made gains in Ontario in 2004, the story of the 2004 election was essentially the failure of the Conservatives to make sufficient inroads into the centre of the country to give them a realistic chance of forming a government. Even the Liberal Party, which often attempts to portray itself as the only truly "national" party, still wins a majority of its seats in a single province. In the 2000 election, the Liberals won 100 of Ontario's 103 parliamentary seats, and it retained all but 31 of the 106 Ontario seats in 2004. Combined with the twenty-one seats that it won in Quebec in 2004, it becomes evident that the Liberal parliamentary caucus heavily reflects the interests of Central Canada. This increased regionalization of politics in Canada is connected to competitiveness in the sense that the regional bases of support for several of the parties are increasingly uncompetitive. In the 2000 election, the average winning margin for Liberal candidates in Ontario was 27.6 percent. In the western province of Alberta, the average winning margin for successful Alliance candidates was an astounding 40.7 percent. Although regionalization and competitiveness are different attributes, it is clear that they are both artifacts of the 1993 election, which redefined the competitive position of the parties across the country in a way that has yet to be reversed (Carty, Cross & Young, 2000).

A further broad trend in Canada that is closely connected with declining turnout is the shift in what we might call the *culture of voting*. Older generations of Canadians thought of voting in elections as civic duty and displayed higher levels of trust regarding politics. But, as we and others have found, this culture of trust has undergone a substantial decline (Pammett and LeDuc, 2003; Blais et al, 2002; Nevitte, 1996). Fewer Canadians, particularly among the young, now believe that voting is an essential social and political act. If voting is not important because one's vote doesn't really count, neither is it important for its own sake as a participatory act. In a multivariate analysis, a factor including civic duty and a number of other items concerning the importance of voting and the relevance of politics to one's life was one of several significant predictors of nonvoting in the 2000 federal election (Pammett and LeDuc, 2003).

In each of these areas where a statistical relationship exists with turnout, a circular pattern appears to emerge. In other words, declining turnout has contributed to the decreased competitiveness of Canadian politics, and that decreased competitiveness in turn fosters further declines in turnout. A similar argument can be advanced with respect to regionalization. As Canadian federal politics has become more regionalized, nonvoting (particularly for supporters of parties that are weak in certain regions) becomes a logical response. This in turn leaves the regionally strong parties even stronger in their regions, possibly leading over time to further turnout declines. As turnout declines in the aggegate, nonvoting becomes more socially acceptable, and nonvoters no longer need to make excuses for their non-participation. Such a decline in the voting culture (as evidenced by a declining sense of civic duty), could eventually bring about even further declines in turnout, particularly when considered alongside some of the broad demographic trends noted earlier.

But because these relationships are circular, they are capable of operating in the other direction as well. If Canadian politics were (and were seen to be) more competitive in 2004, that could work to increase the turnout rate. If the party system were less regionalized, with fewer one-party bastions, that would accomplish the same result. If the extensive education and advertising campaign in 2004 served to persuade young people that it was important to exercise their voting franchise, this might begin to stem the tide of youthful apathy towards the election process. It was arguably true in 2004 that some of these more positive trends were operating. The Conservatives were more competitive than their forebears, the

Alliance and the Reform Party, had been. They made some inroads into the Liberal bastions of Ontario and the East. The Liberals, under their new leader Paul Martin, had hopes before the campaign started of improving their showing in the West and possibly also in Quebec. And the barrage of media coverage and advertising made a serious effort to shame or entice apathetic youngsters into going to the polls. Yet turnout nevertheless declined, albeit only slightly. Were it not for the existence of some of these new factors, it is entirely possible that turnout might have been lower than it was in 2004. Based on the demographic trends alone, turnout *could* have declined a further 3 or 4 percent. But given the increased competitiveness of the parties, some moderation of regionalization, and the active attempts to reinstill a culture of voting among the public, the decline that actually occurred in 2004 turned out to be more modest than it otherwise might have been.

PROVINCIAL TURNOUT PATTERNS

In fact, much of the improvement that *did* take place in voting participation occurred in Ontario, which showed an increase of 3.2 percent in turnout in 2004 (Table 3). British Columbia, which had an increase of 0.6 percent, was the only other province to show any increase at all in turnout in 2004 from the levels of the 2000 federal election. In all other provinces, turnout declined, and in several instances (notably Newfoundland, New Brunswick, Quebec, and Manitoba) it declined quite substantially from the 2000 levels (Table 3). Almost certainly, the improvements in participation in Ontario and British Columbia were attributable to the increased competitiveness of the parties in those two provinces. In Quebec, on the other hand, the dominance of the Bloc and the weak showing of the new Conservative Party continued the pattern of increased regionalization and decreased competitiveness that began in 1993. Quebec voters in 2004 who sought an alternative to the Bloc were more likely to be disappointed in the choices available to them.

Table 3: Turnout by Province, 2000 and 2004

	2004	2000	Net Change
Newfoundland	49.2	57.1	-7.9
Prince Edward Island	70.7	72.7	-2.0
Nova Scotia	61.7	62.1	-0.4
New Brunswick	62.1	67.7	-5.6
Quebec	58.9	64.1	-5.2
Ontario	61.7	58.0	3.7
Manitoba	56.5	62.3	-5.8
Saskatchewan	59.1	62.3	-3.2
Alberta	59.4	60.2	-0.8
British Columbia	63.6	63.0	0.6
Total Canada	60.5	61.2	-0.7

Of course, variables such as competitiveness or regionalization can be thought of at several levels — national, regional, provincial, or individual ridings. Parties that are not competitive in a particular province or region may nevertheless be competitive in certain constituencies, as the Liberals were in a few Alberta ridings or the NDP was in some urban areas in Ontario. Thus, we want to consider the choices that were presented to voters in 2004 at the constituency level, as well as their perceptions of a party's chances of forming a government or gaining a significant level of representation in Parliament. In a previous analysis (Pammett and LeDuc, 2004), we examined the competitive position of the parties at the constituency level, together with the perceptions of survey respondents regarding the question of whether their votes could "make a difference."

By combining the aggregate variables of turnout and constituency competitiveness with attitudinal variables in our 2002 survey of non-voters, it was possible to gain some further insights into the interaction between the objective competitiveness of constituencies and respondents' perceptions of the choice presented to them in an election. Of course, voters do not always perceive accurately the competitive situation in their local riding, particularly if their level of interest in politics is low. But when they do perceive it, it is likely to have an effect on their decision whether or not to cast a vote. Those who understand that the choice being presented to them in the local constituency is not very meaningful are more likely to feel that their vote will not make any difference in the outcome. And those who feel this way are often less likely to vote.

Table 4 shows substantial variations in the levels of voting turnout in constituencies with different levels of competitiveness. Here, we combine the objective level of competitiveness in constituencies (quartiles) as measured by the size of the winning candidate's margin of victory, with responses to the survey question "How much chance was there that your vote would make a difference in your electoral district?" In the most competitive constituencies where respondents perceive that their vote can make "a lot" of difference, voting levels rise above 80 percent. At the other extreme of the table, where constituencies are relatively uncompetitive and respondents feel that their vote can make little or no difference, turnout rates begin to fall towards 40 percent.[6]

The implications of this pattern are clear. If Canadian federal politics continues to become more regionalized and less competitive, as the trend since 1993 suggests, citizens will increasingly perceive that their vote can make little difference. If this happens, turnout rates will continue to fall, not only because of the demographic patterns that have been depressing them, but also because the perceived effectiveness of one's vote has also diminished. Whether the improvements in competitiveness and regionalization in 2004, modest though they were, can make any real difference in persuading Canadians that their votes can indeed make a difference remains a subject for further investigation.

Table 4: Percent Voting in Constituencies with High and Low Levels of Competitiveness, by Perceived Effectiveness of Vote[1]

	Level of Competition (Quartiles)			
	High			Low
Vote can make a difference	1	2	3	4
a lot	82.5	81.4	75.6	74.4
some	72.5	71.5	65.9	66.7
a little	50.8	56.9	59.3	53.6
none	44.1	49.1	46.7	40.0

Chi^2 sig. < .001
Cramer's V = .26
N = 1,902*

1. Text of question was: "How much chance was there that your vote would make a difference in your electoral district?"

* Table is weighted to simulate entire electorate.

EFFECTIVENESS OF THE VOTE

We have already pointed out that the regional dominance of certain parties in Canada creates an overall impression of noncompetitiveness nationwide. In addition, we have seen that there are a large number of ridings in all parts of the country where the gap between the first- and second-place finishers is substantial enough that potential voters might have felt their votes would not count for much in deciding the outcome. Of course, those with high levels of political interest or civic duty were likely to cast a ballot regardless of the competitive situation at the time, but those with more marginal feelings about the importance of voting may have felt that there wasn't much point to it.

Table 5: How much chance was there that your vote would make a difference in the country?

	Voted in 2000?		Total
	Yes	No	
A lot	14.4	7.0	10.4
Some	22.7	18.9	20.6
A little	34.9	33.4	34.1
None	28.0	40.8	34.9
	100.0	100.0	100.0

V = .116 $p < .000$

Table 6: How much chance was there that your vote would make a difference in your electoral district?

	Voted in 2000?		Total
	Yes	No	
A lot	23.1	10.1	16.2
Some	32.3	22.9	27.3
A little	26.1	34.4	30.5
None	18.5	32.7	26.1
	100.0	100.0	100.0

V = .243 $p < .000$

Tables 5 and 6 show that a substantial majority of the sampled respondents believed their votes would make little or no difference in either the country as a whole or their own electoral district. This feeling that their votes would not matter was stronger in the larger arena of the whole country, as we might expect given the large number of votes involved. More telling are the figures for the respondents' own ridings. Here, the feeling that their votes would make no difference is felt particularly strongly by those who did not vote (Table 6). The table shows that two-thirds of nonvoters felt their votes would make little or no difference in their local constituency contest, as opposed to less than half (44.6 percent) of those who voted who felt this way.

Table 7: Correlations (tau b) between Belief That Vote Would Make a Difference in the Electoral District and Selected Variables

Likelihood of voting in the next election	0.33**
Importance of voting in elections (civic duty)	0.27**
Interest in politics	0.25**
Interest in the 2000 election	0.26**
Satisfaction with the way federal elections work in Canada	0.14**
Satisfaction with the present electoral system	0.12*
Support for proportional representation	0.04**

** statistically significant at < 0.01

* statistically significant at < 0.05

The feeling that one's vote would make a difference in one's electoral district has a number of substantial relationships with electoral consequences. First and foremost, those believing that their votes were effective were more likely to express the intention of voting in the next election. The vicious circle, however, is the reverse relationship. Those who do not feel their votes will make a difference are much less likely to say they will make the effort to vote the next time. They are less likely to take an interest in politics, thereby making it less likely they would be informed of any potential change in the competitive situation. They also have a substantially lower feeling of civic duty, which might have gotten them to the polls regardless of the competitive situation in which they consider the political forces to be. In fact, those who do not feel their votes can make a difference are generally less satisfied with the operations of Canadian elections. The attitudinal measures in the 2002 Elections Canada Survey did not include evaluations of the performance of many Canadian political institutions. However, a few measures directly related to the electoral system and regulations were included. People who felt their votes were not effective in making a difference in the election show some indications of dissatisfaction with the electoral system as it currently exists (Table 7). However, they were not more inclined to favour proportional representation as a potential solution to "wasted votes." In fact, those who felt their votes were effective were actually marginally more favourable to proportional representation.

CULTURE

Voting in elections is part of a larger cluster of values and beliefs that are part of our political culture. We have seen that feelings of political trust and being represented are associated with voting, and that low feelings of efficacy are associated with not voting. The most often discussed cultural characteristic associated with elections is civic duty (Blais, 2000). Civic duty is the feeling that participation is to be valued for its own sake, or for its contribution to the overall health of the polity, and does not need to be justified on instrumental grounds. For the believer in the importance of participating out of duty, neither is it important that the prospective voter be enticed to cast a ballot by a particularly attractive bevy of candidates, parties, or policies, nor is it essential that the race be close and the vote more likely to count in determining the outcome. Rather, the conscientious voter motivated by civic duty feels that voting is important for its own sake. Conceptualized in these terms, a sense of civic duty may be measured by the question reported in Table 8, "In your view, how important is it that people vote in elections?" with the alternatives starting with "essential" and working their way down to "not at all important."

Table 8: Civic Duty by Vote in the 2000 Federal Election

In your view, how important is it that people vote in elections?

	Total	2000 voters	2000 nonvoters
Essential	36.2	55.9	19.2
Very important	37.6	37.9	37.3
Somewhat important	20.5	5.4	33.6
Not at all important	5.7	0.8	9.9

V = 0.475 (p< 0.001)
N = 2,029

The overall results in Table 8 show that a majority of Canadians still thinks voting in elections is either "essential" or "very important." Only about a quarter of the total sample gives it a "somewhat important" or "not important" rating. The breakdown offered in the table, however, shows that there is a strong relationship between having an attitude of civic duty and actually voting. Among voters, almost everybody thinks it is at least "very important" if not "essential," whereas nonvoters show a much lower level of civic duty. This bivariate finding is very much what we would expect after viewing the importance of the factors involving civic duty as predictors of voting/nonvoting in elections. The conditions exist for a vicious circle involving voting and civic duty, whereby nonvoters decrease their belief in the importance of voting and therefore become less likely to vote in future elections. And, of course, those who for whatever reason come to believe that voting in elections is not important will be less likely to vote.

CONCLUSION: CAN THE DOWNWARD TREND BE REVERSED?

Can the vicious circles connecting these trends be broken and the pattern of continuing decline in voting turnout reversed? The directions of possible solutions are not hard to discern, but it is impossible to predict whether they can be accomplished. The problem with the regionalization of the party system might be alleviated if one or more of the main opposition parties eventually succeeds in presenting itself as a viable national alternative to the Liberals. The gains made by the new Conservative party in Ontario and the East in 2004 are encouraging in this regard, but the resurgence of the Bloc in Quebec has partly offset this trend towards a less regionalized polity. Although the Liberals are no longer as dominant as they were in the three previous elections, we continue to have a parliament in which the new Conservatives will claim a mandate to speak for the West, the Bloc for Quebec, and the Liberals for the rest of the country, even though none of these parties actually attained a majority of the votes within the region in which they are dominant. In all three instances, the majority of voters who did not cast their ballots for the dominant party in a region may rightly tend to feel that their views are not properly represented. This is partly an artifact of the party system that has existed in Canada since 1993, but also of the electoral system, which continues to magnify these trends and to give greater advantage to parties that concentrate their votes within a particular region.

The problem of decreased party competition and the ensuing lack of representation has already served to put the issue of electoral reform on the nation's policy agenda. Citizen movements like Fair Vote Canada are publicizing the possibilities of implementing a mixed member proportional (MMP) electoral system in the hopes of energizing those currently feeling unrepresented. While there is no large-scale dissatisfaction with the current electoral system per se, survey evidence shows that there is, at the same time, an interest in implementing proportional representation in some form (over 70 percent are supportive). Several of the largest provinces, (Quebec, British Columbia, Ontario) are also studying the possibility of implementing electoral system changes at the level of provincial elections (Milner, 2004). While electoral system reform is no panacea for increasing turnout, it does have the potential to demonstrate the responsiveness of politicians to public concern about lack of effectiveness of voting in the current system and to attract the attention of the disaffected and/or the young.

Cultural attitudes involving the apathy of the population towards politics and towards the essential nature of electoral participation present a particularly intractable problem. Because of the circular nature of the relationship with other factors, any of the institutional changes described above might help to reverse this trend as well. In the meantime, efforts to improve the nature of civic education can help (Milner, 2002). Improved civic education curricula in the schools, implemented by better qualified civics teachers employing participative methods, can make a difference in interesting young people in electoral politics. Innovative advertising campaigns employed by the electoral authorities (e.g., Elections Ontario in 2003 and Elections Canada in 2004) can help to draw the attention of those hesitating about voting to the desirability of making their own choice of representatives rather than leaving this choice to others.

Finally, the possibility exists that new forms of technology can allow and encourage participation in ways that engage the interest of those who feel marginalized from the current forms of electoral participation. Experimentation with methods of electronic voting is occurring simultaneously in many countries (e.g., Britain and the United States), and we have some indications that their use, if security concerns can be addressed successfully, would have a small/modest upward impact on the turnout rate (Pammett and LeDuc, 2003; 55–59). More important than their actual use, however, might be the implied responsiveness to public demands.

The circularity of the relationships between the forces surrounding the phenomenon of the turnout decline makes it possible to be optimistic or pessimistic about the future. At the moment, the pessimistic view seems more realistic. Whether the period of minority government that we are now entering can bring about some moderation of these trends, or whether it will in the end merely reinforce them, remains a question about which we can only speculate. Declining turnout, increasing regionalization, decreasing party competitiveness, lesser cultural importance given to civic attitudes and participation — all of these are contemporary trends that have been developing for some time and will not be dislodged by a single election result. And all of these developments appear to reinforce each other. But it is difficult to believe that these trends can continue indefinitely. Sooner or later, voting turnout will stabilize, a coherent national alternative government will emerge, competitiveness will improve, and exhortations toward civic-mindedness will have some effect, and such developments in one area can affect the others. The prospect of a trend reversal, operated by a virtuous circle as opposed to a vicious one, could be just beyond the horizon. Or further away.

REFERENCES

Blais, Andre. *To Vote or Not to Vote: The Merits and Limits of Rational Choice Theory* (Pittsburgh, Pa.: University of Pittsburgh Press, 2000).

Blais, Andre, Elisabeth Gidengil, Richard Nadeau, Neil Nevitte. "The Evolving Nature of Nonvoting: Evidence From Canada," paper presented to the annual meeting of the American Political Science Association, San Francisco, 2001.

Blais, Andre, Elisabeth Gidengil, Richard Nadeau, Neil Nevitte. *Anatomy of a Liberal Victory* (Peterborough, Ont: Broadview, 2002).

Carty, Kenneth, William Cross, and Lisa Young. *Rebuilding Canadian Party Politics* (Vancouver: University of British Columbia Press, 2000).

Franklin, Mark N. "The Dynamics of Electoral Participation," in Lawrence LeDuc, Richard G. Niemi, and Pippa Norris, eds., *Comparing Democracies 2* (London: Sage, 2002).

Franklin, Mark N., et al. *Voter Turnout and the Dynamics of Electoral Competition in Established Democracies Since 1945* (Cambridge: Cambridge University Press, 2004).

Milner, Henry. *Civic Literacy: How Informed Citizens Make Democracy Work* (Lebanon, NH: University Press of New England, 2002).

Milner, Henry, ed. *Steps Toward Making Every Vote Count: Electoral System Reform in Canada and Its Provinces* (Peterborough: Broadview, 2004).

Nevitte, Neil. *The Decline of Deferrence* (Peterborough, Ont.: Broadview, 1996).

Norris, Pippa. *Democratic Phoenix: Reinventing Political Activism* (Cambridge: Cambridge University Press, 2002).

Pammett, Jon H. and Lawrence LeDuc. *Explaining the Turnout Decline in Canadian Federal Elections: A New Survey of Non-voters* (Ottawa: Elections Canada, 2003).

Pammett, Jon H. and Lawrence LeDuc. "Four Vicious Circles of Turnout: Competitiveness, Regionalization, Culture and Participation in Canada," paper presented to the European Consortium of Political Research Joint Sessions Workshops, Uppsala, Sweden, April 14-18, 2004.

Seidle, F. Leslie, ed. *Youth Participation in Elections* (special issue of Electoral Insight, vol. 5, no. 2) (Ottawa: Elections Canada, 2003).

NOTES

1 Overall, turnout in provincial elections has declined by an average of about 5 percent since the 1980s.

2 Turnout in Britain, for example, also registered a historic low of 59.4 percent in the 2001 general election.

3 For a more detailed report of findings from this survey see Jon H. Pammett and Lawrence LeDuc, *Explaining the Turnout Decline in Recent Federal Elections: Evidence from a New Survey of Nonvoters* (Ottawa: Elections Canada, 2003).

4 A more detailed analysis of competitiveness at the constituency level in the 2000 election may be found in Jon H. Pammett and Lawrence LeDuc, "Four Vicious Circles of Turnout: Competitiveness, Regionalization, Culture and Participation in Canada," paper presented to the European Consortium of Political Research Joint Sessions Workshops, Uppsala, Sweden, April 14–18, 2004.

5 On the role of competitiveness in other countries and under different electoral systems, see Mark N. Franklin, "The Dynamics of Electoral Participation," in *Comparing Democracies 2,* ed. Lawrence LeDuc, Richard G. Niemi and Pippa Norris (London: Sage, 2002); and Mark N. Franklin et al., *Voter Turnout and the Dynamics of Eectoral Competition in Established Democracies Since 1945* (Cambridge: Cambridge University Press, 2004).

6. The pattern becomes stronger if a control for subjective perceptions of party competition is added, using responses to the question "How competitive do you feel the the political parties were here in this electoral district?" In the most competitive constituencies, where respondents perceived them as such and also felt that their vote could make a difference the turnout rate was 88 percent. At the other end, where the constituency was in the most uncompetitive quartile, and respondents perceived that the riding was "very uncompetitive," the turnout rate was 26 percent. Because of the problem of small cell sizes, a complete breakdown of these combinations is not given here. But the overall direction of the pattern shown by the combination of objective and subjective indicators of competitiveness in Table 4 is quite clear.

KEY TO APPENDICES

BQ	Bloc Québécois
CA	Canadian Action Party
CHP	Christian Heritage Party
COMM	Communist Party
Cons	Conservative Party
GP	Green Party
IND	Independent
Liberal	Liberal Party
Libert	Libertarian Party
MP	Marijuana Party
ML	Marxist-Leninist Party
NDP	New Democratic Party
No Affiliation	
PCP	Progressive Canadian Party

Appendix A

Results of the 38th General Election by Percentage of Votes and Number of Seats Each Party Received

	Canada		Alta		BC		Man		NB		NFLD & LAB		NWT		NS		NT		ONT		PEI		QC		SASK		YN	
	# seats	% votes	# seats	% votes	# seats	% votes	# seats	% votes	# seats	% votes	# seats	% votes	# seats	% votes	# seats	% votes	# seats	% votes	# seats	% votes	# seats	% votes	# seats	% votes	# seats	% votes	# seats	% votes
BQ	54	12.4																					54	48.8				
CA	0	0.1	0	0.1	0	0.3	0	0	0	0.1	0	32.3							0	0			0	0				
CHP	0	0.3	0	0.2	0	0.3	0	0.9	0	31.1					0	0.1			0	0.5	0	0.1	0	0	0	0.3	0	0.9
COMM	0	0	0	0	0	0.1	0	0.2											0	0			0	0				
Cons	99	29.6	26	61.6	22	36.2	7	39.1	2		2		0	17.2	3	28	0	14.5	24	31.5	0	30.7	0	8.8	13	41.8	0	20.9
GP	0	4.3	0	6.2	0	6.4	0	2.7		3.4	0	1.6	0	4.3	0	3.3	0	2.9	0	4.5	0	4.2	0	3.2	0	2.7	0	4.5
IND	0	0.4	0	0.1	1	0.3	0	0		0.2	0	0.6			0	0.1	0	16.2	0	0.3			0	0.1	0	4.6		
Liberal	135	36.7	2	22	8	28.6	3	33.2	7	44.6	5	48	1	39.4	6	39.6	1	51.2	75	44.7	4	52.5	21	33.9	1	27.2	1	45.9
Libert	0	0			0	0.1													0	0			0	0				
MP	0	0.3	0	0.2	0	0.2	0	0.4		0.1					0	0.1			0	0.2			0	0.5			0	2.4
ML	0	0.1	0	0	0	0.1									0	0			0	0.1			0	0.1				
NDP	19	15.7	0	9.5	5	26.6	4	23.5	1	20.6	0	17.5	0	39.1	2	28.5	0	15.3	7	18.1	0	12.5	0	4.6	0	23.4	0	25.4
No Affiliation	1	0.1			0	1													0	0					0	0.1		
PCP	0	0.1	0	0											0	0.3			0	0.2								
	308		28		36		14		10		7		1		11		1		106		4		75		14		1	

APPENDIX B

PERCENTAGE OF VOTES RECEIVED BY CONSTITUENCY

NEWFOUNDLAND

AVALON

LIB	58.3
CONS	29.3
NDP	11.0
GP	1.4

BONAVISTA—EXPLOITS

LIB	48.2
CONS	41.6
NDP	8.1
GP	1.1
IND	1.0

HUMBER—ST. BARBE—BAIE VERTE

LIB	62.6
CONS	23.0
NDP	13.1
GP	1.4

LABRADOR

LIB	62.2
CONS	15.8
IND	10.4
NDP	9.6
GP	2.0

RANDOM—BURIN—ST. GEORGE'S

LIB	46.8
NDP	33.2
CONS	18.2
GP	1.8

ST. JOHN'S NORTH

CONS	41.4
LIB	36.7
NDP	19.8
GP	2.2

ST. JOHN'S SOUTH

CONS	39.6
LIB	35.3
NDP	23.7
GP	1.5

PRINCE EDWARD ISLAND

CARDIGAN

LIB	53.4
CONS	33.2
NDP	10.2
GP	3.2

CHARLOTTETOWN

LIB	49.4
CONS	27.6
NDP	18.4
GP	4.1
CHP	0.6

EGMONT

LIB	55.4
CONS	29.1
NDP	11.6
GP	3.9

MALPEQUE

LIB	51.9
CONS	32.5
NDP	10.1
GP	5.5

NOVA SCOTIA

CAPE BRETON—CANSO

LIB	53.3
NDP	24.3
CONS	20.2
GP	2.2

CENTRAL NOVA

CONS	43.3
NDP	27.7
LIB	26.4
GP	2.7

DARTMOUTH—COLE HARBOUR

LIB	42.1
NDP	32.5
CONS	21.1
GP	3.2
PCP	1.0
ML	0.2

HALIFAX

NDP	41.6
LIB	39.1
CONS	14.6
GP	4.7

HALIFAX WEST

LIB	47.5
NDP	27.9
CONS	21.0
GP	3.6

KINGS—HANTS

LIB	46.6
CONS	30.1
NDP	17.7
GP	3.6
CHP	1.3
IND	0.6

NORTH NOVA

CONS	50.5
LIB	26.5
NDP	18.9
GP	3.1
PCP	1.0

SACKVILLE—EASTERN SHORE

NDP	45.8
LIB	28.7
CONS	21.4
GP	2.6
PCP	1.7

SOUTH SHORE—ST. MARGARET'S

CONS	37.9
LIB	32.1
NDP	25.7
GP	4.3

SYDNEY—VICTORIA

LIB	52.1
NDP	27.7
CONS	15.9
GP	2.3
MP	1.3
IND	0.7

WEST NOVA

LIB	42.6
CONS	33.0
NDP	21.1
GP	3.2

NEW BRUNSWICK

ACADIE—BATHURST

NDP	53.9
LIB	32.7
CONS	10.9
GP	2.5

BEAUSÉJOUR

LIB	53.3
CONS	28.2
NDP	14.7
GP	3.8

FREDERICTON

LIB	46.8
CONS	33.5
NDP	17.4
GP	2.4

FUNDY

CONS	44.8
LIB	34.8
NDP	16.2
GP	3.1
IND	1.1

MADAWASKA—RESTIGOUCHE

LIB	44.7
NDP	27.6
CONS	24.0
GP	3.7

MIRAMICHI

LIB	48.1
CONS	29.0
NDP	18.4
GP	4.5

MONCTON—RIVERVIEW—DIEPPE

LIB	59.3
CONS	23.5
NDP	12.5
GP	4.7

ST. CROIX—BELLEISLE

CONS	53.1
LIB	31.5
NDP	11.7
GP	3.1
ACTION	0.6

SAINT JOHN

LIB	43.3
CONS	33.6
NDP	19.1
GP	2.2
MP	1.0
IND	0.8

TOBIQUE—MACTAQUAC

LIB	48.2
CONS	39.6
NDP	8.5
GP	3.7

QUEBEC

ABITIBI—TÉMISCAMINGUE

BQ	57.7
LIB	31.0
CONS	5.6
NDP	3.4
GP	2.4

AHUNTSIC

LIB	43.8
BQ	41.3
NDP	6.2
CONS	5.2
GP	2.7
MP	0.7
ML	0.2

ALFRED-PELLAN

BQ	49.2
LIB	39.6
CONS	5.1
NDP	3.5
GP	2.1
IND	0.4
IND	0.2

ARGENTEUIL—MIRABEL

BQ	57.4
LIB	26.9
CONS	7.0
GP	5.1
NDP	3.0
CHP	0.4
ML	0.1

BEAUCE

LIB	41.4
BQ	36.3
CONS	17.1
NDP	3.1
GP	2.2

BEAUHARNOIS—SALABERRY

BQ	50.7
LIB	34.6
CONS	9.2
GP	2.7
NDP	1.9
MP	0.9

BEAUPORT

BQ	49.7
LIB	25.6
CONS	16.0
NDP	4.1
GP	3.4
MP	1.3

BERTHIER—MASKINONGÉ

BQ	59.9
LIB	22.8
CONS	11.3
NDP	3.4
GP	2.7

BOURASSA

LIB	50.0
BQ	37.8

CONS	5.3
NDP	4.0
GP	1.6
MP	1.0
ML	0.4

BROME—MISSISQUOI

LIB	42.1
BQ	39.7
CONS	11.1
GP	4.6
NDP	2.7

BROSSARD—LA PRAIRIE

LIB	45.9
BQ	41.0
CONS	5.9
NDP	4.4
GP	2.6
ML	0.2

CHAMBLY—BORDUAS

BQ	60.9
LIB	22.8
CONS	7.6
NDP	4.8
GP	4.0

CHARLESBOURG

BQ	51.6
LIB	25.7
CONS	15.8
NDP	3.5
GP	2.6
MP	0.8

CHARLEVOIX—MONTMORENCY

BQ	60.9
LIB	20.6
CONS	12.6
GP	3.4
NDP	2.5

CHÂTEAUGUAY—SAINT-CONSTANT

BQ	57.3
LIB	30.0
CONS	5.7
GP	3.7
NDP	3.3

CHICOUTIMI—LE FJORD

BQ	45.3
LIB	43.4
CONS	5.2
NDP	3.7
GP	2.3

COMPTON—STANSTEAD

BQ	46.7
LIB	36.0
CONS	10.5
GP	3.5
NDP	3.3

DRUMMOND

BQ	56.3
LIB	22.8
CONS	16.9
GP	2.2
NDP	1.8

GASPÉSIE—ÎLES-DE-LA-MADELEINE

BQ	55.7
LIB	32.7
CONS	6.8
GP	2.8
NDP	2.1

GATINEAU

LIB	42.1
BQ	40.3
CONS	7.6
NDP	5.7
GP	3.1
MP	1.0
ML	0.3

HOCHELAGA

BQ	60.1
LIB	25.6
NDP	5.5
CONS	4.1
GP	3.0
MP	1.1
COMM	0.4
ML	0.3

HONORÉ-MERCIER

LIB	46.1
BQ	40.4

CONS	6.0
NDP	4.1
GP	1.8
MP	1.3
ML	0.3

HULL—AYLMER

LIB	41.9
BQ	32.5
NDP	11.9
CONS	8.2
GP	5.3
ML	0.2

JEANNE-LE BER

LIB	41.1
BQ	40.9
NDP	6.9
CONS	5.5
GP	4.1
MP	1.1
ML	0.3

JOLIETTE

BQ	63.4
LIB	22.7
CONS	6.4
NDP	3.6
GP	2.4
MP	1.5

JONQUIÉRE—ALMA

BQ	54.9
LIB	29.1
IND	6.0
CONS	4.8
NDP	3.4
GP	1.5
COMM	0.3

LAC-SAINT-LOUIS

LIB	63.9
CONS	12.1
BQ	10.2
NDP	7.5
GP	5.1
MP	1.2

LA POINTE-DE-L'ÎLE

BQ	66.5
LIB	22.9
CONS	4.2
NDP	3.8
GP	2.6

LASALLE—ÉMARD

LIB	56.6
BQ	30.7
CONS	5.0
NDP	4.4
GP	2.2
MP	0.8
ML	0.5

LAURENTIDES—LABELLE

BQ	58.4
LIB	29.4
CONS	5.9
GP	3.6
NDP	2.7

LAURIER

BQ	60.1
LIB	17.7
NDP	12.1
GP	6.1
CONS	2.6
MP	1.2
ML	0.3

LAVAL

BQ	50.1
LIB	36.2
CONS	6.4
NDP	4.1
GP	2.2
MP	1.0

LAVAL—LES ÎLES

LIB	47.9
BQ	37.1
CONS	7.0
NDP	4.4
GP	2.4
MP	1.0
ML	0.3

LÉVIS—BELLECHASSE

BQ	44.3
LIB	27.6
CONS	19.1
GP	4.8

NDP	3.9
COMM	0.3

LONGUEUIL

BQ	60.9
LIB	25.6
NDP	5.2
CONS	4.9
GP	2.6
MP	0.8

LOTBINIÉRE—CHUTES-DE-LA-CHAUDIÉRE

BQ	46.0
CONS	24.1
LIB	21.5
NDP	4.8
GP	3.7

LOUIS-HÉBERT

BQ	43.1
LIB	34.0
CONS	13.5
NDP	5.6
GP	3.8

LOUIS-SAINT-LAURENT

BQ	38.4
CONS	31.1
LIB	22.3
NDP	3.1
GP	2.8
IND	1.3
IND	0.7
COMM	0.3

MANICOUAGAN

BQ	58.5
LIB	24.9
NDP	10.3
CONS	4.9
GP	1.4

MARC-AURÈLE-FORTIN

BQ	58.9
LIB	27.7
CONS	6.0
GP	3.9
NDP	3.6

MATAPÉDIA—MATANE

BQ	56.5
LIB	30.5
CONS	6.2
NDP	5.0
GP	1.9

MÉGANTIC—L'ERABLE

BQ	44.7
LIB	36.7
CONS	11.4
NDP	3.7
GP	3.5

MONTCALM

BQ	71.2
LIB	16.4
CONS	5.9
GP	3.3
NDP	3.2

MOUNT ROYAL

LIB	75.7
CONS	8.6
BQ	7.0
NDP	4.9
GP	2.8
MP	0.8
ML	0.3

NOTRE-DAME-DE-GRÂCE—LACHINE

LIB	53.2
BQ	22.0
CONS	10.2
NDP	7.9
GP	5.0
MP	1.1
LIBERT	0.4
ML	0.2

NUNAVIK—EEYOU

BQ	45.2
LIB	43.2
CONS	4.6
NDP	3.9
GP	3.1

OUTREMONT

LIB	41.4
BQ	33.9

NDP	13.5
CONS	6.1
GP	4.2
MP	0.7
ML	0.3

PAPINEAU

LIB	41.1
BQ	40.0
NDP	8.8
CONS	4.8
GP	2.6
MP	1.2
IND	0.6
COMM	0.6
ML	0.4

PIERREFONDS—DOLLARD

LIB	63.6
BQ	16.0
CONS	10.8
NDP	5.5
GP	3.0
MP	1.1
ML	0.2

PONTIAC

LIB	38.4
BQ	29.2
CONS	22.2
NDP	5.8
GP	4.2
ML	0.3

PORTNEUF

BQ	42.9
LIB	27.6
CONS	21.5
GP	4.5
NDP	3.6

QUÉBEC

BQ	50.6
LIB	27.0
CONS	11.1
NDP	5.6
GP	4.3
MP	1.1
ML	0.5

REPENTIGNY

BQ	70.1
LIB	18.3
CONS	4.8
NDP	3.0
GP	2.9
MP	1.1

RICHELIEU

BQ	64.7
LIB	22.7
CONS	7.7
NDP	2.1
GP	1.7
MP	1.2

RICHMOND—ATHABASKA

BQ	55.6
LIB	27.2
CONS	10.4
GP	3.6
NDP	3.3

RIMOUSKI—TÉMISCOUATA

BQ	57.6
LIB	23.8
CONS	8.9
NDP	7.1
GP	2.6

RIVIÈRE-DES-MILLE-ÎLES

BQ	61.4
LIB	24.2
CONS	6.7
GP	4.3
NDP	3.4

RIVIÈRE-DU-LOUP—MONTMAGNY

BQ	57.1
LIB	29.6
CONS	9.1
GP	2.2
NDP	2.0

RIVIÈRE-DU-NORD

BQ	66.3
LIB	21.6
CONS	5.5
NDP	2.9
GP	2.6
MP	1.0

ROBERVAL

BQ	59.4
LIB	23.2
CONS	8.7
NDP	5.1
GP	3.6

ROSEMONT—LA PETITE-PATRIE

BQ	61.8
LIB	22.9
NDP	7.7
GP	4.3
CONS	3.1
COMM	0.3

SAINT-BRUNO—SAINT-HUBERT

BQ	55.1
LIB	30.4
CONS	6.3
NDP	4.4
GP	2.7
MP	1.2

SAINT-HYACINTHE—BAGOT

BQ	62.4
LIB	22.1
CONS	11.0
NDP	2.5
GP	2.0

SAINT-JEAN

BQ	60.1
LIB	26.0
CONS	7.9
NDP	3.4
GP	2.7

SAINT-LAMBERT

BQ	48.8
LIB	36.9
CONS	6.1
NDP	4.7
GP	3.1
ML	0.3

SAINT-LAURENT—CARTIERVILLE

LIB	66.9
BQ	17.2
NDP	6.3
CONS	6.2
GP	2.1
MP	0.7
ML	0.3
ACTION	0.2
COMM	0.2

SAINT-LÉONARD—SAINT-MICHEL

LIB	63.9
BQ	21.9
NDP	6.0
CONS	5.3
GP	2.3
ML	0.7

SAINT-MAURICE—CHAMPLAIN

BQ	55.3
LIB	30.6
CONS	8.8
NDP	2.4
GP	1.8
MP	1.2

SHEFFORD

BQ	46.6
LIB	39.7
CONS	7.9
GP	3.3
NDP	2.4

SHERBROOKE

BQ	58.7
LIB	31.0
CONS	4.3
GP	3.0
NDP	2.9

TERREBONNE—BLAINVILLE

BQ	68.1
LIB	19.7
CONS	5.6
GP	3.4
NDP	3.2

TROIS-RIVIÈRES

BQ	56.5
LIB	27.4
CONS	9.4
NDP	3.5
GP	3.2

VAUDREUIL-SOULANGES

BQ	44.3

LIB 38.8
CONS 8.2
NDP 3.9
GP 3.8
MP 1.1

VERCHÈRES—LES PATRIOTES
BQ 67.6
LIB 20.2
CONS 5.6
NDP 3.7
GP 2.0
MP 0.9

WESTMOUNT—VILLE-MARIE
LIB 55.8
BQ 14.8
NDP 12.0
CONS 10.1
GP 6.1
MP 1.0
ML 0.3

ONTARIO

AJAX—PICKERING
LIB 49.8
CONS 33.6
NDP 12.1
GP 4.5

ALGOMA—MANITOULIN—KAPUSKASING
LIB 40.9
NDP 31.7
CONS 23.2
GP 4.2

ANCASTER—DUNDAS—FLAMBOROUGH—WESTDALE
LIB 39.7
CONS 34.6
NDP 20.9
GP 4.8

BARRIE
LIB 42.7
CONS 40.1
NDP 10.7
GP 6.6

BEACHES—EAST YORK
LIB 47.9
NDP 32.3
CONS 14.1
GP 4.5
MP 0.8
IND 0.2
COMM 0.1
ML 0.1

BRAMALEA—GORE—MALTON
LIB 49.5
CONS 30.6
NDP 14.9
GP 4.5
ML 0.6

BRAMPTON—SPRINGDALE
LIB 47.7
CONS 27.5
NDP 19.8
GP 4.7
COMM 0.2

BRAMPTON-WEST
LIB 45.3
CONS 40.0
NDP 10.5
GP 3.4
IND 0.8

BRANT
LIB 38.1
CONS 33.1
NDP 22.0
GP 5.1
CHP 1.1
IND 0.7

BURLINGTON
LIB 45.0
CONS 38.4
NDP 10.8
GP 5.2
CHP 0.7

CAMBRIDGE
CONS 37.1
LIB 36.7

NDP	20.2
GP	4.9
CHP	0.8
IND	0.3
IND	0.2

CARLETON—LANARK

CONS	50.0
LIB	34.0
NDP	10.4
GP	5.6

CHATHAM-KENT—ESSEX

LIB	39.6
CONS	38.7
NDP	17.1
GP	4.2
ML	0.3

CLARINGTON—SCUGOG—UXBRIDGE

CONS	40.7
LIB	38.3
NDP	15.1
GP	4.1
CHP	1.8

DAVENPORT

LIB	50.7
NDP	34.1
CONS	9.3
GP	4.2
MP	0.8
COMM	0.4
ACTION	0.3
ML	0.2

DON VALLEY EAST

LIB	54.6
CONS	28.0
NDP	13.2
GP	2.9
CHP	0.9
COMM	0.4

DON VALLEY WEST

LIB	59.8
CONS	28.3
NDP	8.6
GP	3.3

DUFFERIN—CALEDON

CONS	42.8
LIB	39.0
GP	8.8
NDP	8.4
CHP	1.0

EGLINTON—LAWRENCE

LIB	60.2
CONS	25.1
NDP	10.4
GP	4.1
ACTION	0.2

ELGIN—MIDDLESEX—LONDON

CONS	43.8
LIB	34.2
NDP	14.6
GP	4.4
CHP	2.7
ACTION	0.3

ESSEX

CONS	36.6
LIB	35.0
NDP	24.4
GP	3.9
ML	0.2

ETOBICOKE CENTRE

LIB	58.3
CONS	28.4
NDP	9.9
GP	3.2
ML	0.2

ETOBICOKE—LAKESHORE

LIB	50.2
CONS	30.6
NDP	14.5
GP	4.4
ML	0.3

ETOBICOKE NORTH

LIB	63.3
CONS	18.7
NDP	12.2
CHP	2.2
GP	2.0
IND	1.0
ML	0.6

GLENGARRY—PRESCOTT-RUSSELL

LIB	47.9
CONS	37.5
NDP	8.5
GP	5.3
CHP	0.9

GREY—BRUCE—OWEN SOUND

CONS	45.0
LIB	35.8
NDP	13.1
GP	4.2
CHP	2.0

GUELPH

LIB	44.6
CONS	26.1
NDP	20.0
GP	7.4
CHP	1.2
MP	0.6
ML	0.1

HALDIMAND—NORFOLK

CONS	42.2
LIB	38.8
NDP	14.4
GP	3.4
CHP	1.2

HALIBURTON—KAWARTHA LAKES—BROCK

CONS	44.2
LIB	34.5
NDP	15.1
GP	4.7
CHP	0.9
IND	0.6

HALTON

LIB	48.4
CONS	38.4
NDP	8.2
GP	5.1

HAMILTON CENTRE

NDP	45.8
LIB	33.7
CONS	15.1
GP	3.2
CHP	1.2
NIL	0.8
ML	0.2

HAMILTON EAST—STONEY CREEK

LIB	37.7
NDP	35.8
CONS	22.3
GP	3.0
IND	0.8
COMM	0.3

HAMILTON MOUNTAIN

LIB	34.8
NDP	32.9
CONS	29.3
GP	2.6
ML	0.4

HURON—BRUCE

LIB	49.8
CONS	31.1
NDP	13.1
GP	3.0
CHP	1.9
MP	1.2

KENORA

LIB	36.2
NDP	32.1
CONS	27.9
GP	3.8

KINGSTON AND THE ISLANDS

LIB	52.5
CONS	23.1
NDP	16.5
GP	6.1
CHP	0.9
IND	0.4
ACTION	0.3
IND	0.2

KITCHENER CENTRE

LIB	47.1
CONS	27.5
NDP	19.3
GP	5.4
IND	0.6

KITCHENER—CONESTOGA

LIB	42.3
CONS	35.4
NDP	15.7
GP	6.6

KITCHENER—WATERLOO

LIB	48.1
CONS	29.5
NDP	15.9
GP	5.6
CHP	0.7
IND	0.2

LANARK—FRONTENAC—LENNOX AND ADDINGTON

CONS	48.8
LIB	31.0
NDP	13.1
GP	4.8
IND	1.5
MP	0.9

LEEDS—GRENVILLE

CONS	50.5
LIB	32.9
NDP	11.3
GP	5.3

LONDON-FANSHAWE

LIB	38.1
NDP	30.4
CONS	26.3
GP	4.0
PCP	1.1
ML	0.2

LONDON NORTH CENTRE

LIB	43.1
CONS	27.4
NDP	24.1
GP	4.8
PCP	0.4
ML	0.1

LONDON WEST

LIB	45.5
CONS	31.5
NDP	17.3
GP	4.7
PCP	0.9
ML	0.1

MARKHAM—UNIONVILLE

LIB	66.3
CONS	22.5
NDP	8.7
GP	2.5

MIDDLESEX—KENT—LAMBTON

LIB	39.7
CONS	39.4
NDP	15.1
GP	3.8
CHP	2.1

MISSISAUGA—BRAMPTON SOUTH

LIB	57.2
CONS	24.1
NDP	14.8
GP	3.5
ML	0.4

MISSISSAUGA EAST—COOKSVILLE

LIB	56.7
CONS	26.0
NDP	11.7
GP	3.0
CHP	2.0
ML	0.4
IND	0.3

MISSISSAUGA—ERINDALE

LIB	54.4
CONS	32.0
NDP	9.8
GP	3.6
ML	0.3

MISSISSAUGA SOUTH

LIB	51.7
CONS	33.6
NDP	10.5
GP	4.0
ML	0.2

MISSISSAUGA—STREETSVILLE

LIB	50.6
CONS	31.7
NDP	9.5
GP	5.4

PCP 2.9

NEPEAN—CARLETON
CONS 45.7
LIB 40.1
NDP 9.1
GP 4.3
MP 0.8

NEWMARKET—AURORA
CONS 42.4
LIB 41.1
NDP 9.9
GP 4.5
PCP 2.1

NIAGARA FALLS
CONS 38.7
LIB 36.5
NDP 20.8
GP 4.0

NAGARA WEST—GLANBROOK
CONS 40.3
LIB 39.0
NDP 14.8
GP 3.4
CHP 2.1
ACTION 0.4

NICKEL BELT
LIB 42.4
NDP 34.5
CONS 18.8
GP 2.5
MP 1.1
IND 0.5
ML 0.1

NIPISSING—TIMISKAMING
LIB 42.3
CONS 37.1
NDP 17.1
GP 3.1
ACTION 0.5

NORTHUMBERLAND—QUINTE WEST
LIB 39.9
CONS 39.3
NDP 15.6

GP 5.2

OAK RIDGES—MARKHAM
LIB 51.7
CONS 33.5
NDP 8.8
GP 3.9
PCP 1.3
CHP 0.7

OAKVILLE
LIB 52.0
CONS 35.4
NDP 7.3
GP 5.2
ACTION 0.2

OSHAWA
CONS 33.2
NDP 32.2
LIB 30.5
GP 3.9
ML 0.2

OTTAWA CENTRE
NDP 41.1
LIB 31.1
CONS 19.0
GP 7.6
MP 0.7
IND 0.2
COMM 0.1
ACTION 0.1
ML 0.1

OTTAWA-ORLÉANS
LIB 45.0
CONS 40.3
NDP 10.1
GP 4.6

OTTAWA SOUTH
LIB 43.8
CONS 34.8
NDP 13.6
GP 5.7
MP 0.8
PCP 0.6
IND 0.4
ML 0.1

OTTAWA—VANIER

LIB	49.2
CONS	24.2
NDP	18.5
GP	6.9
MP	1.1
ML	0.2

OTTAWA WEST—NEPEAN

LIB	41.8
CONS	39.4
NDP	13.0
GP	4.8
MP	0.8
ACTION	0.2
ML	0.1

OXFORD

CONS	44.9
LIB	30.5
NDP	14.5
GP	4.3
CHP	3.3
MP	1.7
LIBERT	0.5
ACTION	0.2

PARKDALE—HIGH PARK

LIB	42.1
NDP	34.5
CONS	15.4
GP	6.9
MP	0.8
ML	0.3

PARRY SOUND—MUSKOKA

LIB	43.9
CONS	36.4
NDP	11.8
GP	8.0

PERTH—WELLINGTON

CONS	42.0
LIB	33.4
NDP	15.6
GP	6.2
CHP	2.8

PETERBOROUGH

LIB	43.6
CONS	31.9
NDP	19.0
GP	5.5

PICKERING—SCARBOROUGH EAST

LIB	57.0
CONS	28.0
NDP	11.3
GP	3.8

PRINCE EDWARD—HASTINGS

CONS	42.4
LIB	37.6
NDP	15.2
GP	4.0
IND	0.9

RENFREW—NIPISSING—PEMBROKE

CONS	55.1
LIB	29.7
NDP	11.5
GP	2.4
MP	1.4

RICHMOND HILL

LIB	58.5
CONS	24.9
NDP	9.7
GP	4.6
PCP	2.3

ST. CATHARINES

LIB	40.4
CONS	34.7
NDP	19.3
GP	3.7
CHP	1.4
ACTION	0.4
ML	0.1

ST. PAUL'S

LIB	58.4
CONS	20.4
NDP	15.7
GP	5.5

SARNIA—LAMBTON

LIB	41.9
CONS	30.5
NDP	16.3

GP	5.4
CHP	3.8
IND	1.6
IND	0.5

SAULT STE. MARIE

NDP	38.3
LIB	36.6
CONS	23.1
GP	1.9
ML	0.2

SCARBOROUGH—AGINCOURT

LIB	64.1
CONS	21.0
NDP	10.2
PCP	2.5
GP	2.2

SCARBOROUGH—CENTRE

LIB	56.7
CONS	23.3
NDP	16.8
GP	2.9
COMM	0.4

SCARBOROUGH—GUILDWOOD

LIB	57.5
CONS	22.7
NDP	16.2
GP	3.0
ACTION	0.6

SCARBOROUGH—ROUGE RIVER

LIB	57.9
IND	17.9
CONS	13.3
NDP	9.3
GP	1.6

SCARBOROUGH SOUTHWEST

LIB	49.5
CONS	23.8
NDP	22.3
GP	4.0
COMM	0.4

SIMCOE—GREY

CONS	40.6
LIB	40.4
NDP	10.0
GP	4.8
CHP	4.1

SIMCOE NORTH

LIB	43.4
CONS	37.7
NDP	11.3
GP	6.4
CHP	1.0
ACTION	0.3

STORMONT—DUNDAS—SOUTH GLENGARRY

CONS	44.9
LIB	36.8
NDP	11.2
GP	7.2

SUDBURY

LIB	44.2
NDP	29.9
CONS	21.1
GP	4.7
ML	0.2

THORNHILL

LIB	54.6
CONS	34.5
NDP	7.0
GP	3.1
IND	0.5
IND	0.4

THUNDER BAY—RAINY RIVER

LIB	39.4
NDP	29.7
CONS	26.3
GP	2.4
MP	1.5
CHP	0.7

THUNDER BAY—SUPERIOR NORTH

LIB	43.0
NDP	29.3
CONS	21.2
GP	4.6
MP	1.9

TIMMINS—JAMES BAY

NDP	41.5

LIB	39.7
CONS	16.7
GP	2.3

TORONTO CENTRE

LIB	56.5
NDP	23.8
CONS	14.8
GP	3.9
MP	0.6
COMM	0.2
ACTION	0.1
ML	0.1

TORONTO—DANFORTH

NDP	46.3
LIB	41.3
CONS	6.2
GP	5.4
MP	0.6
ML	0.2

TRINITY—SPADINA

LIB	43.6
NDP	42.0
CONS	8.6
GP	4.2
PCP	1.0
ML	0.2
ACTION	0.2
NIL	0.2

VAUGHAN

LIB	63.0
CONS	23.7
NDP	8.8
GP	3.5
LIBERT	0.8
ACTION	0.4

WELLAND

LIB	39.6
NDP	29.5
CONS	26.2
GP	2.9
CHP	1.5
ML	0.2

WELLINGTON—HALTON HILLS

CONS	42.8
LIB	38.2
NDP	11.9
GP	5.4
CHP	1.7

WHITBY—OSHAWA

LIB	45.0
CONS	36.1
NDP	14.1
GP	4.9

WILLOWDALE

LIB	61.4
CONS	23.1
NDP	9.6
GP	3.7
PCP	1.8
IND	0.5

WINDSOR—TECUMSEH

NDP	41.9
LIB	33.9
CONS	20.5
GP	3.4
ML	0.4

WINDSOR WEST

NDP	46.0
LIB	31.3
CONS	18.9
GP	3.5
ML	0.3

YORK CENTRE

LIB	54.8
CONS	26.3
NDP	13.7
GP	3.2
IND	2.1

YORK—SIMCOE

CONS	45.2
LIB	35.5
NDP	11.3
GP	5.5
PCP	1.4
CHP	1.2

YORK SOUTH—WESTON

LIB	59.8
NDP	21.2
CONS	15.0

GP 3.5
COMM 0.5

YORK WEST
LIB 64.7
NDP 15.3
CONS 11.3
CHP 5.7
GP 3.0

MANITOBA

BRANDON—SOURIS
CONS 51.7
LIB 24.2
NDP 19.2
GP 3.6
CHP 1.0
COMM 0.3

CHARLESWOOD—ST. JAMES
CONS 44.3
LIB 42.6
NDP 10.2
GP 2.1
MP 0.8
COMM 0.1

CHURCHILL
NDP 43.4
LIB 38.4
CONS 15.1
GP 3.1

DAUPHIN—SWAN RIVER
CONS 54.0
NDP 22.0
LIB 20.4
GP 2.0
CHP 1.7

ELMWOOD—TRANSCONA
NDP 52.0
CONS 26.1
LIB 16.8
GP 2.5
CHP 1.3
MP 1.1
COMM 0.3

KILDONAN—ST. PAUL
CONS 37.3
LIB 36.5
NDP 22.5
GP 2.1
MP 0.8
CHP 0.8

PORTAGE—LISGAR
CONS 65.9
LIB 17.7
NDP 9.3
CHP 4.2
GP 2.5
COMM 0.3

PROVENCHER
CONS 63.0
LIB 24.9
NDP 9.0
GP 3.1

SAINT BONIFACE
LIB 46.6
CONS 31.0
NDP 18.0
GP 2.4
CHP 1.0
MP 0.8
COMM 0.2

SELKIRK—INTERLAKE
CONS 47.3
NDP 26.5
LIB 22.9
GP 2.5
CHP 0.9

WINNIPEG CENTRE
NDP 45.4
LIB 34.7
CONS 13.6
GP 4.3
MP 1.3
COMM 0.4
IND 0.3

WINNIPEG NORTH
LIB 51.3
NDP 48.2
LIB 36.6

CONS	12.3
GP	2.0
CHP	0.5
COMM	0.4

WINNIPEG SOUTH

CONS	34.0
NDP	11.2
GP	2.7
CHP	0.8

WINNIPEG SOUTH CENTRE

LIB	46.6
CONS	27.0
NDP	21.3
GP	3.9
MP	0.8
ACTION	0.3
COMM	0.2

SASKATCHEWAN

BATTLEFORDS—LLOYDMINSTER

CONS	58.3
NDP	20.3
LIB	17.4
GP	2.9
CHP	1.2

BLACKSTRAP

CONS	41.5
LIB	31.4
NDP	23.6
GP	3.1
CHP	0.5

CHURCHILL RIVER

CONS	37.4
LIB	29.9
NDP	20.1
IND	9.9
GP	2.8

CYPRESS HILLS—GRASSLANDS

CONS	60.6
LIB	18.7
NDP	16.5
GP	4.2

PALLISER

CONS	35.9
NDP	35.5
LIB	24.8
GP	2.5
CHP	1.4

PRINCE ALBERT

CONS	47.3
NDP	25.2
LIB	24.1
GP	3.4

REGINA—LUMSDEN—LAKE CENTRE

CONS	33.2
LIB	32.8
NDP	26.8
IND	4.9
GP	2.3

REGINA—QU`APPELLE

CONS	35.8
NDP	32.7
LIB	27.8
GP	2.3
CHP	1.1
NIL	0.4

SASKATOON—HUMBOLDT

CONS	26.8
NDP	25.6
LIB	25.5
IND	20.0
GP	1.9
NIL	0.2

SASKATOON—ROSETOWN—BIGGAR

CONS	44.8
NDP	36.2
LIB	15.8
GP	3.2

SASKATOON—WANUSKEWIN

CONS	46.6
LIB	32.6
NDP	17.8
GP	3.0

SOURIS—MOOSE MOUNTAIN

CONS	36.9
IND	27.4
LIB	19.6
NDP	13.7
GP	1.8
CHP	0.6

WASCANA

LIB	57.2
CONS	24.2
NDP	16.0
GP	2.6

YORKTON—MELVILLE

CONS	62.9
NDP	18.6
LIB	14.8
GP	2.0
IND	1.7

ALBERTA

ATHABASCA

CONS	60.3
LIB	24.1
NDP	10.5
GP	5.2

CALGARY EAST

CONS	61.1
LIB	21.3
NDP	9.9
GP	7.1
COMM	0.7

CALGARY NORTH CENTRE

CONS	54.2
LIB	21.4
NDP	12.1
GP	11.2
IND	0.7
ML	0.4

CALGARY NORTHEAST

CONS	62.2
LIB	24.6
NDP	7.6
GP	4.7
ACTION	0.8

CALGARY—NOSE HILL

CONS	64.4
LIB	22.9
NDP	6.7
GP	6.0

CALGARY SOUTH CENTRE

CONS	51.2
LIB	29.9
GP	9.9
NDP	8.5
ACTION	0.5

CALGARY SOUTHEAST

CONS	71.0
LIB	16.4
NDP	6.6
GP	6.1

CALGARY SOUTHWEST

CONS	68.4
LIB	18.4
GP	6.2
NDP	5.6
MP	1.0
CHP	0.4

CALGARY WEST

CONS	55.9
LIB	29.3
GP	7.6
NDP	6.5
ACTION	0.6
ML	0.2

CROWFOOT

CONS	80.2
LIB	7.7
NDP	6.9
GP	3.8
MP	1.4

EDMONTON—BEAUMONT

LIB	42.8
CONS	42.5
NDP	9.7
GP	4.7
COMM	0.3

EDMONTON CENTRE

LIB	42.5

CONS	41.1
NDP	9.1
GP	4.9
MP	1.0
PCP	0.9
IND	0.4
ML	0.2

EDMONTON EAST

CONS	46.0
LIB	32.4
NDP	14.7
GP	5.6
CHP	1.2

EDMONTON—LEDUC

CONS	55.1
LIB	29.3
NDP	9.4
GP	6.2

EDMONTON—ST. ALBERT

CONS	57.7
LIB	24.2
NDP	11.6
GP	6.6

EDMONTON—SHERWOOD PARK

CONS	57.9
LIB	24.5
NDP	11.0
GP	6.7

EDMONTON—SPRUCE GROVE

CONS	60.4
LIB	25.6
NDP	8.9
GP	5.1

EDMONTON—STRATHCONA

CONS	39.4
LIB	29.0
NDP	23.8
GP	6.5
MP	1.1
ML	0.2

LETHBRIDGE

CONS	62.6
LIB	21.6
NDP	9.7
GP	2.7
CHP	2.3
MP	1.2

MACLEOD

CONS	74.8
LIB	12.1
GP	6.7
NDP	6.5

MEDICINE HAT

CONS	76.2
LIB	10.9
NDP	9.2
GP	3.8

PEACE RIVER

CONS	65.1
LIB	19.0
NDP	11.1
GP	4.8

RED DEER

CONS	74.8
LIB	11.8
NDP	7.8
GP	4.8
ACTION	0.8

VEGREVILLE—WAINWRIGHT

CONS	73.5
LIB	11.7
NDP	8.3
GP	6.5

WESTLOCK—ST. PAUL

CONS	66.7
LIB	19.4
NDP	8.8
GP	5.1

WETASKIWIN

CONS	73.7
LIB	11.9
NDP	7.3
GP	6.2
ACTION	1.0

WILD ROSE

CONS	70.6
LIB	12.6

NDP	8.5
GP	8.3

YELLOWHEAD

CONS	68.6
LIB	11.5
NDP	11.5
GP	6.6
CHP	1.9

BRITISH COLUMBIA

ABBOTSFORD

CONS	61.4
LIB	20.0
NDP	13.6
GP	2.9
CHP	1.2
MP	0.8
ML	0.1

BURNABY—DOUGLAS

NDP	34.6
LIB	32.5
CONS	27.6
GP	3.7
LIBERT	0.6
IND	0.6
COMM	0.3

BURNABY—NEW WESTMINSTER

NDP	33.7
LIB	32.9
CONS	28.4
GP	3.9
ACTION	0.8
COMM	0.4

CARIBOO—PRINCE GEORGE

CONS	46.7
NDP	26.5
LIB	19.9
GP	4.3
IND	1.1
ACTION	1.0
LIBERT	0.4
ML	0.2

CHILLIWACK—FRASER CANYON

CONS	53.7
NDP	20.6
LIB	18.4
GP	3.2
CHP	2.6
MP	1.3
ML	0.2

DELTA—RICHMOND EAST

CONS	45.6
LIB	33.2
NDP	14.6
GP	6.6

DEWDNEY—ALOUETTE

CONS	38.5
NDP	32.7
LIB	21.9
GP	5.3
NIL	1.7

ESQUIMALT—JUAN DE FUCA

LIB	35.3
NDP	30.6
CONS	24.2
GP	9.2
IND	0.4
ACTION	0.3

FLEETWOOD—PORT KELLS

CONS	35.8
LIB	29.5
NDP	28.0
GP	6.3
ML	0.4

KAMPLOOPS—THOMPSON

CONS	40.4
LIB	28.3
NDP	26.2
GP	4.3
IND	0.9

KELOWNA

CONS	48.0
LIB	26.5
NDP	16.8
GP	7.3
MP	0.8
ACTION	0.5

KOOTENAY—COLUMBIA

CONS	52.0
NDP	23.8
LIB	17.9
GP	6.2

LANGLEY

CONS	47.7
LIB	24.7
NDP	16.8
GP	6.1
IND	4.7

NANAIMO—ALBERNI

CONS	39.1
NDP	32.3
LIB	19.9
GP	7.4
MP	0.9
ACTION	0.3
ML	0.1

NANAIMO—COWICHAN

NDP	43.7
CONS	32.8
LIB	16.0
GP	6.6
ACTION	0.5
IND	0.4

NEWTON—NORTH DELTA

CONS	32.8
LIB	31.6
NDP	29.2
GP	6.2
COMM	0.2

NEW WESTMINSTER—COQUITLAM

CONS	32.9
NDP	32.6
LIB	27.4
GP	5.6
CHP	1.5

NORTH OKANAGAN—SHUSWAP

CONS	46.4
NDP	24.2
LIB	22.5
GP	4.5
MP	1.0
NIL	0.8
ACTION	0.5
NIL	0.2

NORTH VANCOUVER

LIB	40.0
CONS	36.4
NDP	15.9
GP	7.3
ACTION	0.3
ML	0.1

OKANAGAN—COQUIHALLA

CONS	49.8
LIB	23.1
NDP	19.6
GP	6.0
MP	1.1
ACTION	0.5

PORT MOODY—WESTWOOD—PORT COQUITLAM

CONS	40.9
LIB	27.3
NDP	26.4
GP	4.3
LIBERT	0.6
ACTION	0.2
COMM	0.2

PRINCE GEORGE—PEACE RIVER

CONS	58.7
NDP	20.7
LIB	13.8
GP	5.7
ACTION	0.8
ML	0.3

RICHMOND

LIB	44.5
CONS	35.3
NDP	15.0
GP	4.3
ACTION	0.9

SAANICH—GULF ISLANDS

CONS	34.6
LIB	26.8
NDP	21.6
GP	16.7
IND	0.3

SKEENA—BULKLEY VALLEY

NDP	37.1
CONS	33.7
LIB	21.6
CHP	3.8
GP	3.3
ML	0.4

SOUTHERN INTERIOR

CONS	36.6
NDP	35.1
LIB	18.0
GP	7.9
IND	1.3
MP	0.8
ACTION	0.2
ML	0.1

SOUTH SURREY—WHITE ROCK—CLOVERDALE

CONS	42.7
LIB	36.8
NDP	14.4
GP	5.7
ACTION	0.5

SURREY NORTH

NIL	43.8
NDP	24.1
LIB	15.7
CONS	12.6
GP	1.9
CHP	1.3
COMM	0.3
ACTION	0.3

VANCOUVER CENTRE

LIB	40.3
NDP	32.3
CONS	19.2
GP	6.8
LIBERT	0.6
CHP	0.5
ACTION	0.2
COMM	0.2

VANCOUVER EAST

NDP	56.5
LIB	25.9
CONS	10.0
GP	5.7
MP	1.0
CHP	0.6
NIL	0.4

VANCOUVER ISLAND NORTH

CONS	35.4
NDP	34.5
LIB	21.5
GP	8.4
ML	0.2

VANCOUVER KINGSWAY

LIB	40.4
NDP	37.3
CONS	16.5
GP	3.6
NIL	1.3
COMM	0.4
ACTION	0.3
ML	0.2

VANCOUVER QUADRA

LIB	52.4
CONS	26.3
NDP	15.0
GP	5.6
ACTION	0.3
LIBERT	0.3
ML	0.1

VANCOUVER SOUTH

LIB	44.5
CONS	25.5
NDP	24.6
GP	3.6
CHP	0.8
ML	0.3
COMM	0.3
NIL	0.2
ACTION	0.2

VICTORIA

LIB	35.0
NDP	31.1
CONS	21.8
GP	11.7
ACTION	0.4

WEST VANCOUVER—SUNSHINE COAST

CONS	35.3
LIB	32.5
NDP	21.7
GP	9.7
ACTION	0.5
ML	0.2

YUKON

LIB	45.7
NDP	25.7
CONS	20.9
GP	4.6
MP	2.4
CHP	0.8

WESTERN ARCTIC

LIB	39.4
NDP	39.1
CONS	17.2
GP	4.3

NUNAVUT

LIB	51.3
IND	15.8
NDP	15.2
CONS	14.5
GP	3.3

CONTRIBUTORS

PAUL ATTALLAH is the Associate Director of the School of Journalism and Communication at Carleton University. He is the author of books in both French and English on communication theory, and of numerous articles dealing with the media.

STEPHEN CLARKSON, who teaches political economy at the University of Toronto, has written the chapter on the Liberal Party of Canada for every federal election book since the 1974 campaign, when the series began. He is currently finishing a book on this subject to be published in 2005 by the University of British Columbia Press, *The Joy of Winning: The Liberal Party of Canada at the Polls, 1974–2004.*

CHRISTOPHER DORNAN is the Director of the School of Journalism and Communication at Carleton University. He has contributed chapters to two previous volumes in the *Canadian General Election* series and was co-editor of the 2000 volume. He writes extensively on the Canadian news media, as well as institutions and industries.

FARON ELLIS teaches political science, history, and research methods at Lethbridge Community College, where he also serves as Director of the Citizen Society Research Lab. He is author of the forthcoming *Limits of Participation: Members, Activists and Leaders in Canada's Reform Party* and various other publications on Canadian politics and Western Canadian history, including three previous contributions to the *Canadian General Election* series.

ALAIN-G. GAGNON holds the Canada Research Chair in Quebec and Canadian Studies and is Professor of Political Science in the Department of Political Science at the Université du Québec à Montréal (UQAM). His recent publications include *Ties That Bind: Parties and Voters in Canada* (Oxford University Press, 1999) with James Bickerton and Patrick Smith; *Quebec: State and Society,* third edition (Broadview Press, 2004); *and Canadian Politics,* fourth edition, Broadview Press, 2004 (edited with James Bickerton).

SUSAN HARADA is an assistant professor with the School of Journalism and Communication at Carleton University. Prior to joining Carleton, she worked for more than two decades as a journalist, for the most part with the CBC, including eight years as a National Parliamentary Correspondent in Ottawa. She contributed to the coverage of three federal election campaigns and numerous national leadership conventions and first ministers' conferences between 1993 and 2001. She also spent seven years as a documentary journalist for the CBC's flagship current affairs show *The Journal,* producing national and international documentaries on a wide variety of issues.

JACQUES HÉRIVAULT is coordinator of the Canada Research Chair in Quebec and Canadian Studies (CRÉQC) at Université du Québec à Montréal (UQAM). After obtaining his MA in political science at UQAM, he served as researcher and political advisor for intergovernmental and foreign affairs to Gilles Duceppe (1997–2001). From 2001 to 2003, he was political advisor to Louise Beaudoin, then Quebec's minister of international relations.

LAWRENCE LEDUC is Professor of Political Science at the University of Toronto. His recent publications include *Comparing Democracies 2: New Challenges in the Study of Elections and Voting* (with Richard G. Niemi and Pippa Norris) and *The Politics of Direct Democracy: Referendums in Global Perspective.*

MICHAEL MARZOLINI is Chairman and CEO of POLLARA Strategic Public Opinion & Market Research, the largest Canadian-owned public opinion and market research firm. Since 1985 he has served as media pollster for CTV News, the *Toronto Star,* Southam Newspapers, Canwest-Global News, Sun Media, and *Maclean's*. He was also the Chief Pollster and Strategist for the Liberal Party of Canada's three back-to-back election victories in 1993, 1997, and 2000.

JON H. PAMMETT is Professor of Political Science and Associate Dean of Public Affairs and Management at Carleton University. He is co-author of *Political Choice in Canada* and *Absent Mandate,* as well as several earlier volumes in the *Canadian General Election* series. He has worked in the fields of voting behaviour, declines in voting participation, political education, and socialization.

TAMARA A. SMALL is a PhD candidate in the Department of Political Studies at Queen's University. Her graduate work is focused on the use of the Internet by Canadian political parties and candidates in the 2004 federal election.

ANDRÉ TURCOTTE is Assistant Professor in Mass Communication at Carleton University's School of Journalism and Mass Communication. He also provides strategic public opinion advice to elected officials at the municipal, provincial, and federal levels. Between 1994 and 2000, he was public opinion adviser to the Leader of the Official Opposition Preston Manning.

CHRISTOPHER WADDELL is an associate professor and holder of the Carty Chair in Business and Financial Journalism at the School of Journalism and Communication at Carleton University. From 1993 to 2001 he was Parliamentary Bureau Chief for CBC Television News and responsible for campaign and election night coverage for the 1997 and 2000 federal elections. Prior to joining CBC in 1991, he worked for *The Globe and Mail* as a reporter in the *Report on Business,* a reporter and then bureau chief in the paper's Ottawa bureau through the 1988 federal election, and then became first the Globe's associate editor and then its national editor.

ALAN WHITEHORN is Professor of Political Science at the Royal Military College of Canada, cross-appointed in the Department of Political Studies at Queen's University and an Associate of the Institute for Humanities at Simon Fraser University. He is the author of *Canadian Socialism: Essays on the CCF-NDP,* co-author with Keith Archer of *Political Activists: The NDP in Convention,* and *Canadian Trade Unions and the New Democratic Party.* He is co-editor with Hugh G. Thorburn of *Party Politics in Canada,* 8th edition. He has contributed chapters to the *Canadian General Election* series since 1988.

PETER WOOLSTENCROFT teaches Canadian politics in the Department of Political Science, University of Waterloo. He has published essays on party politics, the politics of education, political geography, the federal and Ontario Progressive Conservative parties, and party leadership elections.